W9-DEO-649

WORLD POLITY

WORLD POLITY

Conflict and War:
History, Causes, Consequences, Cures

by
James P. Speer

Q. E. D. Press
Fort Bragg, California

WORLD POLITY
Conflict and War:
History, Causes, Consequences, Cures

Q. E. D. Press, **Publishers**
155 Cypress Street, Fort Bragg, CA 95437

Library of Congress Cataloging in Publication Data
Speer, James P.
World Polity.
Conflict and War: History, Causes, Consequences, Cures
Includes bibliographies and index.
1. International relations. 2. International Organization. I. Title.
JX1391.S74   1985   327   85-30056

ISBN 0-936609-00-1

Book Production by Comp-Type
Fort Bragg, CA 95437

Jacket Design by Mendocino Graphics
Fort Bragg, CA 95437

First Printing, February 1986

Printed in the United States of America

987654321

This book is dedicated to this planet's nicest people:
Librarians

SI ID PRETIUM EFFICERE OMNINO
PRETIUM IN MADUS EXTOLLERE

TABLE OF CONTENTS

TABLE OF CONTENTS

INTRODUCTION

The fate of the Earth may be a world polity instead of nuclear war.

This is a book about international relations, also known as international politics or world politics. It deals with the way nations have conflicted with each other through history, why they conflict the way they do, why conflict always overrides cooperation and what the result always is, why statesmen do so poorly in foreign policy, what will happen if we keep on going the way we are, and what we would have to do if we didn't want that to happen.

But politics is a term that comes to us from the Greek *polis*, which meant one of their little countries like Athens or Sparta that consisted of a city and a hinterland under a government. Politics has come to mean most any activity that determines who will boss whom. But the word "polity," from the same root, still refers to the institutions of government as well as the parties, groups, and individuals that want to run those institutions. So the name of this book, *World Polity*, may be an indication of the direction it will take.

An Introduction is the place to thank those who helped. That is quickly done: Dr. Robert W. Rinden, a China expert in the US Foreign Service, cut several hundred pages from the first draft. But a reader might be more interested in the elements that have gone into the book.

First, there is a lifelong interest in war and peace, dating from a religious experience at age twelve, then a decision to study for the Foreign Service, leading to a B.A. in International Relations from George Washington University.

Second, there were posts as a Foreign Service Officer in Mexico, Chile, India and China, with time out for service in the infantry and counter-intelligence as well as for a year of graduate work at Yale in Far Eastern studies and the Chinese language.

Third, there were several years with the Standard Oil Co. of Ohio, including an unsuccessful try at negotiating an oil concession with the

1

Guatemalan Government; then several years as a stockbroker in New Mexico, including an equally unsuccessful try at the U.S. Senate, then an autumn off at Harvard Divinity School where I argued some of the points in this book with Reinhold Niebuhr and Paul Tillich.

Fourth, there were two good years with the Methodist Church, lecturing on war and peace, followed by several years at the University of Colorado in Boulder to take a Ph.D. in Political Science.

Fifth, there were ten years of teaching international relations at the university level as well as courses in the comparative politics of Europe, Asia, and Latin America, plus U.S. Constitutional Law.

The argument in this book is based on history, indeed on a lifetime's habit of reading history for pleasure plus a close observation of world events since the early 1930's. History is where the evidence is. But I have also called upon some thirty years' worth of scholarly articles found in the bound journals in our university libraries plus every book I know of, scholarly or otherwise, that offers something pertinent and different. All this, of course, is likewise history—though sometimes in miniature—as seen through the spectacles provided by the writers' training and experience. And a good deal has come from newspapers; some from popular magazines and films.

Throughout I've made the effort to include the studies and opinions that go against my argument as well as the many that support it, while permitting my own view of the world to come through loud and clear, especially at the end.

The Index and the notes at the end of each chapter will supply to scholars and other experts the names of the writers whom I have drawn upon most heavily, whether as friends or foes, as well as the names of the periodical publications I consider pertinent to this kind of a study. But in their totality the books and articles are so many that a bibliography would run to tiresome length.

The interested citizen or student, to whom this book is primarily addressed, can probably best keep posted on world affairs by reading the *Christian Science Monitor* or the London *Economist* with an occasional look at *Foreign Affairs,* where members of the foreign policy establishment often publish their views, and *World Politics* or *International Studies Quarterly,* whose scholarly articles are usually not too plagued by jargon.

At any rate, this book is offered as the most thorough study of the causes of international conflict yet published. Indeed, one may hope that, except perhaps for Chapter 7 on Prediction, it may prove to have a certain timelessness—if there is that much time left.

James P. Speer
Alpine, Texas
19 July 1985

PART 1

WHAT HAS HAPPENED

This Part consists of a single chapter in two sections. Section A is a much condensed summary of international history. Section B is made up of general statements drawn from that history.

Chapter 1

A SUMMARY OF
INTERNATIONAL HISTORY

A nation is one of several kinds of states. Throughout history there have also been nomadic states, city states, princely or kingly states, and imperial states in addition to today's national states. A state is usually defined as a territory with a population under an independent government, although nomadic states traveled from one territory to another. Also, the definition does not fit too well a federal state in which the overall government is independent in some things while the regional governments are independent in other things.

For the most part we'll use terms like "nation," "national," and "international," because these are the familiar terms. When we speak of an international *system* we mean a group of nations in frequent enough contact with one another so that change anywhere is apt to have some effect everywhere.

A. Review of International History

1. We begin with ancient China, not because it had the earliest international system we know of, for it did not, but because it is convenient to start there, move on to India, then through the Near or

Middle East to the classic Greek and Roman underpinnings of the European international system.

China's Period of the Warring States during the fifth to third centuries B.C. followed the disintegration of the Chou and the still earlier Shang empires. The Chou Dynasty, lacking a centralized bureaucracy, was unable to control its empire by a feudal arrangement. By diplomacy, intrigue, subversion and war, a thousand small states were integrated into twelve large nations, and then into seven. These were ultimately conquered by Ch'in. Competition arose among four philosophies, and there were peace parties within nations that opposed war parties. Ch'in, under the Legalist philosophy that held the business of government was to keep order, foster agriculture, and make war, unified China and made it into one of the earliest totalitarian nations, complete with book burnings and severe punishments. Improvements included a central administration and the enhancement of weapons, as chariots were superseded by cavalry while iron displaced bronze.

The Han Dynasty which followed expanded the empire and installed Confucianist philosophy and a bureaucracy. China later had periods of disintegration, owing apparently to ambitions of subordinates, misrule, the large size of the country, and perhaps the diverse spoken tongues. But during disintegration there were only a few large nations which were rather soon reintegrated by conquest into one nation. Reintegration might have been helped by the tradition of imperial unity, the widely shared mixture of Confucian, Taoist and Buddhist beliefs, and a single written language. Unified, China did not interact much with other nations. It received tribute from lesser countries while defending itself from or conquering the nomadic tribes to the West and North.

Except for three rather brief periods of integration by conquest, the area in what is now India was usually divided into two or more warring international systems prior to the Mogul Empire in the 16th century A.D. Until then there was no adequate administrative technique for so vast a land, and India's rigid caste system contrasted with China's relative ethnic unity. India's large number of spoken languages was not transcended by a widely shared written language. India did not suffer greatly from religious cleavage until the Moslems came, yet there was no unifying ideology, for Buddhism competed with Hinduism for a time and Hinduism itself was a highly diverse thought-system.

The techniques of international interaction were much the same as in China, but more highly developed in the elaborate *Mandala* system of circling friends and enemies, and there was perhaps more reliance on deceit and treachery. According to the *Arthasastra* writings on statecraft, war was the main business of a prince, and he was also to rely on force to keep order in his kingdom, much as in Ch'in Legalism.

But China lacks a full parallel to the way Maurya unified much of

India in the 4th century B.C. He first seized his home state of Magadha, then systematically used the gains of the last war to pay for still wider conquests, a practice condemned in later India because war, it was said, ought to be waged for glory only. Indian thought agreed with China's Mandate of Heaven idea: so soon as a prince could not keep civil order and protect against foreign enemies, he lost his right to rule.

India, whether unified or not, always interacted with other strong empires or systems to the Northwest, often some Persian dynasty. India also furnished its religions and statecraft to most of Southeast Asia.

In the Middle East and Egypt, as empires rose and fell, the area of international interaction expanded. Tiny systems along one of the great rivers were brought under a single rule by conquest. Then these larger kingdoms—the Egyptian, Hittite, Assyrian, Babylonian—conflicted until Cyrus the Persian conquered all of them and added regions as far east as the Indus. Alexander later took over the Persian domains, adding his Greek homeland and Northwest India (where young Maurya saw him enter in triumph and got the idea).

But by the time Alexander's empire had been divided into three parts by his successors, the arena had expanded again, for Rome was impinging upon Greece so that some sort of international system existed from Mauryan India to Roman Spain.

In the Middle East language was not especially divisive. Rulers, merchants and cosmopolitans shared a succession of international languages: first Akkadian, Aramaic and Persian, then Aramaic and Greek. Yet there were many dialects and these could have aggravated international conflict while fostering disintegration of empire. But Alexander's empire divided along the administrative lines he had drawn, while conquest too tended to proceed by administrative divisions, for province after province was taken over as their governors or satraps were defeated in turn.

It is hard to evaluate the role of religion. The city-states were the main political actors, and each had its patron deity who was supposed to protect it in battle. Yet all the cities of Mesopotamia and Syria shared a pantheon of some 4,000 gods, many of whom had equivalents in Anatolia and Greece. Egypt, though sometimes bent on conquest, seems never to have tried to export its peculiar religion. Nor did the Persians try to impose their Zoroastrianism with its dual powers of Light and Darkness; they practiced toleration. Certainly none of these empires was unified by any specific world-view. Egypt and Persia, with their unique religions, were able to maintain their national identities through all vicissitudes.

The Middle East, even more than India or China, was invaded by Indo-European and other Central Asian tribes driven by drouth or famine or by other tribes. These invasions might unify the area by conquest if it was in a period of fragmentation, or fragment it if it were integrated.

These incursions out of Central Asia are a recurring theme in history up to the 16th century A.D. when Persia put down the last one.

Indo-European tribes, like the early Sumerians and the earliest nations along the Ganges, practiced a limited monarchy similar to a republic. But in the Middle East, as in India and China, absolute monarchy seems to have prevailed from the late 3rd millenium B.C. onwards. The king-god (Egypt) and the king-as-the-god's-representative (Mesopotamia) were concepts that tended toward unlimited monarchy. Monarchs were restrained, however, by the priesthood in Egypt and by the merchant class in Mesopotamia.

Omitting for the moment the Greek and Roman period, a look at the later history of the Middle East reveals that the Arabs, led by Mohammed in the 7th century A.D. and by the caliphs who succeeded him, united most of the area by conquest and expanded across North Africa into Spain. They had no advantage in military technology; merely a fierce and inspired cavalry. They adopted Persian-Alexandrine notions of administration. Arab tribesmen settled the provinces, like the Hittite and Chou in earlier times, as a new military and landed aristocracy. Arabic prevailed over Latin, Greek, and Persian. Christians, Jews, and Zoroastrians were permitted to live in their own autonomous communities subordinate to Arab rule; others often had to choose between Islam and death.

The Arabs created the theocratic state, with all military, civil, and religious authority concentrated in the caliph, though there was a separation of authority below him. The empire tended toward fragmentation, owing probably to the highly personal nature of Arab rule, the tradition of equality among Arab tribesmen, schisms over who was the rightful caliph, and the ravages of Genghis Khan and Tamerlane.

The Arab caliphate at Damascus was succeeded by a more Persian one at Baghdad. There was recurring war with the Byzantine empire. The caliphate became by the 12th century a hollow shell, presiding over a system of warring states. Such centralized authority as there was belonged to the caliph's Turkish guards, then to the Seljuks and then the Ottoman Turks. These last finally extinguished the Christian Byzantine Empire in the 1400s and ruled most of what had been the Arab empires. The Ottomans threatened Vienna but fell into decline under inept rulers in the 18th and 19th centuries, with each *Bey* or *Dey* acting independently of the Sultan. These independencies were incorporated by colonialism into the European international system.

In these Islamic empires there was to a high degree a common language, religion, and culture, backed by a centralized administration. Yet each disintegrated into a system of independent nations. But none of them fell apart into the units that had been originally merged together. Instead, they mainly dissolved into new nations which had lately been administrative divisions.

The classic Greek international system was marked by competition between the democratic ideology represented by Athens and the oligarchic ideology represented by Sparta. Each of these city-states was often the center of a coalition against the other. Democratic states were just as prone to knavery and violence as were non-democratic ones. Moreover, states did not always ally with states of the same ideology or on the basis of traditions of tribal kinship.

In time of war, democratic states would often name a dictator for the duration of the crisis, and sometimes he stayed on. In democratic states, public opinion determined foreign policy but leaders could manipulate opinion.

It is puzzling that the Greek city-states failed to devise any larger political unit, other than the Achaean federation which came too late, for these people spoke and wrote substantially the same language; they shared a polytheistic religion; and their notions of class, marriage, property-holding, and other customs were similar. Instead, they continued as tiny sovereign entitities, making coalitions and war until they were so weakened by the Peloponnesian War that they succumbed, first to Philip of Macedon, Alexander's father, and later to Rome.

The political thought of Plato and Aristotle was original, complex, and forever interesting, but never able to rise above the level of the city-state. The later Stoic school talked of the universal state reflecting the unity of God in the brotherhood of all men—men who through right reason and good conscience could understand the universal Natural Law. Stoicism was to become the philosophy of the Roman ruling class.

2. Let us now look at the foundations of the European international system, beginning with Rome whose empire came to include Greece.

Rome, like Athens, was originally a kind of federation of clans governed by clan law. Eventually civil law largely displaced the clans which were too divisive for the good of the city. Rome, like Athens, evolved from monarchy to oligarchy, but whereas Athens went on to democracy, Rome stopped with a "mixed form of government" (variously defined by Aristotle, Polybius, and Cicero) whereby the citizens had the final say, true, but the Roman Senate and other officers kept a high degree of control, especially over foreign policy, until imperial times.

Rome interacted with other states in larger and larger arenas of conflict, swallowing up one interstate system after another through alliance, counter-alliance and war. After finally defeating Carthage, Rome then faced east and eventually conquered most of the kingdoms that were successors to Alexander's empire. This is not to say that Rome was especially aggressive; it was successful in defending itself, then success began to feed upon success. Its military advantage lay more in good discipline than in any technological superiority. Presumably, too, once the decision was made on war, public opinion supported it more than if the decision had been made by a monarch or oligarchs.

In diplomatic machinations, the Roman proclivity for offering protection to one city in an interstate system, thus stirring up trouble which ended with Roman conquest of the whole system, is worth noting. Rome used this technique also among the barbarian tribes. It is to Rome we owe the phrase, "divide and conquer," though the technique was old even then.

So long as Rome was a republic the conquests continued, even during the civil wars of the triumvirates, but they trailed off with Augustus' imperial rule. Thereafter, most emperors were on the defensive, installing better central administration while keeping the barbarians at bay. Eventually, when the Praetorian Guard began deciding the imperial succession, emperors were more concerned with keeping their crowns than anything else and the less secure the empire and emperor, the more despotic the rule.

Could such an empire disintegrate as a result of the lack of a unifying belief system? Rome was substantially Christian after Constantine's reign. Or was the empire too large? The Romans were not fertile in technology except for their roads. It was not the lack of a unifying language, for Latin remained the official language of the Eastern as well as the Western Roman empire, not giving way to Greek until about the 7th century A.D. And, although Greek had all along been the *lingua franca* of the East, and even though there was a split between the Bishop of Rome and the Patriarch of Constantinople over power and doctrine, the empire was divided in two for administrative rather than religious purposes, a division that became permanent.

Class war? Class conflicts were intense from early on. Coupled with ambitious men, they destroyed the Republic. But it was a struggle among these men, not among classes, that was resolved by Augustus' ascendancy. The Empire then persisted, with all its old socio-economic injustices, for five centuries, and thereafter the Eastern (Byzantine) Empire for ten more, with the same inequities.

A failure of leadership? Perhaps. It is plain that the Republic produced able leaders at the right time far more consistently than did the Empire. Consuls elected by citizens were abler than emperors elected by soldiers.

After the Western Empire collapsed under barbarian invasions and was followed by several vague systems of small states, the Eastern Empire at Constantinople continued as a great power interacting with the Islamic empires.

The rise of Charlemagne briefly restored political unity to most of Western Europe, though it was an empire of rags and patches. He reluctantly permitted himself in 700 A.D. to be crowned Roman Emperor by the Pope, who claimed this right under a document of Constantine later proved a forgery. Thus began the long uneasy relation between Church and State.

Charlemagne, who interacted with Byzantium for a time, followed the

Frankish tradition by dividing his realm among his three sons, thus influencing the development of France, Germany, and Italy. This division was somewhat reversed by Otto the German who was crowned by the Pope as "Holy" Roman Emperor. Later still, the "marrying Hapsburgs" were sometimes able as Emperors to transcend the fragmentation of Western Europe. at least to the extent of controlling most of Germany and much of Italy. The emperor was elected by several princely or ecclesiastical states, and the "empire" was no more than a loose league. The Hapsburgs' personal domains later made Austria-Hungary a great actor in the European system.

Meanwhile Europe had disintegrated into several hundred petty states. Under the fear of Norse and other barbarian incursions, the feudal arrangement developed. Peasants sought the protection of a baron who in turn owed his lands and loyalty to a count, and so forth up the chain through marquis, duke, king, and eventually the titular emperor. Beginning, however, with William the Norman's conquest of Saxon England, the great kingdoms began to emerge through merger—often by conquest, not infrequently through marriage, sometimes by imperial or papal intervention.

Christian crusaders sacked Christian Constantinople on their way to save the Holy Land and brought back some Greek and Roman learning. Plato and Aristotle, the most-read philosophers in the Islamic lands, were translated from Arabic into Latin and came into Europe. Roman law was rediscovered, strengthening the Emperor's arguments against the Pope. Commerce revived, and merchants became creditors to princes, so that "free cities" run as republics by merchants became common.

Europe by the year 1200 was in the High Middle Age as contrasted with the earlier Dark Age. Scholars had to reconcile Aristotelian reason with faith. With Imperial authority in low repute, and the Church in decline, partly because it could not adjust to the new money economy, the kingdoms of England, France, and Spain became the great actors, along with the Hapsburgs.

The Italian interstate system of principalities and republics became the principal arena of activity. Here, relatively self-contained for a time, was a scene of deceit, intrigue, assassination, bribery, threat and violence which was perhaps matched only in feudal India. Dozens of states were reduced to a few, usually by violence. Machiavelli wrote his advice to princes. The Pope was a principal actor, along with Florence, Milan, Genoa, Venice, Naples and Sicily. Ideology was significant, with Guelph (pro-Pope) and Ghibelline (pro-Emperor) parties in every state. Mercenary captains sold their little armies to state or faction. Personal feuds mingled with high policy.

We cannot know whether some one prince might have unified Italy, as Machiavelli wished, for the Italian system was soon subordinated to the European when the Emperor and the kings of France and Spain became involved in the Italian wars. But modern diplomacy, with its exchange of resident ambassadors, was born here though it drew upon papal precedents, Roman jurisprudence, and German chivalric practices. So ruthless was the interstate conflict in Italy, however, that diplomatic immunity often was not respected.

In political thought, apart from Machiavelli's power realism, the post-Roman period is noted for Augustine's emphasis upon the universal state under God and his notion that peace and order are probably necessary to salvation itself. Catholic doctrine of defensive and other "just" wars owes something to him. Much was written in behalf of papal supremacy or of imperial rule. Dante wanted a world government under the Emperor, with some local autonomy, and with the Pope restrained pretty much to the spiritual sphere. The foundations of Western secular political thought were laid late during this period, mainly by ecclesiastics. The great kingdoms would soon find their apologists in Bodin and others.

The "medieval synthesis" was further threatened by the flood of classical learning brought into Italy by Byzantines fleeing Constantinople in 1450. In the 1500s the synthesis was wrecked by Luther's Protestant Reformation which spread rapidly in Germany. The Emperor Charles V tried to uproot heresy. Francis I of France upheld princely autonomy in religion. Germany, with seven large states and hundreds of smaller ones, became the main theater of a war marked by mixed motives of religion and princely ambition. There was a similarity to the Italian quarrels between Guelphs and Ghibellines, to the Crusades between Christians and Moslems, to wars in feudal India between the Left-Hand and Right-Hand factions, and among Chinese states which embraced differing philosophies. There were conflicts within each German state over religion. Peace was restored in a deal whereby each prince or free city could opt for Catholicism or Lutheranism.

But some items were not settled, nor were the rising Calvinists included in the deal, so a complicated politico-religio-economic quarrel erupted again in the Thirty Years' War. Protestantism had become an issue in every great nation, and had evoked the Counter-Reformation featuring the Jesuits. Yet it was not unusual for a country predominantly Protestant to cooperate with a Catholic nation against another Protestant land. This ignoring of ideology had happened also in the Italian wars and in the Crusades, especially in Spain. Alliances changed frequently. All Europe, even Russia, was involved. France, Spain, Austria, England, and Sweden were the principal actors. But Germany, where attempts to integrate the Empire more closely had failed, was again the main theater of war and did not recover from its devastation until the 19th century. France emerged as Europe's strongest nation, and Brandenburg (Prussia) began its rise.

The war ended in 1648 with the Peace of Westphalia. The modern national-state system is usually dated from this time. The Peace did away with the subordination of princely state to Emperor except in ceremonial matters, while even in the counter-reformed states of southern Europe papal claims to temporal supervision were ignored. The system of sovereign, secular states was the reality, with princes claiming to rule by "divine right" without papal approval. Jean Bodin, a French philosopher, asserted that sovereignty resided in the several "estates" of each realm (nobles, clergy, burghers, etc.) but so emphasized the need for a supreme law-giver to keep order that he was interpreted as arguing for absolute monarchy. The estates prevailed in some countries, especially Poland where any noble could veto state action. In Germany, Althusius argued for a cooperative "federalism" among the estates. Elsewhere the trend was toward absolute kingly sovereignty, and the estates were rarely called into session.

During the "Age of Discovery" European nations reached out, with their new technologies in sailing and navigation, to incorporate the rest of the world into the European system. "Mercantilism" developed, whereby the king's government moved into the economic realm and raised trade barriers around itself and its colonies. Territories acquired by sea-land power increased the wealth of the nation so that more territories could be taken, and prince and people might prosper. It was reminiscent of Maurya in India, and to a degree of Ch'in Legalism. Mercantilism foreshadowed state socialism.

Hugo Grotius and others developed international law. Nations were sovereign but their practices, including war, were held to be subject to the norms of right reason, good faith, and moderation. These norms came out of "natural law," stemming from the Stoics and preserved by the Roman church. But whether sovereignty meant supremacy only within the nation, or implied the imposition of that supremacy on other "sovereign" nations, remained a matter of dispute.

As the great kingdoms expanded by conquest and intermarriage, the number of states decreased. The methods of alliance and counter-alliance, and the techniques of threat, deceit, and so forth, revealed nothing new. The influence of religious public opinion on state policy was noteworthy, though not unique, and it seems significant that religious animosities declined remarkably after the Thirty Years' War. Despite the wars, the Italian Renaissance swept Europe during this period, and it was a time of freshness, optimism, and individuality.

We turn now to Cromwellian England where in the mid-1600s the first national state was being created, in contrast to the Age of Despots that described most of Europe. Presbyterians and Independents (Puritan Congregationalists), most of them commoners, defeated royal armies of noblemen and retainers who upheld the established Anglican Church and the King's prerogative to determine policy despite Parliament.

Cromwell created the first modern army, enforcing discipline and making equipment and dress uniform. Prussia, then other nations, emulated him. A republican constitution was written, though not implemented, and there were movements aimed at redistribution of property. Much of modern ideology dates from England's civil war. England had possessed elements of a national state. Charles I was considered un-English, threatening notions of life, liberty and property that went back to Magna Charta—ideas now shared by the people. It was their war. It was out of the yeoman army that the republican document came, asserting the sovereignty of the people. Cromwell's constitution, making him Lord Protector for life, was approved by popular referendum, the first in modern times. Cromwell had a secret police force which monitored people's private lives.

It is suggestive that "sovereignty" was originally a theological concept meaning lordship or supremacy, and that it was transferred from God to the monarch, then from him to the people and from them to the national state, coming at last to justify the unlimited power of the modern totalitarian state over its people. Thus does the concept of sovereignty tend toward absolutism. Much of this process is seen in Cromwellian England. He reigned in the people's name and by pointing to enemies in England and on the Continent was able to arrogate to himself totalitarian authority.

After Cromwell's death, the Stuarts were restored to the throne for a time, but then William and Mary were brought in as Europe's first constitutional and limited monarchy, subjected largely to Parliament in domestic policy.

Thomas Hobbes wrote, against the background of the civil war, that man without government is prey to fear, greed and hate, but that he can assert his reason long enough to covenant with others to place a sovereign—one man, several, or many—over themselves, thus creating a viable society by creating a government which can preserve order. Only then is morality possible, a notion shared by the Chinese Legalists and probably by Augustine. John Locke, writing after William and Mary had been crowned, argued that men could live fairly peacefully without government, hence did not have to give up their natural right to life, liberty and property when they eventually found it convenient to create government.

The Age of Despots flourished on the Continent from the end of the Thirty Years' War until the French Revolution. Its principal figure was Louis XIV of France. He centralized French administration and made war for his own glory. Again and again, most other European nations had to form coalitions against him. William of Orange, later England's king, forged several of these, and in the end Louis was contained.

Louis introduced a new technique in power politics. He would work out some legal claim to a foreign territory, get a favorable verdict from his own courts, then "enforce" it by diplomacy and war. All nations practiced mercantilism to the hilt, emphasizing the economic dimension of international conflict in the manner of Genoa and Venice in their heyday. Because France was the richest country, Louis was notable for using money to buy allies and to subvert officials of other nations.

Prussia became a great nation, using its army to acquire new territories, then administering them frugally and well, so as to afford the means for further conquests, in much the fashion of Maurya in India. Hapsburg authority was extended over Hungary and then the South Slavs as the Ottoman tide receded. Only in the Dutch federation, the Swiss confederation, and in veto-fraught Poland did despotism not flourish on the Continent. In Russia the Tsar brought the nobles under control, then the Orthodox Church, thus completing "caesaro-papism," the Byzantine practice whereby church and state are led by one person. Moscow saw itself as The Third Rome.

Louis might have conquered Europe if Russia had not entered the European system, thus making Louis' ally, the Ottoman Sultan, more cautious; or if Holland and England as well as Spain had not begun to draw strength from activities outside Europe. And it is noteworthy that England and Holland, though Protestant and tending toward republicanism, cooperated with despotic and Catholic Austria against despotic and Catholic France. Religion and political ideology did not seem to count for much during the high time of Europe's balance-of-power system.

3. We look now at the Industrial Revolution in England in the early 1700s, noting that its beginnings can be traced to the development of cannon and gunpowder in the 1300s which spelled the end of the feudal castle's viability, hence of the feudal economy and state. The Industrial Revolution grew out of the commercial revolution of the High Middle Age in Italy and of the Hanseatic towns in Northern Europe. England's new technology included central banking and techniques of managing the national debt. England would soon call for free international trade in place of mercantilist protectionism. With similar developments occuring in Holland and France, Europe's advance was unchallenged, for there was decline in Africa, the Middle East, and East Asia.

After Louis' demise there was no general war from 1714 to 1740 but Russia defeated Sweden in a long war and became a major power in a European system no longer dominated by France. The usual balance-of-power maneuvers ended in the general war of the Austrian Succession, 1740-48. The nominal issue was whether a woman could succeed to the Austrian throne. In the following peace, Prussia acquired Austrian Silesia. Then there was the general Seven Years' War, 1756-63, whose main result was that France lost its positions in North America and India to Britain. Coalitions changed frequently. Prussia, Austria and Russia cooperated briefly in the first partition of Poland. From 1775 to 1782, France and Spain saw gains in helping the American colonies win independence; US signed a separate peace with England in violation of its alliance with France. France, though victor, was economically weakened for the revolution to come.

David Hume, a Scot, remarked that Europe's vaunted balance system did not really work very well because England, though in good position to do so, did not act as the "balancer;" other nations could always count on England to side against France. Rousseau, the Genevan-Frenchman, sketched a plan for a European confederation based on St. Pierre's earlier effort. Kant, a Prussian, added his own version, a mere league of nations. Bentham, an Englishman, offered still another scheme. Evidently there was unhappiness with the way the system was working.

The French Revolution was preceded by the Enlightenment, a rationalist movement centered in the philosophers and encyclopedia-writers of France. Rousseau was principal prophet, asserting that in France, where the despots had been less enlightened than elsewhere, government originated and preserved inequality and poverty. US republicanism was admired in France where liberty, equality, and fraternity became slogans. Louis XVI was forced to call the Estates into session; there the middle-class commoners combined against clergy and nobility. Taking their cue also from the Cromwellian period, the Estates created the first thoroughly national state based on popular rather than kingly sovereignty. Merchants and lawyers substituted *laissez-faire* ("let-do") economics for the mercantilism marked by government interference.

The Revolution proceeded from supporting a constitutional monarchy to executing the king and queen and creating the First French Republic. The kingly nations were alarmed; French emigrants connived in foreign capitals. French nationalism-republicanism became messianic in fervor. While this was going on, the partition of Poland, where a republican constitution was being written, was completed by Poland's neighbors, thus violating the principle of the European balance system that a nation had a right to exist.

The French National Assembly, alarmed by counter-revolution, had declared war on Austria and Prussia. Marked by new techniques of mass conscription in France and the dissemination of republican propaganda in the monarchial states, this war went on from 1792 to 1795 when France won. But, in the process, France had changed under increasingly radicalized regimes (Jacobins, Girondins, Montagnards) from a republic to a police state, culminating in the Terror and Robespierre's guillotine regime. There were wage and price controls, and paper currency was issued recklessly. France was again victor but bankrupt.

In an effort to restore internal order, Robespierre was executed and the new multiple-executive Directory relied heavily on the army. Its hero was Napoleon Bonaparte who had won victories in Italy. Babeuf's first communist uprising in modern history had already been put down and elections were suppressed with the help of one of Napoleon's officers. The Directory was glad to send Napoleon to Egypt in 1798. He easily conquered the land, revealing Ottoman weakness and creating the science of Egyptology. Insurrection broke out again in France. Napoleon, though the English had sunk his fleet, traveled overland to France and was hailed as First Consul, then Life Consul, then, in 1804, Emperor.

If revolutions tend toward greater extremism, France's may be considered worse than Cromwell's because in France the revolution was constantly threatened by international war. Was it the revolutionaries or the European monarchs and their aristocracies who were responsible for the wars? Given the idealogical chasm, coupled with French confiscation of landed estates and hostility to the Church, war was probably inevitable.

Generally, the more oppressive the old regime, the more extreme the ensuing revolution, and the more extreme the revolution, the more hostile the reaction of other nations. War abroad coupled with a counter-revolutionary threat at home seems to produce tyranny at home, and domestic tyranny coupled with war-weariness seems to produce popular support for any stable government that offers peace abroad and order at home. Napoleon seemed made to order.

He of course instead went repeatedly to war. Eventually, there were six great coalitions against him, not counting the final defeat at Anglo-Prussian hands at Waterloo in 1815. Meanwhile, however, he abolished the Holy Roman Empire, reordering and combining the German states. He put his brothers and in-laws on thrones. He ruled an empire from the North Sea to the Balkans divided into 130 departments. He preserved the socio-economic reforms in France and instituted them everywhere he administered. He was ruined by the long war on the Iberian peninsula and a disastrous victory in Russia. In effect, he lost out to the foreign nationalist fervor that French nationalism had evoked. He returned from his first exile, offering Frenchmen a new democratic and pacific empire, but many did not believe him. In final exile on St. Helena his apologia was that he had hoped to integrate Europe and establish perpetual peace.

Although Napoleon was for a time far more successful than Louis XIV, he failed to unify Europe, perhaps by allying with nations he defeated instead of administering conquered lands directly, perhaps because of the ability of Russia and England to call upon resources outside the European system. This enabled England to control the seas.

Moderation was exercised at the Congress of Vienna in 1814-15 where Napoleon's foreign minister, Talleyrand, now acting for the restored Bourbons, was the central figure. The new European system consisted of many secondary and tertiary nations plus Britain, Austria, Prussia, Russia, and France. The Ottoman Empire was less highly regarded now. US had fought to a tie in the War of 1812 against a Britain pre-occupied with Napoleon, but was not yet a major power.

The Iberian colonies in the Western Hemisphere achieved

independence, thanks in large part to Napoleon's conquests of the home countries where he instituted reforms that frightened conservative colonials.

The Congress of Vienna marked the beginning of what is now called "functional" international organization, with agreements on navigation of the Rhine and Danube and the slave trade. The Tsar failed in his pioneering effort to achieve disarmament and raise an international army to enforce the Vienna settlement, but the Quintuple Alliance— sometimes called the Holy Alliance or the Concert of Europe—served for a long while as an "organ of consultation" among principal monarchs and prime ministers.

Accord at Vienna was followed by a period of black reaction against the Napoleonic reforms. But this "return to throne and altar" was uneasy and in many places short-lived. From 1815 to the Crimean War in 1854, the focus was upon civil conflict, with widespread insurrections in 1820, 1830, and 1848.

St. Simon and Comte believed that natural laws of society could be discovered and that a nation should be administered by experts, thus creating an early French version of the field of sociology. Elsewhere, the romanticism touched off by Rousseau's view that intuition is more reliable than reason took the form of "romantic nationalism." The state was seen by Hegel and many others as an organism of a rather mystic type endowed with historical purpose. Hegel said the state that embodies "Absolute Idea" will win out in war. Old languages were resurrected and new histories written extolling certain ethnic groups. Transnational Pan-Slavism vied with Pan-Germanism. The heterogeneous Austro-Hungarian empire was wracked by contending romantic notions of nationhood.

From the extremisms of the French Revolution, Hegel, Burke and others drew the lesson that change should be gradual, but romantic nationalism allied itself with liberal notions of limited monarchy or of republicanism, and squared itself off against throne-and-altar monarchy. Somehow, Metternich of Austria was nearly always able to muster enough of a temporary international army to overcome the liberal, capitalist insurrectionists; and he was helped in the revolutions of 1848 when Marxism first appeared and frightened the middle-class liberals. Only Britain did not cooperate with Metternich, for long-deferred reforms were taking place there and the nation was in a period of withdrawal from the European theater.

While romanticists on the Continent were praising common law, including old Germanic law, Britain was cleaning up its bloody common law. Britain never abandoned rationalism, though Carlyle, like Fichte and later Nietzsche, extolled the role of the hero in history. As the great sea power, Britain was moving toward free trade while unilaterally enforcing an end to the slave trade.

The Industrial Revolution speeded up, helped by steamship, telegraph and cable, and railways. Prussia bound North German states to it in the first modern customs union, the *Zollverein*. Austria remained head of the German Confederation established at Vienna.

Darwin and Wallace enunciated evolution as the survival of the adaptable, but romantic nationalists interpreted it as a struggle for survival of the strongest among those organisms called nations. Similarly, internal civil struggle was viewed by many in the same light; hence Social Darwinism was born.

Russia expanded to the Pacific, Austria-Hungary farther into the Ottoman domains. Britain coerced China into the international system through the Opium Wars. Louis, Napoleon's nephew, used expert propaganda to win election as President of the Second French Republic which arose out of the 1848 revolutions. As prototype fascist dictator, he played on the fear of Marxism, divided the opposition, became emperor by *coup d'etat* and had himself confirmed by plebiscite. He began, in Algeria, the colonial takeover of Africa, and later made an effort in Mexico.

Marxism claimed to be "scientific," as opposed to Babeuf's "utopian" socialism and to those versions of non-state socialism pushed by Fourier and Owen. Marx declared the inevitability of the triumph of socialism as the most efficient way of organizing production, then (with Engels) the withering away of government, and a new type of human being in the final, communist phase. He had drawn upon Hegel's view of the way philosophical ideas advance through thesis, antithesis, and synthesis, but to him this "dialectic" was materialist rather than idea-list. He held that the organization of the means of economic production determines the political, social, philosophical, and moral aspects of society, hence "economic determinism." He adopted the view of Ricardo, an Englishman, that Adam Smith was wrong, that there is no "hidden hand" that makes every man's greed work to the good of all; instead, the laborer is deprived by the capitalist of the product of his labor, thus alienating him from himself and from others.

The Concert of Europe, long weakening, fell apart in 1854 when Britain, France, and Austria intervened to prevent Russia from acquiring further Ottoman domains. Thus began what has been called the era of "power realism." It was a return to ordinary balance-of-power politics, featuring Bismarck and Prussia.

Prussia defeated Austria, then France, and in 1871 had the prestige to unify all of Germany except Austria in a federation dominated by Prussia and headed by the Prussian King-Emperor. Emperor Louis Bonaparte fled to England where he died. Briefly, a socialist commune held Paris and continued the war, causing great fright among French liberals before it was put down and the Third French Republic was established. Italian liberals such as Garibaldi, Mazzini, and Cavour took advantage of

France's preoccupation and drove the Austrians out, unifying Italy in 1871 under the King of Sardinia-Piedmont. Like Germany, Italy was a liberal constitutional monarchy. The number of independent states in the European system had been drastically reduced.

Though liberalism had lost most of the battles of 1820, 1830, and 1848, it had in the end triumphed in large measure everywhere except in Russia, either by evolutionary reform as in Britain or by revolution as in Spain and Portugal or by wedding liberalism to the cause of national unification as in Germany and Italy. But some were already beginning to question liberalism's *laissez-faire* economics. J.S. Mill, an Englishman, suggested that liberalism must be amended to include responsibility by the government for the poor. In effect, he was adapting Marxist appeal into liberalism, foreshadowing the democratic socialism of later decades. Bismarck helped things along by giving the German socialists much of what they wanted in social welfare programs.

Meanwhile, in the writings of Schopenhauer, a German, romanticism's anti-rationality and sentimentality (ridiculed by Mill) was turning into an irrationalism that would become increasingly pessimistic as it mingled with German sin-fixed Protestant theology. German industrialism deepened pessimism, causing a yearning for the Middle Ages when true community was thought to have existed.

4. We come now to the period after 1871 when the European system was completed with the addition of unified Germany and Italy. Called the Age of Imperialism, but perhaps better named the Age of Nationalist Extremism, it simply carried on the earlier Power Realism. The period saw the ultimate expansion of the European system in a final burst of colonialism which linked the planet into an economic whole through the technology of transport and communication. The period ended when this new global international system experienced its first world war.

Germany under Bismarck was industrializing rapidly, as was Japan under the Meiji oligarchs who had ousted the Shogun and now ruled in the name of the Emperor. They had patterned their new form of government on the one designed by Bismarck for the Second Reich, except that Japan was a unitary rather than a federal state. Both constitutions gave the emperor (or his advisors) broad emergency powers and gave the military access to the emperor over the heads of the civilian ministers.

At the German universities, which were arms of the government, professors lectured on *Realpolitik* which was to a degree Machiavellian. An Englishman, Mackinder, invented "geopolitics." Developed further by a German, Haushofer, the concept held that Eurasia was the "world island" that could dominate the rest of the world, and that the "heartland," occupied mainly by Germany, Austria-Hungary, and Russia, was the key to controlling Eurasia, and hence the world.

In Britain, still the most industrialized nation, the economic value of colonies was being questioned. But other nations wished a greater "place in the sun" and merchants and industrialists wanted government to protect them by tariffs while using army and navy to advance the flag around the world. Bismarck refrained at first from the colonial competition, being content with Germany as the "big land rat" and Britain as the "big sea rat." Indeed, he encouraged France's colonial ambitions to divert that nation from seeking revenge in Europe.

But eventually Bismarck and others succumbed to the lure of empire. Between 1870 and 1890, Britain, France, and Russia added eight million square miles and 100 million people to their empires. Germany, Austria-Hungary, Italy, Japan, and US likewise pursued their "manifest destinies." Most people, including those of the middle class and even the workers who were supposed to be socialists, took seriously "the white man's burden" and "the civilizing mission." Racism, mingled with Darwinism, held sway. At a Congress in 1884, the powers agreed that any nation might add colonies by gaining control and notifying other states.

Despite Germany's hegemony on the Continent and Bismarck's careful policy, there were war scares with France in 1873 and 1875. In 1878 Russia, in the name of Pan-Slavism, quickly defeated the Ottoman and dictated a division of the Slavic Balkans into independent states. But at the Congress of Berlin the other powers virtually robbed the Tsar of his victory. He blamed Britain and Germany, yet Bismarck was able in 1881 to negotiate the "Three Emperors" understanding with Russia and Austria-Hungary. Bismarck went on to forge an alliance with Austria, then drew in Italy, forming the Triple Alliance. He completed his work in 1887 with the "reinsurance treaty" whereby Russia agreed not to intervene in case of war between Germany and France.

Then, in 1890, the new young Kaiser Wilhelm II dropped Bismarck, and somehow failed to renew the treaty with Russia, while in France the able Delcassé became foreign minister. He adjusted old quarrels with Italy, which privately declared its alliance with Germany and Austria as purely defensive. He went on to win over the Tsar to an *entente* (understanding) in 1891, transformed in 1894 into an alliance.

Russia was busy in the Far East. Japan had defeated China in 1894-95 in a war over Korea. Russia forced Japan to disgorge some gains, though Japan kept Korea, Taiwan, and certain places in Manchuria. Russia got concessions from China in Manchuria and began to turn most of that vast province into a colony. Germany, in effect, held China's rich province of Shantung, while France and Britain administered much of China's public services. All great nations had extraterritorial rights, meaning they and their citizens were not subject to Chinese laws.

Ottoman power was low and Germany displaced Britain as the Sultan's protector. Britain bought controlling interest in the Suez Canal and had its own secure lifeline to India. The Kaiser was building the Hamburg-to-Baghdad railway. With Austria-Hungary and the Ottoman under his wing, he could control much of the Eurasian heartland. He made a deal with Russia, which had taken over Moslem Central Asia, for permission to complete his railway.

These decades saw a great arms race featuring seapower. Admiral Mahan, an American, was its prophet. Germany, feeling like "a mollusk without a shell" without a great navy, set out to build one. Britain said in 1889 it would build a navy equal to the navies of its two closest rivals and the race was on. Britain, bogged down in the Boer War, resented Germany's unofficial sympathy for the Boers, then was alarmed by German naval budgets in 1898 and 1900. Moreover, German goods were underpricing British goods in world markets.

In this situation, Delcassé was able to bury the ages-old enmity of Britain and France by pointing to Germany as the common enemy. In 1904 the *Entente Cordiale* was reached. There remained the problem of bringing Russia into cordial understanding with Britain, for Russia was seen as a threat to India. The two nations had come close to war in 1895.

At this juncture, in 1905, France made demands upon the Sultan of Morocco. The Kaiser announced himself Morocco's protector and demanded France dismiss Delcassé. He was dismissed; both France and Britain were having domestic difficulties with the socialists, and so were not bold. But by the time the great-power conference was held, French and British public opinion had rallied and Germany suffered diplomatic defeat, backed only weakly by Austria. Russia had been defeated by upstart Japan in 1905 in the Far East, and the Tsar was unhappy because the Kaiser had encouraged him to take a strong line against Japan. The Tsar was even more unhappy with the 1905 Russian revolution, triggered by the losing war, which forced him to give Russia its first constitution.

France was thus able to get Russia and Britain to negotiate their colonial quarrels and in 1907 the Triple Entente became a reality. It was less than an alliance, yet its significance was clear. Delcassé's "diplomatic revolution" had been completed; Germany's hegemony had been displaced by a near equilibrium of power.

In 1908 Austria-Hungary, which had administered Bosnia for some time, annexed the Adriatic province outright. Austria feared the Young Turks, who had installed a liberal regime in Istanbul (Constantinople), might convince the other powers to restore Bosnia to Turkish administration. The Kaiser announced his support of his fellow emperor against the wishes of Russia and Italy. He carried the day, for France and Britain did not take a strong stand.

In 1911 France, with Delcassé back, made Morocco a full protectorate. The Kaiser took a strong line, but this time France did not yield. Foreign capital began to be withdrawn from Germany; the German army was not ready for war; and the crisis passed with another defeat for the Kaiser.

In 1912 the German-trained Turks were defeated by Italy in a war over formerly-Ottoman Tripoli in North Africa. Then Serbia, Bulgaria, and

Greece attacked the Turks who were again defeated before Germany or Austria could intervene. At a great-power conference, Bulgaria got less than it wanted, so in 1913, with Austro-German encouragement, struck Serbia and Greece. Bulgaria lost, and again Pan-German prestige suffered.

This was the situation when the Austrian archduke and heir to the imperial throne was assassinated in Bosnia in June 1914.

One should look closely at the tragi-comedy of events—their escalation amid shrill, vain cries of nationalism; the stupidity and carelessness of leaders; the deception of ally by ally; the deception of chiefs of state by their ministers and generals; the disregard of sober and well-meant warnings; the failure to take timely action; and, on the other hand, the over-reaction that led to world war. Ultimatum evoked mobilization, then counter-mobilization, then declaration of war. The events of the summer of 1914 are worth being studied in detail.

We should also briefly note the development of democratic socialism during this 1871-1914 period, a non-revolutionary form of Marxism which sought its gains in collective bargaining and the parliamentary process. Syndicalism and anarchism were subordinated to Marxism in most of Europe, but then Marxists in some countries split into evolutionary and revolutionary factions, as in Russia where Mensheviks opposed Lenin's Bolsheviks. Lenin conceived of a small disciplined party, the "vanguard of the proletariat," which would use violence to attack capitalism at its weakest point, Russia, which was still more feudal than capitalistic.

It is interesting that Lenin and the tsarist prime minister both believed the revolution could win only in the event of international war. In no nation of Europe did the socialists of any stripe refuse to back the war effort. Nationalism had won the day.

During this period pessimistic irrationalism developed further in Nietzsche's writings, and in Bergson's emphasis on action for action's sake. Schopenhauer's concept of blind will was quite popular in the years leading to World War I.

It is curious that it was the Tsar, who called the Hague Conferences of 1899 and 1907 but failed to get disarmament or anything except some rules of war and voluntary (not compulsory) arbitration of disputes, who lost both crown and life in the war which followed.

At this point two generalizations tempt us: that international history is the record of little men trying to cope with situations quite beyond their capacities, so that even the work of "great" men like Bismarck is singularly narrow and national and temporary; and that international systems seem to arrange themselves into two competing coalitions which somehow always involve all the great nations.

The war was initially declared between Germany and Austria-Hungary on the one hand and Serbia, Russia, France and Britain on the other. Japan came in quickly, for Britain had friendly relations and had fostered an accord between Japan and Russia. Japan wished the German position in Shantung plus holdings in Oceania. The Young Turks, fearing Russian designs on Istanbul, joined Germany and Austria, as did Serbia's enemy, Bulgaria. Italy remained neutral until promised Austrian territory, then despite its Triple Alliance declared war on Austria.

As initial Austro-German offensives bogged down in trench warfare, peace talks began in 1916 involving President Wilson. Austria wished peace; Germany did not. Then Wilhelm renewed unrestricted submarine warfare, necessary to prevent the Allies from bringing outside resources into the European theater. Britain too was violating international law by stopping neutral ships that carried no contraband. Then Britain intercepted and released the Zimmerman telegram suggesting that Mexico, which had bad relations with US, become involved. Pro-German sentiment in US was quashed. In March 1917 the liberal revolution in Russia erupted, enabling Wilson to see the war as between democracy and autocracy. US declared war in April.

All great nations were now involved. Even China, where the Manchu Dynasty had been supplanted in 1912 by a shaky quasi-republican regime, declared war and sent laborers to the Allies in Europe. Peking hoped for Allied support against Japan which in 1915 had forced China to accede to some of its "Twenty-One Demands." These hopes were dashed after the war, turning Sun Yat-sen away from the West and giving rise to the Chinese Communist Party.

With stalemate in Europe, US entry in the war turned the military-economic balance against the Central Powers. Despite Germany's introduction of poison gas and the launching of projectiles from aircraft (both in violation of the Hague Conventions), its last offensive failed, even though Russia's collapse had freed up resources for the Western front.

Russia's defeat produced successively more revolutionary and extremist regimes, culminating in seizure of power by a tiny minority led by Lenin, whom the Germans had shipped back to Russia to foment discord. The Allies sent ships and troops to Russia, ostensibly to keep supplies from falling into German hands, but ended up by backing the White armies against the Red, an event which was to have lasting consequences. Lenin and Trotsky expected revolutions elsewhere but eventually had to sign the Brest-Litovsk Treaty and give up much territory; and this draconic peace was exemplar for the peace imposed at Versailles.

The moderation of Vienna in 1814-15 was not present at Versailles in 1919-20. Worst of all perhaps, owing to war deaths old statesmen with old viewpoints dominated the 1920s and much of the 1930s, during the ensuing Era of Totalitarianism.

5. The period from the end of the first world war until the present is the

most tragic in international history. 19th century visions of infinite progress and human perfection surrendered first to pessimistic irrationalism and then to raging belief systems. Optimistic formal-legalism, with its assumption of a natural harmony among nations that need only be recorded in treaties, shuddered under the failure of the League of Nations and then collapsed with the inability of the United Nations to cope with international conflict and other worldwide problems. Pervasive pessimism concerning the human venture has been accompanied by pervasive power realism in world politics.

After World War I the Romanoff, Ottoman, Hapsburg, and Hohenzollern dynasties were gone. USSR gave up considerable territory on the western edge of the Russian empire; Lenin began the New Economic Policy which permitted capitalism to repair somewhat the damage caused by war. Ataturk salvaged Turkey from the Ottoman disaster and modernized it. Britain received League mandates over Palestine and Iraq; France received mandates over Syria, including Lebanon. Saudi Arabia became an independent kingdom while other sheiks accepted British tutelage. Egypt and Sudan were in effect parts of the British Empire; Tunisia, Algeria, and Morocco part of the French; while Italy retained Tripoli (Libya). In North Africa, as in the Near East, even nominal Ottoman sovereignty was gone.

Austria-Hungary was broken up in accordance with the principle of romantic national self-determination, except that Austria was denied union with Germany. Austria and Hungary became small republics while Serbia was aggrandized, including non-Serb Slavic elements, into Yugoslavia. Czechoslovakia, an amalgam of Slavic peoples plus some Germans, was economically viable because it had industry; the rest of the former empire was not, and attempts to form a customs union failed.

Peasants demanded land, and most East European countries moved first to the left in sympathy with the Russian revolution, then back to the right as army and landowners asserted authority. This was also true of Poland, now back on Europe's map.

Germany, now under a democratic socialist government, gave back Alsace-Lorraine to France and accepted French occupation of the Saar Basin and part of the Rhineland. Germany lost all its overseas empire as Japan became the dominant power in the Far East. China was divided into warlord provinces, though Sun Yat-sen and his brother-in-law, Chiang Kai-shek, would shortly start their unification process, helped by Soviet advisers.

As for the Covenant of the new League of Nations, President Clemenceau of France said that if the League had no international police force the Covenant would be only a philosophical document, but Woodrow Wilson believed the US Senate would ratify nothing stronger.

Section 16 of the Covenant offered statesmen scant assurance that the "collective security" principle would in fact provide security to any nation. Basically, each member-nation had a veto as to its own participation in any military or economic "sanctions" to enforce the peace. So the world international system was left to look to arms and alliances for security, as usual. There were new international agencies with specialized functions to perform and a new World Court that could hear only disputes that nations wished to refer to it and had no means of enforcing its decisions.

During the interwar period the world system focused again, possibly for the last time, on Europe. The war had been fought and won by regimes which, though liberal, had had no time for socio-economic reforms. In the 1920s, most governments were conservative and did not want reforms. Anti-communism was strong in Europe and America.

In the 1920s there were many small wars but no big one, as the nations tried to recover and to adjust to the postwar settlement, and to shore up the League Covenant by other treaties. US and Britain turned away from Europe. France desperately sought "guarantees" that the peace settlement would not be undone. The Locarno treaties of 1925, involving principally France, Germany, and Italy, helped temporarily. There was also an understanding between Germany and that moral leper, the Soviet Union. Germany started rearming with Soviet help. A later French effort at "guarantees" produced the amusing Kellogg-Briand pacts of 1928 which "outlawed war" except for reasons of defense.

But World War I brought totalitarianism not only to Russia but to Italy as well. Mussolini, combining syndicalism and socialism with anti-communism, and using Lenin's idea of a disciplined party but his own notions of the charismatic leader, led disgruntled war veterans in the March on Rome in 1922. Fascism represented worship of the organic state and glorification of war—a rather full expression, politically, of pessimistic irrationalism.

Yet, once in power, Mussolini permitted capitalism its profits under government tutelage, made a deal with the Church, and ran a cautious foreign policy. Indeed, if Europe had a balancer in the 1920s, it was Italy. Mussolini's ability to bring order and a measure of prosperity to Italy was admired by many in the liberal nations. They said he made the Italian trains run on time.

Hitler probably copied Mussolini, though each was said to travel with a copy of Machiavelli's *The Prince* in his luggage. Like Mussolini, Hitler coupled nationalism with an economic appeal in his "national socialism," but he added anti-semitism and offered to undo the Versailles peace. He made his first move in 1923, the year of the great German inflation. He ended up in jail, but all he needed was another great economic crisis. This came in 1929 with New York's stock market collapse which touched off a worldwide deflationary type depression. Germany's fragile prosperity was based on infusions of outside capital, mainly dollars, which were supplied in a complicated effort to handle

French demands for war reparations from Germany. What with currency imbalances and trade deficits made worse by high tariffs, every great nation except USSR suffered disaster during the Great Depression (USSR of course had its own economic problems).

In Germany the democratic socialist regime, remembering the 1923 inflation, practiced "sound money" principles until there were six million unemployed, a third of the work force. Its representation in the *Reichstag* dropped to a third; the Communists had a third; the Nazis and the rest of the extreme right, the remaining third. Germany was scarcely governable. President Hindenburg used the emergency clause in the "model" Weimar Constitution to authorize first one and then another chancellor to rule by decree. Eventually, in desperation in 1933, he named Hitler, who jailed the communists, then got a majority of what was left of the *Reichstag* to vote him dictator "temporarily."

Hitler's coming to power ended the Geneva disarmament talks of 1932-33, and he shortly took Germany out of the League. In 1922 the Washington Naval Treaty had fixed warships in the ratio of 5-5-3-3-2 for US, Britain, Japan, France, and Italy, respectively. A few ships were actually destroyed or deactivated to meet this ratio. Further efforts were made toward other disarmament in 1927 and again in 1932 at Geneva when the talks were noted for their domination by military men and arms makers.

Japan had already walked out of these talks and out of the League, which had criticized Japan's take-over of Manchuria in 1931 and its creation of the puppet state of Manchukuo. Japanese militarists had justified this venture at home on the grounds that development of Manchuria would mitigate the Depression's effect. When other nations refused to revise the Washington Treaty, Japan in 1934 denounced it and began building warships. Japan had its "State Shinto" cult but was an autocratic military state rather than a fascist state. Yet fascism was an active movement in nearly every nation in the 1930s, as was communism.

The 1930s are said to be the decade of appeasement. But ideology played a role. Pierre Laval, French foreign minister, was pro-fascist and anti-communist. He helped assure that the Saar plebiscite in 1935 would turn out in Germany's favor. He paved the way for Mussolini's invasion of Ethiopia in 1935 and connived with Samuel Hoare, British foreign minister, to weaken League sanctions against Italy. This spelled the end of the League. Mussolini's invasion may have been evoked by his fear Hitler would outdo him by uniting Germany and Austria, thus posing a threat to Italy's northern frontier. And, in fact, this shortly happened.

Germany was rearming rapidly, thus buying temporary prosperity. In 1936, when the French parliament ratified a defensive treaty with USSR, Hitler said this violated the Locarno pact so he sent troops to reoccupy the Rhineland, supposedly "demilitarized." He told his troops to withdraw if they met resistance. But as usual the balance of power was not operative; France, Britain, and Belgium couldn't decide what to do.

The final try-out for World War II was Spain. In 1936 General Franco raised a rebellion against the Republic, then governed by a "popular front" of liberals, socialists, and communists. With Mussolini and Hitler sending more help to Franco than the government got from USSR and France, Britain and US maintained a neutrality that favored Franco. A complicating factor was that, under pressure of war, the government was increasingly dominated by its communist element. Franco finished occupying Spain in 1939.

By then all Europe was about ready for war. In the fall of 1938 at Munich, Britain and France had persuaded Czechoslovakia to cede to Germany the *Sudetenland* where many Germans lived. USSR and France were Czech allies but Czech leaders did not wish Soviet troops to intervene. USSR was not even informed of the deal, though Moscow had said it would stand by its ally. USSR thereafter doubted it could depend on Franco-British support against Germany. French and British public opinion was opposed to the Munich deal and began to turn toward war as the only way of coping with Hitler who already occupied most of Czechoslovakia and now forced several other East European nations, some of them already under fascist regimes, to ally with him.

Britain and France gave their guarantees to Poland, the next target. They extended guarantees to Rumania and Greece in April 1939 when Mussolini invaded Albania; then to Turkey, whereupon Hitler and Mussolini announced their Axis "pact of steel." Britain and France had military talks with USSR but could reach no agreement, partly because Poland's almost feudal regime would not welcome Soviet help. Litvinov, Soviet foreign minister who had consistently supported collective security through the League, was displaced by the tough Molotov. At the end of August came the Nazi-Soviet Pact, for which USSR was expelled from the League. The real damage to Moscow came from the worldwide communist outcry against so infamous a pact; it seemed to many true believers that the communist movement was only a tool of Soviet policy.

World War II began in September 1939 when German troops crossed into Poland, which was defeated before any help arrived and then partitioned between Germany and USSR. The Baltic states were reincorporated into USSR and Stalin launched an invasion of Finland. His "revolution from above" provided the industrial base for a major war effort, yet Soviet arms won only some strategic ground in Finland, not glory, and the army was still unprepared in June 1941 when Hitler invaded USSR. Presumably this was part of the cost of Stalin's purges of Soviet leaders.

Hitler took Denmark and Norway, which caused changes in the British and French cabinets, then in June 1940 Germany's "lightning war" forced French surrender, even though Churchill offered federal union with France at the last moment. The British had been driven back across the Channel but Churchill vowed Britain would fight on alone, which it did, with increasing US moral and material support.

Mussolini entered the war, vowing to regain Nice and Savoy from France, but instead followed up his invasion of Albania by unsuccessfully invading Greece. Germany had to rescue him after occupying Yugoslavia and then go into North Africa where Italian forces were losing to the British. Mussolini's new Roman Empire could boast of triumph only in Ethiopia; henceforth he would be Hitler's puppet.

In late 1940 President Roosevelt leased destroyers to Britain, and US had its first peacetime draft in history. In early 1941 US lend-lease aid began reaching Britain, then, after Hitler's invasion, USSR. On December 7, 1941, Japan attacked Pearl Harbor. Seven hours later, Japan caught MacArthur in the Philippines with his planes on the ground. In 1937 Japan had invaded China proper and forced the removal of Chiang's Nationalist regime to the far Southwest. Now it swept most of the Far East, capitalizing on anti-colonial sentiment in Indochina, Burma, Malaya, Singapore, the Philippines, and Indonesia. Chiang was inactive, more afraid of the Chinese communists than of the Japanese. Mao Tse-tung was headquartered in the far Northwest but his cadres and guerrillas infiltrated and controlled much of North China other than the cities and railheads which were occupied by Japanese forces.

After Pearl Harbor, Germany and Italy declared war on US even though their defensive treaty with Japan did not require them to do so. Roosevelt was thus free in the eyes of US public opinion to give priority to the war in Europe while conducting little more than a holding operation in the Pacific. A successful Allied invasion of French North Africa gave substance to De Gaulle's "Free French" regime. Then Sicily and Rome were taken, forcing Mussolini to flee. He was for a time head of a regime backed by German troops but eventually he and his mistress were taken by Italian partisans and hanged upside down.

The anti-Axis alliance was christened "The United Nations" but USSR never participated in any unified command. Stalin wanted a second front in Western Europe but didn't get it until June 1944. By that time Hitler's disaster at Stalingrad in early 1944 had been followed up by a Soviet advance to Warsaw. Many Jews perished in the Warsaw uprising when Soviet troops refused to enter the city. These were some of the six million Jews killed by Hitler's orders throughout Europe, most in calculated cold blood.

Hitler had once held more of Europe than Napoleon, but his empire quickly dwindled. Again, US industrial might and manpower had denied Germany victory. Hitler and his mistress committed suicide and Germany surrendered unconditionally.

Allied leaders had discussed the war and the postwar settlement at various conferences. At Yalta in early 1945 occupation zones in Europe were agreed upon. As the Cold War soon prevented any overall peace settlement, these zones remade the map of Europe. Millions of long-time German residents in East Europe were shipped back to a shrunken fatherland west of the Oder-Neisse line. At Yalta it was agreed too that USSR, upon Germany's defeat, would enter the war against Japan. Truman, who succeeded Roosevelt in the spring of 1945, is sometimes accused of using the atomic bomb on Hiroshima and Nagasaki to forestall Soviet gains in the Far East. He claimed he was trying to shorten what promised to be a long war despite US military superiority in every respect. At any rate, the human race entered its nuclear era on August 6, 1945. USSR joined the war immediately, occupying much of Manchuria and Saghalin Island. Japan surrendered a week later.

The UN Charter was a pre-nuclear document, signed at San Francisco on June 26, six weeks before Hiroshima. The Charter is substantially a longer version of the League Covenant. Roosevelt thought the League failed because US was not a member. Like Wilson, he wanted a document that the US Senate would ratify. Much preliminary work had been done; Truman had no apparent influence on the Charter.

The Security Council, where the five great nations have permanent seats and each possesses the veto, has sole responsibility for keeping the peace. All others surrendered on paper their sovereign right to take independent action; all are required to join in military or economic or diplomatic sanctions, as determined by the Council. But their obligation to provide forces and facilities was made subject to special agreements to be negotiated by the Council with them. This proved not possible owing to mutual suspicions and the veto. Nor has the Military Staff Committee under the Council ever been agreed upon.

Indeed, statesmen who gave the Charter a close reading knew from the outset that, so soon as great-power unanimity broke up, the UN could provide no security to any nation. Security would depend, as in the past, on the vicissitudes of the balance-of-power game. National power would continue to determine effective sovereignty, modified by skill in diplomacy and by chance. The UN, like the League, never would preside over the international system but would be made an instrument of national policy.

To understand recent international history it is important to consider the sequence and coincidence of events. The following few paragraphs describe how the Cold War got started:

> Mutual suspicion which prevented Franco-British accord with USSR in 1939 persisted through the wartime cooperation. Soviet suspicions were aroused by Western slowness in opening a second front. British-backed and Soviet-backed groups already contended for governance of Yugoslavia and Poland after the war should be won. At Yalta in February 1945, Stalin was persuaded by Roosevelt to agree to free elections in the East European states; Churchill would have accepted a more realistic delineation of "spheres of interest."

Just after Yalta, Soviet authorities ousted the all-party regime they had permitted in Rumania and required the king to install a communist administration. USSR then denied to the Allies facilities promised them in East Europe; refused to agree on an occupation of Austria; announced the Soviet foreign minister would not head its delegation to the UN conference at San Francisco; and accused the Western Allies of trying to make a separate peace with Germany.

And it is true that German generals tried to hold back Soviet armies so as to surrender to the Western Allies; that Churchill tried, in April, in violation of the Yalta agreement, to persuade General Eisenhower to push on to Berlin; and that, after Germany surrendered, Churchill and Truman were slow in drawing troops back to their assigned zones.

The Cold War began at about this point, before the German surrender, rather than in 1947 or 1948 as some assert.

The inter-allied commission set up to govern Germany deadlocked. Western statesmen, with Truman replacing Roosevelt, took a strong line with USSR on East Europe at the Potsdam meeting in July 1945. France feared Germany's postwar industrial competition so refused in October to treat all Germany as an economic unit as agreed at Potsdam. Truman terminated lend-lease aid to USSR as soon as Japan surrendered, and somebody "misplaced" a Soviet request for postwar help, thus hampering Soviet effort to rebuild a war-shattered land. USSR shipped vast quantities of industrial machinery back home from its zone in Germany as reparations. This angered the Western allies; and USSR was supposed to ship food from its zone to their zones, but food was scarce so none was shipped.

The inseparability of events in a worldwide system is seen, during this same autumn of 1945, in the failure of US and USSR to agree on a common administration for Korea, and in USSR's virtual exclusion by US of any influence in the administration of occupied Japan.

And that is the way the tit-for-tat sequence has gone on for more than forty years. International history since World War II is dealt with in some detail in Chapter 6 on foreign policies. Here we shall content ourselves with brief descriptions of the main themes during the post-war period.

The dominant theme is of course the Cold War. With US-USSR relations worsening, and the UN powerless to do anything about it, US monopoly of nuclear energy ended in 1949 when USSR exploded its first atomic bomb. Truman responded by forming an alliance with Canada and West European nations called the North Atlantic Treaty Organization (NATO). In 1955, after NATO decided to re-arm West Germany, USSR formed a counter-alliance with East European nations called the Warsaw Pact. By this time USSR had matched US by testing a fusion or H-bomb and the world had entered the Nuclear Balance of Terror.

There were repeated crises while Dulles, Eisenhower's Secretary of

State, was running an anti-communist crusade, and this culminated, during the Kennedy administration, in the Berlin Crisis of 1961 and the Cuba Crisis of 1962. Kennedy and Khruschev then signed a partial Nuclear-Test-Ban Treaty in 1963, the first thaw in the Cold War. But Kennedy was shot and the Cold War resumed under the inept Johnson, with Vietnam as its centerpiece. Nixon continued the Vietnam war, but at the same time made new approaches to USSR and to China, now Enemy No. 2. Under Nixon, Ford, and Carter, arms control agreements were reached with Moscow and US recognized communist China, so that in the mid-1970s there was another thaw, called *detente*. But this ended in 1979 when USSR intervened in Afghanistan, an intervention still continuing and highly criticized by US and China. Reagan's anti-communist rhetoric, with Moscow's responses, has put the Cold War back into a deep freeze not seen since Dulles' time.

The Cold War's hot wars are: (1) the Korean War of 1950-53 in which Truman intervened in the UN's name—after China intervened it ended in a draw, with Korea divided as before; (2) the Vietnam war of 1945-74 in which the communists in the North, helped somewhat by China and USSR, defeated their colonial French masters and then the Americans, who backed the non-communist South; and (3) the Afghan war, in which a puppet regime supported by USSR troops has been bogged down since 1979 in combat with Afghan guerrillas backed by Pakistan and US.

Another main theme is the liquidation of colonial empire. Before the war ended, US promised the Philippines independence. Britain, under a Labour government, followed shortly by granting independence to India and its other dependencies in South Asia. After the Mau-Mau troubles, Britain granted independence to its colonies in Africa and, eventually, to its mandates in the Middle East. The Dutch tried to hold on in Indonesia, and the French in Indochina and Africa, but after much violence both had to give up, with De Gaulle making the decision that France should terminate its losses but keep the profits by maintaining cultural and economic ties. Belgium turned the Congo loose suddenly, leading to a chaos that the UN tried to pacify. Finally, when Portugal and Spain returned from quasi-fascist to liberal government in the late 1970s, most of their colonies achieved independence. Now only a few fragments remain of European overseas empire, but most of the former colonies are in deep trouble.

An aspect of the unburdening of the white man's burden can be seen in the defeat of Chiang Kai-shek's Nationalists by Mao Tse-tung's Communists. Whereas Chiang *tried* to rid China of the Europeans, Mao actually did it, then went on to drive MacArthur out of North Korea and make China a nuclear power. But in trying to produce the "New Communist Man," he brought the country near chaos and upon his death in 1977 was supplanted by moderate modernizers who appear to be turning away from Marxism.

Also related to the end of colonialism is the Arab-Israeli problem and the concomitant energy crisis. Britain, under pressure from US and Zionists, gave independence to Palestine after dividing it into Arab and Israeli parts. Violence ensued; the Israelis won, and many Palestinian Arabs became exiles. Israel has fought three wars against them and a combination of Arab nations, chiefly Egypt, Syria, and Jordan, winning them all. Meanwhile the Palestinian Liberation Organization became terrorists (as indeed the Israelis had once been) and have shown other minorities and individuals how, by murders and hijackings, they can at least get attention.

The 1973 Arab-Israeli war evoked an embargo by the largely Moslem Organization of Petroleum Exporting Countries (OPEC) against oil shipments to US and European nations which were supporting Israel, followed by a tremendous increase in the price of oil. Then in 1979 the Shah of Iran, whom Nixon and Kissinger had established as their great ally with vastly greater oil revenues, was overthrown. These disorders caused a further jump in the price of oil, to over $30 a barrel compared with about $2.50 before the 1973 jump.

Since then the Western DCs (Developed Countries) have suffered almost chronic recession while the LDCs (Less Developed Countries) have been hard put to find the dollars to buy oil to make fertilizers to grow food. The Moslem oil producers banked most of their dollars in US banks, which then lent them to LDCs. Several of these owe enormous debts and can't pay unless the banks lend them more. As most of this is owed in turn by the banks to the Arabs, a monetary and trading collapse of the 1930s type is possible. The only good thing is that a lot of new oil has been discovered in Mexico and the North Sea, so that the price of oil in mid-1985 fell below $30.

Another theme since World War II has been the spread of industrialization to all of the Soviet bloc nations; to the Pacific Rim countries, namely Taiwan where the Chinese Nationalists took refuge, South Korea, the city-states of Hong Kong and Singapore, and mainland China to some degree; and to Brazil and Mexico, both now heavily in debt. Japan, already industrialized before the war, now rivals USSR as the second greatest industrial nation and outdoes US in many products.

Allied to this economic development is the rise of customs unions and common markets in Central and South America, Black Africa, and Europe. Of these, only the European Common Market is significant. It was organized after the US Marshall Plan helped Western Europe rebuild, and it was intended to lead eventually to a federal union of Western Europe. Its main achievement was the creation of a relatively free-trade area throughout most of non-socialist Europe, but its prosperity has waned in the recent recessions. There is much bickering and its future is now in doubt. The same is true of NATO which includes all the Common Market countries except Ireland, plus US and Canada, Spain, Portugal, and Turkey. Meanwhile the Soviet bloc's Council for Mutual Economic Assistance (COMECON) has been of some significance, but most of the economic gains appear to be owed to departures from Marxist economics as practiced in USSR. Moscow, while permitting a modicum of free enterprise by its allies, has shown by its armed interventions over the years in Poland, Hungary, and Czechoslovakia that there is a near limit to their autonomy.

The remaining great theme is the great increase in population in most places other than Europe and Japan, but especially in LDCs that are least able to feed the increase. This problem will be discussed in detail in Chapter 7.

Allied to the population explosion is a lesser theme: environmentalism, which is a worldwide rising concern over pollution, much of which is transnational, and over depletion of natural resources, especially top soil and petroleum. This too will be dealt with in Chapter 7.

Actually, this presentation of international history since 1945 suffers in that while the first world war gave focus to the events of 1871-1914 that led up to it, and the second world war similarly was the culmination of the events of 1919-1939, in contrast, the events of the past forty years have as yet no such culmination or focus. But of course the complete history of this period may never be written.

A final theme of these four decades has been a quantum jump in most branches of science and technology, especially in biology and electronics. The most publicized of these advances has been the use of missile-launching technology to place satellites and reusable shuttles in orbit, to put men on the moon and to send probes throughout the solar system.

If, in addition to splitting the atom, we can do these things, why can we not build a durable peace among nations?

To answer this question, we must first understand the causes of international conflict. In Chapters 2 and 5 we shall undertake this.

But first, let us draw from our summary of international history some generalizations that will help us find out why nations behave as they do.

B. Generalizations Drawn from International History

Our procedure will be to work up what seem to be the most significant regularities of behavior of (1) international systems, then of (2) leaders within nations, then (3) we shall try to integrate this into one statement.

1. *The Behavior of International Systems.* A system comes into being when two or more nations engage in frequent contact. The earliest systems probably formed when one group and then another was attracted to some grassy plain or irrigable valley which then became their arena of interaction. These little states would grow as newcomers arrived or as

colonies were planted by older states or by extension of the arena to impinge on other independent groups. We know there were several hundred states in pre-Han China; in the Mediterranean in classic times; in Europe in medieval times; at least several dozen in old India, Middle America and the Andes; plus many hundreds in Indonesia and Oceania, Black Africa, and North America when the Europeans arrived. So the total must have come to several thousand, in hundreds of systems, even though the planet's population was small.

An international system is more or less self-contained. To operate as a system, most of its states must interact more frequently and significantly than with outside states. Even the most self-contained systems have been permeable: the Yellow River system from Central Asia and the Andean from the Amazon Valley, for example. The European, with its monopoly of technology, was almost self-contained for a time, but the only wholly self-contained system is the present planetary one.

Once nations come into contact, they seem to have no choice but to interact. International behavior begins and takes the form of cooperation or conflict; or first one and then the other; or some of both; or cooperation with some and conflict with others. Conflict transcends cooperation in all systems we know much about, repeatedly issuing in violence and war. War may have been rare among the very early Eurasian agricultural states overrun by the Central Asian peoples; the Eskimo tribes did not make war, we're told; and there appears to have been little if any war among the Mayan city-states, though they made war against outsiders. But such behavior is deviant for independent states, in the light of international history as a whole.

For some reason, even cooperation produces conflict. A trade agreement between two nations is seen by other nations as a threat to them. Similarly, conflict produces cooperation, as when citizens of one nation are denied resident-trader rights in another, and the first nation seeks the help of other nations to correct the situation.

Clearly, there is some obscure dynamic which sets up a dialectical movement between conflict and cooperation. But it is a many-sided movement with multiple dimensions or axes within a system and difficult to discern. The overriding thrust of this dynamic is toward conflict: in both examples in the last paragraph, the situations move toward conflict. More importantly, the weight of history is that cooperation is tentative, being recurrently transcended and cut off by conflict and violence.

The thrust toward conflict is accompanied by enunciation of state goals backed by strategies to achieve them. The goals are diverse: the getting of wives or slaves; princely or national glory and honor; territorial aggrandizement or national self-determination; economic advantage; the spread or protection of religion or ideology; the white man's burden or black nationalism; and self-defense. The strategies are actually only one:

the balance of power, sometimes called power politics, its hallmark being coalition-building or the forming of alliances. The tactics of the balance of power are appeals for help including the identification of one's goals with those of other nations, cajolery, lying, spying, trickery, assassination, bribery, foreign aid, cultural exchange, propaganda, subversion, insurrection, appeals to international law and public opinion, and the calling of conferences. All these tactics are aspects of diplomacy.

Once a system has come into being it will have form, structure, configuration. Three such configurations can be discerned. One is the One-Nation Predominant configuration, as in the Europe of Louis XIV and of Napoleon, when one nation is by far the strongest in population, resources, and other capability. Another is the Two-Nation Predominant, as in the cases of Athens and Sparta, Rome and Carthage, Charles V and Francis I, and US and USSR. The third is the Multi-Nation configuration, typical of most systems through most of their histories. The same system can move from one configuration to another.

The configuration is linked to coalition-building. In the first type, secondary and tertiary nations typically combine against the predominant nation, which finds a few tertiary allies, while others remain neutral. In the second, each of the two predominant nations builds a coalition of secondary and tertiary nations with itself at the center, while some remain unaligned. In the third, in which there usually have been three to seven nations of more or less equal power, it somehow happens that two opposing coalitions develop, including lesser nations, while some lesser nations remain neutral. It is difficult for small nations to stay unaligned but it is for some reason virtually impossible ultimately for a great nation to do so.

Thus, whatever configuration one starts with, an international system ends up repeatedly in a bi-partite arrangement of two opposing coalitions. One could add the uncommitted and call it tri-partite, but the uncommitted are formless as a group, hence not a party. There is of course cooperation within each coalition, but it is wary, uneasy, secretive, tentative. Through the tactics of the balance of power, and answering to whatever is the hidden dynamic, coalitions change. Nations that blew hot blow cool, some drop out and join the other coalition, some withdraw into the uncommitted, some grow in power, others decline. A prince may die, a president leave office, or a cabinet lose a vote of confidence, hence policy may change.

What does not change is the outcome of coalition-building, for this persists through its waxings and wanings until it ends in violence, in war. Coalitions, being conflictual divisions, are oriented toward violence, made in anticipation of war. Somehow the process always ends in war.

We have spoken of the balance of power. Logically the word balance can refer only to an equilibrium, an equipoise. If the system thrust is toward equilibrium, why is it not attained? And, if it is, why do not things stop there, in balance, in *status quo*, with the system maintaining itself by adding or detracting in small increments, without proceeding on into violence?

Evidently the thrust is not toward equilibrium, or equilibrium is too difficult to weigh or is too easily altered if achieved and thus is not satisfactory as a goal to the nations concerned. Clearly, no international system has been stable if violence shows instability, although some systems, such as the Greek and the European, have perpetuated much the same principal members despite repetitive violence.

At any rate, the recurring course of events is plain enough: If there is contact, then there is conflict; if there is conflict, then there are coalitions; if there are coalitions, then ultimately there is war. At all points, cooperation is subordinated to this overriding sequence.

Here we have just departed from straight description and discussion. By using statements of the "If, then" type we have set up a sequence of events which may suggest some causal connection.

The outcome of violence, in all systems to some degree and in most to a high degree, is merger of nations by conquest into other nations so there are progressively fewer nations. Hence, If war, then integration. But since it is not war alone that produces international integration, but the whole tactical bag of power politics that conflict brings into play, and since these can end—under threat or not—in merger by princely intermarriage or by agreement, the better generalization is, *If* conflict, *then* integration.

Conflict tends to reduce the number of system members until there remains only one and the system is extinguished. Examples are the Chinese system unified under Ch'in; the Indian under Magadha; the Nile reduced to two kingdoms, then one; the Mediterranean under Rome; and the Andean under the Incas. These unified nation-empires then, sooner or later, become actors in broader international systems.

Conflict also produces integration by weakening states so their system can be subdued and incorporated by an exterior power. After the Near Eastern arena had been reduced to three main actors—Egypt, Assyria, and Babylonia—conflict among them paved the way for Cyrus' Persian conquest. The Peloponnesian War wrought such attrition that Macedon, a state peripheral to the Greek system, could impose its will on the Aegean. At a later era, conflict among Alexander's successors permitted Rome to conquer them. Conflict among states of the Western Mediterranean enabled Carthage and Rome and then Rome alone to prevail. During the centuries of colonial imperialism, the European colonizers would have found the job much more difficult if the states in the systems they conquered had not been fighting among themselves.

The degree and kinds of authority exercised by the conquerors vary. But there is a trend throughout history, often afforded by advancing technology, toward greater depth and reach by the central authority. The

Hittite empire, like the Aztec, was only a military hegemony over autonomous states, whereas Persia had garrisons throughout its empire controlled by centralized communications. So too did the Inca empire. The Islamic empire headquartered at Baghdad was more centrally administered than the Arabian caliphate at Damascus, and the Ottoman more so yet. India had been integrated under the Mauryas and Guptas but got its first rationally and hierarchically organized administration under the Moguls; and the British centralized it further.

An empire is an amalgam of formerly independent units under a central authority which decides, as a minimum, the military and external policies of the whole. If an empire lasts, internal diversities are lessened, while externally it becomes a state among states. This is true of China, India, USSR, and US. Germany, if not now divided, would be included. But it should be noted that Italy, as a late example, and indeed all states of any size today, are likewise empires—amalgams of pre-existing independent entities.

The coercive force needed to maintain integration is in proportion to the change that is desired, and how quickly it is desired. More force was needed to make people embrace Islam than to content Jews, Christians, and Zoroastrians with living in their own communities while paying taxes to caliph or sultan. Usually it is not necessary after a time to employ much coercion if cultural peculiarities are respected; cultural homogenization may then occur rather rapidly. The old ruling classes and ambitious young men learn any new language required. Many, especially those of the highest and lowest classes, adopt the dominant religion. There is inter-breeding. Law codes become commingled. Systems of mathematics and calendar-keeping spread throughout, as do art forms, musical notations, and philosophies.

Peoples resent settlement of aliens among and over them, but the tendency is to accept the inevitable, especially if the new government maintains order and is in other respects not much worse than they were accustomed to.

International conflict produces much cultural homogenization, as in the Crusades, even if it does not result in political integration. But such homogenization does not of itself lead to political integration, for integration by agreement is rare.

Integration can come by agreement, but successful, enduring examples are few, and conflict among the parties or between them and outsiders has always prompted agreement. We do not include here religious associations such as Greece's Amphictyonic League or kinship associations such as the Ionian League, or such loose associations as the Holy Roman Empire, the Arab League, Organization of American States, or Organization of African Unity. We do include the Achaean League which was a true federal union; the United Provinces of the Netherlands, federated under the House of Orange; the Swiss Confederation, when changed in 1848 to a federation; the United Kingdom, formed by succession of a Stuart to both thrones but confirmed by agreement; the United States, once the Constitution was adopted; Bismarck's Second Reich, a federal union brought more by agreement than violence; Italy, unified by agreement and violence; and others.

Thus we can generalize, If agreement, then integration, but we bear in mind that conflict elicits agreement.

Integration is not a one-way street. We have noted disintegration of empires in China, India, the Near East and the Mediterranean, and of the Austro-Hungarian in Europe as well as the short-lived empires of Napoleon and Hitler, and now the dissolution of the colonial empires.

Political disintegration correlates with dynastic decline whereby rulers become less capable or less interested, more removed from administration, less apt to provide order or justice, less quick to apply timely force, or less convinced that the the game is worth the effort. This is accompanied by the rise of palace guards in the capital and of military governors in the provinces, so that the center is shaken and the peripheries become independent.

Romantic nationalists emphasized divisions within nations along linguistic, cultural lines, some of which were approved in the Versailles settlement, but the more common disintegration has been along artificial administrative boundaries. The rarest thing has been a disintegration back into the independent units originally incorporated into the greater nation-empire, and then it must occur quickly, as with the empires of Napoleon and Hitler or in the case of Syria which left Egypt's "United Arab Republic" after only three years. Statehood and ethnic peculiarities are distinctions which commonly are so blurred during integration that they do not reappear in disintegration.

Even though integration is not a one-way street, the evidence of history is clear enough. As against the thousands of independent states once on this planet when its population was probably a few millions, there are about 170 today, most of them comparatively insignificant, when its population is upwards of five billions. The world international system has about the same number of significant actors as the European had, far less than the Greek. Despite ebb and flow, the dominant process is toward international integration, and our overall generalization for this Subsection 1 must be:

If there is an international system, then it moves through conflict, coalition-building, war and/or agreement toward integration into one nation-empire and extinction as an international system, whereupon the new nation-empire becomes an actor in a larger international system.

Why, then, has the present global international system not extinguished itself?

For the same reason that the European system didn't. As we noted in Section A of this chapter, even as early as the wars of Louis XIV, the coalitions that opposed him were able to rely upon resources drawn from their new overseas empires. And Napoleon's bid to integrate the European system by conquest was frustrated in part by Russia's ability to draw upon its farther land empire but mainly by Britain's ability to draw upon its own overseas empire while denying to Napoleon the overseas resources of the European states he had conquered—specifically the Spanish, Portugese, and Dutch empires.

In essence, what had happened was that the seafaring European nations, in the process of using their superior technology to acquire overseas empire, had extinguished by conquest many small interstate systems and several large ones but at the same time they had rendered the European system permeable from overseas and therefore no longer self-contained.

Similarly, both the world wars began as European wars which spread out from the European subsystem to include all the principal independent nations in the world system as well as all the European overseas empires. Indeed, during the second war the principal event in this process was the linking up of a pre-existing conflict in the Pacific subsystem with the one in Europe. The Japanese attack on Pearl Harbor signaled that Europe would no longer be the single main arena of conflict in the world system.

There were, in effect, two wars, though the contending coalitions straddled both Europe and the Pacific, with US the main victor in each theater. With its nuclear monopoly, US could have integrated the world system in all likelihood, exclusive of Soviet Eastern Europe perhaps, but it settled for the UN Charter. The consequences have been grave.

We turn now to the national or foreign-policy level where we shall generalize on the behavior of leaders and publics within nations as it affects national action within an international system.

2. *The Behavior of Leaders and Publics within Nations.* There is an interplay between internal and external conditions. The international situation affects the domestic situation; a nation's politics influences international politics.

External and internal forces both focus upon the national leaders who make both domestic and foreign policy. Increasingly in modern times, however, there are economic, cultural, and ideological forces which cut across national frontiers and affect many publics. Leaders and the elite groups that support them cannot wholly control these forces so must take them into account. At the same time leaders may consciously direct such forces across the frontiers of other nations to serve their external policies.

If there is indeed a dynamic within an international system that thrusts toward opposing coalitions, it must operate through the national leaders. Leaders have personalities. Some, like Richelieu and Bismarck, seem well-adapted to the game of coalition-building and play it with skill and relative moderation. Some, like Emperor Louis Bonaparte and Prime

Minister Chamberlain, play it poorly. Others, like Napoleon assisted by Talleyrand or Hitler assisted by Ribbentrop, are adept but try to pile success on success until they achieve failure. Still others, like Cyrus the Persian and Alexander, are equally immoderate but more skillful and achieve total success.

Of these four types, all except the Bismarcks are elements of instability which move the system on past balance into war and possible integration. The Louis Bonaparte types and the Alexander types are especially responsible for integration, the latter type being opposed by such inept leaders of the former type that they are able to integrate systems into empires. In contrast, leaders of the Napoleon type such as Louis XIV have been opposed by such able coalition-builders as William of Orange that they have been denied even temporary integration.

Leaders of the Napoleon and Alexander categories are not content with a mere balance of power; clearly they have sought imbalance and conquest. They, combined with inept leaders such as Chamberlain, vastly outnumber the Bismarcks. And Richelieus and Bismarcks are not only scarce; their work is temporary. The accomplishments of the first were ruined by Louis XIV; those of the second by Wilhelm II.

Some leaders are intelligent, others dull; some patient, others not; some faithful to their word, others faithless. Coalition-building begins too quickly; it is completed too late. Indecision can be fatal, as in the case of US on the eves of both world wars; decision can be fatal, as with the Kaiser and the Tsar in 1914. A leader cannot control his allies, especially in a "cockpit" subsystem such as the Balkans or the Middle East. A leader cannot control his generals, as in the case of Wilhelm and the advance of his army into Luxembourg. A leader cannot control the purity of his information: Wilhelm I was misinformed in the "Ems dispatch" by Bismarck; his son suffered the same from the Austrian foreign minister; in both cases, deliberately.

Thus the decision-making process in every nation is fraught with mishaps; among the several national governments of a coalition, the situation is worse; among the many such governments in both coalitions, worse still. The wonder is that the balance of power manages conflict even temporarily without violence, for the situation is absurdly unstable.

In early stages of conflict situations, leaders and their supporting elites manage foreign policy with little reference to publics. But as conflict moves on toward crisis, they increasingly appeal to the rank-and-file. They at first arouse merely a generalized patriotism but later spell out that such things are at stake as the gods, ethnic peculiarities, Lutheranism, communism, or the greatness of the nation. They justify coalitions by pointing to any commonalty with allied nations or, if that is lacking, by stressing need for common defense.

In early stages, some part of the public will heed other leaders who urge a different policy: Cato saying Carthage must be destroyed, Lindbergh telling Americans to stay out of World War II, a French labor leader denouncing the coming World War I. But as conflict deepens, publics become ever more homogeneous in support of official leaders until, with outbreak of violence, dissent is silenced by social as well as governmental pressures. This occurs whether government is autocratic or democratic; policy is no longer that of leaders-elites only but of all the people; and the nation is essentially autocratic, its society closed.

Yet it has not been rare, especially in later centuries, for public opinion to lay down broad limits within which leaders must maneuver. In the religious wars, a wise Protestant prince did not take sides with other such princes if most of his own subjects were Catholic. Liberal opinion within monarchical countries made it difficult for them to combine against revolutionary France. Anti-fascist opinion, some of it inspired by Roosevelt, would have made it impossible for him to align with Germany, while he was at pains to explain alliance with communist Russia. Anti-communism, some of it instilled by Truman and his aides, produced a public opinion which tended to rigidify policy thereafter.

The more united the public—or the dominant elite, if the masses do not count for much—is on internal policy, the bolder and more consistent the nation's external policy can be. Leaders are sometimes bold abroad to abridge dissension at home: the Church proposed the Crusades in part to divert dissension within Europe; some Austrian leaders in 1914 welcomed war as a means of uniting a fissiparous empire; Mussolini and Hitler may have rearmed to get their economies moving and quiet discontent. But sometimes internal dissension has caused leaders to speak softly, as for example France in the first Moroccan crisis, or to withdraw from the international situation, as in the cases of USSR in the 1920s and China during the Cultural Revolution of the 1960s. Yet civil conflict always destabilizes the international system, for it adds to or detracts from the nation's normal weight, making policy calculations difficult.

Because war or its ever-present threat tends to silence domestic discord, and because resources are diverted from internal needs, internal socio-economic change is postponed. But this holds true only if the nation is successful abroad or so long as it is not unsuccessful. Britain in the Napoleonic years and US during the world wars and the Cold War are examples. But when war goes badly, as with tsarist Russia in 1917, or is lost, as with Germany in 1918, or is won but lost, as with Italy in 1918, dissension breaks out again and internal change comes rapidly under new leaders-elites proposing new solutions.

Indeed, the principal thrust of international conflict is toward drastic internal change. It does this by discrediting old regimes, as in the examples just given, but also by deferring evolutionary change so that internal pressures ultimately demand great changes even in liberal countries, as in the British reforms of the 1830s and the American ones in the 1930s. Also, there is imposition of change on the vanquished by the victors, witness Germany and Japan after World War II. In all these variations, pressure for change and willingness to accept it are heightened by destruction of material and human resources.

Hence we could say: If civil conflict, then international instability; and, If international conflict, then civil conformity but then drastic civil change. We shall return to this theme in Chapter 7 on prediction.

But our focus is upon international conflict and integration, so our generalization on Subsection 2 is:

The instabilities of national leaders who vary in their abilities and intentions, and whose tenures are uncertain, together with public permissiveness or dissent, and of unpredictable incident, tend to destabilize coalitions and to move the international system into violence and thus into integration.

3. *Summary Statement.* Bearing in mind that the more general and all-inclusive we become in our generalizations the more detail we lose, we combine Subsections 1 and 2 to say:

In an international system, national leaders-elites are driven or permitted, by their publics and by the instabilities of the domestic and international situations, to push their coalition-building past the threshold of violence, so that ultimately, by conquest and/or agreement, the international system extinguishes itself by integration under an overall government.

True, the present planetary system, in existence now for about one hundred years, and produced by millenia of international conflict in ever-fewer-but-larger systems, has resisted thus far its integration under one government. But in a sense the world system has filled itself out only with the collapse of colonial imperialism, for we now have new significant actors like India and China.

4. *Other Trends in History*

Technology. The thrust toward integration has taken place in an environment of advancing technology. We mean all ways of doing things more efficiently, including hierarchical bureaucracy and quick communications which permit control of larger territories and populations. Technology's military applications have been significant: weapons of bronze instead of stone, and then of iron; the horsedrawn chariot of the Indo-Europeans, then Assyrian cavalry; the Macedonian phalanx, then the Roman square; the rowboats of Phoenicians and Greeks and Vikings, Persian and Arab dhows, European sailing ships with sextants and compasses; bows and lances, gunpowder and cannon; steamships, railroads, airplanes, tanks; telegraph, telephone, wireless; nuclear warheads and inter-continental-ballistic-missiles (ICBMs).

The role of technology in international history has been to inter-relate nations ever more closely in the economic, cultural, and military senses; to broaden the arena of international conflict; to give an advantage in weaponry to some nations while making violence ever more deadly and destructive; and to make possible the control of ever-larger territories under one over-arching government.

Loyalties. Individuals throughout history have had difficulty in identifying their interests with anything beyond their families and their localities. But at some very early time the individual found it possible to identify with the extended family or tribe which, whether nomadic or sedentary, was independent of any other and was therefore a nation. As the nation grew in scale through history the individual transferred his loyalty from the tribal state to the city-state, to the principality and to some great kingdom, then to today's national states and superpowers. There are even some individuals now who think of themselves primarily as Europeans or simply as members of the human race.

The Justification of Government. From the time of the Four Schools of pre-Han China, up through India's statecraft writings and the "Mirrors for Princes" written during the Arab and Islamic empires, to Hobbes and Hamilton and Reinhold Niebuhr, philosophers have discussed how government—that is, some men telling other men what to do—can be justified.

But there are two requirements that all philosophers lay down: government is justified if it preserves order within the nation and if it defends that nation against other nations; otherwise not. Many writers make further requirements; for example, that government also provide social or economic justice. But all political theory requires those two functions as the minimum: order, and defense. Even Marx-Leninism requires that government do those two things until the socialist phase is finished and the state (government) can wither away.

It is interesting that the two basic requirements are, optimally, only one: peace. And one can jump from the old philosophers to the latest research in biology and game theory to find suggestions that governments are instituted to (a) restrain greed, (b) prevent cheating, and (c) make cooperation possible.[1] Here too the ends are order and peace.

The Scourges of Mankind. As of 1985, after several millenia of organized society, cannibalism and human sacrifice have disappeared. Slavery is virtually extinct but there is still some serfdom and more peonage. Women and boys are rarely sold for sexual use but prostitution persists in most places. Polygamy is becoming rare, divorce common, and the parents-children family is everywhere displacing the extended family. Physical torture and capital punishment have declined but they do persist, while no solution has been found for those adjudged criminal or insane. Child labor is disappearing except in farming, and children generally are well-treated. Women approach closer to equality everywhere, but especially in the industrialized nations.

Politically, the republican form of government has displaced virtually every other form, and colonialism is all but wiped out. Yet representative government with its party competition and freedoms of speech, press, and association has disappeared in most ex-colonies, has not reappeared in the socialist nations, and is not grappling effectively with problems even in the old liberal capitalist nations. Nearly all adult males can vote, and most females, for whatever that is worth. But the norm is the nation ruled by one man, one faction, one party, or by wealth, with the military elite everywhere dominant or influential. Democracy is rising as a slogan, declining as a practice.

Economically, the world's gross product has increased dramatically owing to technology but the LDCs have only about 15 percent of it, hence they experience chronic malnutrition and face mass starvation. In socialist and capitalist DCs, including China, incomes are tending toward equality with minimums at or above subsistence levels, but in capitalist DCs drastic inequality of wealth persists. In DCs, "cradle to grave" economic security at some tolerable level has been the trend, but there is a widespread conservative reaction in the 1980s.

Socially, the rigid class or caste stratifications noted in all civilizations at a certain stage have broken down dramatically in the last few generations, though they persist in DCs as well as LDCs. The landholding aristocracies that used to run things were displaced by civil and military hierarchies and by businessmen entrepreneurs, and these in turn have been succeeded by specialized managerial elites that operate industries, government bureaus, political parties, the armed forces, research complexes, and so forth. They are the upper class. The other class consists of the white or blue collar workers. The old four- or five-tiered stratification exists almost nowhere except in India, but there remain in most parts of the world invidious distinctions based on color, caste, and ethnicity that have blurred rather than disappeared.

Yet, while most of the scourges of mankind have declined to a degree that few realize, there is a threatening trend toward total control by government over the political, economic, and social aspects of people's lives. The Ch'in emperor tried to burn all the books he didn't like; a Roman emperor tried to fix wages and prices; and the Inquisition burned heretics. But the phenomenon is largely recent, beginning with conscription in Cromwell's England in the 1600s and culminating in the totalitarianisms of Mussolini, Hitler, and Stalin.

This totalitarian trend is associated with uptrends in nationalism, ideology, and the threat of apocalyptic war.

Many political theorists, including ourselves, believe that liberal, representative government occupies the high, middle ground between the need for social order on the one hand and the desire for individual freedom on the other. Thus one of our concerns as we move along will be to identify the circumstances in which that kind of political system can flourish. Those circumstances will no doubt include a reversal of the totalitarian trend just mentioned.

Chapter 1 Notes

1. Kathleen Stein's "The Biology of Power Plays" and Bill Lawren's "Interview with Robert Trivers," both in *Omni* 7:10 (1985), pp. 68 and 76 ff. See also our page 133.

PART II

WHY HAS THIS HAPPENED?

There is a chain in which the first link is international history and the descriptive generalizations drawn from it. The second link is explanation based on description. The third is prediction based on explanation. The fourth and last is prescription based on explanation and prediction. Clearly, the most important link is explanation, which we undertake in the next four chapters.

Few efforts have been made to work up categories for getting at the causes of international conflict, despite the immense body of writings on international relations.[1] The most comprehensive and useful scheme, though it was developed more than 25 years ago, is that of Kenneth N. Waltz who found that the alleged causes can be grouped into three categories: first, in the nature of man; second, in the natures of nations; and third, in the nature of the international system.[2]

Our analysis will be couched in categories which are adapted from those of Waltz.

Chapter 2

BECAUSE WAR IS INHERENT
IN HUMAN NATURE?

The first hypothesis is that international conflict originates in the nature of individual man, or anyway in his behavior. This statement covers two basic views of human nature, plus variations. One holds that man is intrinsically sinful and from this flow those secondary characteristics called hatred, greed, vainglory, and the like. The opposing view asserts that man's nature is intrinsically good and that if he were living in a condition of nature or under a good socio-political system his behavior would be uncorrupted and good.

In between are other views that man is a mixture of good and bad, or that some men are naturally good while others are bad, or that man is evil but is capable of redemption or transformation, or that man is merely ignorant and can be enlightened and made good by education.

A view that may be gaining ground is that man is a still-evolving organism whose next great step will be to adapt himself to living harmoniously with his fellow men. This theory, coming from trained biologists, has imparted some scientific validity to the humanist hope that man can work out his social problems.[3]

We go now to the specific qualities and behaviors that are said to cause international conflict.

A. Man as Sinful

Any argument that human nature is the cause of international conflict must necessarily go on to say that such conflict is inevitable until human nature itself changes. This is especially true of that form of this argument which declaims flatly that men are sinners and that there will be "wars and rumors of wars" until the end of time.

Most of Christian theology, from St. Paul up to the neo-orthodoxies of Reinhold Niebuhr and Karl Barth, has accepted the doctrines of sin and grace, with some disagreement whether grace improves behavior in this life or merely redeems the soul in the hereafter.

But it does not follow from this that Christian theology has taught that war is caused by defects in human nature. Instead, it has for the most part been silent. Augustine may have thought that war, like private property and government, is an evil thing which man gets because of his sin, but he was conscious that peace was possible for he had seen peace maintained by the Roman empire in a Mediterranean world made up of many diverse peoples. He watched its breakup through civil war and barbarian incursion with dismay, speculating that even individual salvation might not be possible without civil peace.

The Roman Catholic Church, until very recently, taught a distinction between just and unjust wars, based on Augustine's work mentioned in the last chapter, so that for example a war of aggression was sinful but a war of self-defense was not.[4] Niebuhr accepts man as sinful but says individual man can transcend his sin and act altruistically whereas it is virtually impossible for a group of men to transcend its group interest; of the societies to which men belong, the state (nation) is the least moral.[5] So Niebuhr, more than Augustine, sees society as corrupting individual morality, and group-man as being more responsible for international conflict than individual man.

Luther left affairs of state to the princes of his day, although he surely got the idea from Paul. And it is mainly among Protestants, armed with the book Luther gave them and applying its phrases automatically to the questions of our day, that one finds at the flattest the assertion that man is sinful and will not have peace until (a) all are converted or (b) the Second Coming. This viewpoint is typically accompanied by a confounding of peace in the sense of civil or public or international peace with peace in the sense of the individual's peace of mind or peace of soul.[6]

Of the traditional Chinese schools of thought, Taoism taught that human nature was good like all nature and that it could only be corrupted by social custom or government or by preachments of morality and love. Mohism accepted human nature as good but sought to make it better through preaching an ethic of unconditional love. Confucianism tried to enhance the good in human nature by building a well-regulated familial and social environment in which selfish impulses would be repressed and generous impulses rewarded. Legalism taught that human nature was bad and could be restrained only by law backed by coercive force, and that war was the proper business of the government, whereas the Confucianists and Mohists opposed war and blamed it on rapacious rulers.

Hinduism assumes that the soul, when first it incarnates, is crude and unenlightened, but that it may learn and progress through many reincarnations, each of which is determined by the soul's accumulation of moral and immoral acts. Buddhism teaches that life is a burden and shows the path by which the soul may become so enlightened that it is freed of the necessity of rebirth. Both originally taught that the soul must progress by its own merit but have developed large sects that teach redemption through intercession by liberated souls. Hindu thought left international conflict to princes, but non-violence was brought over into Hinduism from Buddhism and Jainism, introducing a pacifist strain, especially apparent in Gandhi's teaching.

Islam adopts much the same attitude toward human nature as Christianity, springing as it does from the the same Judaic roots. War was the main business of the Arab tribes that Mohammed converted from polytheism to monotheism. He gave this activity a new direction, holding that the only good wars were those designed to spread or maintain Islam. This theme is similar to that of the Roman Church during the Crusades.

Summary Comment. Theology and philosophy are metaphysical, beyond the physical, and to the extent that they elaborate upon divine revelation are supernatural as well. They are incapable of proving how accurately they reflect reality. But we cannot conclude that this body of thought is not based on a great deal of human experience or that it does not show insight into the human heart.

B. Man as Aggressive

Unlike theologians, modern psychologists have not been much interested in whether man is innately sinful, or even in whether he is good or bad. They are interested in the wellsprings of man's behavior—in his basic instincts and in the degree to which many generations of living in a culture have caused him to override or redirect those instincts.

Albert Einstein once wrote to Sigmund Freud giving his own ideas on the causes of war and asking for Dr. Freud's views as a psychoanalyst. Freud replied that the aggressive or death instinct contends with the *eros* instinct which seeks to conserve and unify, and tends to prevail when "a nation is summoned to engage in a war." Then, patriotic appeals speak also to the *eros* instinct and line it up in partial support of the aggressive instinct. Working against this aggressive instinct are whatever "produces ties of sentiment between man and man" plus the growth of culture and the strengthening of the intellect. These forces may, he says, possibly bring about a time when all men are pacifists like himself and Einstein.[7]

Freud does not explain why most individuals are non-pacifist with regard to international conflict but pacifists as to civil conflict. Nor does he follow up his own suggestion that the aggressive instinct may be diverted "into a channel other than that of warfare." One thinks of money-making, sports, politics, and other competitive activities, as well as high endeavors such as mountain-climbing, venturing to the moon, or doing research in psychology or physics.

Freud elsewhere gave an apparently different account of aggression. A recent psychology textbook lists five types of behavior systems, two of which are "dependency" and "aggression," the one deriving from the infant's helplessness and the other from consequent frustration. Then:

> A suggestion, deriving from Freud and widely accepted by others, is that aggression is one of the consequences of frustration....
>
> We have to be careful in the case of aggression to distinguish between aggression as a means to an end and aggression as a motive in its own right...This is a matter of some dispute, but in the behavior-theory interpretation the answer is that aggressive behavior, having been in some way rewarding in early childhood, comes to be a motive in its own right...
>
> However the aggression comes about, some children and some adults develop strong tendencies to injure themselves or others.[8]

Thus we do not know whether aggression is an innate, basic instinct or is something culturally derived. Here the latter is emphasized. Also it would appear that only some persons develop strong aggressive tendencies. Dependency and aggression certainly appear less basic than the other three "behavior systems" listed: the oral, the anal, and the sexual, which have clear physiological bases in hunger, elimination, and sex.

Frustration occurs when an individual's progress toward a goal is thwarted. The consequences of frustration, in addition to aggression and destructiveness, are restlessness and tension; apathy; fantasy; sterotypy, meaning blind, repetitive, fixated behavior; and regression, meaning a return to childish behavior. These are more or less immediate reactions to frustration. There are also habitual ways of adjusting to frustration, called "defense mechanisms," which we'll discuss in Section E on irrationality.[9]

Carl G. Jung emphasized the role played by family, group, and society in determining individual personality. He spoke of a "collective unconscious" in which racial memories, so to speak, were stored up from generation to generation and affected individual behavior.[10] A major trend in psychology seems to be toward emphasis on social psychology, not only as to what is peculiar to groups as groups, such as the crowd-mentality,[11] but as to the degree to which group influence may shape individual personality. Erich Fromm, a "dynamic analytic" psychologist, writes that "man is *primarily* a social being, and not, as Freud assumes, primarily self-sufficient and only secondarily in need of others in order to satisfy his instinctual needs," that "individual psychology is fundamentally social psychology."[12]

This seems to mean that, to the extent man is aggressive, he is so because of the social organization more than because of his natural impulse.

Fromm, a psychoanalyst, has written on international conflict. He deals with aggression only as it relates to (a) paranoia, the conviction that "they are after me," which takes the form of believing, because something *can* happen, such as that the USSR could take over the US, that it *will* happen, thus abandoning what is *probable*, which must always be the basis for rational action, in favor of what is *possible*; (b) projection, whereby the individual sees in the enemy (say, communism, or capitalism) all the evil he feels in himself; and (c) fanaticism, a condition of excitement one achieves by drowning his emptiness in a total submission to some idol such as country or ideology or race.[13]

Jerome Frank, a psychiatrist who has given much thought to international conflict, writes that "the clinician is inclined to view war as a form of aberrant human behavior and to explore the ways in which psychopathological processes in individuals may foster it." He speaks of how "denial" may impede full realization of the destructiveness of nuclear weapons, and of how the "repetition compulsion," aggravated by anxiety, may hamper the search for solutions. Further:

> Each member of a group internalizes its values. They become part of himself, and their loss represents a kind of psychological death that many find much harder to contemplate than losing their lives in defense of their values, an attitude summed up in the slogan, "Better dead than Red."[14]

Frank lists four group standards that support international conflict: (1) national sovereignty; (2) that violence is a feasible and proper way of pursuing the interests of the group; (3) that armed strength is the same thing as courage and determination; and (4) rejection of the outsider.[15]

Werner Levi, a political scientist, suggests that aggression is leader-inspired, for in "modern wars there are never enough 'aggressive' men flocking to the recruiting stations" so "everywhere men are drafted into armies;" that their fighting spirit must be aroused by government effort; that in some armies more than half the men who were supposed to shoot did not pull the trigger; and that the stimulus of revenge or defense of the fatherland soon has to be replaced by "war aims" conjuring up visions of a beautiful, peaceful world.[16]

Aldous Huxley, son and brother of famous biologists and author of *Brave New World*, writes that war is a purely human phenomenon, that only man among the animals organizes the mass murder of his own species. He ridicules the Social Darwinist notion that war acts as "nature's pruning-hook," for it eliminates the young and strong while sparing the unhealthy. "War is not a law of nature, nor even a law of human nature," he asserts, and the wish for war, as a matter of historical fact, has varied from absolute zero to a frenzied maximum.[17]

As for animal behavior, Robert Ardrey in *The Territorial Imperative* recounts F.F. Darling's conclusion that motivation for territory is psychological, not physiological. It arises from twin needs for security and stimulation, the one satisfied by the territorial heartland and the other by the periphery. Ardrey speculates that identity is another animal need that territory satisfies—identification with a fragment of "something larger and more permanent than the animal itself." He believes these same needs are the keys to human behavior. Their opposites are anonymity, boredom, anxiety. Human war, he says, satisfies all three, hence war "has been the most successful of all our cultural traditions." "While general warfare has in our time become something too fissionably hot to handle, the result has been not so much to reduce war's basic appeal as to introduce frustration into our lives; we are denied what we want."[18]

So, reasoning from animal behavior to history and his observation of human behavior, Ardrey takes issue to a degree with Frank, Levi, and Huxley, saying man is happy to go to war because thereby he finds his identity, defends his territory, and experiences excitement. But Ardrey intimates that aggression is merely the secondary reaction to these three more basic needs.

In a study of the behavior of animals, birds and insects, as well as of primitive man, a behavioral physiologist, Konrad Lorenz, asserts in his *On Aggression* that the original function of the instinct of aggression was to ensure the spacing out of members of the same species, a genetic adaptation to the environment to preserve the species, hence more physiological than psychological in its origin.

Apart from rats, he says, which also engage in clan wars in the murder of their own species, only man engages in war. Man, unlike the heavily armed carnivores who can kill at one blow, did not develop sufficiently reliable inhibitions (behavior mechanisms that function in a way similar to morality) to prevent the self-destruction of the species. Man has acquired killing tools, from the club to the atom bomb, too quickly for his inhibitory mechanism to keep pace. Man thus has an excessive remnant of his aggressive instinct in relation to his present environment.

To Lorenz, customs as well as instincts are produced by adaptation to changing circumstances. Customs are not behavior patterns rationally conceived and consciously brought about. Human beings very early developed taboos or prohibitions to preserve the social unit, and this practice has continued through history even though the size of the social unit has increased dramatically. The making of custom lags in relation to instinctual aggression, and man is hard put to find "compensatory mechanisms" which might drain off this predisposition. This predicament is noticed among American plains Indians and head-hunters of Borneo who have been forced by civilized man to give up their bloody activities while civilized man retains his international wars.

Lorenz says custom gets it strength from (a) "militant enthusiasm" by which a group defends its ways against another group not sharing them and (b) group cruelty to any members who fail to conform. But social norms, like instincts, may miscarry due to environmental change not "foreseen" in their "programming." All values, "good" or "bad," have an instinctual, emotional base, and even problems which are rationally examined are examined from the standpoint of emotional values.

Fortunately, Lorenz asserts, social norms can disappear in one generation because they cannot bear disruption of their continuity. For example, the head-hunters not only no longer hunt heads but their whole culture is in collapse.

There is also "rational responsibility" which must control the "militant enthusiasm" evoked by instinct and social norms. This developed originally to defend the small, concrete, face-to-face community. Nowadays it defends abstract values, and all obstacles in its path become unimportant. The inhibitions against hurting or killing one's fellow men lose much of their power. To impose rational control, one must first know that militant enthusiasm is aroused when (1) the unit the individual identifies with appears threatened; (2) the threat comes from a hated enemy who is seen as threatening the unit's values; (3)there is a leader-figure who inspires the individual; and (4) many others are present and agitated by the same emotion.

Lorenz, having said in sum that aggression originated as a way of preserving the species that would become human, and that this residual instinct can interact with social norms to produce militant enthusiasm, warns that adherence to social norms must not be mistaken for "responsible morality." Instead, responsible morality means getting control by conditioning the instinct to respond to a "genuine value." This, he says, is most successful if applied to teenagers.[19]

The role of instinct in human behavior is reduced to almost nothing by M.P.A. Montagu, a geneticist and anthropologist. In *Culture and the Evolution of Man* he says primate nature has changed into human nature by gradual supplanting of instinctual drives by intelligent adaptation to environmental challenges; that man retains, of his instincts, only his automatic reaction to a sudden loud noise or to a sudden withdrawal of support. In another work he asserts that aggression is taught, as are all forms of human violence.

In 1969 Montagu and others published essays attacking the conclusions of Lorenz and Ardrey, based mainly on study of animal behavior, that human aggression is instinctual rather than acquired; also that the scientific evidence of animal aggression comes from cases of relatively high population density, and that it is this rather than instinct that produces fighting within many species.[20] A peace researcher said in 1980 that the ethological-biological approach has something to offer but that Lorenz does not because his work is seriously flawed on several counts.[21]

A study by the Committee on Violence, made up of psychiatrists at Stanford University, distinguishes sharply between aggression and violence, saying the first is a biological characteristic, the other not an inherited trait. Man developed violence to adapt to an environment of saber-toothed tigers and maintained the trait to safeguard his territory when food was scarce. But violence is no longer adaptive, the Committee says, and man must adapt to his present environment by learning fast how to express aggression in non-violent ways. Fortunately, "We have marvelous adaptive abilities for coping with varying, even extreme, situations."[22]

Recent research in biology and animal behavior suggests that war is not so rare among animals as was thought and that through natural selection humans are genetically prone to irrational hostility. This research, which undergirds rising disciplines called psychobiology, sociobiology, and biopolitics, tends to emphasize "nature" over "nurture." But Edward O. Wilson, whose books *Sociobiology* (1975) and *On Human Nature* (1978) pioneered this field, believes that aggressive behavior, as it relates to military action, is learned.

Summary Comment. It appears that human aggressive behavior may (1) stem from profound, animalistic instinct, aggressive in and of itself, and/or (2) be a reaction to frustration of deep instincts; and/or (3) be a culturally derived quasi-instinct instilled by countless generations of human experience including behavior within the family and perhaps hostility to those outside it. These three sources of aggressive behavior probably lie mainly within the unconscious, whether individual or collective, and category (3) may be much the same as category (2).

Human aggression may also stem from (4) custom, including most forms of hostility to others outside one's group, whether the group is small or is seen as including one's nation, and/or from (5) rationally calculated behavior, as when the individual "psyches up" hostility within himself or when this is done by his fellows or by his leaders. Source (4) would appear to lie largely in the conscious mind and source (5) wholly so.

Individual men may identify with the whole human species. But group-man persists in his observed behavior as hostile to other groups and becomes willing to kill members of other groups of his species, as do rats. The explanation may be that individuals bring themselves, or are brought by others, to visualize other groups as belonging somehow to some sub-human species. This contrived view belongs to source (5) and can be abated, according to Lorenz, by an equally contrived "conscious morality" which reconditions man's ingroup-outgroup response by presumably making him identify with his species as a whole.

It is between Freud and Lorenz that we find the greatest difference of opinion whether the aggressive instinct is basically species-destroying or species-preserving, yet they agree that the cure lies in cultural reconditioning. Likewise, those who see aggressive behavior as deriving from culture rather than instinct find the cure in cultural reconditioning. Ardrey appears to insist that human behavior is still determined mainly by instinct, yet his "identity, stimulation, and security" can scarcely be anything but culture-conditioned. We must note here Lorenz' statement that long custom can disappear in a single generation.

We have been discussing human nature or behavior as seen in the average or mass man, and not the special case of the leader who behaves aggressively and involves his nation in conflict. We'll deal with this in Chapters 3 and 4.

C. Man as Greedy and Selfish

We noted earlier that behaviorist psychology lists five basic behavior systems, three of which have physiological bases in hunger, elimination, and sex.

The more obvious basis for greedy and needy behavior is of course hunger, but there is a derivation from the sex drive too. Every human must satisfy his hunger, if he can, and must find the means outside himself. If he is frustrated, then he will seek the more aggressively. Thus, presumably, some display more than others the behavior grounded in hunger—or sex. Plato said the few are dominated by their minds, by the love of knowledge; some by their hearts—they are courageous; and the many by their appetites. But he did not say how members of the first two classes react when they are hungry.

Most of humanity has had to contend throughout history with an economy of scarcity. Lorenz says aggression was originally a species-preserving instinct. But the motive underlying that instinct was hunger. Man's prototype had to keep the number of his species thinned out to accommodate to the supply of food. Modern man's propensity to overindulge is said to be an instinctual remnant from the time when meals might be few and far between. Today, feeding occurs regularly for most, yet malnutrition is chronic for much of our species. Scarcity of food and clothing and shelter is known to all, hence the determination to maintain and enhance one's standard of living. To the undernourished Indian or Bangladeshi this determination by people in the developed nations appears as greed and selfishness, but to them, mere need.

Plato identified greed, the "pursuit of wealth," as the main cause of war.[23] Hobbes, the 17th century English philosopher, said that where there is no government men use "violence to make themselves masters of other men's persons, wives, children, and cattle," so that "if one plant, sow, build or possess a convenient seat, others may probably be expected to come prepared with forces united to dispossess and deprive him, not only of the fruit of his labor, but also of his life or liberty."[24] Locke and Rousseau believed men could live together for a time in the absence of government but that trouble would begin so soon as some began to fence off a piece of land or store up property in the form of money. All these three philosophers related these views to international conflict.

Quincy Wright, the international lawyer, in writing of the "drives of war," speaks of "peoples which became involved in war through behaving according to prevailing psychological and economic patterns."[25] Paul Hoffman, an industrialist active in UN aid programs, writing of "certain forces that breed war," speaks of "widespread impoverishment and ignorance, gnawing hunger and frustration."[26] Kenneth Boulding, an economist, in writing of overpopulation and poverty, speaks of "paranoid nationalist leaders" who divert people from "seemingly insoluble real problems to never-never lands of national glory and aggressiveness."[27] Gunnar Myrdal, a Swedish economist, believes that owing to hunger in an overpopulated world "we will be skirting a disaster of such proportion as to threaten the peace and stability of the western world."[28]

Psychologists have been more interested in relating aggression than greed to international conflict. They tend to treat the "need for acquisition" as basically a need for prestige and have dealt with it as part of the achievement motive.[29] In this sense it is related to aggression and also to the search for glory which will be discussed shortly.

It is reasonable to believe that so soon as man was conscious of the need to provide for himself he turned aggressive in order to do it. From very early on, youths were schooled in taking the necessities of life from others as well as in hunting animals and picking edibles off of trees. Need was not the only cause of inter-tribal conflict: we know from anthropological studies of peoples still in the Stone Age that even at that stage conflict had been routinized and institutionalized. But material goods, together with wives and slaves and glory, were the ordinary stakes in inter-tribal violence.

We find need as a cause still operative at the beginnings of recorded history, but it has become sophisticated into greed as barbarians invade the great river valleys, there to settle and enjoy the material benefits of rich cities. Greed was indeed a prominent motive in the imperialism of Athens, where Plato wrote, and doubtless in other commerce-minded city-states in that era. Phoenicians and Carthaginians were thus motivated. Many crusaders hoped for fiefdoms in the Levant or in Moslem Spain. The economic motive was uppermost in the policies of Venice, Genoa, and Aragon.

In mercantilist times, from the 16th century on, merchant-venturers traded abroad in partnership with the royal exchequer and founded colonies. In the 19th century whole populations supported national policies designed to find markets and raw materials abroad and to protect industries at home, even though the beneficiaries were men of capital while high tariffs meant the masses had to pay more for what they needed. And today, although colonies as a means toward national prosperity and self-sufficiency have been abandoned, and although there is less faith in trade restrictions, every trade-tariff negotiation arouses the greed of the interests affected, thus influencing international conflict.

Whatever the motives of high policy, common soldiers knew until recently that success would provide plunder. This was true even of disciplined troops in Roman and high European times. If soldiers were paid, they still looked to plunder; and if, for good reasons, a conquered city was spared pillage, commanders had to deal with discontent. With regularization of armies by Cromwell and the kings of Prussia, this practice abated, yet as late as the 19th century naval commanders and crews shared the value of ships taken in action.

As for the present day, trade and tariff negotiations do indeed aggravate relations among allies as well as among enemies. But the closer connection with international conflict probably lies in what President Eisenhower called the "military-industrial complex." Here, greed takes the form of a combination of military men, defense contractors, politicians, and the labor unions and local communities affected by defense spending. Such an alliance is influential in any nation where there are profits or other benefits to be gained out of military appropriations. George Kennan refers to the military-industrial complex as a "national addiction" and believes that defense spending has inflationary consequences besides.[30]

Summary Comment. We noted in the *Summary of International History* that the cry against "the merchants of death" goes back at least to the 19th century and that defense contractors worked to kill the Geneva disarmament talks in the interwar period. And, even today, like the battleship captain who took prizes, all military officers know that quick promotion, with its increases in pay and allowances, depends upon opportunities afforded by war.

That the influence of the complex on national decisions should be on the side of peace is scarcely to be expected. But its influence in terms of urging a nation on to violence is not known. We do have studies indicating that high military expenditure in relation to gross national product correlates with future involvement in war.[31] This does not explain why so much was spent but no doubt the greed of the complex is partly responsible.

In looking back over this section we note that in nearly all the historical instances of governments which pursue the economic motive on into war, the governments have been dominated by commercial or industrial oligarchies. This suggests that they have been nations of a particular "nature," so we must pursue this matter in Chapter 3.

We might add that the widespread hope of two and three generations ago that international violence would cease because businessmen knew that war was bad for business is moribund if not dead. This hope, which said in effect that greed would bring an end to war, was wrecked by the circumstance that the period during which business had maximum control over the principal nations coincided with the two world wars.

D. Man the Glory-Seeker and the Bored

Here the allegation is that war results from those facets of man's nature which motivate him to seek fame in war or respite from peacetime boredom. The connection of glory with conflict is more obvious than that of boredom. The remembered myths of the race and the literature of all languages are replete with accounts of heroes and of brave battles fought in the name of some group small or large. Western literature is especially devoted to such accounts, from Homer's epic poems to the latest prose item in praise of some Israeli general.

Hobbes pinpointed glory as a cause of conflict. The spur to glory is not gain but "trifles, as a word, a smile, a different opinion, and any other sign of undervalue, either direct in their persons or by reflection in their kindred, their friends, their nation, their profession, or their name."[32] Hobbes thought only some men would be brought to violence by vainglory, while Rousseau believed every man has at least the urge to stand forth in the company of his fellows.

Politicians and military men seek fame, like princes formerly, for their professional success depends on it. Some hunger and thirst after it. General David Shoup, retired commander of the US Marine Corps, says that "Civilians can scarcely understand...that many ambitious military professionals yearn for wars and the opportunities for glory and distinction afforded only in combat. A career of peacetime duty is a dull and frustrating prospect of a normal regular officer."[33]

Yet the same thirst has driven many whose names never made the history books. A fair sampling of letters sent home by soldiers in the US Civil War reveals that a fierce glory in combat was widespread. Despite *The Red Badge of Courage* and Ambrose Bierce's short stories about that war, and Sherman's statement that war's glory is all moonshine, a new generation carried the same glory-pride into the first world war. That war, with the anonymity, obscurity and infinite misery of trench warfare, marked for most the end of chivalric notions of combat.

And, indeed, few modern writers even refer to glory as a factor. Jerome Frank, previously quoted on aggression, remarked there that one of the group standards which support war is that which "equates armed strength with determination and courage." And Judd Marmor, another psychiatrist, writes that

> Virtues such as heroism and courage are regarded as being "manly" and are traditionally associated with waging war. Conversely, the avoidance of war or the pursuit of peace are generally regarded as "effeminate," passive, cowardly, weak, dishonorable, or subversive.[34]

But, as we saw, Huxley and Levi indicate that neither glory nor duty has been a sufficient motive for a long while now. For that matter, thousands bought their way out of conscription during the Civil War. Seamen had to be impressed (kidnapped) by both British and French navies in the Napoleonic wars.

One may conjecture that glory never motivated large numbers of individuals to risk their lives, and glory is certainly no longer an important motive for the rank-and-file participant in war, although some who know they will not be called still speak loudly of national glory—older people, mainly.

Glory as a motivating factor in princes and elites will be dealt with in Chapter 3.

Passing now to boredom, the first thing to stress is that this is a more important factor than might be thought at first mention. In the imaginative literature, especially, there are many references to boredom as the latency out of which the martial spirit emerges. If there have been "heroic" wives who cheered their men into battle, there have been at least as many others who knew their husbands wished to get away from them and the children and the hum-drum frustrations of everyday life. Indeed, boredom may be seen as another manifestation of that frustration out of which aggression develops. Huxley writes:

> In their studies on suicide Durkheim and, more recently, Halbwachs have shown that the suicide rate among non-combatants tends to fall during war-time to about two-thirds of its normal figure. This decline must be put down to the following causes: to the simplification of life during war-time (it is in complex and highly developed societies that the suicide rate is highest); to the intensification of nationalist sentiment to a point where most individuals are living in a state of chronic enthusiasm; to the fact that life during war-time takes on significance and purposefulness, so that even the most intrinsically boring job is ennobled as "war work"; to the artificial prosperity induced, at any rate for a time, by the expansion of war industries; to the increased sexual freedom which is always claimed by societies, all or some of whose members live under the menace of sudden death.[35]

Levi lists, among the psychological causes of war, boredom and the thirst for adventure, and mentions a study which found that factory workers began to enjoy dull work so soon as it contributed to the war effort.[36]

Ardrey's need for "identity" is maximally satisfied by military glory, but mere military rank enables many to "know who they are," while the need for "stimulation" is thoroughly satisfied by war:

> The flight from boredom has never been presented with such maximum satisfactions for maximum numbers. No philosopher, viewing the horrors of war through the astigmatic lenses of the pain-pleasure principle, can grasp the attraction which war presents to civilized men. It is the ultimate release from the boredom of normal existence...In all the rich catalogue of human hypocrisy it is difficult to find anything to compare with that dainty of dainties, that sugared delicacy, the belief that people do not like war.[37]

Garibaldi, in his wars of Italian unification, sent out the call to "Come and suffer," and they came. The spirit of England in the fall of 1914, after war had broken out in August, has been described as "a kind of deep, solemn, sacred joy."[38]

Nels Ferre, a theologian interested in imparting meaning to life, says boredom is occasioned by meaninglessness and lists boredom, along with frustration and fear, as the deeper causes of war, multiplied by crowd psychology and intensified by mass communications.[39]

Boredom, and the pervasive unease which seems to underlie it, are related to "alienation," a condition prominent in Marxist and Existentialist thought. Marx held that the laborer was alienated from others and from himself by the fact that the product of his labor, over and above mere subsistence for himself, was taken from him by the capitalist. This was so because a man knows himself and realizes himself only in his work. Marx also speculated—and this was taken from Feuerbach, a contemporary German philosopher and theologian—that man is alienated from himself by the requirement that he believe in a God outside and over against himself.[40] Existentialism finds the cause of alienation mainly in the brevity and ultimate meaninglessness of life.

Margaret Mead, an anthropologist, wrote of the Nuclear Era that now,

> Without a future for anyone, anywhere, human life loses its meaning. There is no rationale for the simplest act, no reason to save or to plan or to build; no reason to vote or to sit in committees; no reason to plant or pray. As men see it, this new possibility of total destruction is not an act of God's vengeance turned against a particular unfaithful people but instead an act which is the outcome of man's fullest development as man.[41]

By "fullest development" Mead refers to science which had earlier evoked an "upsweep of faith in the future." Similarly, W.E. Hocking, a philosopher, says that "When human life and its meaning can be thus abruptly broken off, something must happen to that *picture of futurity* which attends all human action, as the field of its fulfilled meaning." Then, "It is in this atmosphere that the youth of our Western lands are moving toward maturity. For them, faith in any total meaning of the world process has become a dubious placebo."[42]

Summary Comment. It would seem that pursuit of glory is of decreasing importance whereas boredom and alienation are on the increase. Boredom is not increasing dramatically because the work week shortens only gradually, while fewer people in proportion are harnessed to the dullest industrial work and more are in the service occupations which offer variety. What has increased dramatically is alienation. Its rise has accompanied the decline in faith in the traditional religions and in the future of life itself. Whether alienation and its cousin, "anomie," which means lack of a personal value system, contribute to international conflict is debatable. But chances are they do, for, like boredom, they contribute to a "don't care" attitude. Existentialism's effort to transform alienation into a Stoic sort of ethic probably does not touch the many, though it may influence the few.

E. Man as Stupid, Ignorant, Irrational and Stubborn

By stupidity, we mean a relative inability to learn; by ignorance, a lack of learning relative to some standard; by irrationality, an inability to follow the processes of reason; by stubbornness, a refusal to accept the dictates of reason based on knowledge, or anyway a refusal to behave accordingly.

The general allegation is that, owing to the prevalence of these traits, humanity in the main does not see where its long-term interests lie, or does not act as though it did.

Whether there has been any increase of intelligence during the past several thousand years is doubtful. Claude Levi-Strauss, an anthropologist, believes the savage mind brought to its environment qualities of observation and abstract thinking similar to ours.[43] The oldest extant writings from the Bronze Age show as much native capacity as we have today, while the thought-systems of China, India and Greece dating from 2,500 years ago match the best that we can produce now. If there is a decrease in stupidity it is developing at a rate so slow as to be imperceptible.

Those who believe international conflict is rooted in the ignorance of man assert that education is the cure. The discovery of new knowledge, and its dissemination through education, have increasingly been considered the cures for all problems.

Boulding, the economist, speaks of three different kinds of knowledge: "folk," "literary," and "scientific."[44] The child receives folk knowledge from his family and friends and from his own perceptions slanted by what he has heard from others. This knowledge, consisting largely of "hearsay" versions of reality, will include images of his own nation and others. If he remains illiterate, most of his knowledge as an adult will tend to be disorderly and oversimplified. Even if he is literate and can acquire "literary knowledge," the view he will get of the international system is likely to be "a melange of narrative history," memories of past events, stories and conversations, plus an enormous amount of usually ill-digested and carelessly collected information.

> When we add to this the fact that the system produces strong hates, loves, loyalties, disloyalties, and so on, it would be surprising if any images were formed that even remotely resembled the most loosely defined realities of the case.[45]

So, two reasons are suggested for the ignorance of man as this relates to international affairs: (a) the thrust of group standards toward a warping of history and current events that the group finds a satisfying perversion of the objective situation; and (b) the scarcity of knowledge that can be called "scientific," that is, theory derived from experience and then verified by enough re-application so there is a high statistical probability that it is correct.

Most literary knowledge that people acquire originates with journalists, politicians, historians and other scholars who write about international relations. As to their objectivity, one need only read magazines of the Cold War 1950s and early 1960s from the vantage point of the 1980s. As Boulding remarks elsewhere, even the scientist has difficulty in getting beyond his own national image.

Yet an awareness of man's predicament in the nuclear age, as well as of some other worldwide problems, does seem to have percolated down through the layer of literary knowledge and into the domain of folk knowledge. Everyone is aware of the situation in its broad outlines. The problem is a part of the general fund of knowledge; but the solution is not. Military preparedness does not seem the full solution, and there is a vague awareness that disarmament never seems to get very far, but apart from these there is only hopeful reference to the UN in elementary and secondary classrooms, cynical reference to it in university seminars. Hence, perhaps, the widespread expectation of discontinuity that Mead and Hocking commented on.

In brief, man is not too ignorant to know that he is in trouble but he is too ignorant to know what to do about it. He does not know a course of conduct that will serve his long-term interests so he is left to serve his short-term interests. It is the hope of the "peace scientists" who apply statistical and other mathematical treatment to the problem of international conflict that there will eventually be a fund of true, scientific knowledge that people can draw on. Others believe that true knowledge can be found out through the "scrupulous use of the human mind" as applied to the history of international conflict. We shall discuss this more fully in Chapter 3.

Irrationality is related to stupidity in that it is an inability to perform well certain mental processes, specifically those that link concepts together such as cause and effect patterns, ends and means, or the deducing of one proposition from another, or the synthesizing of bits and pieces of evidence into a whole.

Only a minority is trained in mathematical deduction; a still smaller minority in empirical induction. Logic, which was studied by educated individuals until recently, is not paid much attention any more except in its mathematical application. Yet, logic in its more informal meaning is practiced by most of us to a greater or lesser extent. If it were otherwise, communication would be impossible. So simple an utterance as "I am hungry" implies a cause, lack of food, and the end of abating hunger is served by the means of food. Hence we can venture the generalization that most individuals not only have enough knowledge to understand the international predicament but also enough rationality to judge proposed solutions for it.

We go on to consider the emotional aspect of irrationality and the psychology of stubbornness.

In Section A we noted that aggressive or violent behavior is one of the principal immediate consequences of frustration. We also listed other immediate consequences and mentioned habitual consequences known as "defense mechanisms." Some of these illuminate emotional irrationality and stubbornness as they relate to international conflict.

"Stereotypy" is a tendency to blind, repetitive, fixated behavior, similar to what Jerome Frank called the "repetition compulsion."

> Ordinary problem-solving requires flexibility, striking out in new directions when the original path to the goal is blocked. When repeated frustration baffles a person, some of his flexibility appears to be lost, and he stupidly makes the same effort again and again, though experience has shown its futility.[46]

Thus one who pinned his hopes for an end to war on the League or the UN may, despite their failure, simply reiterate his support for the UN or call for some new collective security organization slightly different from what has been tried. Another, despite the failure of military preparedness to provide durable peace, may call monotonously for greater defense expenditures. Not only laymen, but scholars and statesmen too, suffer from stereotypy.[47] Once the habit has taken hold it may become an obsessive fixation in which alternatives dictated by reason cannot be entertained.

"Scapegoating" is displaced aggression, which occurs when the individual "cannot satisfactorily express his aggression against the source of the frustration."[48] This applies to frustration induced by expectation of international violence, because its sources seem too obscure or, even when rationally examined, too complex and diverse to afford hope and satisfaction. Hence the finding of simplistic scapegoats and release of pent-up aggression on communism or capitalism or colonialism or something else.[49]

"Fantasy," another reaction to frustration, means that the individual escapes into a dream world, perhaps the 19th century when things were simpler. "Regression" means a return to more primitive modes of behavior, as in "nuke them."

If the foregoing are active forms of irrationality and stubbornness, "apathy" is a passive form. It is marked by "indifference, withdrawal, inactivity, inattentiveness;" apathy may be the "normal" or typical reaction to "extremely frustrating situations of long duration where there is no hope of escape."[50] Here there is a refusal to act or think, whether rationally or not. Apathy applies to those who have found the problem of international conflict too difficult and have withdrawn themselves to the extent that they are inattentive to any proposed solutions. Probably most people nowadays simply refuse to think about nuclear war or the population explosion, though this may be changing.

"Rationalization" means to justify impulsive or improper conduct so that one seems to have acted rationally. This can be done consciously or unconsciously. Thus a young man may avoid conscription because he is frightened but tell himself and others it is because he is morally opposed to war. An older man might support war on grounds that he is opposed to communism or capitalism whereas he actually takes vicarious joy in the spectacle of death and destruction.

"Projection" means protecting oneself from recognizing one's own undesirable traits by assigning them to others. A common example is the individual who looks upon the international enemy as the aggressor, regardless of the facts. US intervention in Vietnam and the Dominican Republic were justified by attributing aggressive designs to Chinese and Cuban communists. Projection is akin to rationalization, as when inhumane acts of war by the enemy are alleged in order to justify one's own similar acts.

"Reaction-formation" occurs when one conceals a motive from oneself by giving strong expression to its opposite. Thus an individual who is most unhappy with his nation may be moved to an extreme manifestation of patriotism. He who disapproves of the situation in his country, and who ought rationally to try to reform it, may be he who approves most unconditionally of his nation as an entity. Many a bitter nationalist is of this stripe. Reaction-formation is related to love-hate ambivalence.

"Dissociation," or the splitting-up of the unity of doing and thinking and feeling, may be manifested as a "compulsive routine" which is indulged in whenever that which caused the splitting-up is in some way touched upon. This appears to be related to stereotypy and, like it, may have something to do with the cool reception usually accorded to proposed new courses of action embracing new ideas.

"Repression" occurs when an individual protects himself from a full awareness of impulses he prefers to deny. It differs from the other defense mechanisms in that it is a partial or total forgetting of the impulse and of the behavior resulting from it. Thus, toward the end of a long and weary wartime, a person may forget that he had been a great flag-waver at its outset. Similarly, after a long and weary peacetime, he may forget the pacific inclinations he had entertained at the close of the last war.[51]

The last of the defense mechanisms is "substitution," meaning that approved goals are substituted for goals unapproved either by the individual or by his culture. Substitution is a strong reinforcer of group standards. Thus we saw many active communists of the 1930s became famous anti-communists in the 1950s. Similarly, many followed sharp turns in the Soviet party-line over the past half-century, while Frenchmen who were Europeanists immediately after World War II returned to ethnocentrism during De Gaulle's second stint in office.

In the set of categories we have been using,[52] substitution includes "sublimation," famous in Freudian psychology as the diversion of the sexual drive into another activity such as painting or poetry. But it is difficult to see why any form of psychic energy, wherever derived, cannot be redirected or misdirected into channels fixed by group standards or charismatic leaders. Indeed, all that we have been considering as irrationality can be seen as varying sublimations of that energy generated by frustration which for whatever reason is not expressed in direct aggression.

Substitution also may cover "compensation," another Freudian term meaning a strenuous effort to make up for failure or weakness in one respect by excelling in a different respect, together with "overcompensation" which means denying a weakness by trying to excel where one is weakest. Thus, poor sexual performance or inability to earn an adequate living might cause a man to become a bold fighter pilot, or the man who thinks himself cowardly may be the first to respond to a call to the colors. Similarly, uncommonly short men often feel the need to dominate and lead others.

All the defense mechanisms are habitual modes of self-deception.[53]

Summary Comment. We have drawn near to several tentative conclusions. Man's intelligence is increasing at a very slow rate, if at all, but most can perform such rational operations as drawing simple inferences, "putting two and two together." Given this, most people have acquired enough knowledge of the broad outlines of world politics and modern weaponry to understand that they are threatened with discontinuity in the human venture.

If they were offered explanations of why things have come to this pass, and were told how the nuclear predicament can be resolved, they have the rational intelligence to understand and to judge. Unfortunately, the explosive increase of knowledge in the physical sciences has not been matched by the knowledge of man and his social institutions including international conflict. Behavioral-social scientists continue to quarrel over what is knowledge; more precisely, By what methods can reliable knowledge about man and society be obtained?

Lacking knowledge that the elites can agree upon as being reliable, men in the mass are bombarded by oversimplifications of the situation which derive from group standards or come from the lips of petty prophets who are able to enlist a following. Men are apt to suspend the critical faculty and to perform irrational psychological operations such as "stereotypy," "scapegoating," and "denial" in order to come to terms with themselves and their society. Thus many an alleged cause and cure for war finds a home. Group standards not merely constrain an individual to conform; they also supply him with all or most of the values, including the moral values, by which he judges himself. His inner and outer comfort both counsel him to deceive himself into accepting the cry of his crowd and his prophet. The absence of rational, scientific knowledge leaves the field to irrational, folk knowledge—that of one's own folk, of course. So men stubbornly hold to old values and old cures, however discredited, or they take refuge in apathy.

Two scholars, however, submit a minority report, saying that "Most wars involve very real incompatibilities between the basic moral objectives of the two sides, and it is historical fact that ordinarily the population of each side deliberately and without any element of crowd irrationality supports the carefully formulated policy of the leadership."[54] One suspects they are young men who have not lived through any wartime.

F. Man as Nationalist and True Believer

Psychologists do not agree on the relative importance to accord the earliest as compared with the later years of life, or to physiological as contrasted with environmental factors. However, there seems to be substantial agreement that the full personality is largely the result of the individual's search for identification through adopting the traits, values and behavior of those with whom his lot is cast: first, his parents and other family members, his neighbors, his class at school, his adolescent peers, and then the ever-larger groupings of the adult, up to the national state.

As he goes along, the individual fits into social roles as son, friend, classmate, citizen, and member of this or that associational grouping. If a blank tablet at birth, as Locke held, he gets his standards ready made when he identifies with his groups; if considered to be born with predispositions, he still must react to these standards and conform if he can.

Humans have a strong drive to form cohesive groups, probably because they cannot survive in isolation, either physically or psychically. But cohesiveness requires rejection of the outsider—the maintenance of an ingroup-outgroup boundary line.

Nationalism is similar to other group identifications. It can be distinguished by defining it as identification with that group which provides—or tries to—security against outside groups and order within the group. Thus nationalism is identification with the security unit. For that reason it is almost always an identification with the largest group that the individual identifies with at all. Exceptions would be the feudal periods in history when a person identified with his particular feudal state and master but also, in more or less equal degree, with Christendom or the Holy Roman Empire or with the Caliphate and Islam. The ambivalence of the American between allegiance to his state and his nation prior to the Civil War would be somewhat the same.

But nationalism, even in its ambivalences, is an effort by the individual to identify with that political unit which is independent and can punish him in order to preserve civil order or can place his life at risk to serve the interest of that political unit against other independent units.

The intensity of nationalism tends to increase with the degree of the nation's control over its citizens or subjects, and this varies with the intensity of international conflict as we saw in Chapter 1. In the 19th and 20th centuries nationalism reached an intensity in large national states comparable to that in the classic Greek city-state or the Italian Renaissance republics.

Nationalism has received many definitions, especially by the romantics of the last century.[55] One of the best is that nationalism is whatever it is that causes a person to prefer the fortunes of his nation over those of any other. Einstein described nationalism as a juvenile disease—the measles of mankind. Nationalism is sometimes called the most powerful ideology of them all in our day. But it is not an ideology because it has no idea content, although it may assimilate ideas and ideologies to itself. Nationalism is simply that boundary in the imagination where identificaton ends.

Nationalism is transferable, as we noted in Chapter 1, as international integration proceeds through history. We do not know for sure how long this takes, but Lorenz said that long customs can disappear in a generation. So long as it is merely a question of identifying with a somewhat larger and altered territory, or of accepting a new lord as symbol of the new state, and no drastic changes in life style such as a new language are to be imposed immediately, it is not difficult and does not take long. But the need to identify with a territory is not easily extended to very large territories. The warm patriotism which the individual can feel for his native land and climate and people tends to be displaced in very large nations by a colder nationalism which must be cultivated and institutionalized.[56]

Thus whereas territorial patriotism is a natural identification, nationalism is to a degree artificial, especially in large or new nations. Whatever can be viewed as peculiar to the nation—its history, government, economy, language, customs, and beautiful women—these are seized upon by publicists, statesmen and orators and praised so the individual will realize the uniqueness and glory of his country. In this way the ingroup-outgroup bare bones of nationalism takes on a content. The process is helped along by what one writer calls "the tendency of men to project on the state unfulfilled personal aspirations and ambitions."[57]

But nationalism receives its most urgent content by its assimilation to a religion or ideology. Groups seem always to have had their peculiar spirits to guard and keep them. The ancestral tablets of the extended family in the Chinese and other cultures, the household gods of the Greeks, the family ikons of the Russians, the spirits evoked by tribal shamans, the totems and taboos, the patron saint of a village or a feudal fief, Spaniards for Saint James and Scots for Saint Andrew, the Cross and the Crescent—these illustrate the point.

Just as man searches for identification with groups, so does he seek aid and comfort from the supernatural, sometimes with an effort toward personal identification with those powers but more typically through rituals of propitiation, worship and entreaty. He listens to those who purport to reveal the Above and its relation to the Below. Out of this come religions such as Christianity and Islam.

But man may content himself with a more philosophical revelation which merely explains life on this plane and what to do about it. Such belief systems are Buddhism in its original manifestation, the Hinduism of the *karma* which Buddhism enlarged upon, and Taoism. As a minimum, man wishes to know how to behave in this life. Here he has been attracted by Mohism, Confucianism, and the Hinduism of the *dharmasastra* (social policy), as well as by the ethics taught by the supernatural religions.

At each of these levels—supernatural, philosophical, and ethical— man is reaching for an explanation of reality which imparts purpose to his life. Thus man knows himself not only as group member but as true believer. Indeed, he is conscious of himself as a member of a community of true believers. But this has been more intensely the case as regards Western than Eastern Man. The *Summary of International History* shows nothing in the history of the East that is truly comparable to the crusades by Christians against Moslems or the Catholic-Protestant wars of religion.

The alliance between state and religion, with religion giving content to nationalism, caused some of the bitterest international conflict in history. Religion is still a factor in some conflicts. But the religious impulse weakened in the 18th century and has been displaced by other belief-systems which we call ideologies. These supply most of the idea content to nationalism today, in East and West.

Ideology has been variously defined. Two psychologists say that an "opinion" is a response to a single question, an "attitude" is a set of responses to a series of related questions, and an "ideology" is a pattern of related attitudes.[58] Their definition could cover any belief-system at all. Ideologies are usually considered to have a strong orientation toward political action. Thus a political scientist says ideologies are links between theories and actions.[59] A political theorist says that "theory aims at the truth and ideology aims at victory over human opponents...an ideology is a deliberately prefabricated set of answers whose effect is to close off inquiry."[60] Saul Bellow says "An ideology is a spell cast by the ruling class, a net of binding falsehoods."[61]

We need not adopt so invidious a definition. Ideologies have been devised by individuals who believed they were honest and right. The point is that ideologies are belief-systems which do not merely imply political action, as when a Protestant state defended its religion against the Catholic Holy Roman Emperor, but which actually call for political action.

A religious belief-system, once established, does not on the whole attempt further change in the prevailing social, economic, and political arrangements. In the West, rational criticism of religion, together with changes that came with the commercial and industrial revolutions, produced reformers aware of the need for social change. These individuals were for the most part a-religious and anti-religious, inclining toward humanism. Men love to speak in terms of principles, and leaders know that men prefer to act in the name of something greater than themselves. Hence, out of new and untried ideas, as well as reinterpretations of old ideas, two great modern ideologies were created.

Liberalism, involving the rights of man, sovereignty of the people, and representative government, got its start in Cromwell's England, as we have seen, but became a full-blown ideology in the late 18th century. Instances of wars fought in its name are those fought by the English and Spanish colonies in America for independence, the wars of the French Revolution and also the Napoleonic wars. There was also many a civil war in the 19th century between liberals and monarchists. Liberalism, with its emphasis on religious freedom and capitalism, had come to prevail in most industrial countries by the eve of World War I. Liberalism was a part of the cement which bound the Allied cause together, once the liberals had taken control in Russia. Germany, Austria-Hungary, and especially the Ottoman empire still seemed sufficiently monarchical so that Wilson could speak of a war to "make the world safe for democracy."

Socialism as an ideology was hinted at in Cromwell's time but became an active revolutionary movement in France during the Revolution, when the liberals ruthlessly crushed it. It got its full explanation of reality from Marx, as we have seen, whose "scientific" historical determinism was a call to political activism buttressed by assurance of success. Democratic Socialism, committed to the liberal political process, has become part of the ideology of many developed industrial nations. Leninist Communism, based on a seizing of power by a disciplined party which then rules on behalf of the proletariat, has become the principal ideological competitor to liberalism in much of the world.

Marxism was overtly anti-nationalist and looked forward to the withering away of the state, that is, of national governments which it saw as mere fronts by which the dominant economic class controlled others. Yet, wherever communist socialism has come to power it has become the ideology equated with the state and with nationalism. It is virtually the established religion. This is not new; liberalism was the religion of French revolutionary nationalism. But it shows the power of nationalism to utilize ideology or religion despite the tenets of the ideology or religion itself, including Christianity.[62]

Fascism is the third and newest of the great ideologies, though it uses techniques that can be traced to the two Bonapartes and even to Cromwell. Fascism is nationalism in which the individual submerges himself in worship of the state as representative of the organic unity of the unending national community. It requires unquestioned obedience to a single party representing that organic state, whose doctrines and policies are announced by its charismatic leader. In the Italian and German versions, a measure of state-directed socialism was involved, but capitalism was by and large left with its profits.

Fascism is offered as the supposed sole alternative to the internal and/or external threat of communist socialism. In the German experiment racism was prominent. In the Spanish version there was little socialism or racism. Fascism encourages the individual to give himself to the mystical destiny of his state. Fascism has overtly and unabashedly tried to establish the power of its nation over other nations. Its natural enemy in international conflict has been the communist nation, but fascism has displayed its contempt of liberalism too.

Fascism is a small body of ideas which fleshes out nationalism to its ultimate screaming perfection. Unlike totalitarian communism, which endeavors to wipe out religion, totalitarian fascism has made use of religion while controlling it.

Thus those involved in World War II were fighting for or against liberalism, communism, or fascism. The Cold War similarly is conceived to be a struggle not just between one's own nation and others but also between communist socialism and liberal capitalism.

Summary Comment. Man as nationalist and true believer is no more than an inquiry into the significance of "group" and of "standards" as applied to international conflict. If one's own nation is the best because one belongs to it and because one's fellows agree that his is so, then other nations must be less than the best. If one ideology is true and explains all, then others must be false. An inquiry into how the mere existence of the nation as a unit in a system of independent nations serves to create the nationalist and true believer must be taken up in Chapter 4. Here we can conclude that, at the level of individual psychology, nationalism and belief help to satisfy the need for indentity as well as the need for reassurance as to one's role in this world and one's place in the Hereafter. Man becomes nationalist and true believer by group acculturation, and his behavior in these capacities is intimately related to international conflict.

G. Man as Fearful

It is rare for laymen or scholars to connect human fear with international conflict, even though few motives bulk as large in general psychology as does fear. Psychologists have not much concerned themselves with sin; they have had a great deal to say about guilt, which is fear of having fallen short of some personal or societal or supernatural norm; they have also said a lot about anxiety and other forms of fear.

Erikson, a psychoanalyst, lists psychosocial crises which occur in the individual's progress from infancy to adulthood: trust vs. mistrust, autonomy vs. shame and doubt, initiative vs. guilt, industry vs. inferiority, identity vs. identity diffusion, intimacy and solidarity vs. isolation, generativity vs. self-absorption, and integrity vs. despair.[63] Clearly, virtually all these crises of development are pregnant with fear. Kohlberg, a psychologist, lists six stages in the development of moral character. He specifies that the earliest stage elicits obedience to avoid punishment while the remaining five are marked by conformity to obtain rewards or to avoid the disapproval or to obtain the respect of others, or to avoid self-condemnation.[64] All this is fear. In a study published by Remmers and Radler, also psychologists, high school students saw the "parent problem" in terms pervaded by fear and anger.[65]

The most basic physiological needs—for air, food, and water—are related to fear because of the possibility of the organism's being deprived of them, and this fear sets up drives which shape behavior. Deprivation of sex will, in the female animal, evoke "tension and restless activity" akin to anxiety, whereas the maternal drive is curious in that fear for the infant tends to exclude all other fears.[66]

When psychologists speak of appetites and aversions, they mean a fear called aversion and also, by implication, the fear that appetites will not be satisfied. Fear is categorized by psychologists as an acquired drive.[67] But this merely means that it is derived from actual deprivation or pain and not that fear is to be interpreted in a superficial or narrow sense.

Mowrer, a noted psychologist, seems almost to make fear the prime determinant of human behavior. He says that although fear is a secondary drive, once learned it acts alongside such primary drives as hunger and thirst to produce "avoidance behavior" and thus habit formation. He notes that by 1940 fear had been commonly recognized by psychologists as an acquired drive and was being referred to as a "secondary reinforcement" of behavior. He traces this view back to John B. Watson and ultimately to Freud. Interestingly enough, Mowrer conceives of "hope" as "decremental fear" while hunger, though a primary drive, can be thought of as "hunger fear."[68]

In the broad divisions which psychologists make of human incentives into pleasure and pain, fear would seem to attach to pain whereas anxiety would seem to be part of the desire for pleasure.

Fear is difficult to distinguish from anger. If a cat is frightened by a dog, adrenalin flows so that the cat is ready to fight. Is this fear or anger? The bodily symptoms of arousal are so similar that one must almost know what stimulus aroused the emotion before one can identify it as fear or as anger. However, a study by a physiological psychologist found that although seven physiological responses were not significantly different when his human subjects were aroused by fear or by anger, four others were more common when angered and three others more common when frightened.[69]

A child psychologist writes that aggression and fear are remarkably similar physiologically.

> Suppose one spoke in terms of extreme arousal; arousal requires responsivity and can lead to flight or fight. The animal generally takes flight—unless he is cornered (an environmental phenomenon) and *then* his response is aggressive. Perhaps aggression is a name we give to responsivity in cornered animals. As man developed, and his brain permitted him the luxury or curse of abstraction, the corner also became abstract.[70]

Anxiety is sometimes defined as a free-floating fear which does not have a known specific cause. In addition, psychologists have defined anxiety as fear of insecurity:

> According to the concept on which this use is based, anxiety is social in its origin, beginning in infancy while the child is dependent upon the adults who care for him. Deprivation, neglect, and loss of affection arouse the feelings of insecurity and the infant comes to fear. This fear of insecurity is considered the basic anxiety, and it is a fear always associated with other people. What is feared is isolation, lack of affectionate responses by other people. When anxiety is used with this meaning, it is distinguished from fear: *things* can cause fear; only *people* can cause insecurity.[71]

This tells us something about why individuals adhere to group standards, including nationalism and its assimilated ideology.

Anxiety is used in a third way by psychologists to mean concern over one's own conduct, that is, guilt. It would appear that it is guilt which evokes the psychological mechanisms we considered in connection with irrationality in Section E. Children are anxious about blurting out their resentments toward their parents; the adolescent may fear to reveal his interest in sex; adults fear to show fear. Thus the inner conflict over mutually-exclusive goals which produces frustration, aggression, and all the irrational mechanisms, is saturated with fear.[72]

A fourth meaning of anxiety is that given by existentialists, who say it arises out of the contemplation of death's inevitability and the sense of one's unrealized possibilities. Kierkegaard, founder of existentialism, used the word "dread" but later existentialists substituted "anxiety."[73]

Freud's psychoanalysis arose out of changes in the social structure which, by the 20th century, had caused the relation of children to parents to lie "under a heavy shadow of vague unconscious fears." The "confusions surrounding family life and the uncertainty regarding the social forms of sexual expression" were related by his patients through their dreams and became the starting point for depth psychology.[74] Freud was interested in the Oedipus complex and its relation to religion, saying that in primitive times sons had killed their fathers and then repented, leaving mankind with a legacy of guilt and sin "that are carried in the unconscious through all generations."[75]

Jung believed the Oedipus complex was only one of many

"archetypes" or "psychoids" (elements in the collective unconscious which are close to instincts) present in all mankind. These reach the individual personality "only via the symbolism of myths and the unconsciously held beliefs transmitted with *national* cultures."[76] If Jung is correct, there can be other things in the unconscious besides the Oedipus complex which evoke guilt.

Alfred Adler, who like Jung separated from Freud, had early been interested in the effect of organic deficiency on personality. He himself had been a weak child due to rickets. He came to believe that sexuality was only one factor in determining personality. He emphasized the weakness of man as a species that had to become social in order to survive. Thus man's inferiority acted as a stimulus to discovery of a "better way and a finer technique in adapting himself to nature." Man herded with others and developed his psyche as an organ of "thinking, feeling and acting" in order to survive.

Yet always he "feels his incapacity before the goal of perfection;" there is ever something more that he must do, something more he must become in order to subdue his sense of insecurity. It becomes clear that to be a human being means the possession of a feeling of inferiority that is constantly pressing on towards its own conquest. The stronger the feeling of inferiority, the more powerful is the urge to conquest, and the more violent the emotional agitation.[77]

So, out of a sort of archetypal fear which has its origins in human evolution, each person develops his "life style" determined by his particular inferiorities as he perceives them and by his particular goals. This "life style" is played out in the company of his fellows and he is torn inwardly between his aggressions and his "social feeling." Hence Adler's famous doctrine of the "inferiority complex" and resultant compensation, overcompensation, and aggression. In short, Nietzsche's "will-to-power" is, in Adler's more scientific opinion, merely a superficial manifestation of the basic fear of inferiority.[78] Similarly, Lasswell, a noted modern political scientist, sees the main drive for power as arising from a damaged sense of personal worth.[79]

Adler spoke of a cosmic meaning to man's evolution whereby the "imperishable contributions of our forefathers" would be realized eventually in an "ideal society," a "universal community of mankind" in which social feeling would prevail over the egotism of inferiority and insecurity. Prior to World War I he had forebodings of catastrophe; after serving in the Austrian army he came to believe that if European culture were not to destroy itself, "its ego-centered struggles for power would have to be overcome by deepened social feelings."[80]

To Adler, then, international conflict was rooted in man's ego-centered aggressiveness, which in turn was rooted in man's fear of his own inferiority.

Otto Rank, cultural anthropologist and psychologist, concerned himself with man's fear of death and his desire for immortality. Man's "main fear was that the group would change or would come to an end."

> Underlying the more obvious and superficial motives of warfare we see, therefore, man's endless struggle toward "self-perpetuation;" and this means, as Rank develops his conception, man's ubiquitous effort, inherent in his evolutionary nature, to secure his immortality by maintaining an identity between his individual will and the continuous historical life of his group.[81]

Adler's view that man must evolve toward an ideal universal community of mankind is supplemented by Rank's assertion that modern man has been robbed of belief in the immortality of his soul and that he needs more than a psychotherapy to inspire a new "collective vitality" in a tired civilization. Meanwhile, man finds his immortality through identifying with his national group; this is his answer, according to Rank, to the fear of death, and is the basic cause of war.

Hobbes, as already noted, said that two causes for quarrel when men live in a condition of nature (without government) are competition for material things and search for glory. The third cause is fear, which he calls "diffidence":

> And from this diffidence of one another, there is no way for any man to secure himself so reasonable as anticipation; that is by force, or wiles, to master the persons of all men he can so long till he see no other power great enough to endanger him; and this is no more than his own conservation requireth.[82]

Because man walks in "continual fear, and danger of violent death," he becomes unlimitedly aggressive in self defense. And, to make sure his readers understand him, Hobbes gives the example of international conflict wherein all are always in the "posture of gladiators."

Finally, a late study of international conflict concludes that "there appears to be a trait cluster of need achievement, rigidity and stereotyping which are all related to conflict or militarism. The presence of such a cluster suggests a basic factor which underlies these separate traits. My research has suggested quite strongly that this basic factor is fear."[83]

Summary Comment. One wonders whether psychologists and related experts realize how frequently they refer to fear in one guise or another. If so, why have these experts who have concerned themselves with the connection between international conflict and individual behavior not had more to say about fear?

They teach that fear and anxiety are reactions to the possibility that basic human drives may not be satisfied. Fear thus arises at the point where frustration *may* occur, hence fear is prior to frustration. And aggression and irrationality arise out of frustration or the fear of frustration. Adler asserts that aggression is the response to the fear of inferiority, and this too is a fear of frustration through incapacity.

Fear is related to behavior other than aggression and irrationality.

Adler says, in effect, that the fear of inferiority begins when the child is taught to seek gain and glory. Hobbes treats fear as the reaction to the search for gain and glory by other men. Desire for gain is basically reaction to fear of hunger or other deprivation, but it can become Rousseau's thrust toward distinction or glory, which is the standard view in general psychology, and in this guise it relates back to fear of inferiority.

Mowrer treats fear as the shaper of responses to almost every stimulus. Freud and Jung, together with Adler, speak of guilt in the collective unconscious, and guilt is a form of fear. Consider how some religions exploit fear as well as assuage it, while ideologies trade on fear. Theologians who think of man as sinful might do well to think more basically of man as fearful—fearful of death, for example, as Rank emphasizes, and of the lack of meaning in life which evokes boredom and alienation and anomie. Fear relates even to ignorance, as most learn poorly if they are anxious.[84]

Fear has to do with group standards, which are important to virtually all the behavior we have reviewed—especially to man as nationalist and true believer. Anxiety arouses affiliative needs in human beings.[85] Thus fear causes the willingness to herd together in groups. Thereafter fear maintains the group against any questioning of its standards, upon pain of social disapproval, outlawry, or exile, because questioning threatens the solidarity of the group.

Conclusions

Fear is more closely related than is aggression to basic human needs for food, air, water, and sex. It is the fear that these needs will not be satisfied that turns needs into "instinctual" drives. Fear *is* that inner conflict between motives which creates frustration, and it is fear of being blocked which produces frustration even before any such goal is actually blocked. Fear thus produces—out of frustration—aggression and irrationality. Indeed, fear seems to be basic to every form of human behavior we have considered except stupidity and, to a degree, ignorance. We must conclude, tentatively at least, that fear is *the* well-spring of human behavior. If, as some say, human nature in its pristine condition is bad, then fear expresses that nature admirably; if good, then fear corrupts it.

Fear is both a cause of and a reaction to danger and to aggression. If it is fear clothed as aggression, greed, glory, or something else, that initiates international violence, then it is fear in the fundamental sense that perceives this violent intent and reacts to it. Once international violence has become certain, individuals in their masses on both sides will react in fear. This was the case with the populations of other states on guard against Ch'in, while the population of Ch'in itself would see its fate also at stake in the war. And so in India when Magadha was rising; in the

Middle East whenever a new empire was in the making; and in all the civilizations of Asia when nomad incursions threatened. Thus also in the Aegean in the high days of Athens and Sparta and later of Macedon, and in the Mediterranean when Rome was on the increase. The same holds true of Europe in the eras of Louis XIV, Napoleon, and Hitler, or when any two coalitions have come near to violence, as in the Cold War crises since 1945.

Fear is easier to communicate when communication is easy, as it was in small city-states and principalities and as it is today with almost instant communications. As stimuli become known almost immediately, so may statesmen go at once before the microphone and camera to imprint upon citizens a perception of threat and evoke a response of fear.

Fear is more intense with the intensity of the threat. Genghis Khan and Tamerlane and many others carried the threat of extinction to their enemies. After a long interval of more limited warfare, modern weapons technology carries the same threat of extinction to national populations today.

Chapter 2 Notes

1. But see Morris Ginsburg, "The Causes of War," *Sociological Review*, vol. 31 (1939); Luther L. Bernard, *War and its Causes* (New York, Holt, 1944); Quincy Wright, *A Study of War* (University of Chicago Press, 1965), 1285-95; and Robert C. North and Matthew Willard, "The Convergence Effect: Challenge to Parsimony," *International Organization* 37:2 (1983) 339-358.

2. Kenneth N. Waltz, *Man, The State, and War* (Columbia University Press, 1959).

3. See Pierre Teilhard de Chardin, *The Phenomenon of Man* (New York, Harper & Row, 1959) or his other less difficult writings. Julian Huxley, also a biologist, has published somewhat similar views; in his *UNESCO: Its Purpose and Philosophy* (Washington, Public Affairs Press, 1947), he writes that a "general philosophy of UNESCO should, it seems, be a scientific world humanism, global in extent and evolutionary in background" (p. 8). Teilhard's theory may be a restatement, on a more scientific basis, of the 19th century "geological prophecy" which said that evolution showed God's foreknowledge of man as the culmination and crowning achievement of His evolutionary process. (See Loren Eiseley, *The Immense Journey* (New York, Vantage Books, 1957).

4. The entire issue of *Peace Research Reviews* 7:6 (1978) is devoted to the "just war" idea, including changes in it in the light of nuclear weapons, especially in Pope John 23d's encyclical *Pacem in Terris*.

5. Reinhold Niebuhr, *Moral Man and Immoral Society* (New York, Scribner's, 1936)

6. See Robert and Rita Kimber, eds., *The Germans* (Princeton University Press, 1974) for Erich Kahler's thesis that Luther is largely responsible for German political immaturity.

7. Letter of September 1932 from Vienna. Reprinted in Robert A. Goldwin and Tony Pearce, eds., *Readings in World Politics* (New York, Oxford University Press, 2d ed., 1970) 89-99, by permission of the Estate of Professor Einstein and the Sigmund Freud Copyright, Ltd.

8. Ernest R. Hilgard and Richard C. Atkinson, *Introduction to Psychology* (New York, Harcourt Brace & World, 4th ed., 1967) 144-149. "Behavior theory" is that interpretation of psychology which emphasizes stimulus-response relationships and habit formation in accounting for behavior. The five behavior systems were described in J.W.M. Whiting and I.L. Childs, *Child Training and Personality* (New Haven, Yale University Press, 1958).

9. *Ibid.*, 508-520. Ivo K. Feirabend traces aggression back to frustration in his "Aggressive Behavior Within Polities," *Journal of Conflict Resolution*, vol. 10 (1966) 249-271.

10. Jung's theory may derive from Emile Durkheim, the French sociologist, who believed mental contents are not strictly individual; that there are collective states of the tribal mind which owe their force as beliefs to their super-personal reality.

11. Gustave Le Bon, in the late 19th century, said crowd-mentality is inferior to the mental level of the same individuals acting separately. Niebuhr's theme in *Moral Man and Immoral Society* may derive from this.

12. In L.N. Riselbach and G.I. Balch, eds, *Psychology and Politics* (New York, Holt, 1969) 256.

13. Erich Fromm, *May Man Prevail?* (Garden City, Doubleday Anchor Book, 1961) 18-26.

14. Jerome Frank's contribution to Elizabeth Jay Hollins, ed., *Peace is Possible* (New York, Grossman, 1965) 96-98.

15. *Ibid.*

16. Werner Levi, "On the Causes of War and the Conditions of Peace," in R.A. Falk and S.H. Mendlovitz, eds., *Toward a Theory of War Prevention* (New York, World Law Fund, 1966) 151.

17. From Aldous Huxley's *Ends and Means* (New York, Harper, 1937), reprinted in Goldwin, *op.cit.*, 76-85.

18. Robert Ardrey, *The Territorial Imperative* (New York, Atheneum Press, 1966) 333-337.

19. This is from Konrad Lorenz, *On Aggression* (New York, Harcourt, 1965), especially Chapter 13. The German version was published in 1963.

20. M.P.A. Montagu, *Culture and the Evolution of Man* (New York, Oxford, 1962) and *The Humanization of Man* (Cleveland, World Publishing, 1962); also M.P.A. Montagu, ed., *Man and Aggression* (New York, Oxford, 1969).

21. Samuel S. Kim, "The Lorenzian Theory of Aggression and Peace Research," *Journal of Peace Research* 13:4 (1976) 253-276.

22. Summarized by John Poppy in "Violence: We Can End It," *Look* magazine, June 10, 1969.

23. Plato, *The Republic*, Book 2. He suggests too that leaders stir up wars to retain their positions.

24. Thomas Hobbes, *Leviathan*, Part 1, Chapter 13.

25. Quincy Wright, *A Study of War* (University of Chicago Press, 1965, unabridged ed.), Vol. 1, Chapter 2, Section 5.

26. Paul Hoffman, "A War on Want," *UN Monthly Chronicle* 1:2 (1964) 92-98.

27. Kenneth Boulding's article in E.J. Hollins, *op.cit.*, 49-53.

28. Gunnar Myrdal's article in E.J. Hollins, *op.cit.*, 54-62.

29 Hilgard and Atkinson, *op.cit.*, 155.

30. George F. Kennan, *The Cloud of Danger* (Boston, Little Brown, 1977) 9-14.

31. Alan G. Newcombe, *et. al*, "An Improved Inter-Nation Tensiometer for the Prediction of War," *Peace Research Reviews* 5:4 (1974) 1-52.

32. Hobbes, *op.cit.*, Part 1, Chapter 13.

33. Quoted in *Between The Lines* 23:11 (1969).

34. Judd Marmor, "Psychological Problems of Warlessness," in Arthur Larson, ed., *A Warless World* (New York, McGraw-Hill, 1962) 124.

35. Aldous Huxley, *op.cit.*, 80.

36. Werner Levi, *op.cit.*, 149, 151.

37. Robert Ardrey, *op.cit.*, 335-336.

38. By James Norman Hall, quoted by W.E. Hocking in his contribution to Arthur Larson, *op.cit.*, 157.

39. Nels F.S. Ferre, "Does Man Really Want Peace?" *Saturday Review*, July 1, 1967, 10.

40. For Marx on alienation, see *Socialist Humanism: An International Symposium*, Erich Fromm, ed. (New York, Doubleday, 1965), contributions by Schatz and Winter.

41. Margaret Mead's contribution in Arthur Larson, *op.cit.*, 134-135.

42. E. Hocking's contribution in Arthur Larson, *op.cit.*, 146-147.

43. Claude Levi-Strauss, *The Savage Mind* (University of Chicago Press, 1965).

44. Kenneth Boulding, "The Prospects of Economic Abundance," in *The Control of Environment* (Amsterdam, North-Holland, 1966) 41-57.

45. Kenneth Boulding, "Learning and Reality-Testing Process in the International System," *Journal of International Affairs* 21:1 (1967) 1-15. See also Stewart E. Perry, "Notes on the Role of the National," *Journal of Conflict Resolution*, vol. 1 (1957), 346-363.

46. Hilgard and Atkinson, *op.cit.*, 510. Psychoanalytic theory speaks of the "compulsive" personality characterized by obstinacy as well as excessive cleanliness, orderliness and stinginess (*Ibid.*, 474-475).

47. Amitai Etzioni, "The Kennedy Experiment," *Peace Research Reviews* 8:1 (1979) 53-89.

48. Hilgard and Atkinson, *op.cit.*, 511. Psychoanalytic theory emphasizes the "authoritarian personality," given to scapegoating as well as to cynicism, destructiveness, and power-lust (*Ibid.*, 475).

49. Francoise Hall, "The United States' Search for Security: A Psychotherapist's Viewpoint," *Journal of Peace Research* 20:4 (1983) 299-309. She says the US Government lacks global perspective—this would be too complex—so it prefers to be sore at the Soviet Union as a more manageable target.

50. Hilgard and Atkinson, *op.cit.*, 511-512.

51. Francis A. Beer, in *Peace Against War: The Ecology of International Violence* (San Francisco, W.H. Freeman & Co., 1981), says that "because of the length of time since prior serious wars, levels of resistance to later wars may wear down, and they may explode more easily" (p. 69).

52. That of Hilgard and Atkinson, *op.cit.*, Chapter 20.

53. Psychoanalytic theory places irrationality into a rather neat three-layered perspective, with dynamic interaction among the layers: the *id* is irrational and impulsive, seeking immediate gratification; the *ego* postpones gratification so it can be achieved realistically and in socially approved ways; while *superego* (conscience) imposes a moral code.

54. Steven J. Rosen and Walter S. Jones, *The Logic of International Relations* (Cambridge Mass., Winthrop Publishers, 1980) 336.

55. See Hans Kohn, *Nationalism: Its Meaning and History* (Princeton, Van Nostrand, 1955).

56. See James P. Speer, "The Nature of Patriotism," *Christian Century*, July 1, 1953, 763-770, for an attempt to explore the distinction between patriotism and nationalism.

57. Kenneth Thompson, *Understanding World Politics* (Notre Dame, University of Notre Dame Press, 1975) 227.

58. T.F. Lentz and Wm. Eckhardt, "Factors of War-Peace Attitudes," *Peace Research Reviews* 1:5 (1967) 6-7.

59. *Ibid.*, 10.

60. Lee C. McDonald, *Western Political Theory* (New York, Harcourt, 1968) 606-9.

61. Saul Bellow, *Him With His Foot In His Mouth and Other Stories* (New York, Harper & Row, 1984) 151.

62. Marx did not think of his system of thought as an ideology. He spoke of ideology as "false consciousness," holding that the way of thinking in each era is determined by the socio-economic conditions of that time, hence no ideology could be the source of normative judgments (of truth) pointing beyond the existing state of affairs. See George Lichtheim, *The Concept of Ideology and Other Essays* (New York, Vintage Books, 1967) 18. Yet Marxism fits the commonsense notion of ideology as well as the definitions we cited earlier.

63. Hilgard and Atkinson, *op.cit.*, 74.

64. *Ibid.*, 85.

65. *Ibid.*, 98.

66. *Ibid.*, 119-127.

67. *Ibid.*, 132-134.

68. O. Hobart Mowrer, *Learning Theory and Behavior* (New York, J. Wiley & Sons, 1960), especially Chapters 3 through 5, and particularly pp. 92, 126, and 162. Mowrer in effect is amending (Watson's) Behaviorism's stimulus-response approach, saying (p. 77) "Thus, where Behaviorism restricted itself to the simple one-step S-R formula, we are here confronted by the necessity of postulating, minimally, a two-step, *two-stage* formula: S-r:s-R, where S is the danger signal, r the response of fear which is conditioned to it, and where s is the fear, experienced as a drive, which elicits (after learning) response R."

69. Hilgard and Atkinson, *op.cit.*, 169-170. Ax, the experimenter, induced fear through the clumsiness of his lab technicians, and evoked anger through remarks made by them. Just how valid these techniques might be, and how distinct the one stimulus from the other, is dubious.

70. Sandra B. McPherson, letter to *Bulletin Of The Atomic Scientists* 23:4 (1967), 36.

71. Hilgard and Atkinson, *op.cit.*, 179.

72. *Ibid.*, 179, 504-508.

73. *Ibid.*, 179.

74. Ira Progroff, *The Death and Rebirth of Psychology* (New York, Julian Press, 1956), 7.

75. *Ibid.*, 159.

76. *Ibid.*, 144. Italics ours.

77. *Ibid.*, 46-57, especially 56-57. Progroff quotes freely from Adler's *Social Interest* (London, Faber & Faber, 1938).

78. See Friedrich Nietzsche, *The Will To Power* (New York, Random House, 1969). He wrote in the late 19th century.

79. Harold D. Lasswell, *Power And Personality* (New York, W.W. Norton, 1948), Chapter 3.

80. Progroff, *op.cit.*, 81-89.

81. *Ibid.*, 213.

82. Hobbes, *op.cit.*, Part 1, Chapter 13. See the treatment of Hobbesian fear in Blair Campbell's "Prescription and Description in Political Thought: The Case for Hobbes," *American Political Science Review*, vol. 55 (June 1971), 376-388, especially 387-388.

83. Mike Pennock, "Psychological Motivation and National Conflict," *Peace Research Reviews* 5:4 (1974), 85-97, 89.

84. Hilgard and Atkinson, *op.cit.*, 147.

85. *Ibid.*, 361.

Chapter 3

BECAUSE NATIONS ARE
DIFFERENT FROM EACH OTHER?

The main allegation here is that nations can't get along because they are of differing natures, each having a distinct set of characteristics such as race, language, culture, customs, ideology, government, economy, and so forth. An allied allegation is that war is caused by certain types of "bad" nations. We'll deal with this first.

A. Bad Nations

The kinds of nations that have been termed "bad" in recent times in terms of causing international conflict and war are monarchical nations, capitalist nations, and totalitarian nations of the communist or fascist variety. It is said that such nations are greedy and aggressive.

1. *Monarchical Nations.* The notion that conflict is caused by monarchies and that conflict among "democracies" would be moderate and not issue in violence is especially connected with President Woodrow Wilson. The idea is that common people do not wish conflict because they must furnish soldiers and money and suffer resultant destruction. In monarchies, where representative government is lacking or weak, the people cannot prevail. The monarch, backed by a martial aristocracy, is free to play the balance-of-power game and to seek or risk violence.

There is doubt that people in the mass have consistently opposed war in the past, but there is also much to support Wilson's view. For we have seen that diplomacy and war have been the sport of princes throughout most of history. Of the individual psychological traits considered in the last chapter, the one most appropriate to the conduct of princes is the search for glory. Princes and the males of great families were born to the martial role. From the time the Warrior Peoples first erupted out of central Eurasia during the Bronze Age through, say, the wars of Louis XIV, the princely search for glory was the commonest cause of war.

Glory in combat for its own sake was not the sole motivation. Glory could shade over into a desire for territorial or other material gain such as plunder and ransom or commercial advantages. But glory-seeking monarchs commonly subordinated the domestic economy to foreign adventure. We see this in Ch'in Legalism as in Louis XIV's Mercantilism or Napoleon's Continental System. Chandragupta Maurya and the Prussian kings used the gains of the last war to pay for the next, but glory was the goal.

The monarchical state continued to play a role in bringing about war through World War I perhaps, and reappeared shortly as the new totalitarian state. But the monarch, from Cromwell's time forward, had increasingly to consult or influence public opinion.

It seems reasonable to conclude that an active agent in causing most international conflict from the beginnings until recently was the monarchical state and that the principal dynamic was the princely-aristocratic search for glory.

Referring back to Wilson's belief that violence would not occur in a world made up of liberal "democracies," it is true that we do not have a clear-cut case of war between nations which offer representative government on the basis of widespread franchise plus the usual guarantees of free speech, press, and so forth, though World War I bordered upon being such an example. We do have many instances of conflict between them, however. And we have many instances of apparently aggressive acts by such nations against other types of nations.

Princely states are rare nowadays, and where monarchs still exist their roles as presently defined no longer require them to seek glory in war. This would appear to be true even of the Arab princes who were personally engaged in war as recently as World War I.[1]

2. *Capitalist Nations.* These are those liberal states with highly industrialized capitalist economies which Wilson called democracies.

Lenin's theory of imperialism is also a theory of the cause of war. Lenin said the collapse of capitalism had been delayed because capitalist nations, having exhausted rich markets at home, had found even richer ones abroad in colonial empire. Only a few large monopolistic industries had survived the cut-throat competition of capitalism and they were linked with equally monopolistic banking corporations. They used the government to promote and protect their colonial ventures. This, Lenin said, was the final stage of capitalism, meaning that capitalist nations were in a competition for colonies, markets, and raw materials which, deepening into conflict, must issue in mutually destructive war.

Actually, Lenin wrote his theory after World War I had begun. It was his way of explaining wars in general during the capitalist stage of history, and that particular war which he expected to end with the collapse of all capitalist nations, paving the way for the socialist stage. Thus the democratic socialists were foolish to work merely for an altered capitalist society, while communist socialists ought to strike at capitalism's weakest point, Russia.[2]

There is some reason to trace the causes of World War I back to the imperial competition of the later 19th century, accompanied by rising tariffs and naval appropriations and culminating in crises over the way Africa would be divided up. However, there were non-economic factors at work, including national pride and stupidity in high places.

Moreover, since World War II we have seen the collapse of Western imperialism, at least as political domination, and this has happened in large part simply because "The final accounting suggests that the colonies brought their masters but indifferent returns."[3]

Lenin's theory is pretty much a dead letter, although we need to remember that what he was really trying to explain was why capitalism had not yet collapsed. His theory's only present validity might be its application to the struggle between developed countries (DCs) and less developed countries (LDCs) over terms of trade and aid. LDC statesmen say the new "economic imperialism" is nearly as bad as old political imperialism. But LDCs are not able militarily to challenge the DCs, even if they wished to do so, and there has been no large-scale violence between them since independence. Nevertheless, the weakness of LDCs for economic and other reasons does invite great-power intervention leading to great-power conflict.[4]

Plato, as we noted, believed that the desire for luxury was the main reason for the Mediterranean wars of his day. Probably, however, this has been a principal cause only in states dominated by merchants such as Athens, the oligarchic republics of Medieval and Renaissance Europe, and to some extent the 18th and 19th century capitalists who persuaded parliaments to enhance their profit-making opportunities abroad. Much depends on the nature of the elite. Commercial-industrial elites tend to subordinate glory to wealth whereas land-holding aristocracies subordinate wealth to glory.

We are left, however, in doubt as to capitalism's blame for conflict in our day. There is that alliance among military men, arms-producing corporations, labor unions, local communities and politicians, but it is difficult to assign a weight to this military-industrial complex. We can be sure only that it is significant in US and other capitalist nations in keeping the Cold War alive.[5] And it would be foolish to assume there is not some rather comparable alliance in USSR among military men, certain government ministries, and Politburo and Central Committee members.

The economic interpretation of history is not so generally accepted in the West as it was a few decades ago. Today it is common in the study of international relations to see the economic factor treated only as a means. For example, Lionel Robbins, a British economist, says:

> The attainment of military power in the narrowest sense involves the control of scarce resources. The attainment of any kind of power, save perhaps the power of the spirit, is similarly

conditioned. This is so whatever the social system of the state in question. Under socialism as much as under capitalism, national power rests on economic factors.[6]

Whether national power is an end in itself, or is in its turn merely a means to a further end, is one of the things we'll be discussing later. What Robbins is telling us here is that "bad" capitalist nations and "good" socialist nations alike seek economic power as a means to state power, and this is rather a different thing from using state power to acquire wealth.

The economic explanation of war suffers a blow from a study by two French scholars. Their investigation of the wars of the past hundred years leads them to conclude that these have been due primarily to political factors, with economic factors having been either secondary or mere tools in the hands of politicians.[7] This period includes the heyday of Lenin's "imperialism." Since their book was written in 1969, the Organization of Petroleum Exporting Countries (OPEC) has executed the greatest transfer of wealth in history into the hands of a few rather insignificant states, and all the great capitalist nations suffered OPEC to do it to them.

The corollary to Lenin's theory is that war will cease when all nations become socialist. Unhappily for him, we have now seen intermittent violence between socialist USSR and socialist China, and between China and socialist Vietnam, as well as Vietnam's invasion of Cambodia to oust the socialist Khmer Rouge regime. We have, too, examples of apparently aggressive acts by USSR, in its invasion of Finland in 1939 and its armed interventions in Hungary in 1956 and in Czechoslovakia in 1968.

A Marx-Leninist might explain those Soviet acts by introducing Stalin's theory of "capitalist encirclement," meaning they were necessary to protect the socialist world from capitalist threat. Lyndon Johnson might have explained his interventions in the Dominican Republic and Vietnam in Wilsonian terms, saying he was trying to "make the world safe for democracy" by resisting communist aggressions.

3. *Totalitarian Nations.* Communists do not like to have socialist countries labeled totalitarian. To them, socialism requires a high if not a "total" degree of social control but only during an interim period to prepare the country for communism and consequent demise of the whole apparatus of control called the state. More specifically, in the highest or communist stage of history, there will be public bodies of some sort to control "things" but no government to control people.

To communist-socialists, capitalist nations are the bad ones, and fascist nations are those in which capitalism has been about to expire due to its own inner "contradictions," but a rightist seizure of power has supervened to preserve capitalism's profits, under state control, and thus defer the transition to the socialist stage.

Liberals pointed to fascism's worship of the state and blamed World War II on its thrust toward aggrandizement. In USSR and elsewhere, however, the war was blamed on fascism's hatred of communism—its use of state power to stamp out communism in Italy and Germany and then to try to wipe out USSR as the only socialist state in existence. Fascism was the Reaction, the Counter-revolution.

The totalitarian state, whether fascist or communist, may be seen as a new form of the monarchical or authoritarian state, but intensified by ideology and modern modes of reinforcing state power over individuals. It engages in international conflict according to the dictates of a Mussolini, a Hitler, or a Stalin, much as states moved at the whim of a Napoleon or a Renaissance prince. The search for glory played as large a role in the policies of Hitler and Mussolini as in the careers of earlier conquerors. The same cannot quite be said of Stalin, for USSR in his time reacted to initiatives of other great nations far more than it initiated action.

We may note again that the thrust toward glory is a search for identification, a form of aggressiveness rooted in frustration and a fear of inferiority which evoke compensation and over-compensation. Individuals who reach the top of the political heap tend to be a queer breed whether dictators or not. Khruschev and Churchill were as short of stature as Stalin, Mussolini, Hitler, and Napoleon. Churchill lisped while Demosthenes stammered. Roosevelt was a cripple. De Gaulle, like Lincoln, was ungainly and ugly. The dictator or the "strong man," even more than the hereditary prince, is apt to have an interesting psychological history.

Late research in primate behavior suggests that certain males are dominant because their bodies carry a high level of the neurotransmitter serotonin, but the level seems to vary with their success, and anyway the linking of biology to behavior in humans is still in its earliest stages.

A 1966 study of the personality traits of both Western and non-Western decision-makers found that most rated high in education, political experience, need for power and achievement, energy and competitiveness. Most were from high socio-economic backgrounds. But totalitarian leaders were something of a category apart, rating low in education and socio-economic background but very high in authoritarianism and need for power and achievement.[8] We might say that monarchs sought glory in war because the roles to which they were born demanded it, whereas totalitarian dictators sought to become monarchs because their personalities demanded it.

But the idea that totalitarian nations cause war, or that dictators cause war, can be turned on its head, for it may be truer that war causes dictators and totalitarian states. The *Summary of International History* indicates that fascism could scarcely have triumphed in Italy and Germany, nor could communism have come to power in Russia, except for the despair and devastation wrought by World War I.

It was the Japanese invasion and World War II which ruined the Nationalist Party of China and produced the conditions for communist take-over. The same war terminated in a situation in East Europe which assured the success of communist factions from Poland to Yugoslavia. International war tends to evoke civil war, and adventurers find their chances in times of troubles. As we noted, the Greek city-states, when threatened by war, often named one man *tyrannos* or tyrant, and sometimes the appointment turned out not to be temporary. In the earlier Cold War period, Americans saw their government arrogate more and more power over them in the name of anti-communism and "defense of freedom." Conscription is the most widespread invasion of individual rights ever conceived. And the Vietnam war is simply a recent proof that war wrecks economies and weakens the body politic.

Herbert Spencer, an English writer famous for *laissez-faire* economics, theorized in the later 19th century that war and militarism lead to an expansion of governmental control and despotism, with increase of social stratification and decrease of self-government, whereas peace tends to call forth the opposite results.[9] Pitirim Sorokin, Russian-born social philosopher, asserts that "The explosion of war or famine or any other great emergency invariably leads to an expansion of governmental regimentation in all societies of a certain kind; and the termination of war, famine, or other emergency regularly leads to a quantitative and qualitative decrease in governmental regimentation."[10]

Summary Comment. We conclude that (a) from at least early Bronze Age times through World War II, states dominated by monarchs or dictators and backed by aggressive elites initiated much of the conflict, although there has been a tendency since the 18th century for leaders to appeal to arms in the name of national glory rather than their personal glory; (b) from time to time through history but increasingly since late Medieval times, states dominated by commercial or industrial elites have initiated much of the other conflict, although there has been a tendency since mid-19th century to believe that the national economic interest cannot be served by violence; and (c) fascist totalitarian nations have been more prone to initiate conflict than have liberal or totalitarian socialist nations.

We express these conclusions without prejudice to the part fear plays in stimulating glory-seeking or greed to take the initiative. Much less do we depreciate the influence of fear in causing other nations to respond hostilely to an aggressive initiative. Also, the existence of "bad" nations does not explain the wars of religion, even though glory and greed were factors in them. Perhaps we need another category of "bad" nation called "religious" or "ideological" nations.

Each type of "bad" nation corresponds to a psychological trait considered in the last chapter: the monarchical or fascist nation corresponds to man as glory-seeker; the capitalist or communist-socialist nation to man as greedy; and the religious or ideological nation to man as true believer. In each of these cases there is a decision-making elite whose members display the appropriate psychological trait. The correspondence varies greatly but the point is that, by focusing on elites, we can to a degree perceive individual psychology in nation behavior.

B. Differences in the Natures of Nations

The argument here is that international conflict can be explained by differences in the make-up of one nation as contrasted with others, and that international cooperation can be explained by similarities. According to Sorokin, the components that make up a nation are (a) its physical-biological endowment, including soil and subsoil, bodies of water, location, topography and climate, vegetation and animal life; (b) its people, including race and language; (c) its material culture, mainly its economy; and (d) its idea culture, meaning its myths and understanding of history, religions or other ideologies, social ethics and personal morals, and its politics and government.

These components are said to give a nation its particular nature. They represent so many variables that no two will have the same make-up. Each is different from any other, although it will have more components in common with some than with others, so presumably it will conflict more with the latter than with the former.

The thesis that nations conflict because they are different is pertinent to explaining conflict but also will be relevant to any attempt to prescribe for peace. For, if nations conflict because they are different, it follows that they cannot cease to conflict until they are similar. Thus there can be no durable peace until a homogenization process takes place whereby all nations acquire a rather uniform race, language, ideology, economy, and form of government along with similar myths, norms, values, and so forth. A further inference can be drawn that this process will take a very long time.

In discussing the nature and behavior of man as the cause of international conflict, we relied mainly on psychology. Here we shall rely most on sociology and anthropology. Socio-cultural peculiarities have been studied by scholars in these fields, and their theories have passed into political science and international relations. They influence understanding of international conflict along the lines of the logical sequence just described, and thus tend to bar prescriptions which offer to resolve our predicament in the foreseeable future instead of only through the long working out of history.

Sociology and anthropology developed out of the body of philosophy during the last hundred years or so. They carried on certain lines of thought which seemed promising or attractive. The most important ones as they have developed, for our purposes, are discussed as follows.

1. *Romantic Nationalism.* Romanticism, as we learned in the

Summary, was a reaction against the cool rationalism of the Enlightenment. Romanticism emphasized feeling and sentiment and intuition. The French nationalism that arose with the Revolution extolled the special qualities of France as well as the Rights of Man. By the beginnings of the 19th century, writers in other lands were searching out and glorifying the peculiarities of their own physical and cultural environments. These were to be loved, not appraised.

The "geographical" school of sociological thought explained socio-cultural characteristics in terms of geography and climate. It developed out of Montesquieu's writings and remained an important line of thought well into the 20th century.

In Italy and Germany, each divided into many states, sentiment became intense as patriots yearned for a unified state to embody what they asserted to be one language and one culture. Hegel held that a particular aspect of Absolute Mind called a *Geist* or spirit illuminates and guides the history of each People until a State is achieved, then the State becomes the march of God in the world. Hegel also theorized that Absolute Mind favors a particular state at a particular era in history and that this favor becomes manifest in the outcome of international war. Hegel was a Prussian.

2. *The Organic State.* Hegel viewed the society-state as an organism, as did many others, especially the Germans.[11] This involved an analogy with biology. Hobbes called his state "Leviathan" but intended an analogy with the whale only in size and power. He actually described a mechanism rather than an organism.

But the romantic nationalists thought of the national state as an organism flourishing within a particular environment, made up of individual human beings who were articulated into a functioning whole by Society. It was Society which imparted nervous system and brain, while State endowed the entirety with a moral will. The state became a person, implicit with the sort of unique worth which most romantics also granted to individuals. But, in Germany and to a degree throughout the Continent, the state-molecule had a worth greater than the human atoms which comprised it.

Sorokin summed up four conceptions of society: the mechanistic image of society as a kind of machine; the atomistic, which sees in society nothing but individuals and does not recognize society as a super-individual reality; the organismic, which views society as a living entity and grants it a superindividual reality, of natural origin and spontaneous existence; and the functional conception which does not care whether society is mechanism or organism, natural or artificial, but which views society as a system of interrelated individuals.

"Among these four conceptions, the organic has been the most popular" and can be divided into three subclasses: "philosophical organicism," which contends only that society is a living unity that originated spontaneously and lives according to natural laws; "psycho-social organicism," which contends that society is "a superindividual organism of ideas, representations, minds, and volitions" and is "a kind of spiritual personality—a real social or group mind;" and "biological organicism" which says "society is nothing but a specific variety of *biological* organism" and "has not only psycho-social, but physical reality."[12] These views were applied to state as well as to society.

The image of the nation as an organism was promoted by racist theories which became part of 19th century romantic nationalism although the basic notion of racial purity and superiority is at least as old as the Hindu *dharmasastra* (social policy). Gobineau, a Frenchman, wrote of superior races, meaning whites and especially "Aryans," and contrasted these with races incapable of progress, saying that "a people and their civilization dies out when the people's fundamental racial constitution is changed or engulfed among other races."[13] Out of this notion grew "the white man's burden," the "civilizing mission," Nordicism, Teutonism, and Hitler's racism. When coupled with romantic nationalism it produced Pan-Germanism and Pan-Slavism. Racism was so prevalent that Theodore Herzl, founder of Zionism, called Jews who opposed Zionism "a degenerate racial strain."[14]

Also related to organicist sociology was the "demographic" theory which said social phenomena result from change in population density. Malthus spoke of a "law" whereby war functions as one effective check on population increase, while W.G. Sumner and others said that a desire for expansion resulting from overpopulation was a cause of war. Thus Hitler later invaded Russia to obtain "living room" for the German *Volk*.

Lest it be thought that the notion of the organic state is outdated, Alexander Solzshenitsyn, a famous modern writer, thinks of a nation as a "crystallized personality."[15]

3. *Community.* Sociology was born during the early decades of the industrial revolution on the Continent. While Germany was yet without its State, Marx saw the new industrial beginnings in Prussia and the Rhineland. He went to France and saw industry at a more advanced stage. He crossed into England and saw these conditions at their most advanced. In his early writings he bemoaned the lost medieval community, the warm village of face-to-face relationships which economic necessity had forced men to leave for the depressed conditions and cold impersonality of the industrial city.[16]

As the industrial revolution moved along in Germany, more writers were impressed by the human cost of industrial prosperity. Friedrich Tonnies' *Community and Society* was an account of the contrast between the continuity and satisfaction he believed inherent in the interpersonal relationships of the traditional *community* and the impersonal contractual relations which regulated individuals in large-scale *society*.[17]

Tonnies' terminology has not always been followed but sociology has combined the idea of the organic state or society with the idea of community, in the sense Tonnies intended, into the concept of the organic communal society-state. Such an entity cannot be deliberately changed. It is not a thing artificed by man, so man cannot alter it, at least not into something better but only into something worse, as the French did in their revolution when they sought change too quickly. Each society will change, as it grows and develops, but always along its own unique axis, and it should be let alone.

For example, Emile Durkheim, a noted turn-of-the-century French sociologist, wrote that "It displeases man to renounce the unlimited power over the social order he has so long attributed to himself" although man's "power over things really began only when he recognized that they have a nature of their own, and resigned himself to learning this nature from them."[18] A modern sociologist says that "it appears like a grandiose dream to think of controlling according to the will of man the course of social evolution."[19]

4. *Priority of Society to State.* This organism of humans with its territory and environment is called by different names. Sociologists say "society." Anthropologists call it "culture." Tonnies and others, as we shall see later, prefer "community." They all mean the same thing.

Locke and Rousseau believed that society can form before the state (that is, government) does. Hobbes disagreed. German scholars thought society was prior because there had been a German society in some sense for centuries before Bismarck created the German state. According to sociologists, society lays the foundations for the state and determines the form of government appropriate for the society. Thus it was the German society which created the Bismarckian state. It was the Chancellor's job merely to bring about unification and then to draw up a unique form of government to match the peculiar configuration of the underlying society.

It would have made better sense to recognize that each of the German states that Bismarck brought together corresponded more closely to communal peculiarities and sentiments than an overall German state could possibly do. But the nationalist feeling was strong enough to establish the overall state as the ideal, corresponding to ties of language and literature and buttressed by recollections of membership in the Holy Roman Empire. The fact that Bismarck's state turned out to be a federal rather than a unitary state like France or England ought to have suggested the idea that community is a matter of degree and that different degrees can be represented by different levels of government, each with its own grant of authority.

The fact of the matter was that German society-culture-community was not so organically uniform that the several state governments could be abolished. Instead, Bismarck created a new level of government with authority over war and peace and a few other matters. Thereafter German society homogenized and prospered until the Kaiser and his ministers risked all in 1914.

5. *The Struggle for Existence.* The "biological organicist" idea of a nation as a separate living entity guided by its own soul or mind or will, when coupled with Malthus' and Darwin's "struggle for existence" or Spencer's "survival of the fittest," was interpreted to mean that it is as natural for nations to conflict as it is for animals. Biological sociology asserts that "Eternal struggle is a universal and everlasting law. Such a struggle goes on among atoms, organisms, human beings, societies, and among all kinds of units." Many organicists have insisted, with Hegel, that the question, Which of two groups is better, more resourceful, more intelligent, and therefore more entitled to survive, could not be decided without war.[20] Darwin and Wallace, in their evolutionary theories, had emphasized the survival of those most adaptable to changing environments, but the "Social Darwinists" tended to think simply in terms of survival of the strongest.

Some organicists disagreed that international violence was not only inevitable but desirable. They said intergroup conflict is inevitable but they agreed with the view of Aldous Huxley that actual violence tends to eliminate the fittest, hence does not advance the human race. Around the turn of the century these theorists were saying that war would disappear because men were learning that struggle could be carried on by non-violent means similar to those used to adjust conflict within nations. This period corresponds to the high hopes of formal-legalism when the meetings at The Hague were being held and arbitration treaties were being signed and agitation for a League of Nations was getting under way.[21]

Social Darwinism became an element in most people's way of looking at things, in America as in Europe, and was important in the rise of fascism. It is by no means dead today, even among scholars, as we see in this statement by a modern anthropologist who was objecting to the idea that if men can find out how to make the atomic bomb they can also find out how to prevent war:

> Wars are not caused by ignorance, nor can "the peace be kept" by the findings of social scientists. Wars are struggles between social organisms—called nations—for survival...No amount of understanding will alter or remove the basis of this struggle, any more than an understanding of the ocean's tides will diminish or terminate their flow.[22]

6. *Modern Systems Theory.* In recent decades most anthropologists and sociologists have dropped the cruder romantic and organismic images, yet the central idea has persisted and has reappeared in "general systems theory" which, like earlier organismic theory, has come into the social sciences from biology. A Soviet scholar defines the "holistic" or unified system as "a totality of objects whose interaction generates new

integrative qualities absent in their isolated parts" and is to be distinguished from a "merely summative system (a pile of stones and the like) whose properties are identical with a mere sum of the properties of its parts."[23] Applied to biology, systems theory means "it is impossible to resolve the phenomena of life completely into elementary units" because the behavior of an isolated part is different from its behavior within the context of the whole. A cell taken out of an organism and allowed to grow in a tissue culture will behave differently from the way it did within the organism. The characteristics of life are altered with alterations in the whole system and disappear when it is destroyed.[24]

It is from biological systems theory that the behavioral and social sciences have obtained notions of dynamic mutual interaction and ordered sequential process. A biological system may be contrasted with a mechanism, which is incapable of self-regulation following disturbances or changes in the environment. The two basic ideas here are that an entity is as it is and behaves as it does because it is part of a whole called a system. A holistic system is capable of correcting and stabilizing itself whereas a mechanism can be put right only through intervention by an outside agency.

Sociology and anthropology borrowed systems theory from biology and began to speak of social systems and cultural systems. Each phrase refers to a "general" system, meaning the whole realm of interaction, although in actual practice the whole realm often turns out to be something less than the whole.

There are "subsystems" of two kinds. There is the subsystem quantitatively less than the whole, such as a state of the American system or a county of the English system. There is also the subsystem qualitatively less than the whole, such as the political system or the economic system, even though spatially they are identical with the "general" social or cultural system.

In the main, adaptation of systems theory to international relations has meant that scholars who use this approach consciously or unconsciously apply the "holistic" assumption to their understanding of national societies. The idea of a "whole" implies that it be distinct and apart, and this means the national state is usually regarded as the "whole" because its geographical boundaries are distinct. It is also a "whole," though the behavioral scholar may not notice it, because the national government has the authority and power to maintain its distinctness. A national government is a "boundary-maintaining mechanism."[25]

A national society may seem to be a better example of a system than is the international system, for it is essential to biological systems theory that the organism be an "open" system. That is, it takes "inputs" (nourishment, etc.) from its environment, processes them through a "matrix" (digestive apparatus), and deposits "outputs" (excrement) in the environment. This part of the biological analogy fails when the systems theorist raises his level of analysis to the world international system which, pending the advent of interplanetary interaction, has to be considered a "closed" system. The systems theorist is simply more comfortable with national systems; they are self-contained enough to look holistic and show much internal interaction at several levels, yet they are not so self-contained as to be "closed" systems.

But a national system is very far from being self-contained, as demonstrated by international history culminating in today's global system in which each nation is daily bombarded by "inputs" from other nations and domestic policy is dominated by foreign policy. The social scientist must give up the biological analogy which requires an open system and admit that there is only one "general" social or cultural system and that it is a closed one coextensive with the planet. Efforts made by some to treat the global system as an open one which receives its inputs from its own subsystems, warp and astigmatize the understanding, especially if one looks for a central "matrix" to process these inputs into outputs.

An American scholar remarked in 1978 that systems theory has not yielded impressive results; that its models have been difficult to apply to real international situations; and that disenchantment is spreading.[26] In 1983 a European peace researcher said he would like to see research done within a sociological framework but he then listed the core elements of sociological theory—norms, roles, classes, institutions—and asked, At the global level, where are they?[27] Other international relations specialists accuse the systems theorists of having relaxed the standards of traditional science to reduce theory to mere analogy, analogy that is obviously biological,[28] or of reifying the nation or the system into an organism instead of an organization in which individual human beings make the decisions.[29]

So far as the international system is concerned, it is enough to say, as we did at the outset of the first chapter, that it is a group of nations in frequent enough contact so that any change anywhere is apt to have some effect everywhere. The system is indeed holistic, in that the nature of the system is such that it affects nation behavior; but more about that in Chapter 4.

7. *Socio-Cultural Differences That Cause International Conflict.* In addition to the extreme view that nations are unique organic beings that naturally struggle against each other for existence, there is the more reasonable assertion that if nations differ in certain specific respects then conflict is made more certain while cooperation is made more difficult. Here we discuss briefly these specific differences.

(a) *Racial Differences.* Racial uniformity is found only in small and remote or primitive social groups. Any sizeable modern nation is a racial conglomerate, and in general the larger and more powerful the nation the greater is its racial diversity. US, USSR, and India are prime examples, while most Chinese, Frenchmen and Britishers display a common color which hides a long process of admixture.

In early history there was a coincidence between race and interstate conflict in so far as tribal states accounted for such conflict. many centuries later European romanticism clothed colonial imperialism with the "white man's burden" justification. The image of the German master race was one of the contours along which World War II was fought. We have romantic nationalism resurrected in Black Nationalism with its praise of *negritude*, and there is a coincidence between racial difference and international conflict in southern Africa. The conflict between developed and undeveloped countries is to some extent a white-colored division, but Japanese and Chinese are not white.

Race has had little correspondence with the lines of international conflict since earliest times. Teutons have been warring upon Teutons and Nordics upon Nordics, Latins upon Latins, Mongols upon Mongols, and Blacks upon Blacks, for too long for any careful observer to believe that racial difference causes international conflict or that similarity causes international cooperation. Not only do semitic Arabs oppose their Israeli cousins but Arab nations quarrel with and fight each other.

Race is not a cultural characteristic but a biological one—a consequence of a certain coincidence in genetic codes. It imparts to large groups of people similarities of coloring, bone structure and so forth, all of a superficial character so far as we know. Our consciousness of race is of course cultural, and we have been slow to realize that the traits we associate with race are likewise culturally induced rather than biologically determined.

Racial difference is a source of civil conflict, especially in US and the Republic of South Africa, although one can stand on a corner in Honolulu and watch all the races of man pass by, living peacefully together.

But at the international level one must conclude that there is no correlation between race and either conflict or cooperation.

(b) *Language Differences.* Differences in languages are often clear-cut and obvious, and language boundaries often coincide with national frontiers. Hence the "folk-knowledge" notion that nations do not get along because they cannot understand each other's speech.

Language difference as an element in international conflict has been emphasized in the European system because nearly all its principal states have a different dominant tongue. Each language has its own literature, including its history, so that a people's understanding of itself is a part of its language.

Language is perhaps the most important element in cultural particularism, and where a language barrier coincides with a national boundary, language reinforces a sense of separateness. But this does not mean that language differences cause international conflict.

The states of Germany, even though their peoples spoke mutually comprehensible dialects, quarreled and fought among themselves for a thousand years before Napoleon merged many of them and then Bismarck united most of those left. Austria remained outside that federation and continued to speak German while belonging to a political union of states speaking Hungarian and some Slavic tongues. The Italian-speaking states of Italy had their own millenium of blood and conflict, until they were united in 1871. In the earlier Mediterranean, before Roman dominion, the Latin-speaking city-states had fought each other, as had the Etruscan-speaking cities, and the Oscan-speaking cities; and the Greek city-states fought each other for many centuries despite a common tongue.

In the early Middle East, the Medes and Persians could understand each other but the latter subdued the former. Before Mohammed's time the Arabic-speaking tribes fought each other continually; then, after Arabic had by conquest been made the common language of an empire, there was disintegration into new independent states which then fought each other. The empires of Rome, Byzantium, and the Ottomans lasted for centuries despite great diversity of languages.

In old India, interstate conflict did not follow language lines or any other lines except state boundaries. China has never had unity in spoken tongues, yet has been one state through most of its history. If it is argued that China was held together by its common written language, how can one explain Latin's failure to hold Europe together?

Switzerland has for centuries managed a viable federation despite three major languages while Canada's federation comprises English and French and South Africa makes do with English and Afrikaans. The Arabic-speaking states bicker constantly and several have been at violence with one another. Perhaps they would bicker less if they could not understand each other so easily.

International conflict often coincides with language differences; often it does not. There is no pattern. Thus one can conclude that language differences cannot be a significant determinant.

(c) *Differences in Myths, Histories, Values, Folkways, and Norms.* Myths are incidents and figures believed to be in a people's past which are clothed with significance and passed down through the generations by oral tradition, as among the Polynesians, or are at some point committed to writing, as was the epic Norse *edda.* Their principal importance has been in more primitive cultures, yet there are scholars who believe that mythic particularism is a cause of international conflict or at least a barrier to understanding and supranational integration.[30]

The definition of myth can be expanded to include such images as "Uncle Sam" and "John Bull," even though these are wholly fictitious, having emerged in recent times.

We shall be on sounder ground if we turn from myth to history and say that historical particularism may be a cause of conflict. For it is from the histories, as written in each nation, that individuals ingest the message of national cultural particularism, whether or not it has much objective basis. From our histories we learn the myths of national uniqueness and superiority, and—depending on changing circumstances—whether we are a warrior race or a peace-loving people, or both, but at any rate a special people with a common past and a common destiny. It is a situation already noted in the preceding chapter, whereby man as nationalist ensures man as ignorant.

A "value" has been defined as the object of an "attitude." An attitude is an aspect of personality that develops under social and group stimuli into a tendency to act in a certain way with reference to some person or object or matter. Behavior is the test of an attitude, so that a value influences behavior toward that which is judged to be of help and away from that deemed harmful. "Mores" are those values which are thought important because the group's welfare depends on them while "folkways" are values prescribing things desirable but of less importance.

Folkways have to do with such things as grammar, dress, modes of greeting and of eating. A folkway may approach a more, as in controversy over proper length of a boy's hair. In some places a folkway may be a more, as in the rules of eating among the castes of India. Mores include prescriptions to respect parents, to honor a promise, to tell the truth, and so forth. When mores are stated negatively they are called "taboos," as in the taboo on incest.

Differences in folkways among the principal nations do reinforce national particularism. There are differences of dress and diet and modes of politeness between Americans and Japanese, Russians and Chinese, Indians and Chinese, and so forth. Institutionalized beggary shocks Europeans in Asia and Africa even though it may have an honored place in, say, Islamic culture.

Values defined as mores are protected by "norms," or prescriptions designed to make behavior conform to values. Norms are rules or laws which may be distinguished according to whether they are enforced by supernatural agencies (gods, angels, demons), by the group, or by the government.

Mores and norms differ less among the great ethical religious systems than from one primitive society to another. They differ less from one modern nation to another than from the modern nation to itself in its past. What we see is a continuum running from the particular to the general, and from the more varied past to the more homogenized present. This goes along with the trend from Tonnies' "community" to his "society," or what Henry Maine, the legal philosopher, spoke of as from "status" to "contract." There is also a historical tendency for norms to be enforced less by the supernatural or the small group as national governments assume more and more authority over their citizens' lives.

However, despite the claims of national cultural particularism, each nation enforces the basic civil norm, that individuals shall keep their promises, while punishing the same criminal offenses from petty larceny to murder and treason. A difference lies in the absence in most nations of many of the procedural safeguards which typify Anglo-American law. Yet it would be wrong to assume that safeguards do not exist elsewhere, or that the Anglo-American guarantees are usually available without disastrous expense to litigant or accused.

With respect to all the cultural attributes we are considering in this subsection, the differences are greater between the DCs on the one hand and the LDCs on the other. The DCs share a lot of history, their folkways have become quite similar, and their values and laws are more uniform than might be supposed. And the principal antagonists in World War III, as in the Cold War and the first two world wars, will be the DCs. It is they who will fight out that war, even though it might start in an LDC which, as we have seen, can be the vacuum that sucks the great powers in.

Nevertheless, to the degree that the "folk knowledge" of hearsay and the "literary knowledge" of ethnocentric history continue to instill a sentiment that *We* are different from *They*, particularism will retain as much subjective reality among the great nations as it lacks objective reality. "Sentimentalists are difficult people."[31]

Actually, customs, values, and attendant norms are less resistant to change than anthro-sociologists presume. For example, the Warrior Peoples imposed a warrior ethic upon much of Eurasia where a relatively peaceful agrarian way of life seems to have prevailed before. It was only a generation after Constantinople fell to the Ottomans in 1450 that classical learning, carried by Byzantine scholars, fleeing to Italy, created the Renaissance.* This new Italian culture did not then seep into France and England; it was installed there under the aegis of Francis I and Henry VIII in a few decades.

---

*In *The Legacy of the German Refugee Intellectuals* (Robert Boyers, ed., New York, Schocken Books, 1972), the introductory article by Henry Pachter says their influence on the social sciences in the United States is comparable to the impact on classical studies in Italy of the Greek scholars who fled Constantinople. Pachter may have a point. But whether their influence on our political thought—their political realism their organismic analogies, their sociology of politics and of law, etc.— has been benign is dubious indeed. They are significantly responsible for amoral U.S. power realism in foreign policy, to be discussed in Chapter 6. They have pushed positivism past common sense. Erich Kahler, himself German-born, asserts that Germany achieved maturity only in the intellectual sphere, never in the political (see Robert and Rita Kimber,

Contrary Views Applicable to Subsections (a), (b), and (c). Edward Sapir, a linguist, writes that

Historians and anthropologists find that races, languages, and cultures are not distributed in parallel fashion, that their areas of distribution intercross in the most bewildering fashion, and that the history of each is apt to follow a distinctive course. Races intermingle in a way that languages do not. On the other hand, languages may spread far beyond their original home, invading the territory of new races and of new culture spheres.[32]

Sorokin says that the culture of practically every individual and of each small or vast social group consists not of one cultural system uniting into a consistent whole millions of meanings, values, norms, and interests but rather a multitude of elements that are partly neutral, partly even contradictory to one another. The map of cultural systems in mankind, he asserts, does not coincide with the map of its social systems.[33]

An anthropologist, writes that:

Nations are not pattered in terms of uniformities of individual behavior. They are extremely heterogeneous entities whose total "pattern" consists of intricately interrelated parts of different kinds. It is only sub-cultural groups—these might be called subsocieties— whose individual members share a substantial core of behavior.[34]

Culture is thus not merely national but sub-national and individual, trans-national or worldwide, depending on which aspects of culture one is talking about. And if there is indeed a correspondence between cultural boundaries and national boundaries, it may be not at all due to "natural" reasons—evolutionary development through history—but to artificial action by the state itself. Sapir says that "in an area dominated by the national sentiment there is a tendency for language and culture to become uniform and specific, so that linguistic and cultural boundaries at least tend to coincide."[35] Another linguist, Bloomfield, notes that "the important lines of dialectical division run close to political lines.

Apparently, common government and religion, and especially the custom of intermarriage within the political unit, lead to relative uniformity of speech. It is estimated that, under older conditions, a new political boundary led in less than fifty years to some linguistic difference.[36]

As we noted in the *Summary*, conquerors have usually imposed their language as at least the medium of official discourse, as the Europeans did in the colonies. Sometimes they have adopted and supported a language of the conquered, as the Manchus did the Mandarin dialect of Chinese. As the kingly states of old Europe emerged out of feudalism, the

---

eds., *The Germans* by Erich Kahler, Princeton University Press, 1974). As someone has said, learning politics from Germans is like seeking advice from a thrice-divorced marriage counselor.

dialect of a particular area tended to prevail wherever the king's writ ran: in France, that of the Isle de France; in Italy, that of Tuscany; in England, an amalgam of Norman French and South Saxon. Often, other cultural traits follow language. In Europe the king's courts and their legal doctrines transcended local law and customs, so that even the law of family and inheritance became uniform in time throughout the land.

(d) *Difference in Religion or Ideology.* Religion and ideology rank with language as strong cultural traits. But history shows a greater correspondence of international conflict with differences in belief systems than with language or racial differences.

Animism, which seems to have been the primitive religion of most peoples, endowed natural features such as rocks and trees with supernatural significance. The spirits were thus localized, and the spirit to be propitiated in one portion of a tribal territory would not be the same as elsewhere. In that sense, animism where it remains today is sub-national.

In polytheism, although particular Middle Eastern and Mediterranean city-states had their particular patron gods or goddesses, as we noted in the preceding chapter the general way of looking at gods and heroes was common to all, and each interstate system had the same overall set of heroes and gods. Religion adhered in part to a state but in its whole to many states. All the Greek states seem to have sent to Delphi for guidance. We do not have a clear example of a religious war in the Middle East or the Mediterranean in ancient times, although the gods were usually consulted and always pressed into service, and religious similarity was one factor in arranging some Greek alliances.

Priests had much to say about policy in ancient Egypt and in the Middle East as far as India, as also in the pre-Conquest interstate systems of Mexico and Peru. Egypt had a religion sufficiently peculiar to itself to suggest that international aggression might have been undertaken to advance it, yet we have no evidence that this happened. The Israelites retained their own god while in captivity, and when Israel was great in the time of David its Jehovah was not imposed on the conquered. A god belonged to the tribe or people and apparently was not something to be propagated.

All the great ethical religions have transcended state boundaries. This is true of Hinduism and Buddhism, of later Judaism especially after the *diaspora*, of Christianity and of Islam. Also, within each state or empire, more than one religion usually has been practiced.

Nevertheless, religious difference has sometimes closely paralleled the lines of international conflict. Religion was the dominant factor in the Arab conquests. It was the secondary factor in the Spanish conquests in the New World. It ranked about equally with glory and gain in the Crusades. It was on a par with similar motives among the Catholic and Protestant princes who fought the religious wars, and was probably uppermost in the motivation then of the Holy Roman Emperor, Charles

V. Since the 17th century, religion has largely failed as a motive in international conflict in the Christian West, and ideology has taken its place, but it remains a factor in Indo-Pakistani and Arab-Israeli conflict and the signs are that, with the rise of fundamentalism, religion may be reviving as a causal factor even as ideology, perhaps, is declining.

We have mentioned the liberal, republican ideological component in the wars of the French Revolution and the Napoleonic wars. This cleavage between liberal and monarchical ideas had some significance in World War I, while ideology was a strong factor in World War II with the lines drawn between fascism and communism and between fascism and liberalism. Ideology has been equally strong in the Cold War, between liberalism and communism.

All three of these modern ideologies have been trans-national. There were republican movements in virtually all states and they triumphed in most. There are socialist or communist movements in nearly all nations today, and communist socialism has prevailed in several important nations. Fascism, though it took over in only a few nations, was an important movement elsewhere, and may yet revive.

A difficulty in assigning weight to belief systems in causing international conflict is that we cannot separate them cleanly from the bare ingroup-outgroup mass phenomenon of nationalism. Another is that the significance of religion-ideology cannot easily be distinguished from the other motives of the princes, decision-makers and elites that we discussed in Section A on "Bad Nations."

One can say, as a minimum, that belief systems have been significant cultural factors in distinguishing the "nature" of one nation from other nations, and that there is more than a little coincidence between differing beliefs and the lines of international conflict. This has been more marked since ideology displaced religion, for we have dozens of examples of war between states of similar religion whereas, among nations of the same modern ideology, we have no clear-cut examples except the violence already mentioned between communist nations.

(e)*Difference in Form of Government.* So far as mere form is concerned, governments today are remarkably alike. Nearly all are republics in which publics elect their decision-makers and there is some differentiation among the legislative, executive, and judicial functions. Representative government is the rule, even in most monarchies, where the prince is mainly a ceremonial figure. To an even greater degree, governments were similar in form prior to the 18th century. Nearly all were monarchies or oligarchic republics.

But the reality behind the republican form nowadays is that on the one hand there is the "open society" in which the electoral process is a competition among parties in an atmosphere for the most part of free inquiry and expression. Distinguished from it is the "closed society" in which a single disciplined party nominates a single slate of candidates and decides questions of public policy with little free inquiry or expression.

The distinction between the two is not so sharp as one might wish, because of the role of private wealth in financing political campaigns in such major open societies as US, West Germany, and Japan. Also, within some closed societies there may be a good deal more debate inside the dominant party than is apparent to outside observers.

Many civil political systems do not fall easily into either the open or the closed category. But those of all the principal nations do, so the categories are germane to international conflict. Yet it is difficult to give causal weight to this form-of-government factor, for it cannot be divorced from ideological distinctions. The liberal ideology goes along with free or open republican government while fascist or communist ideologies accompany dictated or closed republican government. Nor can these be divorced from economic system, to be discussed next.

Whereas Section A had much to say about ideology, form of government and economic system as features of "bad nations" that cause international conflict, we are concerned here with whether or not mere difference in these three respects coincides with the lines of international conflict, and whether similarity coincides with cooperation. We have seen that race, language, and other cultural traits do not so coincide, but it begins to appear that ideology, form of government, and economic system may do so.

(f)*Difference in Economic System.* The liberal ideology implies a more or less unrestricted capitalist economic system (a "market economy") as well as a representative form of government based on party competition. Fascism features a state-directed capitalism and a one-party dictatorial form of government. Communism of course requires state ownership as well as control of the economic system along with—for at least interim purposes—a one-party political dictatorship.

We have here a sort of three-ply rope of differentiation, in which one ply is ideological, another economic, and the third political or governmental.

Marx's economic determinism would say it merely appears this way, that the economic strand actually determines the ideological and political strands, and thus the "nature" of the state. Social philosophers Max Weber and Pitirim Sorokin, who saw religion or worldview as determining the other aspects, might say that the ideological is basic, the other two superficial. A political scientist such as Hans Morgenthau, who insists on the "autonomy" of the political factor, might argue that it is the struggle for political power that determines who shall manipulate the controls of the government and thus determines what shall be the nation's ideology and economy.

It might throw light on this problem if we focused on Lenin's career. First, did the "contradictions" which Marx saw in capitalism destroy

Tsarist Russia and usher in the socialist stage, carrying Lenin to power on the tide of history? Or, second, was it Marx's ideology rather than the "objective facts" of the mode of capitalist production that caused Lenin to act, and was it the soul-satisfying and arrogant inevitability of Marx's view of history that impressed other Russians enough to permit him to come to power? Or, third, was Lenin a power-lusting individual who attracted enough other such individuals to his disciplined Bolshevik camp so they could blandish and bluff their way to political power and then install a new ideology and economy?

Or, did Russia's defeat in the first World War, and the collapse of the Tsarist regime in terms of its politics, ideology and economy, have more to do with Lenin's success than the other three factors just described?

At any rate we are dealing here with three determinants of the "natures" of nations which are interrelated and have some causal relation to international conflict, or at least some coincidence with it. We can say this even though all three may be caused by international conflict, when war or the threat of war so weakens a nation that its "nature" is susceptible to change. As we saw in Chapter 1, there is an intricate interplay between the international and domestic situations.

The experience of the Russian system since 1917, the American since 1787, the French since 1789, the German and the Italian since 1870, the Mexican since 1910, the Chinese since 1949—these and many more suggest that heavy weight must be assigned to the political factor in terms of creating a new kind of state or a new "nature" for an old state.

The profounder impulses for change may be socio-cultural and economic, but these must manifest themselves politically and seize the government to put their changes into effect. They will often alter the form of government to do so. With government as the instrument, socio-cultural and economic change can be brought about rapidly, and an ideology with a tiny following can quickly be made the dominant belief system of the society. If society-culture were so organic and evolutionary as some suppose, revolutionary change simply could not happen. Yet it does; nations change their natures drastically and quickly, upon occasion.[37] Organicists love the dictum that *Natura non facit saltum* (Nature does not make leaps). Perhaps not. But men do.

In all international systems prior to the present global one, every significant nation had a variation of basically a market economy, whether the labor was done by all, by slaves or serfs, or by industrial proletarians. There was no more than moderate governmental control of the economy, as for example in mercantilism. All economies being essentially of the same type, differences were of no consequence for international conflict.

But in today's planetary system, some nations have communist-socialist economies with minor "market economy" elements while others have capitalist economies with some elements of socialism. This difference has been related closely since World War II to lines of international conflict and cooperation. Thus the Western bloc plus Japan is made up of capitalist nations while the Soviet bloc plus China is composed of socialist nations, and each has seen defeat as the end of its economic system, ideology, and form of government.

It is not possible to say which of these three strands in the "natures" of nations is most intimately related to the incidence of international conflict. What can be said is that these three together coincide so closely with the lines of conflict—and, for the most part, with the lines of cooperation too-that they must be taken into account as a causal factor.

C. Regional Cultures as Determinants of International Cooperation.

We have been dealing with socio-cultural particularisms mainly as determinants of international conflict. Here we consider whether cultural similarity at the trans-national, regional level produces cooperation among nations.

The organismic historical theories of Danilevsky, Spengler and Toynbee that history is the record of great civilizations that are born, live, and then die, have evoked interest in studying cultures believed to be trans-national or regional instead of national or sub-national. Increasing doubt that the national state is the ultimate in human social organization contributes to that interest.

An Austrian "cultural morphologist" named Othmar Anderle writes:

> The lethal threat to which the Western World has been exposed since the end of World War II, has awakened an awareness among the peoples of the Occident that they form a community with a destiny...Thinking in terms of civilizations has supplanted thinking in terms of nations.

Anderle says these civilizations or cultures reveal a systematic unity, internal articulation, and interdependence of parts, and are therefore holistic structures.[38]

Feliks Koneczny, Polish historian, says civilizations are the largest "fraction of humanity" that exist as "natural associations." He speaks of seven main civilizations today: the Jewish, Brahmin, Chinese, Turanian, Arabic, Byzantine, and Latin.[39] He thus indicates preference for religion and language as civilization boundaries.

Doubtless there is a degree of cultural similarity at a level above the nation, although Steward, Sorokin and Sapir warn us not to go so far as to describe this similarity as holistic or organic or closed. There are cultural traits which correspond in a rough way to geographical regions that are subjects nowadays for "area studies." Such regions are East Asia, Southeast Asia, South Asia, the Arab world or the Moslem Middle East, Sub-Saharan or Black Africa, Europe including Soviet Asia, North

America, and Latin America. Culturally, North and South America are sub-cultures of the European, as are the Republic of South Africa, Australia, New Zealand, and other places.

It is the notion of regional culture that suggest regions as alternatives to national states. The argument is essentially the old one that similarities of culture make for cooperation in place of conflict and, thus, that any political integration beyond the national state must be founded in a pre-existing cultural homogeneity.

If we grant the premise that cultural unity makes for international cooperation, we must go on to say that enough such unity evidently does not exist at the regional level to create even a pattern of international cooperation, much less a basis for supranational political integration.

The Arab world holds more cultural elements in common than any other region, yet as we have seen its states conflict and cooperate in changing alignments, managing only a more or less steady opposition to Israel. Despite the tradition of having belonged to the Arabic, Islamic, and Ottoman empires, the union of Egypt and Syria lasted only two years; the federation of Egypt with Yemen was no more than an incident of Nasser's attempt to win his war with Saudi Arabia over Yemen and has not been heard of for years. The proposed "federation" of Egypt, Libya, and Syria was to be a federation only in name. The union of Libya with Tunisia died the week after it was announced. Libya's recent union with Morocco is little more than an alliance against Tunisia and Algeria. Arab cultural unity has not even produced a customs union, much less political union.

Latin America has almost as great a degree of cultural unity, but Bolivar's federation of northwest South America, as well as the federation of Central America, was short-lived. There have been several serious international wars since independence. Honduras and El Salvador fought a brief war in 1969. Honduras is presently the base for US efforts against the Nicaraguan government. Plans for customs unions in South and Central America make little or no progress, and the one for the Andean nations not much more.[40]

US and Canada share substantial cultural similarity, but the former tried twice to annex the latter before establishing a peaceful relationship, and Canada not long ago was threatening to leave the NATO alliance.

Black Africa has a high degree of cultural similarity, buttressed by common opposition to the Republic of South Africa and to "economic imperialism" by the former colonial powers. Yet, despite much talk, no supranational integration has materialized except the union of Tanganyika and Zanzibar, called Tanzania, and it is uneasy.

Europe as a region continues to be marked by international conflict, mainly between Western and Eastern Europe, but also within each of those sub-regions. The hope that economic integration in the Common Market would lead to political integration of Western Europe is faint, while communist Yugoslavia is excluded from Comecon, the Soviet bloc's economic arm.

In East Asia, China and Japan were at war a generation ago, and the Koreans, though now divided, hate their erstwhile masters the Japanese.

In Southeast Asia there was violence during the 1960s between Indonesia and Malaysia, and conflict just short of violence between Indonesia and the Philippines and between the Philippines and Malaysia. Vietnam is in a condition of violence with China and Cambodia.

In South Asia, India and Pakistan, possessing substantial cultural similarity and historical background, have been in chronic conflict and three times at war, while Bangladesh split off from Pakistan in violence.

On the whole, then, international violence has been much more common within the cultural regions than between them, though conflict between states does sometimes coincide with lines dividing regions. In remoter history, this was the case between the Central Asian tribes and the high cultures they invaded; between great empires such as the Byzantine and the Islamic; and in the Crusades. Today, the Israeli-Arab conflict can be seen as between Koneczny's Jewish and Arabic civilizations, and the Sino-Indian conflict as paralleling his Chinese and Brahmin cultural boundaries. The Sino-Soviet dispute might conceivably be viewed as between his Chinese and Byzantine cultures. But the parties at dispute are national states, not regional cultural groupings. And the total of conflict between regions is a small part of the whole of international conflict.

In sum, regional cultural similarity does not produce cooperation among the national states that make up a region.

D. A Universal Culture?

As we are spending this chapter on the relation between society-culture on the one hand and war and peace on the other, we may as well inquire while we're at it into whether there is a universal culture, a planetary society, a world community. How much do all members of the human race hold in common, and what are the trends? This matter will come up in the next chapter, and again in the final chapter, so we'll deal at least briefly with it here.

Some anthropologists are aware that their comparative method, derived from matching primitive cultures with their own, has emphasized contrast more than a balanced view of the differences would allow, because comparison is inevitably expressed in terms of contrast. The following statement by Edward Tylor, one of the early great names of anthropology, might well have been given more attention by his successors:

> Surveyed in a broad view, the character and habit of mankind at once display that similarity and consistency of phenomena which

led the Italian proverb-maker to declare that "all the world is one country," "*tutto il mondo e paese.*" To a general likeness in human nature on the one hand, and to general likeness in the circumstances of life on the other, this similarity and consistency may no doubt be traced, and they may be studied with especial fitness in comparing races near the same grade of civilization.[41]

Another noted older anthropologist, Franz Boas, believes that "The organization of mind is practically identical among all races of men."[42] But if one is studying a small and remote tribe, its peculiarities are about the only things worth talking about; hence emphasis on uniqueness and neglect of similarities, a defect shared with many sociologists whose focus has been on small groups rather than nations and empires, but fortunately not with all.

A sociologist named Clark Wissler developed in the 1920s the concept of a universal cultural pattern into which all other cultural patterns fit. Specifically, all peoples have a family system; all have communications systems, or languages; all have systems relating to food, clothing, and shelter, and occupational systems. Every tribe and nation has some kind of government and social control patterns. People in most groups worship a higher power and have art patterns in one or more fields. Informal educational patterns function among all mankind. Wissler adds the universality of ways of making war.[43]

Another sociologist, Charles Morris, found in his research on universal human values that college students in US, India, Japan, China, and Norway could all at least respond intelligently to five values: social restraint and self-control, enjoyment and progress in action, withdrawal and self-sufficiency, receptivity and sympathetic concern, and self-indulgency or sensuous enjoyment. The approval given each value varied widely by nation but Morris also found a substantial variation within his US sampling.[44]

What seems reasonably certain is that (a) there is a greater variation in the gamut of cultural traits among individuals within any sizeable national society than there is between the *average* of individuals in one national society and the *average* in another national society; and (b) the traits which the individual shares with *all* others simply by virtue of being subject to the human condition are more numerous, and certainly—when we think of birth, childhood, marriage, parenthood, work, sickness, old age, and death—more weighty than those he shares only with individuals in his national society or in smaller groups.

The cultural homogenization process may be further advanced—and advancing faster—than is generally supposed. Cultural diffusion is the process by which a culture pattern in one area is spread to other areas. A culture pattern is in itself lifeless so must be carried either in person or by media such as literature, newspapers, film, radio or television. If the "imported" culture patterns appeal by their utility or for any other reason, culture diffusion occurs.[45]

History's greatest cultural diffusion has been that carried out of Europe by missionaries, soldiers and merchants into other regional cultures since the 15th century. Western culture was implanted as a whole in some places, with earlier peoples liquidated, as in most of North America. In other places, as in Mexico and parts of South America and Africa, it was imposed upon native peoples who became the slave and servant class of the new society. Elsewhere, mainly in Asia, native high cultures resisted this cultural diffusion with some success.

But Western culture was implanted everywhere, in a process of "lead" and "lag," meaning that some patterns of the native cultures changed quickly while others remained unchanged or changed slowly. Western ships and guns had an obviously superior utility, so the Japanese accepted enough of Western culture to make Japan militarily strong. (But China's Dowager Empress took money appropriated for a navy and spent it on a marble boat at her Summer Palace.)

In most culture diffusion it is technology which leads while other aspects lag. Marx's theory, shorn of its identification with the class struggle, is that technology is the determinant of culture. Others have developed other theories of change. They have in common the idea that a cultural system has two parts. One is identified with *homo faber*, technical and fabricating man, and has to do with material components, the practical and applied sciences, the mechanical arts, and the economic and political systems. These are elements that serve as means rather than ends. The other part consists of culture in its more rarefied sense: *homo socius* with his poetry and philosophy and fine arts, his theoretical and non-applied sciences, his speculative preoccupations with religion, magic, or ethics. These are elements valued as ends in themselves. The two categories correspond to Sorokin's "material" and "ideational" cultures mentioned earlier.[46]

Non-Western societies have almost always sought to preserve their non-materialistic culture while embracing Western material culture. But there is increasing evidence that if the new technology is received the rest of the old culture tends to break up as other components follow technology, usually in a jerky fashion and sometimes in a revolutionary collapse of the society.

How far Western culture has penetrated is difficult to say. It would be necessary to list the elements of culture and then determine which have changed and how much. The results could probably be quantified in some meaningful way. Meanwhile, the Singer sewing machine has invaded nearly every nook of the planet, followed by Coca-Cola and the transistor radio. The nuclear family is displacing the extended family almost everywhere. Nearly all nations have military and civil bureaucracies modeled on the Western pattern; most have modern weapons and many can manufacture some of them. Few nations lack a socialist, a communist, and a liberal political movement, as previously noted, and the republican form of government is the standard.

Virtually every city is growing as people flock in from villages. Except in certain European countries these cities have a rapidly expanding core or fringe of poverty as the population expands. Western literature, movies, music and art are available almost everywhere. Western dress is worn by at least certain classes in all nations.

Economies differ as to how much is included in the private sphere as opposed to the public, but housewives everywhere count their money and young couples shop for furniture. Education has a high value, universally, and the Western model is the rule. Science is the ideational base of a worldwide cultural supersystem.

Eastern religion and philosophy maintain their cultural ground and are influential in the West. They have much to cope with: movement, change, disequilibrium—these are everywhere, prompted by grave problems some of which are planetary and whose solutions are but dimly seen if at all.

Meanwhile, Interlingua, Esperanto, and other proposed universal languages have not caught on, but there is a barely discernible tendency toward a universal *patois* which evidently will have a good deal of English in it because English is becoming the second language taught in most nations.

Conclusions

Between the primitive community and the planetary whole there is no society that is a cultural unity. Hence it is absurd to speak of nations as organisms that struggle for survival. nor is it productive to think of nations or of the world in terms of "systems theory." Any analogy is in some degree false; biological analogies are especially so.

The kernel of truth in the organismic explanation of international conflict is that people tend to believe that their national societies possess far more cultural homogeneity than in fact they do; that theirs is a good deal more different from others than in fact it is.

Actually, cultural homogenization is proceeding at all levels of human society, including the regional and world levels. But it proceeds faster within a national society because the people live under a common government that promotes homogeneity, and it is this which gives each such society much of the homogeneity that it manifests.[47]

Differences of race, language, and customs do not explain international conflict, nor does similarity in these respects produce cooperation. Historically, nations have gone to violence much oftener with culturally similar nations than with dissimilar ones.

But in modern times differences in ideology, economic system, and government have tended to coincide with the lines of international conflict and cooperation. Hence this three-ply rope of differentiation may have explanatory value. And, incidentally, it is differences in these same three elements that define each of the "bad nations" discussed in Section A of this chapter.

Chapter 3 Notes

1. Joseph Schumpeter, noted early 20th century sociologist and economist, believed war was caused by warrior classes in feudal societies, so it should disappear in industrial capitalist economies (Introduction to R.A. Falk and S.S. Kim, eds., *The War System: An Interdisciplinary Approach*, Boulder Colo., Westview Press, 1980).

2. Lenin's theory of imperialism was borrowed from the Englishman, J.A. Hobson, but Lenin used it also to explain war and for other purposes whereas Hobson said international financiers would not wish big wars (his *Imperialism*, London, Allen & Unwin, 1902, 1938, p. 58).

3. Wm L. Langer, "Farewell to Empire," *Foreign Affairs* 41:1 (1952) 115-130.

4. Inis L. Claude Jr. advanced this thesis in his 1966 "Clay Malick Lecture" at University of Colorado. The Congo crisis of 1960-61 is a leading example.

5. See David Horowitz, ed., *Corporations and the Cold War* (Monthly Review Press, 1969) for an extreme view. This book of essays was sponsored by the Bertrand Russell Peace Foundation.

6. Lionel C. Robbins, *The Economic Causes of War* (New York, Howard Fertig Inc., 1958), 60.

7. Pierre Renouvin and Jean-Baptiste Duroselle, *Introduction To The History of International Relations*, Pall Mall Press, 1969.

8. John R. Raser, "Personal Characteristics of Political Decision-Makers," *Peace Research Society (International) Papers*, vol. 5 (1966), 161-181. Hugh L'Etang, physician and editor of the British medical journal, *The Practitioner*, has done much research in the pathology of leadership.

9. See Wm. Ebenstein, *Great Political Thinkers* (New York, Holt Rinehart & Winston, 4th ed., 1969), 668-670.

10. Pitirim Sorokin, *Sociological Theories of Today* (New York, Harper & Row, 1966), 18.

11. These included Burke, Fichte, Herder, Muller, Lessing, Schlegel, Shelling, de Bonald and de Maistre. However, the comparison of a society or a state with an organism, especially with man or with his body or soul, may be found in ancient Hindu, Chinese, Greek and Roman thought. (See P. Sorokin, *Contemporary Sociological Theories*, New York, Harper, 1928, p. 197.)

12. Sorokin, *Contemporary Sociological Theories*, pp. 195-197. Sociologists who have developed organic interpretations include K.C. Krause, H. Ahrens, F.J. Schmitthenner, G. Waitz, F.A. Trendelebourg, J. von Gorres, C.T. Welcker, F. and T. Nohmer, K. Volgraff, F.J. Stahl, F. Lilienfeld, A. Schaffle, R. Worms, and J. Novicow (*Ibid.*, pp. 200-201). The preponderance of German scholars is noteworthy.

13. *Ibid.*, p. 224. The quotations are from Arthur de Gobineau's *Essay Upon The Inequality Of The Human Races* (English translation, New York, 1914), vol. 1, Chapter 3.

14. *Saturday Review*, February 22, 1975, p. 36.

15. Harold R. Isaacs, "Nationality: End of the Road?" *Foreign Affairs* 53:3 (1975), 432-449, 444, 445.

16. Karl Marx, *The Economic & Philosophic Manuscripts of 1844*, D.J. Struik, ed., New York, International Publishers, 1964.

17. English translation by C.P. Loomis, ed., New York, Harper & Row, 1963. In the German title, *Gemeinschaft und Gesellschaft*, the first word connotes togetherness while the other has the connotation of a commercial enterprise.

18. Quoted in Morton H. Fried, ed., *Readings in Anthropology* (New York, Crowell, 1959), vol. 2, p. 548.

19. *Ibid.*

20. Loren Eiseley, an anthropologist, describes Victorian biologists' acceptance of nature as "red in tooth and claw," then gives reasons for doubting that man evolved through "intergroup struggle." (His *The Immense Journey*, New York, Vintage Books, 1957, pp. 118 ff.)

21. Peter Kropotkin, the anarchist, and others urged, in opposition to the struggle-for-existence view, evidence that humans and other animals have a natural propensity toward "mutual aid."

22. Leslie A. White, "Man's Control Over Civilization: An Anthropocentric Illusion," *The Scientific Monthly*, vol. 66 (1948), pp. 235-247, reprinted in Fried, *op.cit.*, pp. 556-557.

23. P. Sorokin, *Sociological Theories of Today*, p. 138, quoting V.G. Afanassiyeff's "Principles of Classification of the Unified Systems," in *Voprosy Filosofii*, No. 5 (1963).

24. *Ibid.*, p. 141, quoting from L. von Bertalanffy, *Problems of Life* (New York, 1960), pp. 9-20. Bertalanffy, a biologist, may be considered the originator of modern systems theory.

25. See Paul Bohannon and Fred Plog, eds., *Beyond The Frontier* (Garden City, The Natural History Press, 1967), 259-60, for an anthropological description of boundary-maintaining mechanisms which tend to "close" a cultural system.

26. Oran R. Young, "Anarchy and Social Choice," *World Politics* 30:2 (1978), 241-263.

27. Tord Hoivik, "Peace Research and Science: A Discussion Paper," *Journal of Peace Research* 20:3 (1983), 267-270. Hoivik also suggests a name for a future "global nation": Terra.

28. Ronald Rogowski, "International Politics: The Past as Science," *International Studies Quarterly*, vol. 12 (1968), 394-418.

29. Fred W. Neal and Bruce D. Hamlett, "The Never-Never Land of International Relations," *International Studies Quarterly*, vol. 13 (1969), 281-305.

30. See for example Ernst B. Haas, *Beyond The Nation-State*, Stanford University Press, 1964. Georges Sorel defined myth as "a complex of remote goals, tense moral moods and expectations of apocalyptic success." Robert K. Merton called myth a self-fulfilling prophecy. "Myth" is too variously defined to be a very useful concept.

31. Edward Sapir, *Language* (New York, Harcourt, 1921 and 1949), 124. Sapir is talking about racist-romanticism among scholars, one of whom "delivered himself of the dictum that, estimable as the speakers of agglutinative languages might be, it was nevertheless a crime for an inflecting woman to marry an agglutinative man. Tremendous spiritual values were evidently at stake."

32. *Ibid.*, p. 208.

33. P. Sorokin, *Sociological Theories of Today*, pp. 216, 32.

34. Steward's contribution to Fried, *op.cit.*, p. 335.

35. Sapir, *op.cit.*, pp. 208, 213.

36. Leonard Bloomfield, *Language History* (New York, Holt, 1965), 343.

37. Modern sociology tends more than the old to recognize the efficacy of directed and administered social change. See a discussion in Clarence C. Schrage, *et al.*, *Sociology* (New York, Harper & Row, 4th ed., 1968), Chapter 20. In the earlier 19th century Saint Simon and Comte emphasized administered change, and it has remained an element in sociological thought, but American scholarship has been heavily influenced by the German school of organismic, evolutionary sociology, especially since the advent of the German refugees in the 1930s.

38. Quoted in Sorokin, *Sociological Theories of Today*, p. 205.

39. *Ibid.*, pp. 209, 212.

40. James Busey of the University of Colorado, a Latin-America specialist, says wars have been comparatively few because those countries are more nearly feudal states than national states.

41. Quoted in Fried, *op.cit.*, p. 7.

42. Franz Boas, *The Mind of Primitive Man* (New York, Macmillan, 1911), 105, quoted in Emory S. Bogardus, *Sociology* (New York, Macmillan, 4th ed., 1954), 38.

43. Clark Wissler, *Man And Culture* (New York, Crowell, 1923), Chapter 5, summarized in Bogardus, *op.cit.*, p. 38.

44. Reported in A.W. and H.P. Gouldner, *Modern Sociology* (New York, Harcourt Brace, 1963), 144-167.

45. Based on Bogardus, *op.cit.*, p. 46.

46. See Sorokin, *Sociological Theories of Today*, pp. 289-296.

47. Matthew Melko, in *Fifty-Two Peaceful Societies* (Oakville, Ontario, CPRI Press, 1973), 181-182, concludes that "Homogeneity within a society may help preserve peace, although many societies that have not been peaceful have been homogeneous" and that "The factor of nation seems to have been a stronger unifier than that of religion or of civilization. Unified nations often fight violently against other unified nations professing the same religion and civilization. On the other hand, differences in civilization do not lead to conflict." When Melko says "the factor of nation" he means a governed national state.

Chapter 4

BECAUSE ANARCHY IS INHERENT IN ANY SYSTEM OF INDEPENDENT NATIONS?

Monarchy means rule by one. Oligarchy is rule by the few. Anarchy means without rule, no ruler, no government. The Greeks, who coined the word, knew how bad it was when one of their city-states lacked government. But very few of them worried about how bad it was that their whole system of city-states was an anarchy, lacking any overall higher level of government. When they did begin to worry it was too late, for they were taken over by Alexander's father, Philip of Macedon, and then later, after Alexander's time, they became part of the Roman Empire.

But a good many of the great minds in the Western world have worried about anarchy among nations as well as anarchy within a nation. This traces back to Augustine who watched the disorder that went along with the break-up of the Roman Empire. Dante worried about it, and wanted a world monarchy. Machiavelli wanted a prince who could unite the warring Italian states. He didn't get him and the Italian system was subordinated to the European system of great kingdoms, a system that was completed at the end of the religious wars in the mid-1600s.

We'll take up our discussion about there, with Hobbes and the writers of the 18th century Enlightenment. The 19th century won't offer us much, for that was the time when, as we have noted at length, nations were organisms that grew their own governments and weren't to be messed with—nations that struggled with each other for existence. But in the late 1800s there arose what are now called the Formal-legalists who believed that the struggle needed to be moderated by treaties that would lay down the rules of war and maybe even the rules of disarmament and peace. They too didn't have much to say about anarchy. But, beginning in the 1930s, the Realists did. They were followed in the 1950s and 1960s by the Behavioralists, who are our old friends the anthro-sociologists plus a good many others including political sociologists.

113

This school, true to its origins in biological systems theory, saw instead of anarchy a natural harmony in the world system which at most would only need to be tinkered with to make work. Close upon the heels of the Behavioralists, and including many of them, came the Positivists, named for the Vienna school of Logical Positivists who said nothing is true unless it can be proven, meaning that dependable knowledge comes only through the scientific method. Positivists, including peace researchers and peace scientists, dominated the 1970s and the early 1980s, though they took their cue from statistical studies of war dating back to the 1920s. But meanwhile, out of this scientific research but also out of disillusionment with it and with Behavioral studies as well, anarchy has received increasing attention in the 1970s and 1980s.

Before we get into the discussion, what do we mean, as in the heading to this chapter, by a "system of independent nations"? We mean that each nation is not answerable to any higher authority. A centralized decision-making process in each nation is recognized as final on matters of both internal and external policy by most of the public of the nation most of the time and by other nations. This centralized decision-making is usually called government. Decisions of a subordinate nature are typically made at the provincial and local levels, which are controlled by the central government in internal policy and have no role in external policy. The central government, being supreme in the policy process, is called sovereign.

A partial exception is the federal state in which governments of the substates have final authority in some things while the federal government has final authority in others. A federal government always controls a federal state's external policy, so it can be termed independent for our purposes.

The national government in a unitary state and the federal government in a federal state represent the culmination of government in the present planetary international system. Above the national level there is no centralized decision-making process whose decisions are recognized as final and which are enforceable. Above the nation there is no government, so nations act and react in a condition of anarchy.

Thus, in what follows, anarchy will often be discussed in terms of its opposite: government.

A. Anarchy and The Enlightenment

The classic statement on anarchy is that of Thomas Hobbes, the 17th century English philosopher mentioned in Chapter 2 as seeing glory, greed and fear as the causes of human conflict. Here he describes that "condition of nature," meaning the lack of a common power or government, which evokes those ugly passions. Despite his archaic language he is worth studying closely.

...if there be no power erected, or not great enough for our security, every man will and may lawfully rely on his own strength and art for caution against all other men. And in all places, where men have lived by small families, to rob and spoil one another has been a trade, and so far from being reputed against the law of nature that the greater spoils they gained, the greater was their honour...And as small families did then; so now do cities and kingdoms...enlarge their dominions upon all pretences of danger, and ...endeavour as much as they can to subdue or weaken their neighbours by open force, and secret arts, for want of other caution, justly.[1]

Hobbes is saying bluntly that in a condition of anarchy it is not against the law of nature for individuals to despoil one another or for kingdoms to conquer other kingdoms. On the contrary, as we noted in Chapter 2, he says this is no more than their own defense requires. Moreover, under anarchy there is no immorality; acts evoked by fear or greed are no sin "till they know a law that forbids them" and can protect them from each other.[2]

Hobbes recognized the inability of alliances and leagues to provide security, saying that "though they obtain a victory by their unanimous endeavor against a foreign enemy," yet afterwards "they must needs by the difference of their interests dissolve, and fall again into a war amongst themselves."[3] And he saw clearly that so long as there is no "common power to keep them all in awe," that is, so long as there is no common government, "they are in that condition which is called war," because "war consisteth not in actual fighting, but in the known disposition thereto during all the time there is no assurance to the contrary. All other time is peace."[4]

Hobbes, writing against the background of England's civil war which brought the nation to something resembling anarchy, is justifying government at the national level. But, to make sure his readers understand precisely what he is talking about, he uses the analogy of international politics, saying that "kings and persons of sovereign authority, because of their independency, are in continual jealousies, and in the state and posture of gladiators," with "their forts, garrisons, and guns upon the frontiers of their kingdoms, and continual spies upon their neighbours."[5]

Hobbes asserts that self-preservation lays down "the first and fundamental law of nature, which is: to seek peace and follow it."[6] Hobbes meant by this, of course, seek government.

Spinoza, the Dutch philosopher, writing a little later, similarly held that independent states are naturally enemies in the same way men are who live together in a condition of anarchy.[7] Montesquieu, the Frenchman whose writings influenced the American founding fathers, recognized that international anarchy results in "the license of all" and to remedy this he proposed a confederation of nations.[8]

John Locke's notion of the condition of nature, or anarchy, is often contrasted with that of Hobbes. By the time Locke wrote, the civil wars were over, the last Stuart king had sailed off to France, and William and Mary reigned as limited monarchs. Whereas Hobbes would settle for most any government including absolute monarchy, rather than none, Locke wanted "good," meaning limited government. His view of the law of nature is that man is born with the rights of life, liberty, and property. He emphasized the sympathetic element in human nature which would enable men to form a society in which these rights would be tolerably secure for a time, without government, hence these rights need not be sacrificed to get government.

Locke was thus a precursor of sociology in that he held society to be prior to the state, though he admitted, as Hobbes did, that "Government is everywhere antecedent to records." Like Hobbes, he was discussing the justification for government, and most especially what kind of government is justified. But he did not think society could endure very long without government. The enjoyment of man's natural rights

> is very uncertain and constantly exposed to the invasion of others; for all being kings as much as he, every man his equal, and the greater part no strict observers of equity and justice...This makes him willing to quit this condition which, however free, is full of fears and continual dangers.[9]

Thus, at some point, possibly about the time that property begins to be held in the form of money, he suggests, men unite themselves under government because in anarchy several things are lacking:

> Firstly, there wants an established, settled, known law, received and allowed by common consent to be the standard of right and wrong, and the common measure to decide all controversies between them....
> Secondly, in the state of Nature there wants a known and indifferent judge, with authority to determine all differences according to the established law....
> Thirdly, in the state of Nature there often wants power to back and support the sentence.[10]

Locke thus tends to agree with Hobbes that a law is no law unless it is enforceable.

Locke gives another reason for government, saying "their first care and thought cannot but be supposed to be, how to secure themselves against foreign force," so they put themselves "under a frame of government which might best serve to that end."[11]

So soon, then, as internal anarchy is eliminated by government and the creation of the state, anarchy at the interstate level begins. Locke went on to prescribe a government giving the Executive a very ample "prerogative" to manage foreign affairs as he sees fit. And this perhaps still haunts the Americans who fashioned their government more on his model than any other.

On balance, Locke's picture of life under anarchy is not very different from Hobbes'. Locke saw some sort of pre-existing society rather than Hobbes' "band of masterless men" whose lives were "nasty, brutish, and short." But Locke knew that, owing to "fears and continual dangers," no society could last without an overarching framework of government. And although he thought of society as natural he saw government as something that men consciously contrive to suit their purposes, and which they may change from time to time, rather than as something that grows up out of society while nobody is looking.

Yet Locke did view the condition of anarchy as more benign than did Hobbes. Lockean man is more sympathetic, less fearful, than Hobbesian man. Thus modern scholars have asked whether the world international system is in a Hobbesian or a Lockean condition of anarchy.

Our *Summary of International History* suggests the answer. There was a long period, from the Peace of Westphalia in 1648 which initiated the modern state system until perhaps around the turn of the 20th century, when the Lockean condition might be held mainly to have prevailed. Nations often did accept restraints and the balance of power did permit only intermittent violence which fell short of total war. The breakthrough of belief systems which had precipitated the religious wars did not recur until the French Revolution. Napoleon was defeated and the peace was kept, more or less, by the Holy Alliance or the Concert of Europe.

But ideas of popular sovereignty, nationalism, and socialism germinated during the 19th century and came to flower in the 20th with whole peoples committed to the national state and embracing the ideology assimilated to that nation. Enormous societal pressures took the place of the milder predispositions of 18th century princes. Thus international anarchy became Hobbesian. In two world wars and the Cold War, and especially with the advent of nuclear and other weapons of mass destruction, whole national populations have come to have a perception of insecurity which encompasses ideology, way of life, and all they hold dear. This is Hobbesian, not Lockean.[12]

This distinction might be kept in mind as we move along.

J.J. Rousseau, a Genevan residing in France, wrote against a background of European war which he considered ruinous by the standards of his day, and of execrable government in France under Louis XV. He believed individuals were more vicious under the wretched civil government he saw than they would be under anarchy, with fear as their dominant trait. Yet he took no brighter view of civil anarchy than Locke did, so he drew up his own version of a city-state republic that would be well governed. But, more than Hobbes or Locke, he stressed anarchy at the international level, saying that princes justify their rule by offering domestic peace but then sacrifice that peace in foreign wars.

Rousseau viewed the nations of Europe as being in a condition of perpetual war, in the same sense Hobbes suggested. Rousseau was contemptuous of international law, which had been derived through the Church from Stoic notions of "natural" law. He said, "With respect to what one commonly calls the law of peoples, it is certain that, lacking enforcement, its laws are only chimeras even weaker than natural law." Each state "feels weak to the extent that there are stronger states than it," so that "its security, its conservation, demand that it make itself more powerful than all its neighbors."[13]

To Rousseau, anarchy was the cause of international conflict, so he interested himself in a "Project for Perpetual Peace" written earlier by the Abbe St. Pierre who had taken his cue from the still earlier "Grand Design" of Henry IV. Rousseau suggested what we would now call a confederal government, with enforcement powers, but only upon nations, with no right of secession.

Immanuel Kant, the Prussian philosopher, said that man's depravity is checked within nations by government, but that this displaces the problem onto the international level, and he proposed his "Plan for Perpetual Peace." However, his was a mere league without centralized decision-making and enforcement, and Kant himself feared it would not work if tried.[14]

But, as we shall see, it is not unusual for experts to diagnose the ailment as anarchy, then fail to prescribe government as the cure.

Alexander Hamilton was not one of them. He wrote against the background of the experience of the thirteen American states under the Articles of Confederation, an arrangement similar to that proposed by Rousseau for Europe, and stronger than a league or an alliance. In Hamilton's argument for the proposed new federal Constitution he implied that common language and culture were not enough to enable the states to live peacefully—after all, they had broken away in 1776 from England's like language and culture—nor was a confederation adequate, much less a league. He said that "to look for a continuation of harmony between a number of independent, unconnected sovereigns in the same neighborhood, would be to disregard the uniform course of human events, and to set at defiance the accumulated experience of the ages."[15]. This is a clear diagnosis of anarchy with a logical prescription for it—federal government.

B. Anarchy in 19th Century Thought

Rousseau himself had no illusion that Europe's common culture would produce perpetual peace. But his philosophy that emotion is a better guide to conduct than is reason touched off the Romanticism that dominated European thought from the Congress of Vienna, which ended the Napoleonic wars, onward. The belief that men could make governments and administer social change, as evoked by the French Revolution and elaborated later by the early French sociologists, St.

Simon and Comte, lost out to mystical German philosophy-sociology.

As we noted in Chapter 3, the nation was seen as an organic being with a unique history and mission. The nation was deemed the be-all and end-all of social organization. As for international anarchy, Jeremy Bentham, the Englishman who with James Mill founded the philosophy called Utilitarianism, produced his version of a league of nations, as did St. Simon. But they lacked Hamilton's clear view of anarchy's cure.

However, Mill's son, John Stuart Mill, had his innings with the organicists of the day. Writing in mid-century about the problems that might be encountered in installing a new framework of government, he asserted that the new government will work if the people accept it or at least do not "oppose an insurmountable obstacle" to it and "are willing and able to do what it requires of them to enable it to fulfill its purposes." Then, responding to the organicists, he said:

> Whatever they mean more than this appears to me untenable. All that we are told about the necessity of an historical basis for institutions, of their being in harmony with the national usages and character, and the like, means either this, or nothing to the purpose. There is a great quantity of mere sentimentality connected with these and similar phrases, over and above the amount of rational meaning contained in them.[16]

And Mill ridiculed the fancy that a government is something that is "aye, ever growing" like a tree. But even in Britain international conflict came to be understood largely as a Darwinian struggle to determine which nation was fittest to survive, hence anarchy was seen as even serving a good purpose.

C. The Formal-Legalists

But there was an increasing minority viewpoint that the struggle was not such a good idea.[17] Preparation for war, especially in the naval arms race, was too expensive. War itself was too destructive of property and killed off too many of the best young men. So why not sign treaties that would limit the severity of war and provide for peaceful ways of settling disputes? The Tsar was especially of this mind, so tried twice at the close of the century and came away with the Hague Conventions which laid down some rules of warfare and set up the machinery to submit disputes to arbitration but didn't provide for the disarmament that the Tsar also wanted.

Early in the 20th century there was agitation in Europe and America for a league of nations. It would look like a government but it wouldn't be one because these people, whom we now call the Formal-Legalists, had little awareness of anarchy and a very big awareness that nations were just too different for any overall government to work.

The Hague arbitration treaties did nothing to prevent World War I, which sure enough did kill off nearly all the best young men, and at the end of it the old men set up a new exchange of promises called The

League of Nations. When it looked like the League wouldn't work, much the same group of old men signed a new set of formal-legal documents called the Locarno Agreements. Then in 1928 came the supreme achievement: in the Kellogg-Briand Pacts they outlawed war, or at least defensive war, maybe. What with the earlier Washington naval Disarmament Treaty and the disarmament conference shortly to convene at Geneva, not to mention the League which was still in business, things must have looked good to the formal-legalist True Believers.

Had they been familiar with the literature on anarchy, they would have known better. Under anarchy, all wars are defensive; you must hit the other nation before it hits you, for this is what your own "conservation requireth." And the law must not only be known, it must also be enforceable; but their treaties lacked "power to back and support the sentence."

Somerset Maugham somewhere has one of his characters, a woman, say, "You know, I am one of the few people I know who can actually learn from experience." So, after World War II, a slightly different group of old men set up another League called the United Nations.

D. Anarchy and the Realists

These are theorists most of whom had intellectual links with the power realism and the sociological thought of the middle and later 19th century in Europe. But, beginning in the 1920s and continuing on into the 1960s, they have rejected the earlier idea that unlimited national power is a good thing and have also rejected the formal-legalist notion that national power can be controlled by mere treaties. At the same time they have tried, with differing results, to rid themselves of older sociological dogma about the relation between society-culture-community on the one hand and government on the other. All this has involved a return to an appreciation of anarchy and its consequences.

R.M. MacIver, the Canadian-American sociologist, wrote in 1928 that community is any common interest and that this interest needs to be coordinated by associations including the several levels of government, and that nations themselves stand in need of co-ordination no less than do their subdivisions.[18] The reason for this, he wrote in 1931, is that beyond its borders the national government becomes an engine of destruction. "Consequently, we face the paradox that the state is, nationally, the great instrument of social security, but internationally, the greatest menace to that security."[19]

In 1964 MacIver wrote that a common interest is best safeguarded by a common organization limited to the range of that common interest and to the means necessary to protect that interest. Then,

> In our day as never before, the most universal of all human interests is protection against the annihilating effects of modern warfare.

The same forces that refused to expand the protection of common interests beyond the limits of the tribe, the limits of the city state, the limits of the petty principalities of the Middle Ages, now resist the organization of security beyond the limits of the nation....

By failing thus to provide security, the state is subordinating its major and age-old function of establishing law and order in favor of secondary or entirely extraneous considerations. An organization is set up to serve the more effective certain interests of its members.[20]

Thus justification of the national state is questioned, for it can no longer provide security.

MacIver believes further that just as the varying levels of community in the form of common interests create the need for varying levels of government, so does government in return create deeper community at each level, even including the creation of customs.

Reinhold Niebuhr, the influential theologian and teacher of social ethics, wrote in 1932 that "one method of making force morally redemptive is to place it in the hands of a community which transcends the conflict of interest between individual nations and has an impartial perspective upon them." But "present international anarchy may continue until the fear of catastrophe amends, or catastrophe itself destroys, the present social system and builds more co-operative national societies."[21]

Speaking in 1941 of the possibilities of justice being done as the result of a balance of powers within a society or as the consequence of government, Niebuhr said that a balance "is a principle of justice in so far as it prevents domination and enslavement; but it is a principle of anarchy and conflict in so far as its tensions, if unresolved, result in overt conflict." Government "stands upon a higher plane of moral sanction and social necessity" because the balance of power, without government, "degenerates into anarchy."[22]

Niebuhr, though an American, was largely German in his education, and to the end of his life he maintained there was not enough sense of community to give much hope of abridging world anarchy. But he came close at times. In 1953 he wrote:

Most important as a force of social cohesion in the world community is the increasing economic interdependence of peoples of the world....

A second factor in the social tissue of the world community is the fear of mutual annihilation, heightened in recent years by the new dimension which atomic discoveries have given to mankind's instruments of death. We must not underestimate this fear as a social force....some culturally pluralistic communities of past history have achieved some cohesion through the minimal conviction that order is to be preferred to anarchy...

The final and most important factor in the social tissue of the world community is a moral one. Enlightened men in all nations have some sense of obligation to their fellow-men, beyond the limits of

their nation-state...The desperate necessity for a more integrated
world community has undoubtedly increased this sense of
obligation...[23]

And in 1955 he seemed to endorse MacIver's definition of community,
saying "We have spoken of 'the community' as if it were an exact entity.
Actually there are communities based upon every common interest, desire
or destiny.[24]

Niebuhr, like other democratic socialists, saw the totalitarian USSR as
a "bad nation" and could not quite conceive of such nations co-existing
with liberal ones. He was organicist enough to require more world
community before anything can be done about world anarchy but at the
same time he could see that anarchy "tends to destroy organic growths of
community."[25]

Frederick L. Schuman, an American, published his *International
Politics* in 1933. He saw anarchy as the principal cause of international
conflict and his book was probably the most influential college text until
Morgenthau came along.[26] Schuman introduced many students to the
new power realism. In another work, in 1951, he said that relations
among nations can be described fairly simply "despite the fervid attempts
of politicians and political scientists to render them fearfully
complicated.

> Whenever two or more States, each "sovereign" and "independent"
> of others, confront one another across landways or seaways familiar
> to all, their relations will tend to be dominated by a competitive
> quest for power and by calculations of relative power. This familiar
> design, observable in all systems of States, from the earliest we know
> about to the system in which we find ourselves today, can scarcely be
> attributed to the circumstance that all statesmen by nature crave
> power (they do of course—otherwise they would not be statesmen)
> or to the supposition that some States thirst after power and others
> do not. The clue to the pattern lies rather in the fact that in such
> systems of independent sovereignties, power is the price of
> continued independence. Unless it be a buffer between rivals who
> checkmate one another, any State lacking power to prevent others
> from imposing their power upon it will almost inevitably lose
> whatever power it has, and ultimately its freedom to act as a
> sovereign. The most effective assurance against any such
> calamity...is to contain, restrain, reduce and, if possible, extinguish
> the power of other States to inflict such a fate.[27]

Schuman becomes more explicit as to the situation in the 1950s, then says:

> In our day the global anarchy of contending States menaces the
> welfare, and the very survival, of the civilization of the West whose
> emissaries, on the wings of science, have flown to the ends of the
> earth and all unwittingly made all men neighbors. That this is a
> truism makes it no less true. Those who would deny it must ignore
> the recurrent miseries of most of mankind since 1914, and question
> the probability that like causes will produce like results tomorrow
> as yesterday.[28]

Schuman says Niebuhr is wrong in believing that "a long history of organic cohesion" must precede government; that the reverse is more nearly the truth, for all the great empires of the past "ruled over vast and diverse societies among which organic cohesion and unity were the slow consequence and gradual result of common government."[29] But those empires were established by conquest, he says, whereas any effort to integrate the global system by conquest in the nuclear era would probably devastate the earth. This leaves the alternative of integration by agreement, and Schuman himself speculates gloomily that this may not be possible without some shared ideology or transcendant faith.

On this point, a 1973 historical study of fifty-two peaceful societies concluded that there are many "instances where governments have maintained control through policies of tolerance, or where the initial power of religion faded without damaging the peace."[30] Sorokin might say that faith in science is the widely shared belief system of 20th century man. But this may not be quite what Schuman had in mind.

Quincy Wright's encyclopedic *A Study of War*, first published in 1942, shows a sharp awareness of anarchy in a shrinking world in these closing passages:

> War tends to increase in severity and to decrease in frequency as the area of political and legal adjustment (the state) expands geographically unless that area becomes as broad as the area of continuous economic, social, and cultural contact (the civilization)...The very efficiency of sovereignty within the state, however, decreases the efficiency of regulation in international relations. By eliminating tensions within the state, external tensions are augmented. International relations become a "state of nature."[31]

Wright's indication that, to get rid of war, government must be as broad as the area of continuous contact, is worth noting.

Herbert Butterfield, the English historian, commented in 1950 on what he calls the "predicament of Hobbesian fear" in international conflict:

> If you imagine yourself locked in a room with another person with whom you have often been on the most bitterly hostile terms in the past, and suppose that each of you has a pistol, you may find yourself in a predicament in which both of you would like to throw the pistols out of the window, yet it defeats the intelligence to find a way of doing it.[32]

This is the predicament of all disarmament conferences. How do you get rid of weapons without getting rid of anarchy first?

Hans Morgenthau's *Politics Among Nations* was first published in 1947. His version of power realism, coming on the market just as the Cold War was well under way, proved even more influential than Schuman's. It yielded finally only in the 1960s to Behavioralism's broad theorizing and to Positivism's "scientific" approach to understanding conflict.

Morgenthau accepts the anarchy hypothesis in the same degree as does

Niebuhr. It is not explicit so much as implicit throughout his work, especially in his discussion of the balance of power, his notion of the obsolescence of the national state, and his ultimate solution for conflict.

He says that the nation, "far from assuring the security and power of its members, condemns them to impotence and ultimate extinction."[33] Having dismissed, as ineffective restraints on national power, international law, world public opinion, cultural exchange, and collective security whether in the League or the UN, he says:

> Diplomacy is the best means of preserving peace which a society of sovereign nations has to offer, but, especially under the conditions of modern world politics and of modern war, it is not good enough. It is only when nations have surrendered to a higher authority the means of destruction which modern technology has put in their hands—when they have given up their sovereignty—that international peace can be made as secure as domestic peace.

But the present hope must be placed in diplomacy, because

> as there can be no permanent peace without a world state, there can be no world state without the peace-preserving and community-building processes of diplomacy. For the world state to be more than a dim vision, the accommodating processes of diplomacy, mitigating and minimizing conflicts, must be revived.[34]

In the 1968 edition of his masterwork, Morgenthau still felt obliged to leave the problem of conflict to a revived, clear-sighted diplomacy, unencumbered by ideologies and public opinion—in much the same style as the 18th century diplomacy which he himself had criticized roundly.[35] Diplomacy must build the world community, then there can be a world state. How much world community is required? At least enough "so that the interests uniting members of different nations may outweigh the interests separating them."[36]

Their thought is so similar that some consider Morgenthau a disciple of Niebuhr. It is more likely that Morgenthau, who was born and educated in Germany, simply read the same philosophers and historians and sociologists that Niebuhr had studied. Niebuhr finds the lust for power in man's prideful, sinful nature; Morgenthau, in man's need for love which, failing of its object, is transformed into a sort of Nietzschean will-to-power.[37] Both apply the lust for power, without much discrimination, to interpersonal relationships, to the group or class struggle within a nation, and to the struggle among nations.

Niebuhr has been enormously influential, especially upon two or three generations of Protestant clergymen and laymen, while Morgenthau had the largest audience among nearly three decades of international relations scholars and students.

Their basic error is that their theory of politics is not consonant with their theory of society. They see politics as a struggle for power by sinful or egoistic man and by self-centered interest groups. This struggle is viewed almost in Darwinian terms. But they see society as a phenomenon in which the sympathetic, loving, community-building aspects of man's nature intertwine imperceptibly over time into a structure of mutually-respected rights and duties. In their notion of politics, the Hobbesian-Mr. Hyde dark side of human nature dominates; in their idea of society, the Lockean-Dr. Jekyll bright side reigns.

These are two separate constructs which, when brought together, do not merge into a concept capable of explaining any socio-political entity. The two are wrought upon differing foundations, differing assumptions as to the nature of man, differing streams of thought. Their one common denominator is 19th century philosophy with its blustering about power but also with its sentimental longings after the lost community of an imagined medieval age. Cultural pessimism afflicts both theories, the political emphasizing what is and the social what used to be, with neither allowing room for change. As they stand, they are as unable to explain why we have order within national societies as they are to explain how to get order in the world society.

Neither Niebuhr nor Morgenthau was educated to understand the theory of federalism which sought to provide unity as to some things while permitting diversity in other things. Niebuhr was, after all, a theologian. But we have seen that he groped his way at least once to an understanding of community almost in the MacIver sense that community exists at several levels of common interest, interest that can be coordinated by several levels of government.

Morgenthau changed too, but unfortunately he never changed his textbook. There he held that since sovereignty means supreme authority it follows that it is indivisible; federalism is a quaint fraud in that it is constitutionally impossible to deny that the federal government is sovereign but psychologically impossible to admit that the individual states are no longer sovereign.[38] But his logical nicety will not bear examination. If sovereignty means supremacy, then one must ask, supremacy as to what? If it means supremacy as to all things, then sovereignty logically is present only in the totalitarian state. If it means less than all things, then sovereignty logically is present where there is supremacy as to only some things. And if this is true, then one government can be supreme as to some things while another level of government is supreme as to other things. It is the essence of the federal principle that different things are done by different levels of government to the same body politic, each government acting within its own grant of authority, with this authority varying from one member-state to another while the overall government's authority is uniform.

Morgenthau went on to underline his misunderstanding by saying that world government advocates urge the "transference of the sovereignties of individual states to a world authority, which would be as sovereign over the individual nations as the individual nations are sovereign within their respective territories." He also appears not to know, as Madison pointed out in Federalist Paper No. 20, that a "government over governments," which is what Morgenthau describes here, is a confederation, not a federation.[39]

But in 1960 and again in 1961 Morgenthau recognized, not only that the national state can no longer safeguard the biological survival of its people, but that the sense of self-preservation may provide the requisite degree of world community and that a world government might perform only supranational tasks including control of weapons of mass destruction.[40] This is federalism.

Emery Reves, a British subject of Hungarian origins who was educated in France and lived in the United States, offered a clear statement of anarchy at the close of World War II. After remarking that "nation-feudalism" deprives people of their freedom and rights just as the old feudalism did, because both regularly produce war, he says:

> Superficially, it looks as though wars have been waged for a great variety of reasons. The struggle for food and mere survival among primitive tribes, feuds between families and dynasties, quarrels between cities and provinces, religious fanaticism, rival commercial interests, antagonistic social ideals, the race for colonies, economic competition and many other forces have exploded in fatal and devastating wars...
>
> Yet, if we analyze what seem to be the manifold causes of past wars, it is not difficult to observe a thread of continuity through these strange historical phenomena...
>
> If we try to detect the mechanism visibly in operation, the single cause ever-present at the outbreak of each and every conflict known to human history, if we attempt to reduce the seemingly innumerable causes of war to a common denominator, two clear and unmistakeable observations emerge.
>
> 1. Wars between groups of men forming social units always take place when these units—tribes, dynasties, churches, cities, nations—exercise unrestricted sovereign power.
>
> 2. Wars between these social units cease the moment sovereign power is transferred from them to a larger or higher unit.[41]

Reves speaks of "the single cause ever-present," meaning that anarchy among sovereign social units is the primary and constant cause, always present along with perhaps secondary causes.

Kenneth N. Waltz published in 1959 his *Man, the State, and War*, from which we get the three categories of the causes of war that we have adapted for our purposes in Chapters 2, 3, and 4. Waltz concluded that the immediate causes of war, often trivial causes, are contained in the first two categories, namely in the nature of man or in the differing natures of states, but that anarchy is the always present "permissive" cause. He quotes Rousseau's view that wars occur because there is nothing to prevent them. He sees that anarchy as the disease implies world government as the cure, but says that if world government were attempted "we might find ourselves dying in the attempt to unite, or uniting and living a life worse than death" and his conclusion is that world government "is unattainable in practice."[42]

The key to Waltz' conclusion may lie in his statement that there is no logical relation between the proposition that "in anarchy there is no automatic harmony" and the proposition that "among autonomous states war is inevitable."[43] This statement is perhaps true in the short run but not in the long run, for reasons to be discussed in Chapter 5. But Waltz' conclusion may simply arise out of a generalized pessimism reflected again in a work published twenty years later.[44]

Inis L. Claude Jr. offers, by implication, a rather novel view of anarchy. Writing in 1962, he asserts that

> To say that governments succeed, if they do and when they do, in maintaining order by sensitive and skillful operation of the mechanisms of political adjustment seems to me to be correct...The more mundane version of government which I have described is not wholly missing even in the international sphere; in my terms, the United Nations is not entirely "un-government-like." Government, defined in terms of the function of promoting order through political management of inter-group relations, is a matter of degree.[45]

To Claude, presumably, anarchy is also a matter of degree.

But he actually is not optimistic. He does not take what is called international law very seriously. He does not, in the end, believe that the conditions which enabled the balance system to manage power in earlier centuries (sometimes) will arise again, given the rigidifying influence of public opinion and ideology. He admits that the collective security system manifested in the League and UN has failed because the collective security principle is unrealistic in assuming that nations will abandon their freedom to take independent action in favor of collective action. The UN, he says, may leave the world in a condition of nature more Hobbesian than Lockean, but the UN at least helps mankind make the best of it.

It is a difficult question, Claude says, whether community produces government or government produces community. World government under present conditions might turn out more Hobbesian than Lockean, with the sacrifice of Western liberal values to totalitarian ones. He criticizes the view that a world federation could keep the peace by enforcing world law upon individuals, for it is the national governments—which the federal principle would attempt to bypass-that would be the main threat. He, with Waltz, sees the possibility of civil war within a world federation.

Finally, in his view too, world government is almost self-evidently impossible for the foreseeable future, so he places his hope in international organization. He means the UN, which tries to perform the security function, and the specialized agencies affiliated with the UN which perform other functions having to do with food and health, communications and the like. Writing in 1964, he said that if international organization continued its rate of growth, it might yet so transform human relationships on the planet as to justify, at some point, the conclusion that the world has come to be governed.[46] This faith is called functionalism, which we'll discuss later.

Raymond Aron, the French sociologist, was probably the Continent's best known scholar of international relations. He is refreshingly aware of the vast difference anarchy makes between national and international politics, which he calls the "Hobbesian situation," and says he is not sure Hans Morgenthau fully appreciates the difference. Aron sees clearly that the anarchy explanation requires world government as its prescription, with abandonment by nations of their "external sovereignty." But, true to his Continental sociological background, he says this will not be possible so long as members of the global society have not developed "relations comparable to those that link the members—individuals or groups—of each national society."

If only "external sovereignty" need be surrendered, why does Aron go on to require a sense of world community equal to that in a national society? But we are familiar by now with the confusion which afflicts sociologists when they address themselves to our subject. And it is no surprise to find Aron saying a few pages later that the world organization "would have to possess an authority absolute in certain respects but strictly limited in its field of application," that its essential function would be "to maintain an indisputable military superiority of the world power over any state or bloc."[47]

This of course is a picture of a world federal government which might not even take over all aspects of external sovereignty, but only the peace-keeping function.

E. The Behavioralists

Anarchy wouldn't matter if, as some anthropologists believe, there are societies that get along without any government. These are "multicentric" political systems in which, if one clan jumps on another, the other clans will intervene to restore order, so that in the tribe as a whole there is peace except that, true enough, there is quite a bit of fighting. Other anthropologists don't go along with this very far, saying that even if it is true of some tiny societies it has no application to large ones. And, actually, the anthropologist who wrote up this tribe admitted that a "multi-centric" system can be compared to the League of Nations and the UN.[48]

In addition to anthropologists and sociologists, Behavioralists include scholars whose original disciplines run the gamut from mathematics and physics to political science but who have been working in international relations for some time. Their focus in the main is on actual behavior of individuals, groups, and national societies rather than upon the way political institutions ideally ought to work. Most are also interested in why the behavior is what it is. They like to use models, to make complicated things simpler, and are rather free in using analogy. Much of their terminology is sociological, and the "systems theory" described in Chapter 3 is probably central to their approach. Their attention to anarchy focuses on its effects rather than on it as cause.

1. *National Interest and Power.* National behavior in a system of global anarchy was described by Morgenthau as the pursuit of "the national interest defined in terms of power." This was the catch-phrase that occupied center stage when the Behavioralists came on the scene. They began to ask whether power is an end in itself or a means to other ends. If the principal end is preservation of the nation, is this goal limited or unlimited? Is it defined in practice to mean self-preservation through unlimited self-extension? If so, will not the demand for power to achieve such a goal be unlimited too?[49] They have suggested that the national interest is not singular but plural; that national interests correspond to national needs at a given time, and these needs might be domestic rather than foreign. But there is the possibility that national needs simply equal national passions rather than the nation's objective needs.[50]

Behavioralists have asked whether "balance of power" means a policy to be pursued, or most any condition of international affairs at any given time, or an equilibrium among principal nations or competing coalitions, or a hegemony—that is, a preponderant imbalance of power.[51]

Some emphasize that power is not an absolute term but is meaningful only in relation to the power of other nations.[52] Others analyze power as manifested in (1) force, meaning violence; (2) domination, when outright force is not used; or (3) manipulation, when the entity being controlled is not aware of it.[53] And there is much attention to how national power can be computed and then brought to bear. This is called "policy-sciencing" and is in that tradition of advice to princes that we noted several times in *The Summary of International History.* We'll deal with it in Chapter 6.

2. *Decision-Making.* This approach is said to derive from social psychology's assumption that the best way to understand the international system is to study the behavior of individual national actors. The decision-making approach lost favor in the 1960s because it didn't produce much usable theory and because it was not based on empirical studies, but interest in it has revived in the late 1970s and 1980s.[54]

At any rate, the focus is on the individuals who make the decisions. If one understands how decisions were reached, one may understand why they were what they were. Decision-making arises not only from interaction among governments but among elements of national societies other than the governments and also among elements within the same national society.

The personal values of a decision-maker and the societal pressures to which he is susceptible will in part determine his decisions. [55] The decision-making environment consists of whatever is perceived or felt by the individual who makes the decision. This includes perceptions of domestic as well as foreign influences. Policy results from interplay between domestic and external conditions.[56] The international system is seen as a constellation of interacting decision-makers who, to avoid abstraction, must be recognized as real persons in specific situations.[57]

(a) *Organizational theory* suggests an official's decision is often already largely formed for him by his organization and the public. Up and down the administrative ladder, there is interaction of ideas, rational or irrational, and control is reciprocal.[58]

(b) *Role* is a sociological concept which means here the image or notion an individual has of his part in the foreign policy process, and of the part others play. If there is agreement as to roles and who should perform them, this is healthy for the nation and its goals. Personality may cause "role-incongruence," meaning one is not suited to the role he plays, as for example a president who understands domestic but not international politics. "Role conflict" may occur, as when a senator attempts initiatives in US foreign policy.[59] Individuals, even sophisticated scientists, may view themselves simply as nationals, e.g., as a Frenchman or a Mexican.[60] Most will also have an image of the role played, or which ought to be played, by their nations. All these roles and images of roles enter into the decision-making process.

(c) *Elite and mass* is another sociological concept related to decision-making. Some behavioralists see the elite as influencers and the mass as influencees, with the political elite as the top power class, yet one compatible with the democratic process. Others think of the elite as overlapping political, military, and economic cliques that are able to control the democratic process whether others like it or not. Both views refer to "The Establishment." But some behavioralists have, like Claude, noted the loss of freedom by decision-makers, due to the rise of popular sovereignty, representative government, and mass ideologies.[61] One writer commented that elites have been discredited owing to the public's weariness with and distrust of its leaders, and its desire for "privatization," that is, to be insulated from public affairs.[62]

(d) *Simulation* is role playing, with each nation represented by players, often one for foreign affairs and another for domestic affairs, who send and receive messages. Referees confine moves to those feasible, and change the situation at times as in real life.[63] Computers are used in simulation. One experiment found that, as between two coalitions in a Cold War type situation, the trend is toward no change or, if any, toward further polarization; that alliances are under constant strain; that there is a tendency toward escalation in an arms race, and a tendency to respond to de-escalation by cheating a bit.[64] However, a policy-maker who wishes to apply computer simulation to real situations is warned that he would have to cope with the problem of "system instability," meaning the change in relationships among variables in the situation.[65]

In 1983 two scholars closely identified with the decision-making approach announced that they were no longer satisfied with it and were trying to find a deeper basis for international relations theory.[66] On the other hand there have been recent calls for more hard research into the individual biological and psychological aspects of international human actors.[67]

3. *Group Theory and Structural-Functional Analysis, Political Culture and National Character.* Some sociologically-oriented scholars see international politics as a struggle among groups called nations.[68] It is said that groups in their struggle must abide by "the rules of the game." For example, outright bribery of a legislator is counterproductive.[69] But just what the rules of the game are in international politics is obscure.

Group theory has been incorporated into structural-functional analysis, which is a part of that general systems theory described in the previous chapter. Groups articulate their demands which in turn are aggregated by political parties and become inputs which are then processed by the governmental matrix into rules. But when this analysis is raised to the world level, as we have seen, there is no governmental matrix. There are no political parties except such things as the Third World, the peace movement, and the environmental movement. There is no government, only the UN and its related agencies and the treaty process. Group theorists do not quite see that whereas a Taft-Hartley Act, once recorded as the outcome of the group struggle, becomes enforceable, a treaty on international trade, for example, does not.

One Behavioralist writes that the global international system is a "null" political system, meaning that the roles needed to organize and maintain it are lacking.[70] This is sort of a sociological description of anarchy which reminds us that "political" comes from *polis* which meant a governed society, specifically the Greek city-state.

Another behavioralist recognizes anarchy in his suggestion that we look at the world as a society without a state which is in the process of developing a political structure appropriate to a worldwide society.[71] Still another offers an analogy between the world and the less-developed countries with their poorly articulated political institutions.[72] Yet another suggests that what the world system needs are homeostatic systems to maintain its temperature in "steady state."[73]

And that is the trouble with the biological analogy that structural-functional analysis is based on. An organism is normally healthy, self-correcting so that all its parts maintain a "steady state" in natural harmony. This school of analysis has been severely criticized for bringing this assumption of harmony into the study of a world system whose principal homeostatic device is war.

"Political culture" is a modern and rational sociological concept related to the "national character" that was so dear to the romantic nationalists. Behavioralists have asked whether national character is meaningless or perhaps can explain what no other idea can. One has suggested that something of a national character can develop out of common childhood experiences within the same culture which shape a "predisposition" to react in a certain way. He mentions the authoritarian German father. But he notes there is a sameness too in childhood training patterns from one culture to another, and similarities such as the tendency of the lower middle class in many nations to react the same way.[74] Another scholar would give weight to what he calls the "normative order of inner beliefs and habits" which is the "living law of each national or cultural group."[75] A German scholar argues that national character is real, adding that German political immaturity—the alternation between the bully and the browbeaten, between independence and submission—is to be blamed on Martin Luther.[76]

Political culture means a national population's ways of doing and thinking, politically. Two scholars, using depth interviews, compared the "civic culture" developed in the more seasoned liberal political systems of US and Britain with the less developed political cultures of Germany, Italy and Mexico, concluding that a "civic culture" provides the basis for a stable polity.[77]

F. The Positivists.

The study just mentioned was based on interviews the answers to which were then collated, counted, and compared. Thus it was a scientific study of the statistical type employing "quantification" or counting. It could have been discussed under the present heading as it appears to meet the positivist standard that nothing is to be accepted as knowledge unless it can be demonstrated. In this case the political attitudes elicited by the interviews in US and Britain correlated with the long histories of comparative stability in those nations, as did the attitudes in the other three countries with their less stable histories. If the two scholars did their job right, then it is likely that their results could be "replicated" if others saw fit to repeat the study. The Positivists include many Behavioralists and differ from them mainly in seeking a more scientific basis for theorizing about international relations.

1. *Game Theory.* These studies are not based on quantification but on the application of sophisticated mathematics to decision-making in an environment where the intentions of other parties are obscure but the situation is both competitive and interdependent.

Strategy turns on what the player expects the other player or players to do. The game takes several forms but all force the player to spell out alternative strategies and the values or "payoffs" he places on each possible outcome. He must concentrate on the crucial aspects of conflict situations and try to get maximum gain at minimum loss. Some games permit coalitions.

Some say that game theory may be too abstract for a practical problem like nuclear deterrence, and that the assumption of rationality may not hold true in real situations, or even be desirable in some. And it may be impossible to calculate payoffs or to prescribe all feasible alternatives in actual politics.[78] A pessimist has wondered if the international system may not represent an "n-person, non-zero-sum" game with negative payoffs for all—a game in which everybody loses.

Games such as Prisoner's Dilemma and Chicken are explicitly anarchic situations. An extremely interesting study says that in Prisoner's Dilemma the actors' dominant strategies lead them to an equilibrium outcome even though all the actors would prefer a greater gain. So international anarchy can be seen as a game in which nations wish to benefit by defecting from mutual cooperation, for example by cheating, and the result of this mutual defection hurts all nations. Hence the "game theory" version of the Hobbes-Locke-Rousseau social contract: individuals abandon anarchy by agreeing to coerce one another and thereby ensure the optimal outcome of mutual cooperation. Thus government is a coercive institution that permits individuals to give up what rationally would be their course; they give up the effort to achieve maximum gain in order to obtain the optimal outcome for all. In this way they solve the dilemma that frustrates the common interest of all.[79]

2. *Content Analysis and Hostility Measurement.* "Transactions," that is, trade and communication across national frontiers, have interested some scholars. They seek to learn whether pairs of nations handle their transactions so as to establish (1) war communities, meaning the usual tone is hostile; (2) no-war communities, where the attitude is neutral; (3) security communities, meaning they have come to feel secure with respect to each other; or (4) political communities, in which they have developed a habit of so working together that a degree of political integration has occurred which might or does support common governmental institutions.[80] In effect, they measure what Claude might call the degree of anarchy.

These scholars count messages or key words in messages to disclose patterns that common sense alone might not detect. "Content analysis" was applied to some 3,000 documents exchanged in the summer of 1914. It was found that Austrian decision-makers thought oftener of Serbia's incapability for war, and of France's and Russia's readiness or unreadiness, than of Austria's. In all five principal chanceries, perceptions of hostility exceeded perceptions of one's own capabilities.[81] A somewhat similar analysis was made of the 1962 Cuba crisis with the finding that, unlike 1914, there was no demand made that Khruschev could not carry out, and none calculated to humiliate him unduly.[82]

That communications in an anarchic world are fraught with dangers may be inferred from those who point out that there is a loss or distortion of information in transmission between nations which may distort the behavior which the communication was intended to elicit. Also, incoming information may be distorted as it comes up through the intelligence-gathering apparatus, in part because intelligence people often have attitudes different from those of higher decision-makers. But a decision-maker, by carefully and consciously shaping his response, can influence the response he will receive in return.[83]

Boulding, the economist, suggested in 1966 that hostility between nations could be measured by as little as two parameters called warmth (love) and pressure (threats) and that these might be measured by content analysis of communications.[84] A good deal of this type of work has been done, as we shall see shortly. Another scholar, writing about decision-making in crises, speaks of "explosive accumulations" of feeling, which by a reaction process give rise to increasingly provocative decision."[85] Another makes the point that hostility has often been whipped up artificially, as by Hitler.[86]

3. *Peace Research.* The empirical method is the way scientists get at a problem. Empirical means to rely solely on experiment or on experience. Experience is that which is factual, that which has happened. The first person to gather data on war and subject the data to statistical treatment was an English mathematician and Quaker named Lewis F. Richardson, who was driven to this work by the horrors of World War I. He is probably the first Positivist in international relations; for example, the "reaction process" mentioned in the preceding paragraph is also known as the "Richardson process" of escalation toward war and has been the subject of many empirical studies in recent decades. Richardson is surely the father of "peace research," although the phrase was coined by Theodore Lentz in the 1950s. What is the difference between positivism and peace research?

An international relations man points out that "Science does not dictate political purposes. Its claim to truth contains no warrant for telling us whether we want world government or issue-specific technology assessment, peace or war, equality or hierarchy."[87] In contrast, the publisher of a peace research journal says that peace research aims at the elimination of war by finding its causes and being able to predict wars.[88] Thus peace research is akin to the "policy-sciencing" we mentioned earlier.

Richardson took the histories of wars written by traditional historians, as did Quincy Wright and Pitirim Sorokin, and subjected the data extracted from the histories to statistical treatment.[89]

Richardson thought there might be a general cause for all wars, for example, human nature, anarchy, the security dilemma (much the same as the Hobbesian dilemma), or the economic scarcity dilemma.

Richardson said he got his hypotheses by intuition or luck as well as by research.

Richardson thought the "gang-up" pattern of general wars could be explained by a general propensity for nations to fight anyone, but that militant ideology is a cause of war.

The data patterns invite the hypothesis that ethnocultural differences in general, and linguistic or religious differences in particular, are irritants.

The findings are not fatal to economic theories of war but they do pose serious difficulties for them and for economically-based peace schemes.

Richardson was strongly interested in the prospects for world government, saying that a world government might pacify the world if a common government tends to prevent fighting. On this point, Wilkinson, who reviewed and updated Richardson's work, says that "once established, the older the government the fewer (civil) wars it will generate."[90]

In summary it would appear that Richardson concluded that anarchy and its Hobbesian dilemma is a major cause of war, requiring world government; that other differences are only irritants; and that the economic cause of war may be over-rated.

In 1969 two Behavioral-Positivists, Pruitt and Snyder, edited a summary of peace research to date, with illustrative articles written by others.[91] The editors say that, by and large, peace research deals with the proximate causes of war rather than the perhaps more basic ones. The theory developed is not macro-theory, but in the main it is not micro-theory; it is what some call middle-range theory: instead of only scattered bits of a vast mosaic, there are at least "islands of theory." What is needed, the editors say, is more islands and some bridges to connect them. Most studies are speculative, they note, with little empirical verification so far.

They think highly of content analysis and of simulation using humans as decision-makers, less highly of computer simulation. They endorse statistical studies of history, and publish one which examined 2,000 years to find that "peace-loving" nations are no less likely to be involved in war than "warlike" nations, even when the former have the military advantages; that cultural exchange is negatively related to war frequency, though barely so; and that older rulers are more apt to get into war than younger ones.[92]

The editors believe that the causes of war are largely psychological. They accept the view that frustration evokes aggression. They are interested in hostility, arms races, perception of threat, tension, and the effect that crisis has in warping the judgment of decision-makers. They accept the vicious-circle theory whereby not just an aggressor nation but several nations share in escalating hostility.

They are not sure Rosecrance is right in his emphasis on insecure ruling elites as the major cause of war.[93] They include an historical-statistical study which found no significant correlation between civil and international conflict, but Rosecrance is not precisely contradicted by the study's conclusion that "the genesis of domestic- and foreign-conflict behavior must be different."[94]

The editors do not deal with anarchy as such. They do include an article which describes the effects of anarchy nicely but which says that the lack of a world government is "merely an indication of the absence of any sense of solidarity among the peoples of the world."[95] And the editors dismiss world government along with universal brotherhood as utopian.

The editors might well have included some reference to a 1962 book by a prominent economist and member of the Center for the Study of Conflict Resolution. Kenneth Boulding's *Conflict and Defense* draws upon Richardson and applies the economic theory of oligopoly—of competition among the few corporations that dominate an industry—to conflict among the principal nations in the world system. But Boulding is quite aware that business firms, including the multinational corporations, operate always under laws that are enforceable against them in some national jurisdiction, whereas international competition occurs within an environment of anarchy. He concludes in part:

> One of the great organizational problems of mankind, then, is the control of violence or, more generally, the control of conflict to the point where procedural institutions are adequate to handle it. The great course of political evolution, from the family to the tribe to the nation to the superpower, and, finally, one hopes, to the world government now in its birth pangs is testimony to the ability of human organization to extend conflict control to wider and wider areas. It is hardly too much to say that conflict control is government, and though government has broader functions than this, conflict control is perhaps its most important single task—the one thing which it must perform or cease to be government.[96]

In the summary of peace research up to 1969 there was a note of disappointment in the editors' observation that this research does not get into the basic causes of war very much and is in bits and pieces of disconnected little theory instead of overall theory. A great deal of peace research has been published since 1969 as well as before, and we have tried to include at the appropriate places in this volume every such significant and pertinent study. But criticism of and disappointment with positivism and peace research appear to be on the increase.

One of the founders of quantification in the study of international relations remarked in 1977 that "the difficulties of working in the scientific mode are now more familiar" while the pay-offs seem less clear than they may have appeared originally."[97] A noted non-positivist says that "if we confine ourselves to strict standards of verification and proof there is very little of significance that can be said about international relations."[98] A European says that some are coming to believe that the problem of peace is rooted in the very structure of international life or is related to almost "anything at all except narrow research criteria borrowed from the behavioral sciences," adding that peace research in US is "diffuse and theoretically impoverished."[99] An American says that positivism abstracts data from the factual environment whereas other approaches deal with the facts themselves, that is, with events or institutions intelligible to people because they have been made by people."[100] Two others reject "the intellectual capitulation to scientism and its myth of quantification."[101] Another says the scientific method produces results that are frequently trivial and irrelevant.[102] And a German who is an editor of the *Journal of Peace Research* says that peace research is helpless when confronted with the broken peace of the 1980s, that now we need action.[103]

A president of the American Political Science Association said in 1979 that political behavioral research suffers from its unsystematic, atheoretical character, meaning that it is not anchored in large-scale, overall macro-theory; from its limited range of research topics; from the circumstance that some 90 percent of social science research is based on "self-reports," meaning interviews and questionnaires; and from an erroneous conception of human nature, namely the assumption that behavior grows out of a self-conscious intellectual act so that attitudes are mistaken for behavior.[104] Somewhat similarly, 1n 1981 a European noted that the results of quantitative research are pretty negligible and suggested that what is needed is a systematic frame of reference.[105]

There is also criticism of empirical studies from the technical standpoint. One reviewer said that a certain book was a "storehouse of empirical findings" but that 19 tables published in it were useless owing to mathematical errors.[106] A statistical study of the period 1816-1965 rejects an earlier similar study, saying that its error lay in the assumptions contained in its statistical techniques.[107] And in a review of four books based on quantitative analysis, the reviewer found them all flawed from a methodological standpoint.[108]

These technical criticisms raise the questions (1) how many empirical studies are reviewed by other quantitative analysts, and (2) how can the rest of us know whether to take seriously the studies that are not thus reviewed?

Wilkinson said that the shortcomings of Richardson's work included no experimentation, no replication, a minimum of direct observation, and reliance on historians. But he said these are "virtually inescapable" and are shared with much political research animated by the scientistic spirit. Therefore "We are justified in weighing such findings against our intuitive or conventional or commonsense beliefs, and accepting— provisionally—only those findings that do not contravene our earlier beliefs but are consistent with them, *plus* those that *do* contravene our beliefs, but which are, however weak the case for them, better grounded than those beliefs themselves."[109]

Even in the *Journal of Conflict Resolution*, which was the first periodical to get into this sort of thing, there are articles which reflect the worry that the Western scientific method may not even be appropriate for the study of the causes of war and peace. But it would appear that there is pretty solid support for statistical studies of history, especially the longer reaches of history, like those of Richardson but more sophisticated. One scholar, writing in the *Journal of Conflict Resolution* in 1974, said that the latest wave in international relations research included "quantitative history."[110] Another, writing in *Polity* in 1975, went further and suggested that the method of history and not of science may take us closer to truths about contemporary international relations.[111]

Singer, who has actually carried out statistical studies of history at his Correlates of War Project, says that we still need non-empirical but scientific thinking, with the generation of hypotheses and models which could then be checked against evidence; that "the right combination of conjectural and correlational research could bring us close to a causal theory of war within a few years."[112]

Perhaps it is as the Nobel Laureate Percy Bridgman said: "There is no scientific method as such, but the vital feature of the scientist's procedure has been to do the utmost with his mind, no holds barred."

G. The Neo-Realists.

Disillusionment with positivism, often by the Positivists themselves, has been accompanied by a revival of power realism with its emphasis on anarchy.

In 1976 John Herz, one of the senior scholars in international relations, re-stated his notion of the "security dilemma," first published in 1951.

> The security dilemma besets, above all, those units which, in their respective historical setting, are the highest ones, that is, not subordinate to any higher authority. Since, for their protection and even their survival, they cannot rely on any higher authority, they are necessarily thrown back upon their own devices; and since they cannot be sure of the intentions of competing units, they must be prepared for "the worst." Hence they must have means of defense. But preparing for defense may arouse the suspicions of others, who in turn will engage in such preparation. A vicious circle will arise— of suspicion and counter-suspicion, competition for power, armament races, ultimately war.[113]

But Herz quotes Niebuhr, saying that world federalists think they can fix the security dilemma by "fiat of international law," taking "legal symbols for social realities," and he criticizes "world governmentalists" for saying that what ought to happen will happen.[114]

In 1977 Hedley Bull, a noted Australian scholar, published a book called *The Anarchical Society: A Study of Order in World Politics*. He finds unconvincing the argument that the international system can no longer serve the goals of world order. The world is not quite Hobbesian; what with trade, navigation and so forth, there is an international society, but it is precarious and imperfect. Wars were formerly fought for economic or ideological gain, but nuclear war would be risked only for security. World government would be destructive of diversity and freedom. It might produce civil wars and an almost medieval disorder. So Bull puts his faith, weakly, in international law, international culture, and balance-of-power diplomacy.[115]

In 1978 a scholar adept in game theory addressed himself to the security dilemma, saying "The lack of an international sovereign not only permits wars to occur, but also makes it difficult for states that are satisfied with the status quo to arrive at goals that they recognize as being in their common interest."[116] Another recognized that "The international polity is an anarchically organized political system" but said this does not mean chaos; the degree of consensus and community have a bearing. Nevertheless the choices are bargaining, coercive diplomacy, and war.[117]

In 1979 Rudolph Rummel said "The international society is governed by a libertarian political system." He thinks the UN and other international organizations serve as a kind of minimal world government but recognizes that nations retain sovereignty and a monopoly of force is denied the central government. Hence nations are insecure and must depend on themselves and their allies, a security dilemma that creates a constant disposition to violence, a state of war.[118]

We shall pursue realism and anarchy further in Chapter 8. And we'll leave to the next Chapter 5 the problem of working the theory of anarchy in with the theories of human nature and the differing natures of nations so as to produce an overall explanation of war.

Chapter 4 Notes

1. Thomas Hobbes, *Leviathan*, Part I. Chapter 17.

2. *Ibid.*, Chapter 13.

3. *Ibid.*, Chapter 17.

4. *Ibid.*, Chapter 13.

5. *Ibid.*

6. *Ibid.*, Chapter 14.

7. Spinoza's *Political Treatise*, Chapter 3, Section 13.

8. See Christopher Wolfe, "The Confederate Republic of Montesquieu," *Polity* 9:1 (1976), 427-445.

9. John Locke, *Concerning Civil Government*, Chapter 9, Section 123.

10. *Ibid.*, Chapter 9, Sections 124-126.

11. *Ibid.*, Chapter 8, Section 107.

12. Jack S. Levy, in "Historical Trends in Great Power War, 1495-1975," *International Studies Quarterly* 26:2 (1982), 278-300, found that wars have declined in frequency, except for a slight upturn in the 20th century, but have become graver owing to increasing technology, interdependence, and total national mobilization to enhance the military power of the state. This is a statistical study.

13. C. E. Vaughan, ed., *The Political Writings of Jean Jacques Rousseau*, vol. 1 (Oxford, · Basil Blackwell, 1962), 297-304.

14. See Ian Clark, *Reform & Resistance in the International Order* (Cambridge, Cambridge University Press, 1980), 40.

15. *The Federalist Papers*, Paper No. 6, any edition.

16. John Stuart Mill, *Representative Government*, Chapter 1, Paragraphs 6 and 11, any edition.

17. Norman Angell's best-selling book, *The Great Illusion* (London, Wm. Heinemann, 1910) is an outstanding example of this viewpoint.

18. R. M. MacIver, *Community* (New York, Macmillan, 1928), pp. x and 274 .

19. R. M. MacIver, *Society* (New York, Ray Long & Richard R. Smith, 1931), 194.

20. R. M. MacIver *Power Transformed* (New York, Macmillan, 1964), 141.

21. Reinhold Niebuhr, *Moral Man and Immoral Society* (New York, Scribner's, 1932), pp. 110-111.

22. Reinhold Niebuhr, *The Nature and Destiny of Man* (New York, Scribner's One Volume Edition, 1941 and 1949), 266.

23. Reinhold Niebuhr, *Christian Realism and Political Problems* (New York, Scribner's, 1943), 27-29.

24. Reinhold Niebuhr, *The Self and the Dramas of History* (New York, Scribner's, 1955), 37-38.

25. *Ibid.*, p. 213.

26. Frederick L. Schuman, *International Politics, New York, Knopf, 1933. E. H. Carr's The Twenty Years' Crisis* (London, Macmillan, 1939) is noteworthy too.

27. Frederick L. Schman, *The Commonwealth of Man* (New York, Knopf, 1952), 22-23.

28. *Ibid.*, p. 486.

29. *Ibid.*, p. 471.

30. Matthew Melko, *Fifty-Two Peaceful Societies* (Oakville, Ontario, CRPI Press, 1973), 181.

31. Quincy Wright, *A Study of War* (University of Chicago Press, 2d Ed., 1965), pp. 1235-1236. This work was first published in 1942.

32. Herbert Butterfield, "Tragic Conflict," from *Christianity and History* (New York, Scribner's, 1950), reprinted in Robert A. Goldwin and Tony Pearce, eds., *Readings in World Politics* (New York, Oxford University Press, 2d Ed., 1970), pp. 67-69.

33. Hans J. Morgenthau, *Politics Among Nations* (New York, Knopf, 1960, 3d ed.), p. 97.

34. *Ibid.*, p. 534.

35. *Ibid.*, Chapter 14.

36. *Ibid.*, p. 502.

37 See Morgenthau's article in *Commentary*, March 1962.

38. Morgenthau, Politics Among Nations, p. 306.

39. *Ibid.*, pp. 469-470. Germany's unhappy experience with confederal arrangements that were too loose, as well as with quasi-federal governments that were too tight, thus mocking the idea of a divided sovereignty, may have clouded Morgenthau's consideration of the more precisely federal principle. Certainly the American experience as a whole baffles yet intrigues him. Much of this argument appeared originally in the present writer's articles on Morgenthau in *World Politics* (January 1967) and on Niebuhr in the *The Christian Century* (March 15, 1967)

40. See Morgenthau's *The Purpose of American Politics* (New York, Knopf, 1960), pp. 10-11, 33-34, 308-310, and his *The Restoration of American Politics* (University of Chicago Press, 1962), pp. 174-175.

41. Emery Reves, *The Anatomy of Peace* (New York, Harper, 1945), 117-121.

42. Kenneth N. Waltz, *Man, The State and War* (New York, Colombia University Press, 1959), 228-238.

43. *Ibid.*, p. 186.

44. Kenneth N. Waltz, *Theory of International Relations*, Reading (Mass.), Addison-Wesley Publishing Co., 1979.

45. Inis L. Claude, Jr., *Power and International Relations* (New York, Random House, 1962), 270-271.

46. Inis L. Claude, Jr., *Swords into Plowshares* (New York, Random House, 1964), pp. 404-405.

47. Raymond Aron, *Peace and War* (New York, Doubleday, 1966), 709, 753, 759.

48. Paul Bohannon, *Social Anthropology* (New York, Holt, 1963), 272-283. The criticisms are contained in the contributions of Hoebel, Steward, and Forde in Morton H. Fried, ed., *Readings in Anthropology* (New York, Crowell, 1959), vol. 2, pp. 77, 296, 307, 335; also the contributions of Levine and Otterbein in R. A. Falk and S. S. Kim, eds., *The War System: An Interdisciplinary Approach* (Boulder, Colo., Westview Press, 1980), p. 174, 220.

49. See Arnold Wolfers' "The Pole of Power and the Pole of Indifference," *World Politics* 4:1 (1951), reprinted in James N. Rosenau, ed., *International Politics and Foreign Policy* (New York, Free Press, 1961), 146-151.

50. See Morton A. Kaplan's "The National Interest and Other Interests," in Rosenau, *op.cit.*, pp. 164-169, which is a reprinting from his *System and Process in International Politics* (New York, John Wiley, 1957), 151-161. Francis A. Beer, in his *Peace Against War: The Ecology of International Violence* (San Francisco, W. H. Freeman & Co., 1981), p. 318, remarks that "Beyond its focus on the nation-state, the national interest presents no firm, objective guidelines for decision-making.

51. See Ernst B. Haas' "Balance of Power: Prescription, Concept, or Propaganda," *World Politics* 5:4 (1953), 442-477, reprinted in Rosenau, *op.cit.*, pp. 318-329.

52. See M. A. Ash's "An Analysis of Power " in Rosenau, *op.cit.*, pp. 334-342, or in S. S. Ulmer, ed., *Introduction Readings in Political Behavior* (Chicago, Rand-McNally, 1961), pp. 376-383, or in *World Politics*, vol. 3 (1951), 218-2832.

53. See H. Goldhamer and Edward A. Shils, "Types of Power and Status," in Ulmer, *op.cit.*, pp. 334-342.

54. R. A. Falk and S. S. Kim, eds., *The War System* (Boulder, Colo., Westview Press, 1980), 459-460.

55. See Richard C. Snyder, *et al*, "The Decision-Making Approach to the Study of International Politics," in Rosenau, *op.cit.*, pp. 186-192.

56. Harold and Margaret Sprout, in *Foundations of International Politics* (Princeton, Van Nostrand, 1962), speak of "environmental possibilism" or "cognitive behaviorism," meaning behavior is governed by what is taken into account.

57. R. C. Snyder and Glenn Paige, in Rosenau, *op.cit.*, pp. 193-208, describe the decision to intervene in Korea in 1950. A study of the Kennedy decisions in the Cuba crisis of 1962 is in Peter Woll, ed., *American Government: Readings and Essays* (Boston, Little Brown, 2d ed., 1965).

58. Organizational theory comes from public administration theory. Principal writers are W. J. Gore, G. Goliembieski, and Herbert Simon.

59. See Ulmer, *op.cit.*, Chapter 9.

60. See Bruce M. Russett's article in Falk & Kim, *op.cit.*, p. 533.

61. For example, see Karl W. Deutsch's "Mass Communications and the Loss of Freedom in National Decision-Making," *Journal of Conflict Resolution*, vol. 1 (June 1957), pp. 200-211. On elite and mass, see Ulmer, *op.cit.*, Chapter 10.

62. H. Speier, "International Political Communication: Elite v. Mass," *World Politics* 4:3 (1952), pp. 305-317. But as an Iranian professor put it in basic English, "The American people support the President on foreign policy because they think he's on their side."

63. H. Guetzkow, "A Use of Simulation in the Study of Inter-Nation Relations," *Behavioral Science* 4:3 (1959), pp. 183-191. See also his article in Douglas E. Knight, *et al*, eds., *Cybernetics, Simulation, and Conflict Resolution* (New York, Spartan Books, 1971).

64. Oliver Benson, "A Simple Diplomatic Game," in Rosenau, *op.cit.*, pp. 504-511. Benson comments that the computer exercise gives an appearance of reality but also of inevitability of result.

65. J. S. Millstein and W. C. Mitchell, "Computer Simulation of International Processes," *Peace Research Society (International) Papers*, vol. 12 (1969), 118-36.

66. Robert C. North and Nazli Choucri, in "Economic and Political Factors in International Conflict and Integration," *International Studies Quarterly* 27:4 (1983), 443-446.

67. Thomas C. Wiegele, reviewing two books on the new "bio-politics," in *Orbis* 26:2 (1982), 527-534. The Books are G. W. Hopple's *Political Psychology and Biopolitics* (Boulder, Westview Press, 1980) and Ralph Pittman's *Biopolitics and International Values* (New York, Pergamon, 1981).

68. According to Trygve Mathisen, *Methodology in the Study of International Relations* (Oslo University Press, 1959), p. 37.

69. David B. Truman has written prolifically on group theory. See his "Political Behavior and International Tensions," *World Politics* 3:4 (1951), 545-554.

70. M. A. Kaplan, *System and Process in International Politics* (New York, John Wiley, 1957), 19.

71. Richard C. Snyder, "International Relations Theory—Continued," *World Politics* 13:2 (1961), 300-312.

72. C. F. Alger, "Comparison of Intranational and International Politics," in R. B. Farrell, ed., *Approaches to Comparative and International Politics* (Northwestern University Press, 1966), 301-328.

73. Charles A. McClelland, "Applications of General Systems Theory in International Relations," in Rosenau, *op.cit.*, pp. 412-420. He finds some sort of homeostatic devices in international organizations, broadly defined.

74. Nathan Leites, "Psycho-Cultural Hypotheses about Political Acts," *World Politics* vol. 1 (1948), pp. 102-119.

75. F. S. C. Northrup, "The Normative Inner Order of Societies," in Rosenau, *op.cit.*, pp. 313-316. Northrup's concept seems similar to what Pareto, an early sociologist, called "residues."

76. Erich Kahler, *Der Deutsche Charakter in Der Geschichte Europas*, Zurich 1937.

77. Gabriel Almond and Sidney Verba, *The Civic Culture*, Boston, Little Brown, 1965.

78. Richard C. Snyder, "Game Theory and the Analysis of Political Behavior," in Rosenau, *op.cit.*, pp. 381-389, or in Ulmer, *op.cit.*, pp. 271-276. For an extended treatment, see Thomas C. Schelling's *The Strategy of Conflict* (Harvard University Press, 1960). Ulmer says game theory may detect departures from rational decision-making; Deutsch says it may be too costly and time-consuming for use in real situations.

79. A. A. Stein, "Coordination and Collaboration: Regimes in an Anarchic World," *International Organization* 36:2 (1982), 294-324.

80. Karl W. Deutsch, *Nationalism and Social Communication* (New York, John Wiley, 1953) and *Political Community at the International Level* (Garden City, Doubleday, 1954), and in collaboration with others, *Political Community and the North Atlantic Area* (Princeton University Press, 1957). Category 4 is scarcely a valid or useful one.

81. D. A. Zinnes, *et al*, "Capability, Threat, and the Outbreak of War," in Rosenau, *op.cit.*, pp. 469-482; also R. C. North, *et al*, *Content Analysis* (Northwestern University Press, 1963).

82. Ole R. Holsti, *et al*, "Measuring Affect and Action in International Reaction Models: Empirical Materials from the 1962 Cuban Crisis," *Peace Research Society (International) Papers*, vol. 2 (1965).

83. T. M. Newcomb, "Communicative Behavior," in Roland Young, ed., *Approaches to the Study of Politics* (Northwestern University Press, 1959).

84. Kenneth E. Boulding, "Arms Limitation and Integrative Activity," *Peace Research Society (International) Papers*, vol. 6 (1966), pp. 1-10. See also D. A. Zinnes, "Hostility in International Decision-Making," *Journal of Conflict Resolution*, vol. 6 (1962), pp. 236-243, and O. R. Holsti, "The Value of International Tension Measurement," *Journal of Conflict Resolution*, vol. 7 (1963), pp. 608-617.

85. Robert C. North, "Decision-Making in Crises: An Introduction," *Journal of Conflict Resolution*, vol. 6 (1962), pp. 197-200.

86. Emile Benoit's comments on R. C. North, *et al*, "Some Empirical Data on the Conflict Spiral," *Peace Research Society (International) Papers*, vol. 1 (1964), pp. 1-14, 11.

87. Ernst B. Haas, "Is There a Hole in the Whole?" *International Organization* 29:3 (1975), p. 875.

88. Alan G. Newcombe, "Dollars and Sense of Peace," *Peace Research Reviews* 7:3 (1977), 1-14.

89. Quincy Wright's *A Study of War* (University of Chicago Press, 2d ed., 1965) covered wars from 1480 to 1940. Pitirim Sorokin's *Social and Cultural Dynamics* (New York, Bedminster Press, 1937), vol. 3, covered wars from the 5th century B.C. to 1925.

90. David Wilkinson, *Lewis F. Richardson and the Statistical Study of War* (Berkeley, University of California Press, 1980) pp. 34, 35, 80, 98, 105-6, 114, 115, 118, 120. Richardson's principal work was *Statistics of Deadly Quarrels*, published in 1939.

91. Dean G. Pruitt and Richard C. Snyder, eds., *Theory & Research on the Causes of War*, Englewood Cliffs, Prentice-Hall, 1969. Their comments are found in their introductions to the several sections.

92. *Ibid.*, the contribution by Raoul Naroll, pp. 150-164.

93. Richard N. Rosecrance, *Action and Reaction in World Politics*, Boston, Little Brown, 1963.

94. The contribution by Rummel in Pruitt and Snyder, *op.cit.*, pp. 219-228, 228. Also the method used, factor analysis, is said to be a useful but crude first step in bringing order out of a chaos of data.

95. Werner Levi's contribution, *ibid.*, pp. 35-38, 36.

96. Kenneth E. Boulding, *Conflict and Defense: A General Theory* (New York, Harper & Row, 1962), 325.

97. J. David Singer, "War and Other Problems," *International Organization* 31:3 (1977), 565-578, 566.

98. Hedley Bull, "International Theory: The Case for a Classical Approach," in F. H. Hartmann, ed., *World In Crisis* (New York, Macmillan, 4th ed., 1973), p. 34.

99. N. G. Onuf, "Peace Research Parochialism," *Journal of Peace Research* 12:1 (1975), 71-78.

100. Robert W. Cox, "On Thinking About Future World Order," *World Politics* 28:2 (1976), 175-196, 178.

101. H. G. Reid and E. J. Yanarella, "Toward a Critical Theory of Peace Research in the United States," *Journal of Peace Research* 13:4 (1976), 315-341. This journal is published in Oslo and many of its contributors are Europeans.

102. John H. Herz, *The Nation State and the Crisis of World Politics* (New York, David McKay, 1976), 253.

103. Ekkehart Krippendorf, an editor of *Journal of Peace Research* speaking of a special issue (vol. 18, no. 2, 1981) devoted to theories of peace.

104. John C. Wahlke, "Pre-Behaviorialism in Political Science," *American Political Science Review* 73:1 (1979), 9-31.

105 K. J. Gantzel, "Another Approach to a Theory on the Causes of International War," *Journal of Peace Research* 18:1 (1981), 39-55.

106. R. J. Rummel, "A Warning on Michael Haas' *International Conflict, Journal of Conflict Resolution* 20:1 (1978), 157-162. Haas responds (pp. 163-4) that Rummel is too far gone on factor analysis.

107. C. W. Ostrom Jr. and F. W. Hoole, "Alliances and Wars Revisited," *International Studies Quarterly* 22:2 (1978), 215-236. See also R. M. Siverson and M. P. Sullivan, "The Distribution of Power and the Onset of War," *Journal of Conflict Resolution* 27:3 (1983), 473-494, for a rather similar complaint.

108. Review by Charles S. Gochman, in J. D. Singer & Associates, *Explaining War* (Beverley Hills, Sage Publications, 1979).

109. David Wilkinson, *Lewis F. Richardson and the Statistical Study of War* (Berkeley, University of California Press, 1980), 105-106.

110. Harvey Starr, in a book review, *Journal of Conflict Resolution* 18:2 (1974), pp. 336-368.

111. Benjamin Nimer, "Great States, Small States, and the Prospects for International Relations Theory," *Polity* 8:1 (1975), 131-146.

112. J. David Singer & Associates, *Explaining War* (Beverley Hills, Sage Publications, 1979), 32-33.

113. John H. Herz, *The Nation State and the Crisis of World Politics* (New York, David McKay, 1976), 9-10.

114. *Ibid.*

115. Hedley Bull, *The Anarchical Society* (New York, Columbia University Press, 1977), esp. p. 319.

116. Robert Jervis, "Cooperation Under the Security Dilemma," *World Politics* 30:2 (1978), 167-214, 167.

117. Oran R. Young, "Anarchy and Social Choice," *World Politics* 30:2 (1978), 241-263.

118. Rudolph J. Rummel, *Understanding Conflict and War* (Beverley Hills, Sage Publications, 1979), 45.

119. Donald W. Hanson, "Thomas Hobbes' Highway to Peace," *International Organization* 38:2 (1984), 829-854.

Chapter 5

WHY WAR?

A. Anarchy and Fear

To say that the world international system is only quasi-anarchical is to overlook the fact that the real means of maintaining an independent stance—that is, arms and men—remain in national hands. Nations can and do change their leaders and their policies and even their belief systems. A "security-community" between two nations can and does change to a "no-war" or "war" community. Nations can be made to keep their agreements, including their alliances, only by persuasion including economic blandishments or the threat of force by other nations. The partners change but the anarchic dance goes on.

In the world system, as we have seen, as in every international system in history, each nation has a self-contained decision-making apparatus. In liberal nations, much of the domestic decision-making process may be visible to anyone who cares to watch. But the foreign policy process in all nations is largely obscure, taking place within the closely-guarded upper reaches of the party or the executive bureaucracy with only occasional references to the legislature, usually for budgetary purposes, and very little to other branches and levels of government.

Foreign ambassadors and other observers may hope, by spying or by keeping their fingers on the public pulse, to predict how the makers of foreign policy will reach their decisions. This effort becomes less reliable as the pressures of international conflict cause even liberal presidents and prime ministers to assert more and more executive authority in foreign policy while publics and legislators acquiesce.

Foreign policy decisions, together with the process by which they are reached, are kept secret if possible. This keeps decision-makers freer from public and foreign pressure. If aid to India is not to be increased next year, neither the Soviet Foreign Minister nor the US Secretary of State would wish to say so. If France is considering furnishing fighter plans to Israel, the French Premier may hint at an affirmative decision for the benefit of French Zionists while the French Ambassador in Damascus hints at a negative decision or simply keeps his mouth shut. In Islamabad, some Pakistani decision-makers may lean toward Peking, others toward Washington, but all are apt to be quiet, awaiting offers.

The point is that in a system of independent nations, one nation cannot control the foreign policy of any other nation. It cannot even know with assurance what is being considered in another capital, though its espionage apparatus does its best. USSR and US have not been able to control—or even penetrate the councils of—their so-called satellite nations. As noted earlier, leaders of one nation cannot predict reliably even what leaders in an allied nation will do. In 1944, would General Montgomery try to carry out his task on the left flank while the Americans advanced in the center and on the right? Will Turkey honor its commitments under the CENTO treaty if need arises? is NATO still whole? Is the ANZUS treaty dead? Is Czechoslovakia indeed a reliable Soviet ally? And so forth.

Among independent nations there is a chronic condition of unpredictability which occasions anxiety. If the matter is important, anxiety may become distrust. Distrust in the mind is apt to become distrust in behavior. Distrustful behavior causes reciprocal behavior which will evoke suspicion. Reciprocal suspicions are apt to produce reciprocal acts of fear. Arms escalation produces reciprocal escalation. This is the "Richardson process," Herz' "security dilemma," Butterfield's "Hobbesian dilemma."

As this process goes along, it tends to become cumulative and hard to reverse, as among the European nations prior to both world wars. It takes on a momentum and reality of its own. Tension, born in the very nature of the anarchic system, heightens as anxiety darkens into fear, then hostility, then aggression.

Fear inspires hatred and hatred elicits fear. The mass media are hard at work, rumors fly about, publics ascend emotional heights while leaders plumb decisional despair. At some point the tension builds too high, so that a resolution of the tension is welcomed at whatever cost, and international conflict is transformed into war.[1]

The equilibrium of anarchy is so psychologically delicate that almost anything will initiate the process of deterioration—cutting off Jenkins' ear, for example, or losing an international soccer match. It is somewhat like a tiny thermal instability in the Pacific atmosphere which, once disturbed, grows into a typhoon. At a point further along, the process is similar to a kettle of very hot water which, if shaken, will immediately begin to boil.

The process can be stopped only by a strong imbalance of power disinclined toward violence, or reversed by an extraordinarily wise and agile diplomacy. At best, the process in the long run can only be delayed, for power ratios are ever changing while wise men are rarely at the helm. After Bismarck was dismissed, Germany, secure in land power, decided to challenge Britain's naval supremacy (the British interpreted it that way), and the Kaiser let Bismarck's treaty with Russia lapse, exposing Germany on two fronts. The European imbalance of power changed by 1907 to an equilibrium of power with consequent heightening of anxiety and tension. The process was similar to a chain reaction. As each mobilization was ordered in 1914, it was defended as a necessary reaction to a previous decision by a nation in the other coalition.

The psychology of anarchy is also important in civil conflict. When a generalized dissatisfaction finds a focus, whether in a council of conspirators or a more fully formed rebel regime, the two centers of authority tend to become like two nations. Each is ignorant of the other's true intentions, anxious and fearful. By the time Lincoln was inaugurated in 1861 the dynamic of anarchy was already far advanced, for President Buchanan had simply done nothing after the November election, thus permitting the Confederate movement to form. Sometimes, as in the Mexican Revolution of 1910 and subsequent years, or in China in the 1920s under the warlords, there are so many centers of power that the civil conflict is similar to an international system.

And, as noted already, international and civil conflict feed upon each other. From at least as early as Ch'in times up to present "wars of national liberation," nations have seen advantage in stirring up conflict in other nations, while civil conflicts like the French and Russian revolutions have led to international conflict.

Also, war places great strains on a nation's ability to manage its internal problems, tending to produce civil disorder whether or not other nations encourage it. Athens' defeat in the Peloponnesian War enabled the oligarchs to seize power. The wars of Louis XIV and his successors helped bring on the French revolution. The defeats suffered by Russia and Germany in World War I made leftist and rightist totalitarianisms possible, and the Cold War has moved American politics steadily to the right. Anarchy between nations transmits its fear into each nation's internal situation.

B. Anarchy's Criticism of the Other Two Hypotheses

The theory that anarchy causes war has important implications for the nature and behavior of man, which we considered in Chapter 2 as the cause of war, and for the theory that war is caused by differences in the natures of nations, which we discussed in Chapter 3.

1. *Anarchy and Human Nature.* Anarchy theory offers a solution to an extremely significant question: If a violent human nature explains international violence, how can that same violent human nature explain peace and order at the civil or domestic level? An innately aggressive or otherwise faulty human nature fails to account for the usual condition of reasonably harmonious order at the local, provincial, and national levels

of society while there is continual fear of large-scale violence at the international level.

The solution offered by anarchy theory is that, first and foremost, human nature is not the main cause of international conflict at all, because anarchy is itself the main cause; and, secondly, that anarchy stirs up and magnifies that human fear which underlies aggressive and violent behavior. Anarchy also has strong behavioral implications, through fear, for man as greedy, glory-seeking, bored, irrational, nationalist, and true believer. in short, anarchical fear intensifies those aspects of the nature and behavior of man which lead to conflict, and directs them toward international violence.[2]

Anarchy theory asserts that it is the existence of government (non-anarchy) as a reconciling and enforcing authority which provides order within a nation, and that the absence of such an authority at the international level explains the violence there.

2. *Anarchy and the Differing Natures of Nations.* Rousseau knew that the Christian kingdoms of Europe had many cultural features in common. Hamilton knew that the thirteen American states had even more in common, including language. Yet the thrust of the Rousseau-Hamilton argument cited in Chapter 4 is that, despite all this, harmony among independent "sovereign" states is not to be expected.

The anarchy argument says that, as we noted in Chapter 3, no matter how great their cultural similarity, nations will continue in conflict and intermittent violence if they are independent. Take for example the histories of the early Chinese, Indian, Greek, Italian and German interstate systems, or the behavior of the Arab nations toward each other today.

The anarchy argument further says that nations whose cultural backgrounds are very different can cooperate, if the balance of power arrangement makes this desirable. Examples are Cardinal Richelieu's use of Swedish Protestant troops against Catholic Austria during the wars of religion, or Christian France's long arrangement with the Moslem Ottomans against Austria, and the alliance between capitalist US and communist USSR in World War II.

That it is the existence of independent nations which causes conflict, rather than the existence of independent cultural entities, is further argued by the fact that nations have successfully contained diverse cultures throughout history, especially in the great empires described in the *Summary of International History*. But the same is true even in small political units: Switzerland is an example, as are New York City at the turn of the century or Hawaii today.

Again, the anarchy argument asserts that there can be no tolerable harmony, however great the cultural unity, without government as a reconciling and enforcing authority. However natural the nation may be thought to be, it is not a nation unless it has a government, and governments are artificed by men. New nations or new forms of government for old nations come into existence, after conquest or intermarriage or revolution or agreement, in accordance with somebody's conscious design, perhaps that of a prince or a constituent assembly of the people, and this government can then usher in other sweeping changes.

Owing to conquest, Arab culture supplanted the gothic in Southern Spain, Spanish culture displaced the Aztecan and the Incan, and American ways prevailed in New Mexico—not wholly but largely, and within one or two generations. Owing to intermarriage, the language and ways of Castile came to prevail in Spain. Owing to revolution, from 1917 onward a thorough-going new way of life was installed in Russia by government decree. After a coup Mustapha Kemal Pasha (Ataturk) remade Turkey in the 1920s. Owing to a mixture of parliamentary and revolutionary politics, within a very few years in Hitler's Germany evil became good and good became evil. By agreement in 1789, the American states abolished the slave trade on a given future day and installed a new political process whereby other drastic changes—abolition, prohibition, women's rights and blacks' rights—have been imposed throughout the republic on a given day.

Anarchy theory emphasizes that the "span of control" available to the government of a modern nation enables it to promote cultural uniformity within, but also to manipulate the public's perceptions of differences in the natures of nations. Thus, when the psychology of anarchy is sufficiently far advanced from anxiety to hatred, leaders arouse an awareness of similarity-dissimilarity and of the threat which "they" pose to "us." The American citizen was urged to alter within a few months in 1945 his perception of the Russians from that of friends to that of enemies; from that of people who, though alien, were doing their best, to that of people, alien, doing their worst; from an emphasis on cultural similarities to one of cultural differences. The same thing happened to the Russians. The ethnocentric view of things comes increasingly into play as the deteriorating psychology of anarchy gains momentum.

In summary, anarchy theory asserts that independent nations cannot get along together because of the fear inherent in anarchy which evokes the worst in human nature and magnifies the contrasts between the culture of one's own nation and the cultures of other nations.

C. A General Theory of War

At the close of our consideration of the causes of international conflict we could try to become very precise. We could attempt to reduce our conclusions to formal logic or to mathematical symbols. But it would be a pretense of precision. We would find ourselves forced to become, first, too simplistic, and secondly, trying to get out of that dilemma, overly elaborate. We would be substituting other language which few understand well for words which most understand fairly well. Words are thought to be imprecise as compared with mathematical symbols, but this is not true if the mathematical symbols stand for things which can be defined (qualified) only in imprecise verbal phrases and which can be counted or measured (quantified) only in the roughest sort of way for manipulation.

For example, a statistician says that "Mathematics per se tells us nothing new about reality" since all the mathematical conclusions depend upon "the original definitions, assumptions, and rules and are not determined empirically." Moreover, these mathematical conclusions then have to be translated back into the verbal language if they are to be useful.[3]

In the interdisciplinary approach to the study of international relations, it may ultimately prove possible to accumulate enough depth interviews and statistics on opinion and voting in different parts of the international system, and manipulate these data by reliable methods,[4] so that we can identify all strands of human psychology and assign weights to them as they relate to international conflict and cooperation. We might be able to identify all categories of socio-cultural diversity, knowing where their boundaries fall, and learn how to measure the degree to which nations actually differ in each category as well as the degree to which populations perceive these differences. We might become able to establish precisely the point on a warmth-hostility yardstick where relations between any two nations can be placed at a given time, and measure exactly the expectations prevalent within the global system or its coalitions. But, as we noted in Chapter 4, the prospects for accomplishing all this do not seem so bright now as they did fifteen years ago.

The most we can do here is to interrelate the causes of war into a "constellation of variables" which is reasonable and logical in the light of our consideration of all the alleged causes. We can rank the variables in terms of their significance as causes, and we can even suggest the weights that seem appropriate for each.

Validation of our explanatory theory must rest in the first instance on whether it corresponds to the judgments of other students of international history, illuminated where possible by positivist studies. In the second instance and on down the road, our theory can be validated or not only by its ability to predict future conflict, as will be attempted in Chapter 7.

1. *The First Variable.* The arguments examined in Chapters 2 through 4 and applied to the historical behavior summarized in the first chapter, entitle anarchy to first rank among causes of war. It explains more than the other two hypotheses, and endows them with much of the explanatory vigor they do possess.

We reach this conclusion, not so much because war is always between independent nations, for this in a way no more than repeats what ought to be obvious. Rather, it is because sovereign independence, attempting to co-exist in an anarchic fear relationship with other sovereign entities, explains so much. For the boundaries of nations shift, and the cultural makeup of their populations changes, while human nature and behavior remain much the same, yet conflict and violence continue to coincide with the frontiers of independent nations.

Sovereignty in its internal manifestation means, as we have seen, that the government, by legislation and administration and because the nation is the nexus of strong social pressures, can impose a conformity of legal and social practice. The national government controls to a high degree individual perception and reaction. Sovereignty in its external manifestation means that the nation and its society must be eternally on guard against other independent national societies. This fearful "posture of gladiators" explains why so few nations have managed their relationships so as to create "security communities" with respect to each other.

The ability of coercive government force to make its dominium real, and thus clothe itself with the legitimate authority of sovereignty, explains why mergers of hitherto independent nations have so often endured and the average size of states has increased through history. The principle of sovereign independence explains why the state resulting from merger has become the new unit in international conflict. The search by independent units for security explains why an international system is always in either a fragile imbalance-of-power configuration or in an even more delicate equilibrium-of-power configuration.

And this condition of anarchy also explains much of international cooperation. A nation needs allies and trading partners—and in our time programs of economic and military aid and of student and cultural exchange—if it is to compete in the competition which anarchy imposes upon all.

The theory of anarchy among sovereign nations emphasizes order within the nation and disorder among nations. Anarchy provides opportunity to leaders and elites to express aggressiveness, glory-seeking and greed in socially approved ways because these are directed against other nations. Indeed, the role of sovereign chieftain is also the role of chief glory-seeker for the nation.

The opportunity thus afforded leaders is an important endorsement of the theory of anarchy. But it is not necessary that statesmen possess such drives. It is enough if they are simply frightened by the external threat and afraid they will not handle it well. The psychology of anarchy is even more powerful if statesmen are irrational, or become so through fear.

The nature of internal sovereignty produces a hierarchy of decisional roles whose responsibilities and authorities are spelled out by national law and custom. All these roles focus internally upon the nation while some focus externally upon the international system from the viewpoint of the nation. These roles are assumed, ready-made and with all their precedents, by individuals who see that they have no status apart from the nation. If a leader comes to office early in a process of deteriorating anarchical relationships, he will have ampler policy leeway than in the later stages, but his role is ever oriented toward the nation and he fills it as nationalist and true believer. Even if he is a sturdy and rational person, when he perceives threat from some point in the international system he probably will respond in kind. And the rarest thing—though not unheard of—is the leader who can transcend this thrust of anarchy toward violence.

For these reasons we give first rank and greatest causal weight to anarchy. It is the principal variable in explaining international conflict. It is innate in the nature of all international systems, up to the point at which they may disappear into empires, and it reappears so soon as empires begin to disintegrate into new international systems. Innate in the world system today, it is greatly intensified psychologically by modern weapons. Its presence is constant. It is a barrier of suspicion between any two independent nations, even Canada and US. But it varies in intensity between any two nations and between opposing coalitions.

Anarchy has great explanatory power, but it explains with great economy. It says simply that sovereign independence creates an entity which is subjectively perceived to be a cultural unity, and that several such sovereign entities, each unable to control or even predict the behavior of others, necessarily interact in covert fear and overt hostility.

The theory of anarchy does not require that all nations be viewed as equally sovereign and independent. They are equally sovereign only in the juridical sense, as entities in international law. They vary widely in their actual capacity to take independent action. But it is important for the theory of anarchy that in foreign policy each nation of whatever size is autonomous and secretive, leaving statesmen in other nations to guess what will happen, knowing only that every nation has some capacity in coercive force and some ability to make trouble.

We can agree that anarchy is a "permissive cause" but it is more than merely latent or quiescent. It engenders such fear and such grotesque perceptions of the differences between one's own nation and others that it is at all times actively rearranging the international system, urging it on toward violence.

Alan Dowty has published a significant study. Using quantification as far as he could, he classified "conflict constellations" of states in the Classical World, pre-Mogul India, Renaissance Europe, and 19th-century Latin America. His results indicate that "disputes," where issues of substance such as border questions or commercial rivalry exist, are far more apt to be peacefully adjusted than are "tensions" where there is fear of one state by another, whether conquest is involved or simply fear of another state's power. The study found too that coalition-building tends to begin with fears, and then goes on, with all the "balancing" being purely incidental to fear.[5]

Dowty's study was aimed at learning how much of international conflict ought to be attributed to sovereignty and anarchy. He appears to conclude that nearly all the conflict that leads to war is so caused.

Robert Wesson, in a more traditional study of the rise and fall of empires, concluded that imperialism is the result of the search for security by states and by men who cling to the illusion that a few more increments of power will bring them security. Moreover—and contrary to the theory of Hobson and Lenin—the struggle for markets and raw materials was far less the cause of imperialism than was insecurity; and "the more insecurity, the less room for morality."[6]

2. *The Second Variable.* We have already drawn into the theory of anarchy as our first variable some important elements of the other two hypotheses, especially in the psychological sense. The individual is slower to perceive differences and threats within his nation, quicker to perceive them abroad. If his interests are threatened by others in his nation, he expects accommodation. If he believes the national interest is threatened by other nations, he expects conflict. There is a self-confirming expectation of accommodation at home and of violence abroad.

Thus his fear is aroused, enhanced and confirmed by international anarchy. His nationalism is simply the reflection of the existence of his nation, which must be the best because he belongs to it (the Ego-We). His belief system is a religion or ideology with his nation's brand on it. His ignorance is in part induced by the government's control of the educational process, which tends to exclude proposals to transcend ethnocentrism or resolve international conflict.

His ignorance and irrationality are heightened by what he learns from leaders, the mass media, and his fellow citizens, who are likewise frightened nationalists and true believers. As international relations deteriorate, social pressures toward conformity make him more frightened not to conform and more willing to hate the common enemy.

Nevertheless, some aspects of the nature and behavior of man are in themselves causes of war. We see this especially in the psychological make-up of leaders and elites—particularly those newly come to power. International anarchy often contributes to the domestic conditions in which such men can seize power, and certainly it invites them then to enter upon a career of national aggrandizement. But in many historical situations the chronic condition of international anarchy would not have produced war had there not been nations headed by leaders who were aggressive or greedy or glory-seeking and who were backed by elites which saw violence as a means to a desirable end or as a desirable end in itself.

Princely glory backed by warrior elites played so great a part from early times through the reign of Louis XIV, while leaders like Napoleon and Hitler have been so significant in more modern times, that we rank this second in our causal variables. Here we include leaders and elites who have sought plunder and promotion in war, as well as those commercial and industrial elites that have used the force of the state to acquire colonies or markets abroad or have made their living on defense contracts.

Leadership that is aggressive constitutes an active agency of international conflict with a causal autonomy of its own. At the same time, nations displaying this leadership intensify the level of anarchy within the international system. And nations merely seem in many cases to have an aggressive leadership, because of operation of fear and we-they standards within the environment of anarchy. Indeed we accept the thesis that the warrior ethic itself may have been a routinized or institutionalized reaction to the environment of anarchy. And certainly the ethic is reinforced in individual men by that underlying fear or conviction of inferiority that begets aggression, greed, and glory-seeking.

We noted in Chapter 2 that leaders tend to have interesting psycho-physical histories, being extraordinarily short of stature or having some other handicap, and in Chapter 4 Schuman's remark that statesmen do lust for power, else they wouldn't become statesmen. Rosecrance says that the dependence of revolutionary elites on mass support gives rise to an elite insecurity which forces the elite to divert mass attention from internal problems by engaging in international conflict.[7] Boulding notes that "all the skills which lead to a rise to power unfit people to exercise it" and that we need world institutions to offset this.[8]

Unfortunately for Rosecrance's thesis, USSR and China have been headed by revolutionary insecure elites for some time now, but they have tended to walk very carefully abroad, and especially when their domestic situations were stormiest. It would be truer to say that national leaders are innately insecure persons anyway but that in today's international system they have every right to feel insecure; more about this in Chapter 6.

In working out the theory of anarchy as our principal causal variable, we subsumed important elements of the nature of man, especially the psychology of fear. We also included important elements of the natures of nations, especially the way state sovereignty produces cultural uniformity within the nation while anarchy magnifies cultural differences between nations. In arriving at the theory of the aggressive nation as the second causal variable, we subsume the more aggressive traits of greed and glory-seeking in the nature and behavior of man, never forgetting that fear underlies them.

Aggressive behavior in one nation will evoke fear in the elites of other nations, followed by reciprocal aggressiveness. Aggressive leadership in a nation will be similarly aggressive in stamping out cultural nonconformity within its frontiers and in emphasizing the cultural foreignness of other nations. Aggressive and defensive nations alike, however, emphasize their cultural similarities with allied nations. This is a part of the dynamic of anarchy, and it is in constant operation, but it operates more intensely when there is indeed an aggressive, expansionist nation within the system—a Ch'in or a Magadha or a Prussia, the Caliphate of Omar, the France of Napoleon, or the Germany of Hitler.[9]

3. *The Third Variable.* We now look for other active agents of international conflict which can touch off or accelerate the dynamic of anarchy and fear. Having exhausted the other two hypotheses, we turn back to the differing natures of nations. These elements of difference, each said to be a determinant of conflict, are race, language, myths and customs, religion-ideology, type of government, and economic system.

As we saw in Chapter 3, there is too little coincidence between most of these differences and the actual incidence of international conflict in history to justify their inclusion in a general theory of the causes of war. They are to be seen not as active causal agents but as latencies, as potentialities. They achieve a certain causal value only when emphasized by national leadership to magnify the we-they relationship in preparation for international aggression, or when exaggerated by the public fears which accompany the deteriorating psychological process of anarchy.

Some of these elements are more latent than others. Myths, histories, customs and traditions are quiescent. The same is true of race and to a degree of language. Consciousness of these elements has to be aroused deliberately. They are resistant to change, although all except race have upon occasion been changed rather quickly.

In contrast, men have frequently been conscious of their government, and forms of government and legal norms have changed suddenly. Men have also been conscious of their religion, and of its difference from other religions, and new religions have been embraced or imposed suddenly.

Until modern times, as we have seen, men were not conscious of their economic systems and these systems changed slowly. With the industrial revolution, however, change came quickly. The type of economic system which a nation ought to have became a political issue, connected with the nation's form of government. Thus ideology entered international history in the 18th century with peculiar vigor. Republican liberalism supported transfer of political authority from monarch and aristocracy to businessmen and lawyers.

Then came socialism and Marxism, democratic socialism, and communist socialism, supporting transfer of political authority from businessmen to workers. As a counter-movement, fascism placed the economy and most other aspects of life under the control of a single extremely nationalistic party and its charismatic leader.

Men have not only become highly conscious of their type of government, economic system, and ideology, but, as we have noted, all three have tended to change rapidly and together. It is this simultaneity of change that prevents our trying to choose one of these three elements and call it the determinant. Instead, we must view them all together as comprising one package which contains governmental, economic, and ideological components. It is this package as a whole which has moved from passivity to activity during the past two or three centuries, so that we may award it a causal autonomy entitling it to third rank among the variables which explain war.

What shall we call this package? Is there some basis on which we can assign to one of its elements a priority in terms of its relation to international conflict? Bearing in mind the causal role played by religion in the Crusades and in Europe's wars of the 16th and 17th centuries, one is tempted to emphasize religion-ideology. The significance of republican ideas in the wars of independence between the Western hemisphere and Europe, the French Revolution and the Napoleonic era, and in the "war to make the world safe for democracy" adds weight to the argument. Similarly significant were fascism and communism in World War II, the conflict between communism and liberalism in the Cold War, and the influence of socialist and communist ideologies in the anti-colonial conflicts of the post-World War II decades.

Moreover, whereas a form of government is particular to a particular nation, for we have no trans-national governments, and an economic system is also peculiar to a certain nation or can be made so by the government, it is the idea of a form of government that is exportable; it is the idea of socialism or capitalism that is trans-national or international. In this sense, ideology as the bearer of such ideas deserves a certain priority. Ideas cannot in the main be stopped at national frontiers. Ideology is not wholly malleable or excludable by the nation's leadership, even in totalitarian countries.

Ideologies have tremendous subversive possibilities, even without the organized support of an outside nation. Americans did not have to go abroad in order to influence republican movements from Spanish America to Tsarist Russia. In the later 18th and 19th centuries, republicans and liberals everywhere looked to France for inspiration. Recently communist parties outside the Soviet Union would have looked to Moscow for leadership even had there been no disciplined apparatus trying to assure adherence to the Moscow party line.

Ideology, as bearer of notions of government and economy which comport to its overall worldview, can hamper or help the initiatives and responses of governments at the international level of conflict, hence it is peculiarly autonomous in helping to explain that conflict.

Ideology is also important in its ability to explain international cooperation. There have been exceptions, but as we have seen nations tend to ally themselves and to form "security communities" with nations of like ideology, although usually their form of government and their type of economy will be similar too. At the least, they are apt to form a neutral "no-war" community with like nations. Alignments in balance-of-power coalitions have been drawn between ideologies with substantial consistency since the wars of the French Revolution.

Thus we shall refer to this group of elements as the "ideological package," bearing in mind that it is a politico-economic-ideological package. It is this package that is a free-floating irritant over and above the condition of international anarchy. At the same time it intensifies the psychology of anarchy and helps determine coalitions as conflict deepens into violence.

Rosecrance, if we understand him aright, holds that the rise of secular ideologies such as French egalitarianism or Soviet communism is primarily responsible for the origin of major conflicts.[10] For the new leaders who rose to power with the new ideology, he says, are so insecure that they embark on adventure abroad to abridge dissension at home, as we just noted. But it is easy to overemphasize the autonomy of the ideological package.

In the hierarchy of causes, the first thing to remember is that any given nation exists as one among an anarchy of independent nations and that its citizens or subjects share an identification with the nation that is called nationalism, as we discussed in Chapter 2. Nationalism has no idea content of its own; it is simply the "we" against the "they." Nationalism is the barren mother who embraces whatever the prevailing religion or ideology of the nation may be. When new leaders install a new ideology-economy-government, nationalism promptly assimilates these components to itself, along with the more latent elements of cultural particularism, enhancing their virtue relative to the politico-economic ideology of other nations. As the psychology of anarchy takes hold, these things become worth fighting and dying for, along with the nation and its leaders.

It is not necessary to decide whether a new ideology lifts new leaders to national power or whether it is the other way round. Probably Mussolini and his Black Shirts were more important than their ideology when they seized power, whereas communism's "Bread and Peace" message had more to do with the success of the October Revolution than did Lenin and his pitiful band of Bolsheviks. Fortunately, from Cromwell's time until now, the new leaders and the new ideology always come to national power together.

But it is necessary to remember that these revolutions are primarily of domestic significance until one of them is successful in seizing control of a national government, whereupon the new leadership and its ideology confront other national governments across the arena of international anarchy.

4. *The Theory of War.* We have drawn our first variable from the third hypothesis, the anarchic nature of the international system, with important connections to the other two hypotheses. Our second variable is drawn mainly from the first hypothesis, the nature and behavior of man, with important connections to the other two. And we have drawn our third variable from the second hypothesis, the differing natures of nations, with strong connections to the other two.

In an imprecise but not arbitrary way, we might assign to anarchy a relative weight of ten, the aggressive elite a weight of four, and the ideological package a weight of three. Alternatively, we might consider anarchy as the constant and the other two as variables which appear in the international system from time to time and interact with the constant to intensify it. At any given time, some national leaders and elites are more aggressive than others, but a Napoleon or a Hitler, or a Spartan or fascist elite, appears only now and then. Similarly, the ideological package has had some influence during much of history but it has become virulent only for comparatively brief periods and in a relatively few international systems. Unfortunately, the present global system is one of them.

Our explanation of international conflict, then, expressed as sparely as may be, is:

> Conflict and violence are inherent within a system of independent nations because the nations must interact in an environment of anarchy and fear, and the level of conflict is raised when there is present in the system at least one aggressive national leadership or at least two competing religions or politico-economic ideologies.

> Conflict moves under the impulse of improving technology through alliance-building and violence to the extinction of the system and its incorporation by conquest, marriage, or agreement into one nation-empire and/or to its subordination in a larger system.

Fleshed out a bit, the theory can take the following form:

VARIABLE I. *Anarchy,* meaning the lack within the international system of centralized institutions to make, interpret, apply and enforce rules of peaceful change;

Hence suspicion and fear, with secret power politics, polarization of alliances, escalating arms races, trade-currency crises, and mounting points of tension;

Hence mutual hostility in which religion or politico-economic ideology and cultural particularities are assimilated to the Ego-We and are seen as threatened by They;

Hence a nationalist aggressiveness which is at bottom a defensive reaction to fear, that is, a false aggressiveness.

VARIABLE II. *Aggressive Nations,* dominated by elites whose values are militant, greedy, and expansionist;

These elites being headed by leaders, often charismatic, who are aggressive owing to fear engendered by inferiority and interpersonal conflict;

These aggressive leaders/elites having come to power through civil conflict and consequent radicalization of the nation.

VARIABLE III. *Differing Religions or Politico-Economic Ideologies,* in our time liberalism, communism, and fascism;

Fascism being innately more militant than the others, though it is a matter of degree, for all ideologies have their messianic phases, as do some religions;

The messianic ideology having come to prevail in a nation through civil conflict and consequent radicalization of the nation.

International conflict moves toward violence in proportion to the intensities of Variables I, II, and III, as these interact in mutual intensification. Their thrust is toward extinction of the international system, usually by conquest but sometimes by agreement including dynastic intermarriage, and the integration of the system into one nation-empire. Owing to improving technology in transport, communication, and weaponry, the arena of conflict expands so that the historical trend—sometimes interrupted—has been for smaller systems and integrated empires to become units in larger international systems, culminating in the present planetary system.

D. Civil Radicalization

In nations on the fringes of the world system there are still coups in which self-important generals seize power rather easily without the help of ideology. But in the great nations since the time of Cromwell, as mentioned earlier, new aggressive elites and raging ideologies have come to power together, not in mere coups but in revolutionary movements which have sought to address very real problems, deeply and widely felt, concerning the distribution of political power, economic well-being, and social equality. As it is out of this process of civil radicalization that we get our Variables II and III, we must set down here the causes of that radicalization, which were developed during a seminar at Wake Forest University.

CAUSE A. *Inability of the national government to cope with external stresses* of

1. International violence and expectation thereof, including diversion of resources to defense and the possibility of foreign intervention in civil conflict; and
2. International trade and currency imbalances, trans-national environmental deterioration, and worldwide depression.

CAUSE B. *Failure of the national government to cope with internal stresses* of

1. Differences of economic or hereditary class, religion or ideology, race or caste, language and culture;
2. Underdevelopment, including economic scarcity in relation to population; or
3. Overdevelopment, including overconsumption with resource depletion and environmental deterioration.

CAUSE C. *Salience of alternative leaders-elites and belief systems*, meaning the availability and prominence of new leaders offering new cures for old problems.

Radicalization occurs in proportion to the intensities of Causes A, B, and C, as these interact in mutual intensification.

In nations with small middle classes, radicalization tends to move toward the extreme left (autocratic one-party socialism); in nations with large middle classes, toward the extreme right (autocratic one-party fascism), but there are typically short-term moves in the contrary direction.

Both are messianic, but the extreme right is more aggressive in international relations than the extreme left. In either case, the moderate center is suppressed.

Cause A is drawn from Chapter 1's *Summary of International History*, especially the description in Section B of the interplay between international and civil conflict, and from Chapter 4 on anarchy. Cause B is derived from the *Summary* and from Chapter 3 on socio-cultural and economic differences. Cause C is based mainly on the *Summary* and Chapter 2 on the psychological origins of aggressive behavior.

In these five chapters we have discussed many alleged causes of war.[11] We've also described several schools of thought concerning the proper way of getting at the causes of war and peace. There is another that perhaps should be mentioned. It seems to be centered at the *Journal of Peace Research* at Oslo and consists mainly of Europeans but with some connections to American scholars. As best one can tell, this school tries to bring a Marxist-Leninist framework of thought to the study of war and peace, somehow managing to see the principal threat of war in the New Imperialism of the industrialized North against the impoverished LDCs of the South. This is baffling, for these countries are indeed poor and they are also disunited and they have negligible economic and military capabilities. Their importance, as already mentioned, is merely that, as they radicalize, they are apt to suck in the competing great nations, and this future process will be discussed in Chapter 7.

Marxist analysis, like sociological analysis, is a framework that cannot productively be brought to bear upon the behavior of the anarchic international system. Their place is to analyze civic radicalization in terms of economic disparities and social cleavages which result in the introduction into the international system of aggressive nations (Variable II) and competing politico-economic ideologies (Variable III).

E. A Way of Looking at the World International System

With the warning that what follows is analogy and metaphor, we offer this "model" in the hope that it will serve to illuminate how the system works.[12]

We see the system from above, as it were, coextensive with the planet. But it is laid out in a circular arena, with some 170 nodes sprinkled around its perimeter, each node representing the decision-making apparatus of a sovereign nation. Most of these nodes are small, some large. From each depends its own national society with its interest groups and political parties and mass media, feeding inputs into the decisional node. Some such inputs affect foreign-policy outputs.

Lines representing force or energy, communications or stimuli, connect each of the nodes with each of the other nodes. Some of these lines are heavy, representing frequent and significant interaction; some are very light, representing little more than mutual awareness of existence as nations. These lines alter in density from time to time.

The nodes can be seen as relating to each other in their actual geographic relationships, but for our purposes they must be seen mainly as clustering in different groupings at different times as determined by their balance-of-power alignments. The clustering is in continual flux, for no alliance or coalition is as tight or loose on Friday as it was on Monday, and, with few exceptions, no neutral nation will be placed tomorrow with respect to the clusterings precisely as it is today.

The clusterings are toward the perimeter of our circular force-field. There is nothing in the center of the arena: no unicentric authority which can determine the behavior of the nodes; no central power house, transformer or homeostatic device; no central matrix. There is, however, a large node representing the United Nations, located off-center. Many smaller nodes nearby represent the international organizations which perform specific functions. There are lines connecting nearly all the national nodes with the UN, and other lines connecting many of the nations with each of the international organizations.

Each line connecting national nodes may be thought of as a cable. The cable consists of many strands, some primarily economic, some primarily cultural or social, others primarily political. Some, especially strands which are ideational or ideological in nature, may by-pass the national nodes and enter directly into the national societies which underlie the nodes.

Our model is not based on a simple behaviorist stimulus-response dynamic. Instead, each national decisional node receives an impulse along some particular cable and in normal times reflects upon it. Before responding, it communicates with the underlying society, and perhaps with other national nodes. The response is a conscious one, not a mere reflex action. The decisional node has a certain leeway within which to formulate its response, and it deliberates and consults before responding. Lest we stray too far afield in a mechanistic model, let us affirm that each decisional node is manned by human beings, each with his life experiences and his psychological traits.

Our force-field has a kind of temperature. Let us say its temperature is, at the moment, well below the boiling point, with no large aggressive node and with ideological competition at moderate levels.

Unfortunately, the decisional autonomy of each node poses a constant threat to this thermal equilibrium. Normally, people and things and ideas flow fairly freely through the cables. But if they are blocked at another node, by intent or by chance, the temperature begins to rise, first along that cable but then along others. The murder or imprisonment of a tourist, the jamming of a radio broadcast, a slight increase in tariffs, a change in the price of oil—any of these can raise the temperature of the system. Its equilibrium is so delicate that any change anywhere threatens it. Even a decrease in foreign tariffs may be disturbing, if the node is in doubt as to what the decrease means or what response it should make. An increase in the value of the German mark may be viewed by some nodes as a threat; a decrease may be perceived by others as a threat.

Disequilibria—thermal instabilities—can arise between any nodes within our force-field. The reconciling energies of diplomacy may act as a substitute homeostatic device, restoring equilibrium and lowering temperatures. For example, the cables in Southeast Asia may become overloaded and hot, but stimuli sent to these nodes from other parts of the force-field may evoke responses within these nodes which will temporarily return the Southeast Asian subsystem to a new equilibrium, thus reducing pressures and temperatures throughout the whole field. Each part affects the whole, and it *can* work either way, toward cooperative cooling or conflictual heating.

Stimuli sent along the cables may be thought of as positive, neutral, or negative, the first working toward "security-communities," the next toward "no-war communities," and the last toward "war communities." Unfortunately, nodal autonomy imparts to the system a built-in bias toward instability due to uncertainty and suspicion and fear, therefore toward negative impulses. Hence diplomacy is in the position of trying repeatedly to sweep back the tide, with a sort of statistical probability that some of the waves will either get by the broom or overwhelm it. Any fuse box can be overloaded, and our system has no circuit breaker devices except nodal diplomacy and the services of the UN. Thus, overload in Southeast Asia or the Middle East may be reduced, with temperatures brought back down, but next year they may be up again, with disappointment evoking stimuli that are even more threatening.

In this way, negative charges along the cables come to predominate with the passage of time. The whole cable, whatever its economic and cultural strands, becomes politicized, perhaps intensified by ideological exchanges and sharp perceptions of aggressive intent. Positive impulses are overridden by negative ones. Ideational strands can bypass the decisional nodes only rarely. Nodal decision-making is less and less deliberate, more and more behaviorist or at least like Mowrer's two-step formula whereby a negative stimulus begets a fear reaction and then an almost instantaneous negative response.

As negative impulses predominate along some cables, positive impulses go out along others in the search for allies. Foreign aid—economic, technical, and military—goes out along the cables; impulses are transmitted to energize subversive movements. Neutral impulses become fewer. Through negative impulses along some cables that repel one node from another, and positive impulses along others that attract nodes together, most nodes and regional clusters are polarized into two large clusters.[13] Ideological forces can be significant determinants of which nodes join which cluster, while if there is a great aggressive node it will drive away more nodes than it will attract to its cluster. The configuration of our force-field at any given time is the totality of these attractions and repulsions at that moment in the continuous process of nodal interaction.

Great-nation nodes are always connected to each other by thick cables of interaction. They are the principal attracters and repellers, as if by their weight or density, so must move to the centers of the two opposing clusters. The decisional apparatus within a great node may yet send out positive impulses that will override the mounting negative currents, so that there will be temporarily a lessening of tensions throughout the forcefield and a loosening within the clusters. But in time the thermal instabilities will reassert themselves and the decisional nodes will move again into Mowrer behavior. Clusters will rearrange for the last time and tighten in a kind of paroxysm of fear to the flashpoint. The system, lacking any homeostatic device, will become overloaded and explode into violence.[14]

F. Correlation of Explanation with Historical Generalizations

Referring back to the descriptive generalizations in Section B of Chapter 1 on the way international systems behave, we understand now why, when nations come into contact and have to interact, they are tentative about whether to cooperate, even though there may be much to be gained by it. For there is ignorance of the others' intentions, so they must be on guard. It is natural that cooperation between two nations should worry third nations, and that even a concession by a nation to one's own nation might be seen as the Greeks bearing gifts. What with innate suspicion and misinterpreted signals, it is not astonishing that conflict repeatedly transcends cooperation in history.

The enunciation of grandiose national goals need not now mislead us. There is one overriding goal, security, and in an anarchic environment even conquest can be justified in its name. And there is one overriding strategy, balance-of-power politics, because fear needs friends, hence the coalition-building. And the list of tactics employed, such as lying, bribery and subversion, sorry though they may be, can be understood as acts evoked by fear or by fear's son, aggression.

There is no mystery about the configurations into which international systems form. If there is just one great nation in the system, the others will be scared and will combine against it unless it can persuade or threaten some of them into joining its side. If there are two great nations, they will fear each other, and among the lesser nations some will fear the one great nation more than the other, so after the bag of tricks has been exhausted, each will be at the center of a coalition. And when there are several great nations of more or less equal power and all of them afraid of each other, like will join with like when feasible, but like will join with unlike if that seems the best hope for security.

Nor need we wonder now why the process always ends up with just two coalitions in the system. The process is fueled by fear so—though perhaps with setbacks—it must go on. Whatever the configuration of the system in peaceful times, fear will set about to line it up into one side and an opposing side. And we understand why lesser nations may be able to stay neutral but a great nation cannot: its size and power are greatly to be feared, so anarchy's mutual hostilities work most strongly upon it.[15]

We understand why coalitions are so uneasy and unstable: the ignorance of one ally as to what another ally will really do in the pinch makes suspicion ever present, so that threats between allies, or between a committed nation and an uncommitted one, are not infrequent.

Small wonder, then, what with an unstable balance of power between two coalitions, each of which is internally unstable, that international systems eventually always stumble into war.

By identifying that "obscure dynamic" mentioned in Chapter 1 as anarchic fear, intensified at times by the presence of an aggressive nation or by competing ideologies, we understand why the historical thrust is necessarily toward an imbalance of power. The fuel that provides the thrust is fear, and fear cannot be allayed by a mere equilibrium of power.[16]

We understand too why cultural likeness between nations does not produce their integration: national governments and their mutual fears stand in the way.

And we understand why integration by agreement is so rare: the nations fear and distrust each other too much, so that the long-term interest is sacrificed to the short-term fear.

Turning now to the generalizations in Section B of Chapter 1 on how domestic behavior affects international systems, we can understand why most national decision-makers perform so poorly, for they operate under conditions biased against well-meant statesmanship. They may have ability and good intentions but they have an impossible job. Blinded by fear of other nations and fear of making wrong decisions, as well as fear of civil conflict arising from internal problems, they are muddled by personal belief in their national ideology and may be hamstrung by a public opinion which they themselves had helped to evoke. They cannot be sure their subordinates are telling them the truth; they do not know even what their allies intend, much less their enemies; they misinterpret and mis-send signals; they are prey to pure chance. Understanding of the situation is not theirs. They over-react or under-react, and in the end tension-weariness overtakes them. Moreover, the vainglory and greed and conviction of inferiority that drove them to seek high office assures that few who become statesmen will be mature, balanced, or wise.

We understand how a national government, even in the most open of societies, can require and obtain conformity as international conflict advances. If the public's fears are great enough, and if the government says it is necessary, controls that approach totality will be accepted. But we can understand too why, when needed reforms have been long delayed by fear of war and by war, and the nation bends or breaks apart under combined internal and external pressures, people listen to new leaders who offer new ideologies and policies, so that civic radicalization occurs.

And we can understand why the advantage in international conflict lies with those hyper-aggressive leaders and elites that come to power as the result of civic radicalization, for they are willing to play the game of power politics by instilling fear abroad without scruple, intimidating, buying, confusing or betraying other decision-makers, and are equally ruthless in stifling internal dissent.

Turning now to the other generalizations found in Section B of Chapter 1, we understand how improving technology throughout history has expanded the arena of conflict and, giving temporary advantage to one side or the other, has combined with the dynamic of anarchy to produce larger nations in fewer systems, culminating in today's planetary system.[17]

We can understand why, as this process has gone along, publics in vanquished nations have accepted their integration under the victor nations, and in time have transferred their loyalties to the larger nations or empires, provided only that the victors afford them peace at home and protection against new threats from abroad, for these are the two basic requirements that justify government.

And, finally, we can marvel that, despite these millenia of turmoil, the scourges of mankind have been removed or reduced as much as they have, while at the same time we must tremble as we confront the old scourge of war in its latest technological terror and the new scourge of overpopulation.

The historical generalizations in Section B of Chapter 1 dealt first with international systems, then with leaders and publics in nations. The principal component in our explanatory theory, anarchy, has to do mainly with the international system seen as a whole, while the second component, the aggressive nation, refers mainly to leaders, and the third, ideology, has to do largely with publics.[18]

G. Old Cures for War, in the Light of Our Causes of War

We said a while back that a plan for peace that is not solidly grounded in the causes of war has no chance, ever. Phrased a bit more elegantly, a means of resolving international conflict that does not address itself directly to the several elements in a sound theory of conflict is not even theoretically adequate, therefore it can never become practically adequate. If the theory of international conflict that we have developed is correct and complete, every alleged cure for that conflict must be examined in the light of that theory. If the cure does not cope with the theory, it must be discarded, for if tried for another millenium it still would not work. If the cure does meet the theory, then it must be examined for its practical feasibility.

We shall deal here with a number of old cures that have been tried and are still being tried. Later we'll deal with several proposed but untried cures.

1. *Diplomacy and Power Politics.* This cure has been tried since the Two Kingdoms on the Nile. Its performance is reviewed in our *Summary of International History.* Hans Morgenthau and others continue to prescribe it. Morgenthau at last had his clear-sighted diplomacy in the person of Henry Kissinger, a veritable Talleyrand. But there is nothing now to show for Kissinger's negotiating genius; he plowed the sea.

Diplomacy and power politics do not deal at all with anarchy. Indeed they are aspects of that anarchy; they are articulations of a system of independent nations. Diplomacy can for a time mollify the results of anarchy and postpone its ultimate violence, though it is used too to promote violence on the best terms available. It can perhaps restrict violence to only some nations. But diplomacy, in success or failure, is simply anarchy at work.

Diplomacy does not deal with ideology. It is its prisoner when popular ideology is strong and cannot be changed or tuned down to suit the changing needs of diplomacy.

Diplomacy, because it does not cope with anarchy, can do little about the external pressures that radicalize nations, though it can patch up trade and currency imbalances for a time, usually in crisis. It deals with internal pressures only peripherally, as for example when a minority within a nation has managed to make its status an international concern, but the usual rule is that outsiders may not meddle.[19] Diplomacy may offer aid to relieve economic stress but also to advance foreign policy goals. This means bilateral and sporadic aid, with the receiving nation free to misspend it. And diplomacy prefers military aid; suppurating internal problems go unchecked.

It is suggested that nuclear deterrence invites a diplomacy in which nations live competitively but not aggressively and stay out of the way of each other.[20] This is a healthy criticism of US as world policeman. But US was unable to remain non-aligned in the two world wars, for example, and if US withdrew now from the Western Pacific, would not Japanese, Chinese, and Soviet power be sucked in there? It does not matter much whether the frontier of anarchy is drawn at the Philippine Islands or the Hawaiian Islands.

A paradox which escapes those who want clear-sighted, tough-minded diplomacy and who sneer at formal-legalism is that they too must continually rest their hopes on formal-legal mechanisms such as cease-fire agreements or arms and trade treaties that are unenforceable and fragile.

Diplomacy is often foolish, sometimes wise, and always temporary, but it is the game until anarchy is superseded.[21]

2. *Collective Security*. The purist who reserves this term for the League and the UN and objects to applying it to military alliances such as NATO should recall that although a greater altruism may inspire the UN the two types are essentially similar.

Both are established by treaties among independent nations. Alliances may run for a term of years, then be subject to renegotiation, whereas treaties of the UN type run in perpetuity. But a nation can withdraw from any treaty at any time. Japan, Italy, and Germany withdrew from the League; Indonesia withdrew from the UN, later rejoining.

An alliance is a coalition of these nations against those nations. Collective security is a coalition of most against any that may break the peace. But one nation may decide no breach of the peace occurred, another may agree that a breach occurred but disagree as to which nation was to blame, while yet another may be sure which is the aggressor but feel too exposed to join the action. Meanwhile the victim nation may be unsure that others will help, hence capitulate to the aggressor. Given the best will to fulfill commitments, shifts in public opinion or anti-war sentiment may preclude it.

Collective security accepts that sovereign independence which we call anarchy. Setting its foundations in the quicksands of anarchy, collective security erects its imposing edifices at Geneva and New York, where they totter and quake for all to see.

Ever since the Charter was signed in June 1945 (a pre-nuclear document, remember), supporters have said it would increase in wisdom and strength and eventually come into adulthood. This is the familiar organismic analogy. In 1985, aged 40, this infant is a case of arrested development. Dating from the Covenant, it is a wizened child past 60, still crawling when ambulant at all.

It is argued there is nothing wrong with the UN's structure that greater good will could not cure. President Johnson said so at the General Assembly in 1965. No serious attempt has been made to strengthen the Charter except (1) the "Uniting for Peace" Resolution which interpreted the Charter to mean that the General Assembly can *recommend* action to meet threats to the peace when the Security Council, owing to the veto, cannot *act*, and (2) the effort to enforce Assembly authority to levy assessments for peacekeeping costs.[22] Both died.

The UN has been left to try on its own to push down roots and put out branches and crowd out the national governments. It remains a stunted sapling. Few scholars or statesmen believed the words of Johnson, whose Dominican and Vietnam interventions showed how little attention he paid the UN. Still, they say, there is no chance of getting an adequate organization. But some do come up with small proposals.

One is that the UN should focus on violence among lesser nations, dispatching observers or fact-finders, or patrolling an area while negotiations go on, using the troops that some ten nations have placed at UN call. They keep order; they have no enforcement authority; yet troops under the UN banner have had a degree of success at this minor sort of thing, certainly more than US troops on a similar mission at Beirut in 1983. Still, as to major threats to the peace, "it is nevertheless true that the U.N. is unlikely to act in the future unless both of the super-powers acquiesce."[23] But neither vetoed the Council's settlement terms after the 1967 war, yet Israel ignored them. What all this amounts to is that the UN does not perform the security function that was claimed for it; it is simply a small, additional factor in the diplomatic process.

Universality was once thought the key to an effective collective-security organization. But take the example of a future crisis between India and Pakistan: even if Washington and Moscow could agree on UN intervention, Peking could veto it. Universality may make an ineffective organization worse.

Removal of the veto is the one structural change that has been widely discussed. The veto means the Council cannot act against any of the five permanent members or against any lesser nation protected by any of the five. With the veto deleted, any eight of the 15 members could commit the UN to effective military action.* Yet, so long as nations retain the arms and men they can be made to participate only by other nations willing to war upon them in order then to war upon the aggressor. We reach the absurd.

Collective security, based on the hope that nations which retain the ability to act or not act as they please will not exercise that independence, rests on a *de facto* anarchy which makes a mockery of a *de jure* collective security. Unable to assure security to any nation, it is a facade without substance, and is recognized as such by nearly all.[24]

Independent specialized agencies, loosely affiliated with the UN, try to do something to lessen the pressures which radicalize nations. They will

---

*There may be loopholes which reluctant members could seize upon, as for example in Article 24, Section 2, and in Article 25. But we assume for present purposes that any such have also been closed by Charter amendment.

be discussed shortly.

3. *International Law.* This is related to diplomacy which creates treaty law and to collective security in that the Covenant and Charter "legislated" new law and cases arose thereunder which added to law.

International law, as such, does not deal with ideology or aggressive elites. It does purport to deal directly with anarchy, asserting that law is the opposite of anarchy. Unfortunately, the only meaningful statement would be that enforceable law is the opposite of anarchy.

The UN Charter's prohibition of self-defense except against armed attack has been held by some nations not to affect the broader right to self-defense under traditional international law. Also, since the Charter permits self-defense until the Council can act, presumably violence can continue so long as the Council does not, in fact, act. So one has here a lawyer's brief permitting a nation to use violence indefinitely once it claims it has suffered armed attack or been threatened by one. The Tonkin Gulf incident is an example, which was followed by US "retaliation" far beyond the limit permitted by international law, and USSR has not even bothered to cloak its invasion of Afghanistan with legality.

It is said that diplomacy does not settle much any more because war, diplomacy's final mode of settlement, is precluded by the Nuclear Balance, but that international law has resolved many disputes; that the old World Court connected with the League never had a decision disobeyed while the present World Court has been disobeyed only once in a contentious case.[25] Divided Berlin, China, Korea, and Vietnam were mentioned as examples of this diplomatic deadlock. But why were these never submitted to the Court? Even if the law is scant on such cases, the rules of equity could be applied. The answer is that these divided nations, like others, have seen too much at stake to risk a verdict they might have to reject. We'll return to this shortly.

One scholar speaks of "inter-bloc rules of public order" such as Khruschev's decision not to push his Cuban adventure further.[26] The US decision not to intervene in Hungary or Czechoslovakia could be added. Other "sociologists of law" see reciprocal decision-making as holding the promise of gradually building a "minimum public order of human dignity" at the world level.[27]

"Inter-bloc law" is not convincing, for it simply means that, so long as the Nuclear Balance endures, each side will be cautious about interfering in the other's backyard. To say that "a legal order is always most effective when it corresponds in certain measure to working day-by-day community practices"[28] is to say that what is is all right. It is at the cost of endorsing actual practice that sociological "realism" gets its law obeyed. And Khruschev's withdrawal of missiles from Cuba may have established a new "norm" in 1962 but it did not prevent US from intervening in Vietnam on China's doorstep in 1965 or USSR from intervening in 1979 in Afghanistan, next door to the Persian Gulf oil reserves.

Treaty law forbidding most nuclear testing, nuclear proliferation, the placing of nuclear weapons in space and other arms control measures has been accompanied by efforts to regulate the economic exploitation of the high seas and the continental shelf as well as the non-weapons aspects of national rights in air space and outer space. But even if all desirable rules were written, signed, and ratified—and US, among others, has refused to sign the Law of the Sea Treaty—anarchy still would not have been dealt with at all because "the effective control over the use of force remains on a national level and governs the expectations and behavior of the participating units in world affairs."[29]

International law therefore ultimately depends on the formal-legalist hope that rules which are merely "self-enforcing" will be obeyed, and that national decision-makers will believe this fiction.

How fanciful the fiction truly is can be pointed up by observing that Reagan's de-stabilization of the Nicaraguan government (like Nixon's de-stabilization of the Chilean government) is a violation of the UN Charter, of the Treaty establishing the Organization of American States, and of traditional international law. Moreover, Reagan has informed the World Court that US will not abide by any decision reached on Nicaragua's appeal to the Court.

International law that national courts are willing to apply is of course real law to that extent, but this is so only because the courts' decisions are enforceable by national governments. This kind of law is mainly private rather than public and has only a peripheral connection with international conflict.

4. *International Organization and Functionalism.* Functionalism is related to structural-functionalism and general systems theory, discussed in Chapters 3 and 4, hence comes to world politics through sociology from biology. It asserts a world order will evolve as international organizations (structures) come to perform for the world society those economic, social, technological, and other functions which make a society viable.

Functionalists look at the political organs of the UN as providing the security function through disarmament, peacekeeping, and the like. But most of their attention is on other international organizations (IOs) and some functionalists, by including churches and anything else trans-national, manage to count hundreds of them.[30] Those most often discussed, however, are the IOs that are specialized organizations independent from but often related to the UN. Each of these—the Food and Agricultural Organizations (FAO), the World Health Organization (WHO), the International Labor Organization (ILO), and some two dozen others—has its own "organic law" in the form of a treaty and usually has a permanent secretariat.

Some functionalists lay claim to the multinational corporations which perform a far vaster economic function than all the inter-governmental IOs combined. Several of the largest corporations have a turnover which exceeds the annual gross national product of most UN member-nations. The UN has studied international registration for them with a view to protecting them from nations, and nations from them. Some say the multinationals are colonizing the poorer nations, building conflict instead of global community. But any sizeable nation can have its way, at least with that part of a multinational which falls within its jurisdiction. Iran kicked out a great British multinational oil company, and so weak a nation as Saudi Arabia has repeatedly dictated terms to four huge US-based multinationals.[31]   Functionalists even point to the UN General Assembly's Universal Declaration of Human Rights, embodied in two draft covenants and a protocol. Quite a few nations have signed, not including US, some of them have not ratified, and the agreements would in any case be unenforceable. They are in the same sad situation as the Vladivostok agreement whereby USSR undertook—or US thought it did—to grant greater human rights to its citizens.

Functionalism seeks to by-pass anarchy, attacking it on its flanks. Functionalists believed that, by taking over functions performed by national governments, IOs would gradually displace those governments in the loyalties of peoples everywhere. A kind of world federalism by stages would come about, and anarchy would quietly have been abridged. But David Mitrany, a founder of functionalism, warned way back in 1943 that "there is an effective minimum" of functions "which must include some essential functions now performed by the national state. Security is first among them."[32]   The functionalist process has been at work at least since the International Telegraphic Union was established in 1865 but, as there is nothing to perform the security function, anarchy remains awesome. Two functionalists mention efforts at international organization by Greek city-states more than 2,000 years ago, then say:

> Despite monumental and continuing failures to eliminate war, the idealism which goes beyond the shelter of the national state has goaded mankind to "Try again" to build upon the orderly, brotherly, and cooperative side of human nature... Why is the concept of international organization such a powerful force that it can overcome centuries of failure and innumerable conflicts?[33]

In addition to this heroic optimism, there is an element of anarchism in the functionalists, as there was in their intellectual forebears, the continental sociologists. Government is a dirty word. These two scholars conclude that despite their failure IOs have proved "adequate to bear all of the international cooperation that existing bonds of community will generate."[34]

But this adequacy is of course not adequacy to deal with anarchy. Functionalism's's fatal flaw is that it does not abate the fears generated by anarchy but is forever limited and frustrated by them. A result of this is that functionalism can do virtually nothing about the external pressures that radicalize nations internally.

National decision-makers have retained absolute control over national participation in IOs, standing between them and their own publics. Functional activities are not visible within the great nations and scarcely even in the developing nations. How then can public loyalties ever be transferred to the world level? National governments hold the purse strings and allot pennies to IOs while they spend dollars on bilateral anarchy-motivated aid and hundreds of dollars on the arms race. How then can IOs do anything about the economic hardships that radicalize nations, bringing aggressive leaders and ideologies to power? Significantly, it is the government, the thing depreciated in principle by functionalism, which defeats functionalism.

One writer noted as long ago as 1966 that the difference between the promise and the performance of functionalism lies precisely in the fact that national governments do refuse to allocate scarce resources to IOs.[35] Functionalists have tried to come to terms a bit with anarchy. They speak nowadays of how "anarchic self-interest" leads nations to institutionalize common interests in, say, trade or the resources of the seas, or common adversions, say against a diversity of air traffic regulations or unregulated radio frequencies.[36]

Their new name for this sort of thing is "international regimes"[37] but it is a very old activity whereby by agreement, explicit or tacit, nations undertake to do or not to do something until it is more convenient for them to act otherwise. One scholar comments that "international regime" analysis is just a fad.[38]

We also have now the "neo-functionalists" whose awareness of anarchy leads them to recognize that political institutions may be a factor in international integration. An early voice in this connection was that of Percy Corbett, an international lawyer, who said that "Specialized functions do not flourish automatically and indefinitely without the coordinating control of central political authority."[39] Ernst Haas, usually considered a leading functionalist, has said that international institutions are crucial causative links in the chain of integration.[40]

There is thus an edging over to the position that supranational governmental institutions will be required if functions are to be performed satisfactorily. Kenneth Thompson, who is not a functionalist, looks to "when the tide turns in the present era of anti-institutionalism" among international relations scholars.[41]

In sociological language, the functions are still looking for structures that are adequate to perform them. Yet, despite all their disappointments, functionalists continue to put political integration at the end of their process instead of at its beginning. Indeed, if the intellectual history of our era is ever written, it may see functionalism as the final attempt to warp world politics into a sociological framework of analysis.

Meanwhile, functionalism suffers from "past failures and present pallor."[42] In the wilderness of anarchy, it is a weak voice, crying.

5. *Common Markets.* Customs unions and common markets are created by national decision-makers, of course, but scholars analyze them and the functionalists claim them as examples of how the performance of the economic function can win trans-national loyalties and lead on to integration. This has something to do with the "regional cultures" discussed in Chapter 3, in that a shared regional culture may undergird a common market which in time will produce enough sense of community to make political integration feasible. The show-case example has been the European Economic Community (EEC) which is actually three related communities and is usually known as the European Common Market.

The original plan, in the aftermath of World War II, was to start with the security function. By merging their armies into the European Defense Community (EDC), the Western Europeans would tie France and Germany so closely together that another war between them would be unthinkable, and the EDC was expected to lead to political federation. But France, after proposing the EDC, had a change of leadership and in 1954 torpedoed it. Europeans took this to mean that economic integration was the only route to political unity, so the Common Market was formed.

Another hope was that if political unity could be achieved by one or the other of these routes, then Soviet expansionism could be halted. Thus the Common Market is an example of how international conflict and fear can produce cooperation. The Soviet army divisions are still there in Eastern Europe but the Western Europeans do not at present fear them so much, hence perhaps the lack of progress on toward political unity. And meanwhile, of course, there is the NATO military alliance for their protection.

A European scholar distinguishes between the three earlier stages of economic integration (free trade area, customs union, common market) which are steps of pure market integration requiring only the negative task of removing barriers, and the last two stages (economic union, total economic integration) which require much greater agreement among national policies. He calls this "positive integration" and says it is far more difficult.[43] This points to the heart of the matter: how do you get national governments, each of them responsive to its own parliament and people and each retaining the arms and men that enable it to pursue an independent policy, to agree on common policies for Western Europe as a whole?

It could be worse. The Market's High Commission, its executive, said in 1968 that "the Commission is astonished at the lengthy battles it has to fight merely in order that its functions under the Treaty shall be respected and that nothing be done to whittle them down." Then, "If the

Communities were to be reduced to a vague intergovernmental organization, their effectiveness would be immediately and irretrievably jeopardized.''

The contempt for the intergovernmental organizations which functionalists hold so dear should be noted. The Commission goes on to stress the importance of the almost-supranational institutions already achieved:

> Alone of all the large European organizations, the Communities have succeeded in building up and administering common policies, and this they owe essentially to their institutional machinery. The same men who did not succeed in framing and implementing common policies in the amorphous framework of other organizations have managed to do so in the framework of the Community, which provided them with the necessary institutional machinery.[44]

Things got worse. The lack of a common currency has been a problem, especially after Nixon moved in 1971 to protect US trade and currency balances, with both Britain and France breaking the agreement tying Market currencies to the German mark. At the Commission's urging, member-nations agreed to work toward a common currency by 1980. Then in 1973 the Arab states imposed their oil boycott, and the scramble by most Market members to make special deals with the Arab oil producers shook the Market to its foundations. Oil prices leaped again during the Iranian civil war in 1979. Recession followed throughout the Market nations, ameliorated in Britain and Norway by discovery of North Sea oil. In 1983-84 there was much bickering over quotas and contributions, with Britain threatening to leave the Market. As of 1985, US economic recovery has led to some improvement in Western Europe, but unemployment is still very high while the Market's industries are thought to be non-competitive in world markets and its agriculture certainly is; that is why Spain and Portugal were kept waiting so long; they will at last be admitted in 1986.

The common currency has not been achieved, but one can now buy bonds denominated in terms of a "basket" of Common Market currencies. Also, the members of the European Parliament are now directly elected by the voters in the member-nations, and the Parliament has its first real authority: the right to approve or disapprove the Market's budget.

Meanwhile, Western Europe's statesmen have been getting a lot of advice from scholars.

Aron, the Frenchman mentioned in Chapter 4, wrote in 1966 that

> The hope that the European federation will gradually and irresistibly emerge from the Common Market is based on a great illusion of our times: the illusion that economic and technological interdependence among the various factions of humanity has definitively devalued the fact of "political sovereignties," the existence of distinct states which wish to be autonomous.[45]

In 1967 Deutsch and his associates, who are experts on the processes of integration, predicted that prospects for European political integration would fade as the Common Market encountered obstacles.[46] But in 1970 Friedrich, another expert, said that such views had already been proved erroneous and that Europe would move on to common government.[47]

In 1972, however, scholars projecting Common Market trends said that the federalist approach had been superseded by the confederal model which recognizes the continued independence of the member-nations; that the Market had stopped far short of its original goals in almost every economic sector except the customs union and agricultural policy; and that there was no certainty that external pressures would provide a unified European foreign policy.[48]

Also in 1972, a study of public attitudes in the Market nations concluded there is little comfort in their results for those who believe community must precede political amalgamation. It was found that such community attitudes as there were had arisen after quasi-political institutions had been created.[49]

A 1979 study by a U.S. scholar concludes that there cannot be much more than a tenuous coordination of foreign policies, even among similar nations, so it is unlikely that the Common Market or NATO will go on to tighter integration.[50]

In 1982 there was a notable statement by the President of the European Parliament. He traced the widespread pessimism regarding the European Community back to France's defeat of the European army idea, saying that 25 years' experience with the Common Market shows the falseness of the hope that economic integration would lead to supranational, federalist integration. And now, he said, even economic prosperity was disappearing. He said that the absence of political unity was pulling the Community apart when political decisions were the only way of solving economic problems and their social repercussions. He saw some hope in the elected Parliament with its budgetary authority but said that Parliament can only reach for power through the European Commission which in turn is dominated by the Council of Ministers where unanimity is required. He said that the interests of Europe and US had diverged. He hopes for a new European Defense Community.[51]

Writing also in 1982, Stanley Hoffman gave him no comfort, saying that he doubted a new European Army could be set up, for this would require "a leap toward more powerful central institutions."[52] And in the same year another scholar said that direct election of the European Parliament appeared not to have brought Community institutions much closer to the public; that there was little understanding of and interest in the Community.[53]

It may be that the Western European eggs are now too scrambled ever to be unscrambled, but the expectation that the Market, like the *Zollverein*, would lead to federation is now only a hope. The *Zollverein* was not enough; it took Bismarck and his prestigious wars to unify Germany. Indeed, a West German leader was quoted in 1982 as pointing out that this was the case, even though everyone in the *Zollverein* member-states had the same cultural nationality.[54]

And in 1984 an American scholar noted that the European unification experience reflects on the validity of functionalist logic, saying that "It should not have come as too much of a surprise to discover that in practice, if not in theory, social and economic affairs are not neatly separable from political considerations."[55] Another said that "After more than thirty years of international institution-building we find ourselves with a plethora of institutions but very little in the way of" a new international structure that will serve the demands of interdependence.[56]

In other words, institutions that lack the authority of government do not amount to much. The Common Market is still alive, but one day its epitaph may record that even though it was able to do something about the economic and social pressures that radicalize nations and introduce aggressive elites and ideologies into the international system, it failed because the leaders of its member-nations could not bring themselves to deal head-on with anarchy.

There have been efforts to form economic unions elsewhere. The Latin American Free Trade Association (LAFTA) amounted to little, partly because it favored its more developed member-nations, namely Argentina, Brazil, and Mexico. This caused Boliva, Chile, Colombia, Ecuador, and Peru to form the group known as ANDEAN, but Chile withdrew and Boliva threatened withdrawal, partly because it too favors the more developed member-nations.[57] In Southeast Asia there is sort of an alliance of non-communist governments (Philippines, Malaysia, Singapore, Indonesia, and Thailand) known as ASEAN which has had some success in the economic sphere.[58] And there was the East African Community which worked rather well for a time, economically, but broke up in 1977 over ideological and other differences.

All the foregoing suggests that one cannot, by trying to perform the economic function, slip up on anarchy's blind side and snare it; instead, the persisting political anarchy may abort even the economic integration that has been achieved.

6. *International Understanding, World Public Opinion, and Cultural Homogenization.* International understanding, an old effort which nowadays is associated with UNESCO (from which US withdrew in January 1985), is based on the proposition that war originates in the minds of men. And it never seems to occur to the proponents of this cure that the normal condition of peace within nations must also originate in the minds of men, therefore they never have to wonder what makes the difference. At any rate, this approach involves changing individual psychology, largely through education, so that perceptions of foreigness, fear, and hostility will be displaced by understanding and good will.

World public opinion is thought to be especially strong in its opposition to nuclear war but also is forming in support of worldwide concerns such as pollution, population control, and resource depletion. Cultural particularism will disappear, it is believed, as peoples' ways of doing things and looking at things become more alike.

The methods of these cures are student exchange, people-to-people programs, technical and medical and economic aid, libraries abroad; exchange of art treasures, musicians, performing groups, films, and scholars who do research and teach abroad; freedom of trade, of travel, and of press, radio, and television; and trans-national associations of various kinds.

All these methods can be frustrated by national governments. They can refuse to take positive action where international agreement is necessary or they can take negative action to keep most of whatever is deemed undesirable from transiting their frontiers.

Much frustration occurs. Cultural exchange agreements between US and USSR have been difficult to negotiate and keep in force; even the treaty for an exchange of consuls was long delayed. There has been little exchange between the two blocs or between either of them and China, although tourists now pass with little difficulty, but only in restricted areas. Communist regimes do not pretend to permit freedom of expression in their mass media, while in other nations the media are state-owned or state-controlled to some degree. There has been much exchange within each bloc, and between each of them and the neutral, largely less-developed countries. But this is not where it might do the good that the advocates of these cures talk about.

Cultural homogenization is going ahead, despite national efforts to frustrate it, thanks to the impact of science and technology, and to the very human curiosity about other peoples coupled with willingness of many to imitate what they admire. This process would move faster if exchange programs were adequately financed, if transit across frontiers were easier as it was in the 19th century, and if national governments did not treat cultural programs as tools of power politics.[59]

But, as we saw in Chapter 3, cultural homogenization has not reduced international violence or produced international integration. Thus, even if global cultural homogenization were to achieve the cultural uniformity that Europe had reached by the 20th century, international understanding and world public opinion would still succumb to national fears and nationalist opinion in the pinch. It has never been difficult for statesmen to cut down these tender shoots. And the person who has achieved international understanding may not afterwards identify so exclusively with his nation, but it is a rare individual who will not go along with his crowd when the nation perceives threat and the clarions sound.

Thus, by failing to deal with national insecurity, these prescriptions

fail. They do not pretend to deal head-on with anarchy. At most they try
to by-pass anarchy, in much the same way as does functionalism but in a
more blurred and less systematic fashion.

Nevertheless, world public opinion, even though it is broken when
national components drop out from time to time over some crisis or when
they think their national self-interest is involved, has been vocal enough
and steady enough to undergird the Nuclear Balance of Terror. For it is
widely feared, even among publics not directly involved, that a nuclear
war might subject them to fallout if not to blast and firestorm. And of
course this fear-opinion is greatest among publics of the great nuclear
nations, though they may have steeled themselves against the event.
World public opinion was a factor in bringing about the Nuclear Test-
Ban Treaty in 1963, while the anti-nuclear movement of the 1980s may
offer a degree of hope, which we'll consider in the final chapter.

As for competing ideologies, these cures may bring even the true
believer to understand that there is at least a historical justification for the
enemy ideology, but education, as we noted in Chapter 2, is everywhere
nationally-oriented. It would be an exceptional individual who, reared in
one ideology, would become neutral or embrace the enemy ideology,
much less announce it openly. Ideological homogenization is unlikely
between national populations that fear each other, though we have noted
the hope that science might become the prevailing planetary worldview.

These cures have no bearing on the rise of aggressive elites, for they do
nothing to avert the external and internal stresses which radicalize
nations.[60]

7. *Arms Control and Partial Disarmament.* Arms control measures do
not involve any disarmament. They are designed to reduce the level of fear
and hostility. They may make the Balance of Terror a little more stable.
Such measures include: Antarctic Treaty, 1959; Hot Line, 1963; Limited
Nuclear Test-Ban Treaty, 1963; Treaty Prohibiting Weapons of Mass
Destruction in Outer Space, 1967; Treaty Prohibiting Nuclear Weapons
in Latin America, 1967; Nuclear Non-Proliferation Treaty, 1972; US-
USSR Treaty Limiting Offensive Missiles, 1972, also known as SALT I;
and the US-USSR agreement in 1974 to limit the size of the underground
tests permitted by the 1963 treaty. The SALT II treaty on the further
control of offensive missiles, signed in 1979, has never been ratified,
owing largely to USSR's intervention in Afghanistan, but both sides say
they are abiding by its terms.

Scholarly discussions of arms control have bogged down in arguments
over methodology. A Pentagon employee, writing in an academic
journal, emphasizes the "long road to theory and from theory to
practice." He lays down "scientific" preconditions for reliable theory in
arms control that even the Pentagon's's resources might not suffice ever to
meet.[61]

But arms control is not conceivably adequate. It does not cope with the rise of aggressive elites and ideologies except to lighten slightly those external pressures which radicalize nations. It does not even purport to abridge anarchy but merely tries to provide an atmosphere of lesser fear in which progress might possibly be made toward disarmament. Its instruments are those familiar formal-legal documents which require so much optimism to take seriously—treaties which can be terminated or disregarded tomorrow, or a "Hot Line" which can be unplugged at either end tonight. As Premier Kosygin of USSR said, after the SALT talks opened in Vienna in April 1970, and Nixon later in the month invaded Cambodia: "What is the worth of international agreements in which the United States is taking part or is going go take part, if it violates so unceremoniously the commitments it has assumed?"[62] He was referring to the Geneva agreements of 1954 and 1962.

Soviet leaders may see that their invasion of Afghanistan in 1979 caused SALT II not to be ratified but they can hardly be blamed if they regard Reagan's conversion to arms control in 1984 as an election-year phenomenon. As the November election came near, both US and USSR published lists of alleged violations by the other party of treaties already in force.[63]

Partial disarmament tries to deal with the weaponry dimension of anarchy by reducing the weaponry which enables nations, if they wish, to make a mockery of formal-legal instruments designed to prevent violence. The idea is that if one can negotiate a little disarmament now, more can probably be negotiated later. Great nations can occasionally agree to keep some area demilitarized, as in the case of Austria, at least for a while. But we know of only one example in recent centuries of actual great-nation disarmament. This was the Washington Naval Treaty of 1922, mentioned in the *Summary of International History*. Some warships were actually decommissioned, but this disarmament was followed by rearmament, first by Japan and then by all.

Far commoner is the situation, also described in the *Summary*, at the Geneva disarmament talks in the early 1930s. They were dominated by military men while a major arms supplier was very busy behind the scenes.

The psychology of arms negotiations in an environment of anarchy is noted by one scholar who says of the test-ban talks prior to the Kennedy-Khruschev era that "the tendency to make frequent concessions while agreement was remote, followed by limited concession-making and even retractions, suggests a pattern of approach-avoidance on the part of the United States and the Soviet Union."[64]

Charles Price, a former President of the American Chemical Society who is a peace activist and at times has been close to national decision-makers, wrote in 1984 that he has come to conclude that time and again during the past two decades important initiatives and even negotiated treaties that would have significantly limited the military activities of US and USSR have been undermined by the powerful US military-industrial complex. He asserts that years ago, in negotiations for a complete nuclear test-ban, USSR abandoned its longstanding refusal and agreed to three on-site inspections per year, whereupon US insisted on seven, so there was no deal. Price goes on to say that in recent negotiations for such a complete ban, agreement was reached on twelve automated monitoring stations in each nation, with international on-site inspection of any suspicious event detected by the monitors, but US has now balked at this draft treaty.[65]

George Kennan, the US diplomat considered the main architect of the policy of containment of the USSR, published an article in 1984 which is only somewhat less critical of the military-industrial complex and of US negotiating behavior on disarmament and arms control.[66]

As we noted in the *Summary*, partial disarmament was tried at least as early as the period of the warring states in pre-Han China. It has never worked, for even if agreement is reached there is nothing to prevent a nation from re-arming when it chooses, so partial disarmament cannot cope with anarchy and therefore cannot long reduce the stresses which radicalize nations.

Therefore, when Gorbachev of the USSR's Politburo says in December 1984 that USSR stands ready eventually to ban all types of armaments, and when Reagan says the same thing in January 1985, we ought not to take them very seriously.

It will have been apparent that virtually all these old cures for war considered in this section place their faith in treaties and other formal-legal documents. These cures accept a promise and leave the means of dishonoring it in national hands, taking the shadow for the substance.[67]

Toward the close of the next Chapter 6 we shall discuss two new cures, that is, cures that have not yet been tried.

The earlier and main part of Chapter 6 will consider how statesmen since World War II have coped with the realities of the international system, or, to express it another way, we'll see whether our causes of conflict explain the way decision-makers actually behaved during this recent period. This will be an application of our causal theory to the past. In Part Three, we'll apply that theory to prediction and prescription.

Chapter 5 Notes

1. Richard W. Sterling, in *Macropolitics* (New York, Knopf, 1974), says that "The balance of power is thus generically a balance of fear" and that "The vicious circle that produces both clash and collision begins with anarchy's divisions. It develops with the fears that anarchy generates." (pp. 60, 329).

2. Matthew Melko, in *Fifty-Two Peaceful Societies* (Oakville, Ontario, CPRI Press, 1973) concludes that "If alleged pugnacious and hostile attitudes are deeply embedded in man, they are often neutralized within peaceful societies. They may be displaced in pageantry, exhibitions of national glory, in personal lives, and in the exhausting labyrinths of bureaucratic institutions" (p. 182).

3. Hubert M. Blalock, Jr., *Social Statistics* (New York, McGraw-Hill, 2d. Ed., 1972), p. 21.

4. There are as yet grave difficulties in measuring attitudes for statistical treatment (see Blalock, *op. cit.*, p. 20) except at the lowest or crudest level of measurement.

5. Alan Dowty, "Conflict in War-Potential Politics: An Aproach to Historical Macroanalysis," *Peace Research Society (International) Papers*, Vol. 13 (1969), pp. 85-103. Also pertinent is K. W. Terhune and J. M. Firestone, "Global War, Limited War, and Peace," *International Studies Quarterly*, vol. 14 (1970), 195-218.

6. Robert G. Wesson, *The Imperial Order* (Berkeley, University of California Press, 1967), especially pp. 18-19. The quoted phrase is a precise confirmation of Hobbes.

7. Richard N. Rosecrance, *Action and Reaction in World Politics* (Boston, Little Brown, 1963), 304-6.

8. Kenneth Boulding, "Future Directions in Conflict and Peace Studies," *Journal of Conflict Resolution* 22:2 (1978), 342-354.

9. John C. Lambert, in "Do Arms Races Lead to War?" *Journal of Peace Research* 12:2 (1975), 123-128, says arms races and wars might occur in a world of good guys only but that the factor "aggressiveness" must be a part of any theory in that, given equal odds, some political establishments may go to war while others may not.

10. Rosecrance, *op. cit.*

11. Pitirim Sorokin, who surveyed wars from the 5th century B.C. to 1925 A.D., cites internal changes such as a growing economy, a rapid rate of population increase, or territorial expansion, as leading to war (his *Social and Cultural Dynamics*, New York, Bedminster, 1937, p. 364). Geoffrey Blainey, who studied all international wars from 1700 to 1970, notes that "Wars usually begin when two nations disagree on their relative strength, and wars usually cease when the fighting nations agree on their relative strength." (His *The Causes of War*, New York, Free Press, 1973, p. 246) Steven J. Rosen and Walter S. Jones identify a whole grab-bag of causes: power asymmetries; nationalism, separatism, and irredentism; international social Darwinism; communications failure; arms races; internal cohesion through external conflict; instinctual aggression, economic and scientific stimulation; the military-industrial complex; relative deprivation; population limitation; and as a device for conflict resolution. (Their *The Logic of International Relations*, Cambridge, Mass., Winthrop Publishers, 1980).

12. Richard K. Ashley, in "The Eye of Power: the Politics of World Modeling," (*International Organization* 37:3, 1983, 495-535) reviews six books on world process models, of which he has rather a low opinion. He hopes Deutsch's project in Berlin will produce a model based on trans-national consensus and community in place of the Hobbesian anarchic model. Our model therefore will not please him. R. A. Falk and S. S. Kim (in *The War System: An Interdisciplinary Approach*, Boulder, Colo., Westwood Press, 1980, p. 531) say that the systemic level of analysis is the most comprehensive; that it assumes that a macroanalysis of the system's dynamics will disclose the variables that cause international conflict.

13. M. I. Midlarsky, in a mathematical treatment of international history, says that the more "polar actors" there are, up to five or six, the more likely war becomes, and that early alliances are more de-stabilizing than others added later (his "Power, Uncertainty, and the Onset of International Violence," *Journal of Conflict Resolution* 13:3, 1974, 395-431). Bruce Bueno de Mesquita, in a similar study, seems to confirm Midlarsky, in his finding that bi-polar systems have less war than multi-polar systems, but that the adding of clusters correlates with an increase in major-power wars within five years (his "Measuring Systemic Polarity," *Journal of Conflict Resolution* 19:2, 1975, 187-216). Another mathematical study concludes that there is no correlation between the number of major actors in the international system and the problem of war (C.W. Ostrom and J. H. Aldrich, "The Relationship between Size and Stability in the Major Power International System." *American Journal of Political Science* 22:4, 1978, 743-771), but this does not speak to the question of their alliances.

14. "Catastrophe theory," involving the use of a geometric "behavior surface," appears to have real value in showing how the causes of conflict accumulate until they suddenly

spill over into war. R. T. Holt, B. L. Job and Lawrence Markus, in "Catastrophe Theory and the Study of War," *Journal of Conflict Resolution* 22:2 (1978), 171-208, say this theory may help understand why the same causes may or may not lead to war. In their model, unsatisfied nations lead to coalitions which lead to military capabilities which limit decision-makers' response time which leads to a certain amount of violence. In their geometric diagram, world federation is at one end and the "war of all against all" is at the other end.

15. Rudolph J. Rummel suggests that great states can never remain uninvolved because their power brings them constantly into contact with all other states, regardless of distance (his "A Social Field Theory of Foreign Conflict Behavior," *Peace Research Society (International) Papers*, vol. 4, 1966, pp. 131-147. Melko, *op. cit.*, generalizes that "Moderate powers seem to have had the advantage over very strong powers in maintaining peace. They are strong enough to resist attack, but not strong enough to become overextended." He says "Great powers seem to succeed in attaining peace only if they conquer all other great powers within range" (p. 184). US, as a great power, was drawn into the two world wars in 1917 and 1941; but, as a minor power in 1812, it was co-opted into Britain's war against Napoleon.

16. Wolf-Dieter Eberwein, in "The Quantitative Study of International Conflict," *Journal of Peace Research* 18:1 (1981), 19-38, says that his survey of quantitative studies indicates that a loss of power status predicts to war but that equal powers are even more likely to fight; and that arms races intended to restore a military balance do escalate into war.

17. Silviu Brucan, a Romanian social scientist and former diplomat, speaks of "technological-interdependence pressure" which "in its one-directional sweep and onrush stubbornly drives things toward integration... This is an objective trend that will ultimately prove over-powering." He sees eventually a single world community. (His *The Dissolution of Power: A Sociology of International Relations and Politics*, New York, Knopf, 1971, p. 32.)

18. R. A. Brody, *et al*, in their "Hostile International Communication, Arms Production, and Perception of Threat: A Simulation Study," *Peace Research Society (International) Papers*, vol. 7 (1967), pp. 15-38, conclude that hostile behavior is a product both of hostile behavior and of perceptions of that behavior; they agree that the structure of the interstate system plays a role in producing hostile behavior, but they do not know specifically what role. We call that structure anarchic and describe the role it plays.

19. A rule violated, as we have seen, if outside states feel threatened enough. See Richard A. Falk, ed., *The International Law of Civil War*, The Johns Hopkins University Press, 1971.

20. The suggestion is by J. W. Burton, in his *International Relations: A General Theory*, (Cambridge University Press, 1965), p. 231.

21. For modern diplomatic practice, see Arthur Lall's *Modern International Negotiation: Principles and Practice* (Columbia University Press, 1966) and Robert B. Harmon's *The Art and Practice of Diplomacy: A Selected and Annotated Guide* (Metuchen, N. J., Scarecrow Press, 1971).

22. The Security Council initiated action in Greece, Lebanon, Jordan, and the Congo where the General Assembly continued the action when vetoes stalled the Council. The Council alone acted in Indonesia, Cyprus, Kashmir, and along Israel's disputed frontiers. Assembly recommendations initiated peacekeeping operations only in Suez and West Irian (New Guinea), with permission of the parties at dispute.

23. Arthur M. Cox, "What Does 'U.N. Peacekeeping' Mean?" *Saturday Review*, May 14, 1966, pp. 19-20.

24. See *American Journal of International Law* 75:3 (1981), pp. 674-679, for how much progress has been made on a UN code of Offenses against the Peace and Security of Mankind.

25. Arthur Larson, "International Relations: Fancies vs. Facts," *Center Diary*, vol. 16, 1967, Center for the Study of Democratic Institutions. Since then the Court's 1971 finding

that South Africa should evacuate Southwest Africa (former German territory mandated by the League to South Africa) has been rejected by South Africa.

26. Edward McWhinney, "Soviet and Western International Law and the Cold War in the Era of Bipolarity," in R. A. Falk and S. H. Mendlovitz, eds., *International Law* (New York, World Law Fund, 1966), pp. 189-231, 228.

27. Myres S. McDougal and F. P. Feliciano, *Law and Minimum World Public Order*, Yale University Press, 1961.

28. McWhinney, *op. cit.*, p. 228.

29. Richard A. Falk, "The Legal Control of Force in the International Community," in Falk and Mendlovitz, *op. cit.*, p. 312.

30. Norman V. Walhek, "Global Public Political Culture," *Peace Research Reviews* 5:2 (1973).

31. For a disillusioning view of the effect of multinational corporations, see *Transnational Relations and World Politics*, R. O. Keohane and J. S. Nye Jr., eds. (Harvard University Press, 1972), which suggests such corporations are the most significant of several private transnational oligarchies such as professional and trade associations, and some churches, which are quasi-governments. They say that when a great state clashes with these private interests the state will almost invariably prevail, if it wants to badly enough. But a weak state may become a colony. A later article says the furore over the effect of multinational corporations on national governments has died down but that governments will resist the fact that so many business enterprises are conduits through which larger states exercise influence over them (Raymond Vernon's "Sovereignty at Bay Ten Years Later," *International Organization* 35:3, 1981, 517-529).

32. David Mitrany's contribution to R. A. Goldwin and Tony Pearce, eds., *Readings in World Politics* (New York, Oxford University Press, 2d Ed., 1970), pp. 545-553, 547. Italics added.

33. J. C. Piano and R. E. Riggs, *Forging World Order* (New York, Macmillan, 1967), p. 3.

34. *Ibid.*, p. 541. Yet Riggs himself voiced his own pessimism in titling a 1977 article "One Small Step for Functionalism" (*International Organization* 31:3, 515-539) in which he notes that US congressmen who get involved in international organizations tend to become more positive toward them.

35. James P. Sewell, *Functionalism and World Politics* (Princeton University Press, 1966), 319-320.

36. Arthur A. Stein, "Coordination and Collaboration: Regimes in an Anarchic World," *International Organization* 36:2 (1982), 299-324.

37. See also Ernst Haas, "On Systems and International Regimes," *World Politics* 27:2 (1975), 147-174.

38. Susan Strange, "A Critique of Regime Analysis," *International Organization* 36:2 (1982), 479-495.

39. Percy Corbett, "From International to World Law," Department of International Relations Research Monograph No. 1, Lehigh University, Bethlehem, Pennsylvania.

40. Ernst Haas, "The Challenge of Regionalism," *International Organization*, vol. 12 (1958), 4404-458). Functionalists tend to define "institution" broadly, so the institutions would not necessarily be political ones. However, Haas says elsewhere that functional integration works better if the people in charge have the goal of federalism in mind.

41. Kenneth W. Thompson, "Policy and Theory in Quincy Wright's International System," *Journal of Conflict Resolution*, vol. 14 (1970), pp. 479-485.

42. Stanley Hoffman, "International Organization and the International System," *International Organization* 24:3 (1970), pp. 389-413, 412.

43. Jacques Pelkmans, "Economic Theories of Integration Revisited," *Journal of Common*

   Market Studies 18:4 (1980), 333-354.

44. *Second General Report on the Activities of the Communities: 1968*, published by European High Commission, Brussels-Luxembourg, February 1969, pp. 19-20.

45. Raymond Aron, *Peace and War* (New York, Doubleday, 1966), p. 748.

46. Karl W. Deutsch, *et al, France, Germany and the Western Alliance: A Study of Elite Attitudes on European Integration and World Politics*, New York, Scribner's, 1967.

47. Carl J. Friedrich, *Europe: An Emergent Nation?* New York, Harper & Row, 1970.

48. Steven J. Warnecke, ed., *The European Community in the 1970s*, New York, Praeger, 1972. See also Paul Taylor, "The Politics of the European Communities: The Confederal Phase," *World Politics* 27:3 (1975), 336-360. Actually, the Common Market is less than an confederation.

49. Barry B. Hughes and John E. Schwarz, "Dimensions of Political Integration and the Experience of the European Community," *International Studies Quarterly*, vol. 16 (1972), pp. 263-294. Also pertinent is Wm. E. Fisher's "An Analysis of the Deutsch Sociocausal Paradigm of Political Integration," in *International Organization* vol. 23 (1969), pp. 254-290, which raises doubt whether "social assimilation" is the precursor of political integration.

50. Wolfram F. Hanrieder, "Dissolving International Politics: Reflections on the Nation-State," *American Political Science Review* 72:4 (1979), 1276-1287.

51. Pieter Dankert, "The European Community—Past, Present and Future," *Journal of Common Market Studies* 21:1 (1982), 1-18.

52. Stanley Hoffman, "Reflections on the Nation-State in Western Europe Today," *Journal of Common Market Studies* 21:1 (1982), 21-37.

53. Martin Slater, "Political Elites. Popular Indifference, and Community-Building," *Journal of Common Market Studies* 21:1 (1982), 69-93. Still, it is said that the Court of Justice of the European Communities, with the cooperation of other legal bodies plus that of national courts, has gained acceptance of the broad principle of direct integration of Community Law into the national legal orders of the states, as well as acceptance of the supremacy of Community Law within its limited but expanding area of competence (Eric Stein, "Lawyers, Judges, and the Making of a Transnational Constitution," *American Journal of International Law* 75:1 (1981), 1-27.

54. Wm. Wallace, quoting Genscher, in Wallace's "Europe as a Confederation; the Community and the Nation-State," *Journal of Common Market Studies* 21:1 (1982), pp. 57, 68. Wallace says the false hopes for the Market were based on the illusion that national governments would allow themselves to be by-passed and undermined.

55. David A. Kay, "On the Reform of International Institutions: a Comment," *International Organization* 30:3 (1984), 534-538. Singer and Small's statistical study of wars from 1816 to 1965 found no correlation between the amount of inter-governmental organization in the system and subsequent warfare (J. D. Singer and Associates, *Explaining War*, Beverley Hills, Sage Publications, 1979, p. 29).

56. John Spanier, *Games Nations Play* (New York, Holt Rinehart & Winston, 1984), p. 507.

57. David E. Hojman, "The Andean Pact: Failure of a Model of Economic Integration?" *Journal of Common Market Studies* 20:2 (1981), 139-160.

58. Stuart Drummond, "Fifteen Years of ASEAN," *Journal of Common Market Studies* 20:4 (1982), 301-319. He says the member-nations are as much concerned with revolutions within as they are with Vietnam as the external threat.

59. See Charles Frankel, *The Neglected Aspect of Foreign Affairs: American Educational and Cultural Policy Abroad*, Washington, Brookings Institution, 1965.

60. Falk and Kim (*op. cit.*, p. 230) suggest that if one takes the socio-psychological "minds of men" approach to the explanation of conflict, one ought to focus mainly on the decision-makers. We have done that in discussing the psychologies of leaders and elites, especially the aggressive ones.

61. See for example the review of David V. Edwards' *Arms Control in International Politics*

(New York, Holt, 1969) by Davis B. Bobrow in *American Political Science Review*, vol. 63 (1969), pp. 1339-1340.

62. Associated Press dispatch, May 5, 1970.

63. For differing views, see Colin S. Gray's "Moscow is Cheating" and Michael Krepon's "Both Sides are Hedging" in *Foreign Policy*, No. 56, Fall 1984.

64. Lloyd Jensen, "Approach-Avoidance Bargaining in the Test-Ban Negotiations," *International Studies Quarterly* vol. 12 (1968), pp. 152-160, 160. See also his "Soviet-American Bargaining Behavior in the Post-War Disarmament Negotiations," *Journal of Conflict Resolution*, vol. 7 (1963), pp. 522-541.

65. Charles C. Price, "The Case for Disarmament: Some Personal Reflections on the United States and Disarmament," *Annals of the American Academy of Political and Social Sciences*, vol. 469 (1983), 144-154.

66. George Kennan, "Letter to a Russian," *New Yorker* magazine, September 25, 1984, pp. 55 ff.

67. See Falk and Kim (*op. cit.*, pp. 585-587) on the fruitlessness of traditional formal-legal hopes.

Chapter 6

AND THAT EXPLAINS WHY
FOREIGN POLICY IS A MESS?

Here we first consider the rational approach to foreign policy, including the systematic way decision-makers ought to plan and execute policies, according to scholars who find statesmen too haphazard in this respect. These scholars are the latest in a three-thousand-year tradition that has seen Mo-tze, Kautilya, Ibn Khaldun, Machiavelli, Haushofer and many others write their advice to princes.

We also look at some of the claims made for the rationality and morality of US policy by individuals involved in the policy process. Then we observe how rational or moral the foreign policies of the principal nations actually have been since World War II.

We then apply to the post-World War II period the explanatory theory developed in Chapters 2 through 5.

Finally, we discuss untried cures for international conflict.

A. The Rational Approach to Foreign Policy

Scholars do not tire of calling for calm statesmanship and rational decision-making,[1] but only a few have produced frameworks within which the whole range of a nation's foreign policy can be systematically formulated and expertly carried out.

S. B. Jones, for example, suggests that foreign policy goals (ends) must be linked with national capabilities (means). In assessing capabilities one should stipulate whether one's power resources are available (a) immediately, (b) upon activation, (c) upon conversion, (d) only after development, or (e) merely hypothetically.[2]

Lerche and Said provide a comprehensive treatment of the rational approach.[3] They define national interest as the maximizing of national values such as freedom, power, justice, honor, or peace, and say "goals" must be set up which serve the national interest. Goals are the most desirable condition of affairs with respect to any issue. Toward achieving a goal, one must select as an "objective" the closest feasible approximation to the goal.

Coupling an objective with the means to achieve it is called "policy." No nation can achieve all its objectives, for means are limited. Hence one must have clear priorities. Assignment of resources to objectives is a compromise in which one tries to get all he can of what he wants. As the first charge on resources is responses to challenges, initiatives should be undertaken only with resources not needed for responses.

The resources or means are the nation's "capability" to cause changes in the situation. This may be exercised as influence or coercion, depending on how conflictual the situation is. One must estimate the capabilities of other nations, for it is the capability ratio that counts. Capability changes with the situation, so one must project whatever trends and variables may account for future change. The means-end (capability-objective) arrangement called policy is a continually altering one.

Capabilities are tangible or intangible. Tangible factors are geographic position, population, resource endowment, productive capacity, and military power. Intangibles include a nation's political, economic, and social structure, its educational and technical level, morale, and the general strategic role played by the nation. Tangibles should be computed as to quantity and intangibles as to quality.

Next, one must decide whether to act or not to act. Action uses the capabilities in four ways: (1) diplomacy, in which influence is applied by persuasion, adjustment, and agreement, up to the point of coercion; (2) economic "carrot and stick" incentives involving aid, tariff changes, foreign exchange controls, boycotts, and similar pressures; (3) psychological techniques of propaganda, subversion, and "cultural imperialism;" and (4) military techniques, meaning use or threat of force.

"Strategy in foreign policy or in war is a very conservative enterprise" because the "inexorabilities of cost and risk in an intrinsically unstable system of action combine to inhibit decision and to limit implementation." Hence "the code of prudence that governs rational policy-making." A rational approach must be cautious because of "incompleteness of information, the possibility of accident or pure chance, and the perverseness of the human personality."

> Game theory teaches that the primary responsibility of the player is to ensure his continued participation in the game; no more graphic summary could be made of the task of the statesman who invests his nation's survival in his ability to match strategies with his fellow policy-makers.

However, "there is no reason why all statesmen should be sane; a lunatic, provided only that he were capable of issuing coherent orders, is as qualified to operate the controls of government as a philosopher-king."

The policy-maker must be guided by what is probable rather than by what is merely possible. Hitler, despite the advice of his generals, acted upon his "intuition" that German armies would defeat the Soviet forces.

A common imprudence is "to conclude that a wished-for result is impossible and thereby to miss a real opportunity for meaningful action." But the rational statesman ought to strive for small victories which require only partial commitments of capability.

Like most policy-sciencers who consider themselves "realists," Lerche and Said eschew moral values, saying a foreign policy is "good" or "bad" only in the extent to which the nation "moves toward its objectives in behalf of its national interest." But they carry their realism further than most, giving it a kind or moral quality:

> Today mankind is the loser each time imprudence takes command of the policy-machine of a state. Wags have suggested a psychiatric examination as a prerequisite to high public office, but most leaders are less than enthusiastic about aspersions on their sanity. The best most of us can hope for is that prudence will continue to shackle the hand of reckless adventure; the stakes are too high to permit any but the cautious to play the game of survival in an age of thermonuclear bombs.[4]

B. Rationality of Post-World War II Foreign Policies

American foreign policy has had three strands from the time of Franklin D. Roosevelt's administration, wrote McGeorge Bundy, assistant for national security affairs to Presidents Kennedy and Johnson, in 1965.[5] These are (1) acceptance of the responsibility of power, (2) a permanent, passionate commitment to the ideal of peace, and (3) a readiness to judge ourselves and to be judged in terms of the effect of our behavior on others.

Strands (2) and (3) promise a morally good and wise foreign policy while strand (1) offers a rational one. Yet a few months later J. W. Fulbright, Chairman of the Senate Foreign Relations Committee, wrote that

> There is a kind of voodoo about American foreign policy. Certain drums have to be beaten regularly to ward off evil spirits—for example, the maledictions which are regularly uttered against North Vietnamese aggression, the "wild men" in Peking, Communism in general, and President De Gaulle. Certain pledges must be repeated every day lest the whole free world go to rack and ruin—for we regard this alliance or that as absolutely "vital" to the free world; and of course we will stand stalwart in Berlin from now until Judgment Day. Certain words must never be uttered except in derision—the word "appeasement," for example, comes as near as any word can to summarizing everything that is regarded by American policy-makers as stupid, wicked and disastrous...

As Winston Churchill once said: "Appeasement in itself may be good or bad according to circumstances... Appeasement from strength is magnanimous and noble and might be the surest and perhaps the only path to world peace."[6]

1. *From World War II to 1961.* The era of the Baruch Plan and the Marshall Plan might seem to exemplify all three alleged strands of US policy. Yet what seemed from the US viewpoint to be magnanimity was perceived in Moscow as threat.

The Baruch Plan was the US proposal to transfer all atomic activities eventually from national to international authority. USSR, refusing inspection and wanting control in the UN Security Council subject to veto, opposed it. Stalin was aware that US intended to maintain its nuclear monopoly until the Baruch proposals might be institutionalized, and according to one writer he must have been aware for some time that the testing of the first atomic bomb in the spring of 1945 had caused the new Truman administration to take a rather aggressive stance toward USSR's interest in Eastern Europe.[7]

Also before those two plans were proposed in 1947, Churchill had made his "iron curtain" speech; Britain and US had merged their occupation zones in Germany despite Soviet protests; and Truman had proclaimed his Doctrine of containing USSR, announcing it in Washington while the Moscow Conference on the German and Austrian peace treaties was in session. USSR had already lost face by having to withdraw under Western pressure from Azerbaijan, even though Iran had been notoriously pro-German until occupied by British and Soviet troops.

Years later a senator who had been a member of Truman's cabinet expressed regret that the administration had done so much to get the Cold War going.[8]

By 1949 the principle of peace had been subordinated to the "responsibility of power," with the creation of NATO (North Atlantic Treat Organization), a military alliance of US, Canada, and Western European nations. US decision-makers were willing to be judged then only by allies and not by neutrals or members of the Soviet bloc. Anti-communism became the absolute morality to which other standards, including rationality, had to give way.

Thus, when the Nationalists under Chiang Kai-shek were driven from China in 1949 and a rational approach required as a new "objective" some tolerable relationship with the communist regime in Peking, plus a moderate "capability" in the form of aid to keep Peking from sole dependence on Moscow, the Truman administration did nothing. Yugoslavia had demonstrated that a communist regime need not be controlled by Moscow, yet Secretary of State Acheson raised one weak trial balloon for recognition of China, then gave up.

The American people had been fed anti-communism for several years, and Republican leaders had convinced much of the public that the

Truman administration had "sold out" China to the communists. So, irrationality prevailed. If US policy toward China had been rational in 1949, would North Korea have invaded South Korea in 1950 and would the Chinese have joined that conflict? In this connection, Acheson's statement in 1949 that US would defend only Japan and the Philippines (by inference, *not* South Korea) was an irrationality indeed, but one surpassed by Truman's decision to let MacArthur drive on into North Korea.[9] At any rate, China remained tied to Soviet policy for ten years, and soon became a target itself of US containment policy, with the Vietnam War as a consequence.

We noted in earlier chapters that public opinion has increasingly prevented even wise decision-makers from pursuing that cool, rational diplomacy which delicate balance-of-power politics requires. Morgenthau writes:

> A popular foreign policy is not necessarily a good foreign policy. As Tocqueville put it, with special reference to the United States: "foreign politics demand scarcely any of those qualities which are peculiar to a democracy; they require, on the contrary, the perfect use of almost all those in which it is deficient."

> Faced with this dilemma between a sound foreign policy and an unsound one supported by public opinion, a government is naturally tempted to sacrifice the sound policy upon the altar of public opinion, abdicating leadership and exchanging short-lived political advantage for the permanent interest of the country.[10]

And of course a public opinion inflamed by ideology is a greater handicap.

But leaders create public opinion; they are not simply its victims until they see the desirability of a new policy which the opinion they helped mold precludes them from adopting. Truman and Acheson had been active in selling Congress and the public on the Truman Doctrine by wrapping it in an anti-communist package, not simply an anti-USSR move. It is not necessary to conclude that they were insincere; quite possibly they shared the fear of communism which they communicated to others. So, too, was the fear of capitalism engendered by Stalin from his seminary days by the study of Marxism. This attitude was buttressed by his experience of Allied intervention in the Russian Civil War and his inability to get a military agreement with France and Britain on the eve of World War II.

Stalin was not much hampered by his public, yet was it rational of him to say in a speech in February 1946 that World War II had been only part of an ongoing conflict among capitalist nations? Churchill's pronouncement the following month that "an Iron Curtain has descended across the Continent" at least had the excuse that he was not then in office. Was it rational of Stalin to quibble and delay on the Baruch Plan? No one knew better than he the cost to Russia of international insecurity throughout its history. Was it rational to refuse the benefits of the Marshall Plan, thus leaving USSR and the East European states to bear all the cost of rebuilding? Was it rational to establish the Cominform in 1947, raising old fears of the Comintern (Communist International), or to expel Yugoslavia from the Cominform in 1948, revealing cleavage within the Soviet bloc so that even Western statesmen might well have seen and remembered it?

Perfect use of the instruments of power politics by Western decision-makers, even within the limits of public opinion, is rare. There is almost no long-range planning in the US Department of State. The policy planning unit, which included representatives from other agencies concerned with national security, was notoriously neglected by most policy-makers. The rational, long-range approach is the ideal, but the reality is hurried response to stimuli from abroad on a crisis-ridden and *ad hoc* basis. The usual substitute for rational planning has been to announce a Truman Doctrine or an Eisenhower Doctrine, or "massive retaliation" or "agonizing reappraisal," then publicize it and thereafter be stuck with it.[11]

Shortcomings in US foreign policy, as presented by one scholar,[12] include lack of long-range planning, reliance on formulas, and a black-and-white image of the world, all noted above. Others are excessive legalism, pragmatism, and optimism, plus a switching back and forth between quietism and activism, between the thrust toward violence and the drive for harmony.

These defects were apparent during Dulles' secretaryship, when irrationality reached a high and Bundy's three principles were especially neglected or abused. The switching back and forth is best illustrated by Dulles' objective of friendship with Egypt and other Arab states in 1955. He assigned substantial capabilities by promising US would bear much of the expense of building the Aswan Dam. In 1956, angered by Egypt's dealings with the Soviet bloc, he suddenly and publicly withdrew US support for the Dam, touching off Nasser's expropriation of the Suez Canal and subsequent events.

A former British prime minister has observed that Soviet policy has also been marked by a hot-and-cold approach.[13] Examples would be Stalin's relaxation of the communization process in Eastern Europe in 1946, his flirtation with the Marshall Plan, and his equivocal relations with Yugoslavia.

But Britain itself, with France, blew hot and cold over Suez in 1956, deciding on intervention despite lack of US support and the certainty of USSR opposition. The two nations failed to gain a quick victory, then withdrew ignominiously when US and USSR acted as expected.[14] Britain's fluctuating attitude toward participation in the Common Market was a hot-and-cold example, as was France's rejection of the European Army idea it had originated.

Dulles' black-and-white perception of reality was demonstrated by his anti-communist moral crusade. His version of Bundy's third principle ("a readiness to judge ourselves and be judged in terms of the effect of our behavior on others") was to threaten allies with "agonizing reappraisal," communists with "massive retaliation," and the neutral countries with moral condemnation.

Dulles demonstrated excessive legalism in promoting such jerry-built alliances as SEATO and CENTO and in insisting that the Latin American states include an anti-communist proviso in the legal structure of the OAS (Organization of American States). He was excessively pragmatic in including in the "free world" any nation whose regime, however unsavory, was anti-communist, as well as when he and his brother Allen, head of the Central Intelligence Agency, contrived the invasion in 1954 which ousted the freely-elected but leftist Arbenz regime in Guatemala.

Also in 1954, Dulles carried his dubious moral crusade to the point that, with Vice President Nixon's support, he favored US military intervention in Vietnam but was restrained by Eisenhower who insisted on Franco-British participation, which was not forthcoming.[15] He even tried to persuade US allies to approve nuclear war, in the event China should intervene, although this probably would have activated the Sino-Soviet Pact and thus led to World War III.

It is not known how far Dulles would have gone in the Suez crisis of 1956 and in the Quemoy-Matsu and Near Eastern crises of 1958 if Eisenhower had not moderated his "brinkmanship."

Dulles ignored the State Department he headed and ran foreign affairs "out of his hip pocket," racing across the planet from conference to conference. He became a perpetually tired man, an example of decision-maker fatigue, with at least a touch of senility. After his resignation and death in 1959, Eisenhower took more active command of foreign policy. In 1960 he went with high hopes to a summit conference ruined by disclosure that the CIA had been flying U-2 "spy planes" over the USSR with his permission. His last significant act was to approve CIA-Pentagon plans for invasion of Cuba, having already driven Castro into the arms of the Soviet Union just as Truman had earlier done with China.

The overriding irrationality of the Dulles-Eisenhower period, however, was failure to pursue Bundy's second principle by seeking peace with the new Soviet leadership in 1953 after Stalin's death. Under Malenkov, a loosening of Stalinist internal controls had begun almost immediately, and USSR shortly agreed to a peace treaty for Austria. A rational policy-maker would have looked on the passing of the aged dictator as an opportunity to reduce tensions.

But even after Khruschev came to the helm, with his new openness of approach, and de-Stalinization was sweeping through USSR and Eastern Europe, US policy under Dulles remained rigidly anti-communist. Apart from Eisenhower's "open skies" proposal in 1955 for mutual aerial surveillance, nothing was done to take advantage of Stalin's departure. No effort was made to prepare US public opinion for a change in policy, even though the world had entered the Nuclear Balance of Terror in 1953, just after Stalin's death, when USSR detonated its H-bomb.

Again, the irrationality was not all on one side; there was plenty to go around. USSR under Malenkov, provoked by rearmament of West Germany, created the Warsaw Pact alliance in April 1955, but a month later under Khruschev it agreed to an Austrian peace treaty and withdrew its troops. And why did not Khruschev accept Eisenhower's "open skies" proposal in July? In September he did abolish the Cominform, he restored relations with Yugoslavia, and went on to exchange ambassadors with West Germany. Yet he then put USSR into foreign aid competition with US, though his motivation may have been that in the meantime Britain, at Dulles' urging, had formed the Baghdad Pact (now Central Treaty Organization, or CENTO) with four nations along USSR's southern frontier.

Why was the common stand taken by US and USSR in 1956 against Anglo-French intervention in Egypt not followed by accommodation? Instead, in early 1957 the "Eisenhower Doctrine" offered to help any country threatened by a communist-dominated nation. It is easy to say that USSR's intervention in Hungary in 1956 demonstrated that it was tough-minded as ever, but not easy to show that it was surer evidence of bad intentions than were US intervention in Guatemala in 1954 or US acceptance in 1956 of Diem's refusal to hold elections in Vietnam as required by the Geneva agreements.

US policy under Eisenhower and Dulles hardly conforms to Bundy's three principles. Nor does Soviet, British, or French policy. Even if we assume devotion to national security, the behavior is still irrational and inconsistent. We see Stalin kicking Yugoslavia out of the communist bloc, and it was this, more than US aid under the Truman Doctrine, that brought communist insurgency in Greece to failure. We see Khruschev breaking with China, thus sundering the so-called communist monolith, while Mao was so stiff-necked as to lose China's only support. Then Khruschev put up the silly Berlin wall, thus risking nuclear crisis while advertising East Berlin as a prison. We see Eisenhower in the Suez crisis alienating his NATO allies, Britain and France, yet US policy-makers were shocked when France under De Gaulle then virtually withdrew from NATO.

2. *JFK, LBJ, and RMN, From 1961 to 1973.* Let us now see how rationality and Bundy's three principles fared during Bundy's own period, the Kennedy and Johnson administrations.

The Eisenhower administration had made elimination of the Castro regime an objective and had assigned capabilities to it, then broke diplomatic relations with Cuba in January 1961, just before Kennedy's inauguration. Kennedy approved the invasion but withheld most of the air-power capability. It failed, and the world quickly learned that US had conceived and sponsored it. One would have to search long for a poorer example of the responsible use of power, the commitment to peace, or a sensitivity to the opinions of others. Anti-Castro public opinion allowed policy-makers ample latitude, yet a more imperfect use of the instruments of policy could scarcely be imagined. As an example of tough-minded power politics, it was merely bad comedy. The Bay of Pigs gambit was wholly irrational.

Kennedy then proposed the Alliance for Progress for Latin America, an example of the way conflict between some nations produces cooperation among others.

Despite the highly significant McCloy-Zorin talks which we'll discuss toward the end of this chapter, Khruschev had first tried to bully the young Kennedy, then overreacted to the Bay of Pigs fiasco. Even though he had learned during the Berlin crisis in 1961 that Kennedy was capable of firmness, he installed missiles in Cuba.

Did he not know US would be sending U-2 photography planes over Cuba, even as it had over USSR prior to the 1960 summit conference, and that Kennedy must be spoiling for a chance to redeem prestige lost at the Bay of Pigs? At any rate, when confrontation came, he withdrew the missiles at great cost to that component of capability called prestige. He salvaged something by appearing as a peacemaker to his public, true, but the publicity attending his ouster in 1964 indicated other Soviet leaders never forgave him this "adventurism."

Meanwhile, like Khruschev in Cuba, Kennedy, still smarting from the Bay of Pigs, had added thousands of US military "advisors" in Vietnam to Dulles' already huge commitment of economic capabilities, and in 1962 and 1963 US was getting ever more deeply involved in shoring up the Diem regime on the doorstep of China.

Foreign policies since World War II display the irrationality and inevitability of classic Greek tragedy, yet Khruschev and Kennedy demonstrated in the Cold War thaw of 1963 that leaders can transcend temporarily the apparent irreversibility of international tragedy. Having learned something in the Berlin and Cuba crises about the irrationality of power politics in a nuclear world, Kennedy said at American University in June of 1963 that peace is possible. He insisted that man's problems are man-made and can be solved by men, that man is not gripped by forces beyond his control:

> Some say that it is useless to speak of peace or world law or world disarmament—and that it will be useless until the leaders of the Soviet Union adopt a more enlightened attitude. I hope they do. I believe we can help them do it...
>
> ...we seek to strengthen the United Nations, to help solve its financial problems, to make it a more effective instrument for peace, to develop it into a genuine world security system—a system capable

of resolving disputes on the basis of law, of ensuring the security of the large and the small, and of creating conditions under which arms can finally be abolished.[16]

The partial test-ban treaty was shortly signed. In September, at the opening of the UN General Assembly, Kennedy spoke again of transforming the UN into an instrument adequate to ensure world peace. The treaty was confirmed in the US Senate by a vote of about four to one. It appeared that the Cold War was winding down with respect to US-USSR relations, if not with regard to US containment of China. But Kennedy was assassinated in November. And probably his last significant act was to instruct Ambassador Lodge in Saigon that he should raise no objection to an effort by Saigon generals to oust the Diem regime.

Kennedy had turned US policy toward an acceptance of Bundy's three principles. Kennedy had saved Khruschev's face, in so far as he could, in the settlement of the Cuba missile crisis. This was responsible use of power. He followed the same principle in using US influence and a demonstration of naval power to help end the Trujillo dictatorship in the Dominican Republic, in keeping with the Alliance for Progress' emphasis on democratic regimes in Latin America. In his June and September speeches, and in concluding the treaty, he showed adherence to the cause of peace and a decent respect for the opinions of mankind. He manifested a higher realism quite different from the narrow power realism of his first year in office.

But, if Kennedy matured, his successor, Johnson, never did.

Interested mainly in domestic policy, where he was far more effective than Kennedy, Johnson was insecure in matters of foreign policy. His contribution as Kennedy's vice president had been a statement praising Diem as the George Washington of South Vietnam while on a tour of Southeast Asia. His ineptitude was quickly shown when the Pakistani foreign minister attended Kennedy's funeral and Johnson dressed him down for permitting China's prime minister to visit Pakistan. Actually, Kennedy had sent military aid to India during the China-Indian border violence of 1962 without exacting a commitment from India to settle with Pakistan over Kashmir, thus offending a nation tied to the Western bloc till then. Thus Kennedy and Johnson contributed in some measure to the border war between India and Pakistan in 1965.

Johnson also inherited Kennedy's commitment in Vietnam. Diem had been removed by his generals, through assassination, and unstable military regimes followed. In January 1964 the head of the regime of the moment, General "Big" Minh, said publicly that he wished US would get out of South Vietnam. Johnson was either unable to respond quickly to this opportunity (an example of the inaction that Lerche and Said warn about) or did not wish to do so. Minh's regime was shortly replaced by another, possibly by US contrivance.

Then occurred the first example of Johnson's irrational tendency to overreact. In August 1964 the US Navy reported North Vietnamese torpedo boats had fired on two US destroyers in Tonkin Bay. Whether this was a fabrication by the military or was the result of a misreading of radar-scopes is not certain, but few now believe an attack occurred. Johnson may or may not have believed so. At any rate he reacted by ordering the navy to retaliate and got a Joint Resolution by Congress— drafted by his Administration months earlier—authorizing him to take any steps necessary to repel further aggression. This was not a declaration by Congress of war but it was the basis under US domestic law for subsequent US escalations in Vietnam. The Tonkin Bay Resolution was repealed in 1970, with Senate Foreign Relations Committee Chairman Fulbright asserting he had been misled about the attack.*

The mood of the times was a smug consciousness of American power, as indicated by the Fulbright Committee's own staff director who wrote that learning to live with the world's criticism was a price US must pay for its greatness.[17] The US Ambassador to NATO said that in the jungle of world politics the US was the lion and must become accustomed to wielding power on a global scale, concerned with the breach of the peace anywhere.[18]

Such arrogant assertions later came to have a certain graveyard irony. Yet the "global policeman" idea had a degree of rationality. The reaction of USSR, France, Belgium, and even Britain to UN peacekeeping in the Congo meant that the UN might never again play so significant a role. The US response, however, was not to strengthen the UN along the lines suggested by Kennedy but to try to fill the vacuum itself, while still carrying on its anti-communist crusade.

While some scholars such as Bundy and his successor, W. W. Rostow, have gone to Washington and participated in the tough-minded, power-

---

*Authority given the President by the Resolution was specifically subjected to the terms of the SEATO treaty, the UN Charter, and international law. Assuming an "armed attack" did occur, US was not required by its Southeast Asian Treaty (SEATO) to retaliate. Also, the retaliation went beyond the right of "self-defense" in the UN Charter as usually interpreted, and violated the rule of "proportionality" which is applied by traditional international law to cases of retaliation in self-defense. If no "armed attack" did occur in Tonkin Bay, US had no case at all, for intervention in civil wars is forbidden by international law except to protect one's nationals and their property. US troops were in Vietnam in violation of the Geneva Accords of 1954. Evidence suggests the destroyers were patrolling within 12 miles of the coast, thus violating the limit claimed by North Vietnam and most nations, but were outside the three-mile limit then asserted by US and a few other states. Moreover, the destroyers were "spyships."

realist policies,[19] or lent themselves to the endeavor through government grants and government-financed institutes,[20] others have pointed out the irrationality of US policy. Two such scholars asserted in 1966 that the "real criticism is that we are acting stupidly...employing our immense strength in increasingly expedient ways in pursuit of causes that are...indefensible in terms of historical and political reality."[21] In their view, the "evangelical interventionism" of the US derives from an ideological sickness closely related to earlier isolationism.

Thus, with Bundy sitting at Johnson's right hand, US policy had little to do with Bundy's three principles. Criticism of this policy has been almost wholly on the grounds of irrationality, rather than of ethics.[22] The accusation of irrationality, even insanity, has been directed too against scholars who hire out to do studies in which the deaths and damage resulting from nuclear "scenarios" are soberly computed. One such scholar defends this activity by saying, in effect, that it is rational and sane within the framework of an essentially irrational and insane world situation.[23]

It is only in the light of an evangelical anti-communism and his own fearful, aggressive ego that the policy of President Johnson can be understood. A few days before ordering US troops into direct combat in Vietnam, he ordered US naval forces to intervene in a civil war in the Dominican Republic. He first announced that his intervention was to protect American lives, a legal purpose under traditional international law although opposed to the doctrine of non-intervention supported by Latin American nations. A few days later he changed his ground, saying he feared a communist takeover there. The anti-communist motive gave a measure of legality to the intervention, owing to the anti-communist provision that Dulles had grafted onto the treaty structure of the Organization of American States (OAS).

A military regime had displaced the legitimately-elected Bosch regime, and his supporters were trying to oust the military. With US troops preventing the Bosch forces from pursuing their advantage, the OAS was called in by US which contended that the UN should not get involved. Eventually new elections were held and a "moderate" who had been a tool of the dictator, Trujillo, defeated Bosch.

No one in Latin America would any longer take seriously the Alliance for Progress' emphasis on constitutional regimes. Few observers saw communists or even Castroites as an important element among Bosch's supporters, but Johnson assumed the worst and overreacted.

The Kennedy initiatives toward USSR were not followed up by Johnson. He was first too busy with domestic legislation, then with the Vietnam war,[24] and finally with his own political survival. US-USSR relations suffered more from neglect than from Cold War rhetoric. Johnson seems to have understood that Yugoslavia and China were independent from Moscow but never saw that Havana and Hanoi could be too. He was above all determined, as was Nixon later, not to be the first American president to preside over a losing war.[25]

The continued relaxation of Soviet control over its "satellites" was not put to good advantage. Instead of endorsing De Gaulle's initiatives toward those countries, the US perceived his activity as a threat to NATO. US decision-makers spent what time they could spare from Vietnam on persuading West Germany and Britain to keep the anti-communist faith. A timely treaty of friendship and commerce with Czechoslovakia, while recognizing the paramountcy of Soviet interest in East Europe, might have dissuaded USSR from using its armed forces in 1968 to oust the liberalizing Czech regime.

The policy of the Brezhnev leadership that succeeded Khruschev was inward-looking, stolid and unimaginative but not at first irrational. Anxious perhaps lest the Vietnam war escalate into a nuclear war, USSR was on the whole content to see US bogged down there and unable to do much elsewhere, so that the cost to Moscow of intervening in Czechoslovakia was limited to a brief revival of the Cold War mentality.

From the foreign policy viewpoint, Mao Tse-tung's "cultural struggle" in the later 1960s was irrational indeed.[26] He virtually paralyzed China's capacity for action abroad, including its ability to intervene in Vietnam in the event that might appear necessary, and impaired China's capacity to defend itself should USSR try to wipe out its nuclear installations. Once the struggle within China was over, violence broke out in 1969 along the Soviet-Chinese border. It might have been spontaneous but it was probably started by China. If so, there is no rational explanation unless Peking hoped simply to worry USSR into ceding some of the disputed territories. Perhaps China's explosion of its first H-bomb in 1967 had been a heady experience for Mao.

Johnson, after allegedly turning down three opportunities in 1964-65 to negotiate the Vietnam conflict, de-escalated the war and went to the peace table in 1968. Vietnam cost him a second term and his place in history. But he could have been even more irrational; he could have used nuclear weapons in a final effort to win that war.

Nixon promised to end the war and began his term rationally with his "Nixon Doctrine" that in future US would help countries defend themselves against aggression by giving economic and military aid, but that they must rely on their own armed forces. Then, however, he apparently tried to win the war. There were secret bombings of Cambodia unauthorized by Congress, then the ouster of Prince Sihanouk, the most deft neutralist in Asia, followed by an overt invasion of Cambodia which invited Soviet or Chinese intervention. But an outraged US public forced quick withdrawal, and Nixon left the puppet Lon Nol regime to fend for itself. The communist Khmer Rouge under Pol Pot took over and proceeded to kill several hundred thousands of its fellow Cambodians, in an effort to reach communism immediately.

Nixon carried on the war in Vietnam for four years, though at reduced levels of US troop involvement. He eventually risked Soviet or Chinese intervention again by mining Haiphong Harbor and "carpet-bombing" North Vietnam to get a face-saving agreement in early 1973 with Hanoi, then withdrew most US military forces.

Clark Clifford made a televised confession on April 10, 1975. He had been an important figure in US foreign policy from the Truman administration into the first days of the Nixon administration. He had been Johnson's last Secretary of Defense and had helped persuade Johnson to give up in Vietnam. Clifford still did not know why he and others acted so irrationally over so many years, but he gave a totally candid and sobering account of the Cold War psychology as it was applied to the Vietnam venture and of how he learned at last to question it.[27]

Nixon, like Johnson, was an exceptionally insecure man, unpredictable, and was probably recognized as dangerous by decision-makers in other nations who also recalled his history as a Cold Warrior.

In 1971, faced by a deteriorating domestic economy and a loss of public support on Vietnam, he reversed a lifetime policy and announced new approaches to Moscow and Peking, those fountainheads of communism, while continuing the anti-communist war in Vietnam. Was he trying to return to rationality, or being expedient?

In 1972, facing re-election, he enhanced his peacemaker image by subsidizing a sale of wheat to USSR and signed the ABM agreement to limit defensive missiles. In late 1973, with Nixon facing impeachment, Moscow apparently proposed that the two nations intervene in the fourth Arab-Israeli war. Nixon declined.

Then, in a bizarre move, he asserted that Soviet military planes were on their way or ready to go to the war arena—though Moscow denied this—and he ordered a worldwide US nuclear alert. He thus risked nuclear war, as indeed did Brezhnev if in fact he was about to intervene unilaterally in the Middle East.

In 1971, Nixon had supported Pakistan in its latest war with India. Pakistan had provoked India's intervention by mass murder of Bengalis in East Pakistan (now independent Bangladesh). Nixon sent a naval nuclear task force into the Bay of Bengal. China prepared to move against India. But both drew back; they learned New Delhi had assurances that USSR would prevent China or US from intervening.[28] Nixon's move to intervene was irrational, for Pakistan had no case in world opinion and was already clearly beaten, but the decision to draw back was rational.

Nixon's policy of supporting peace in the Arab-Israeli conflict was also rational. No US president can abandon Israel, owing to domestic political considerations, but US and especially its allies are dependent on Arab oil, so peace is the only rational policy. But a policy of seeking peace is not a policy of scrupulous neutrality, and US policy had so favored

Israel that the Moslem states retaliated with their oil embargo, causing the first great increase in the world price of oil. Thus, in retrospect at least, US favoritism toward Israel was irrational, though politically expedient. And this was followed by the vast irrationality, in terms of substantive national interests, whereby US, its Western allies and Japan let OPEC (Organization of Petroleum Exporting Countries) get away with the embargo and price jump. But, as mentioned in Chapter 5, this merely underlines how unimportant economic interest is as a cause of war. Also, there is some indication that Nixon and Kissinger saw the price rise as a good thing, in that the Shah of Iran would be able to afford the kind of military build-up that would make him the principal ally and surrogate of the US in the Middle East.

The extent to which irrationality might reach was underscored by Secretary of Defense Schlesinger's disclosure that in the last days before Nixon's resignation in 1974 all US military commanders had been warned not to act upon any orders from Nixon that were not placed through the Secretary's office. No doubt Schlesinger recalled the extraordinary military alert in 1973.

After Nixon was discredited by Watergate and other scandals, Kissinger received most of the credit for US foreign policy. But Kissinger, who like Bundy was from Harvard, is a specialist in 19th century European politics who believes in a flexible balance-of-power diplomacy, and back in the 1950s, anyway, saw value in limited nuclear war in some circumstances.[29] He is also a brilliant negotiator, especially famous for his "shuttle diplomacy" in connection with the Arab-Israeli conflict, but nothing remains now of anything that he attempted.

Kissinger was intimately involved in all the Nixon administration's foreign policy decisions, whether rational or irrational, including the CIA's successful effort to "de-stabilize" Allende's leftist but constitutional regime in Chile. This act sufficed to complete Johnson's undoing of all that Roosevelt had accomplished with his Good Neighbor Policy and Kennedy with his Alliance for Progress.

Kissinger, in an article published in the Dulles era and speaking of the need for long-range planning, had said that intellectuals are indeed able to transcend the requirements of the moment but they are asked by the decision-makers to solve problems, not to establish goals. But during his many years as the nation's No. 2 decision-maker, Kissinger himself had no long-term goals, so far as is known. The explanation may lie in Kissinger's recognition in the same article of something we noted earlier. He observes that foreign policy-makers are harried, over-worked, go from crisis to crisis, have no time to think and no time to plan for the future.[30] Fortunately for his own health, Kissinger had greater vitality than Dulles. But his distrust of group judgments, as indicated also in the article just noted, was so great that he ran the country's foreign affairs out of his hip pocket, just as Dulles did. And he had the fatal delusion that, "if you don't solve immediate problems, you can never solve long-term problems."[31]

Among nations of the second rank, France's policy under De Gaulle displayed high rationality, regardless of how irrational some of his motives may have been. France had already disengaged in 1954 from its colonial war in Vietnam. Under De Gaulle, France similarly ended its war in Algeria. De Gaulle appears to have seen the wisdom of giving independence to all the French colonies while maintaining cultural and economic ties with them. It was a way of getting rid of most of the costs while keeping most of the profits.[32]

Judging by his acts, De Gaulle saw the desirability of disengaging France from the US-USSR confrontation by withdrawing French forces from NATO and ordering NATO headquarters out of France. His opposition to the development of the Common Market into a political federation conceivably could be explained on the same grounds, for the other members of the Market were all members of NATO and solidly within the US bloc. His talk of a Europe of fatherlands reaching from the Atlantic to the Ural Mountains possibly was an attempt to bridge the gap between East and West.

France under De Gaulle enjoyed the greatest prosperity in its history, due in part to economic reforms made by the preceding Fourth Republic, and French prestige reached its highest point since the 1920s. Thanks to him, disarray within the communist bloc was almost matched by disarray within the capitalist bloc,[33] and peace was perhaps the beneficiary.

There is little doubt that De Gaulle's deep antipathy for the Anglo-Americans, arising from his cavalier treatment by Churchill and Roosevelt in World War II, and his Joan-of-Arc vision of France's grandeur, had much to do with the genesis of these rather rational policies. Foreign policies that are rational in terms of a nation's long-term best interests, whether De Gaulle's or some of Nixon's, are so rare that one must be grateful for whatever evoked them.

But De Gaulle's glee over shipment of gold from US to France to settle US payments deficits, and his bald appeal to French separatism in Quebec, were senile. As a British historian has noted, old age is frequently impetuous, careless, and incapable of concentration.[34] As De Gaulle himself once put it, speaking of Marshall Petain, "old age is a shipwreck."*

---

*An alleged cause of war that we did not think worth considering, but which may be worth mentioning here, is that old statesmen make wars and send the young men to fight them so as to get at their women. It might be nearer the truth to say that old men who soon must die anyhow may be less motivated to assure a future for others.

Whereas Nixon's new approach to Moscow and Peking appears to have been a diversionary tactic evoked by a worsening domestic situation, Willy Brandt's rational policy after he became Chancellor of West Germany in 1970 seems to have been of a higher order. With the slightest of parliamentary majorities and at considerable domestic political risk, he tried to lead West Germany out of the Cold War. Agreements were ratified with USSR, Poland, and even East Germany, which in effect accepted the division into two Germanies and provided for virtually normal diplomatic and trade relations. Brandt also had much to do with persuading the other Common Market states to admit Britain.

3. *1974-1985*. President Ford was rational enough in presiding over US withdrawal from Vietnam, and in following up the Nixon-Brezhnev SALT I arms control agreement with a meeting at Vladivostok where the Soviets made certain promises concerning human rights. Ford's only irrationality was the Mayaguez incident in which several US military personnel were killed in rescuing others aboard a US ship which the Cambodian authorities had already agreed to let go.

The Cold War, which had been a distinctly milder affair since the Partial Nuclear Test-Ban Treaty of 1963, seemed to have every chance of growing milder still.

President Carter exemplified Bundy's three principles more than any president since the Kennedy of 1962-63. US ratified the Canal Treaty giving Panama ultimate control. Agreement was reached limiting the size of underground nuclear tests. China, under the moderate Deng Xiao-ping, was granted full diplomatic recognition. Carter announced US support of human rights around the world and held to it pretty closely. He withheld US support of Somoza, the Nicaraguan dictator, who was ousted by a broadly-based revolution, and sent substantial economic aid to the new regime, as Eisenhower ought to have done when Castro took over from Batista.

Carter and Sadat brought Egypt and Israel to the Camp David accords which ended their series of wars. When the Shah of Iran, that slender reed whom Nixon and Kissinger had built up into a supposedly powerful ally, was brought down by a coalition of Marxists, students and Islamic fundamentalists, Carter was wise enough not to intervene. Perhaps he had talked with US Peace Corps volunteers who had served in Iran and knew how shaky the Shah's regime had been all along. When US embassy personnel in Teheran were made hostages, Carter showed restraint, and after the US military bungled a rescue attempt, he brought the hostages home alive.

But in a two-nation-dominant configuration of the international system it takes two to sweep back the tide of anarchy. And Brezhnev in 1979 committed the vast irrationality of replacing a friendly but bumbling regime in Afghanistan with a puppet regime. Carter responded by cancelling US grain sales to USSR, increasing the

Pentagon's budget, and sending aid to the Afghan guerrillas, but was otherwise content to let the Soviets experience their own Vietnam. The SALT II arms control agreement, though negotiated and signed, was not ratified by the US.

Carter might have become a truly transcendant leader, rising above the vicious anarchic cycle of mutual fears, as Kennedy became in his last months, if his two principal advisors in foreign policy had been men of vision and if Brezhnev in his senility had not invaded Afghanistan. Yet it was Carter, under criticism for events in Iran, who intervened, however cautiously, to help the Salvadoran military junta put down Marxist guerrillas, and who equivocated on support for the moderates in Nicaragua. At any rate, his moderation in foreign policy, together with high interest rates and inflation, cost him re-election.[35]

President Reagan, by his anti-communist rhetoric and his sharp escalation of the Pentagon's budget, brought the Cold War back to a virulence not seen since Dulles' time. This was not rational in terms of nuclear deterrence and *detente*, but it did serve him by rallying an American public still smarting from the hostage affair and defeat in Vietnam. Reagan abandoned Carter's emphasis on human rights abroad, except in the Soviet Union where Brezhnev was backsliding from his Vladivostok commitments. Reagan sided entirely with the right-wing regime in El Salvador, sending large-scale aid and US advisors, thus risking deeper involvement in another civil war. He persuaded the right-wing government of Honduras to let US use that country as its military base in Central America. He terminated aid to the Nicaraguan regime, accusing it of helping the Salvadoran rebels. Using the CIA, he fostered a civil war within Nicaragua, employing Somoza's supporters and others who dissented against the partially-Marxist government. The CIA's inanities were such that Nicaragua brought suit in the World Court against US, whereupon Reagan announced that US would not be bound by the Court's decision.

That El Salvador and Honduras are enemies, having been at war not so long ago, merely adds to the absurdity of the Central American situation. But in early 1985, Reagan's remarks at his press conference suggested that a degree of senility may have set in and that he intends to have his way in Central America. Later in the year he imposed an embargo on US trade with Nicaragua, so the Sandinista regime promptly sought economic help from Moscow.

Reagan's other irrationality was his decision to send US marines into Lebanon to help keep the peace while Israeli troops withdrew and to prop up a Lebanese government which was Christian in a predominantly non-Christian land. After 241 marines and sailors were killed in a Moslem suicide attack, Reagan withdrew the US force at considerable loss of face, as well as life.

Just two days after the marines were killed, Reagan ordered US troops to occupy the tiny island of Grenada in the Caribbean where, he said, Marxist disorder threatened US citizens (mainly students at a medical-school diploma mill) and the US strategic position in the Caribbean. Reagan gained a great victory and the US military awarded themselves thousands of medals. But the sequence of events reminds us of Kennedy's decision, after his Bay of Pigs fiasco, to try his luck in Vietnam.

Reagan opposed the new Nuclear Freeze movement in US that had begun in 1980 and had gained strength in 1982 with the publication of Jonathan Schell's book, *The Fate of the Earth*. But he had to moderate his rhetoric when the movement spread to Europe and threatened to prevent the installation of a new generation of US missiles in certain NATO countries. He did not, however, attempt any new initiatives when Brezhnev died and was succeeded by Andropov, or when Andropov, soon dead, was followed by Chernenko.

Reagan moderated his stance toward the USSR still further in the presidential campaign of 1984, asserting that he was, after all, in favor of arms control and disarmament. But Andropov and then Chernenko seemed unconvinced. With the Afghan mess still going on, and with their top leaders dying off seriatim, Soviet policy-makers by and large have kept to the Kremlin and attempted no foreign policy initiatives. They did withdraw from arms talks as an effort to stop the placement of the new NATO missiles, but agreed to new talks in 1985, as they are upset about Reagan's "Star Wars" defense against nuclear missiles, which we'll discuss in Chapter 7. They also replaced the food aid which Reagan denied to Nicaragua and are continuing to send aid there, which is the way these things escalate.[36]

Finally, on the matter of irrationality, the columnist Jack Anderson alleges that Reagan in 1981 secretly informed USSR that he would never agree to the SALT II arms control treaty, hence he has no right to complain if in fact the Soviets have built beyond the limits set forth in the treaty. The curious thing is that both sides say they have abided by the treaty, even though it was never ratified.

But Reagan had no monopoly on irrationality during 1980-85.

Israel, under a new right-wing regime, invaded Lebanon in 1982 to oust the Palestine Liberation Organization (PLO), which led to the massacre by Christians of Moslems, the blowing up of the US marine barracks, a vast increase in Syrian influence, and something approaching the fiscal if not the moral bankruptcy of Israel.[37] Under a new Labor government, Israel was trying in 1985 to extricate itself from Lebanon.

President Hussein of Iraq foolishly invaded Iran, forgetting (as US did in Vietnam and again in Nicaragua) that revolutionary Iran was bound to respond with fanatical resistance. Now Hussein seeks vainly for the peace which the old Ayatollah denies him.

The right-wing military regime in Argentina, hoping to divert public attention from its human rights transgressions and economic follies, invaded the Falkland Islands, bringing itself to ruin while enabling the conservative Thatcher government in Britain to gain a great victory in the eyes of the public.

Vietnam, backed by USSR, continued to waste itself in sad Cambodia, trying to oust its fellow communists backed by China.

And in sad Poland, with the support of the new Polish pope, the Solidarity labor movement overreached itself, leaving Poland as usual in a condition which a cynic might describe as "desperate but not serious." Reagan helped things along, making noises about ultimate liberation of the East European countries.

There is an almost heroic quality in the rigidity of statesmen in Washington, Moscow, Peking, Tel Aviv and other capitals who intervene abroad to support sure losers. Often they do it in the face of both right reason and good conscience. US has an especially long list of losers: Rhee in South Korea, Chiang in China, Diem in South Vietnam, Lon Nol in Cambodia, and the Shah in Iran. To this list the Marcos regime in the Philippines will probably soon be added.

The irrationality of supporting sure losers is one that many presidents and foreign policy advisors have shared since World War II. There are other absurdities, described in 1985 by the *Washington Monthly*:

When the US Senate was getting ready to vote on the NATO alliance, Acheson assured the senators that there would be no permanent commitment of large numbers of US troops. Today, 35 years later, 325,000 troops are committed to NATO, and roughly half the US defense budget goes to support them and European defense in general. US spends 7.2 percent of its GNP on defense compared with West Germany's 4.3 and Italy's 2.6. Cannot Europe, with twice the GNP of the Soviet Union, and with only one front to defend compared with USSR's two, now pay for its own defense? If it did, the US budget deficit could be reduced by half.

And *The Washington Monthly* observes, with respect to the Japanese economic miracle, that "The main miracle is how the Japanese have gotten us to pay for their defense for so long. If we spent as small a portion of our economy on defense as they did, we'd have more than $150 billion dollars to build better factories and cars and to train better engineers. As it is, we buy their cars for dollars and we provide their defense virtually for free."

The same publication goes on to discuss US policy in the Persian Gulf, saying that although US gets less than four percent of its oil from the Gulf, US is embarked on a $20 billion project that would commit over 200,000 US forces to contain conflicts in the area such as the Iraq-Iran war.

Then who does care about Persian Gulf oil? Japan for one, which relies on the Gulf for over one half of its oil, and Western Europe, which gets around a quarter. Japan is also the number one or two trading partner with every country in the Gulf except Bahrain, where it is number three. It is the number one trader with both Iran and Iraq. France is selling weapons to the latter.

Given this sizeable financial interest on the part of our allies, you'd expect them to help pay for the Gulf's defense. But would you pay, if you had a soft touch like Reagan eager to do it for you? While Japan and our allies merrily make money off the Iran-Iraq war, we pay the bill to contain it.[38]

This inability to change policies after Europe and Japan have become at least as prosperous as US, and after US has reduced by conservation its reliance on Persian Gulf oil to nearly nil—this too is rigidity, irrational rigidity. Thus two scholars speak of "immobilism" in foreign policies.[39]

The picture we actually get of policy making is such that a psychologist has made rather a good case of generalizing from the behavior of college undergraduates to the behavior of foreign policy decision-makers.[40] It is even more like the tit-for-tat acts of small children during recess.

Two scholars suggest that the assumption that decision-making is done by rational statesmen may be quite wrong, especially in crises.[41] Another speaks of international craziness caused by the seeking of unreasonable goals, a propensity for high risk-taking, ritualistic policy styles, and a simple inability to grasp means-ends relationships.[42]

It may be worse than that. A statistical study of personality effects on American foreign policy, published in 1978, concludes that it is a fantasy that rational choice prevails; that US politics frequently elevates to high office "high-dominance individuals with greater personal predispositions to threaten or use force."[43] And in a book published in 1984 Saul Bellow says that "true personality did not exist at the top of either hierarchy, East or West. Between them the superpowers had the capacity to kill everybody, but there was no evidence of human capacities in the top leadership. On both sides power was in the hands of comedians and pseudo persons."[44]

But Henry Kissinger, who is experienced and intelligent even though he has no vision, is probably closer to the truth in writing, in 1979 after he had left office, that

The superpowers often behave like two heavily armed blind men, feeling their way around a room, each believing himself in mortal peril from the other, who he assumes to have perfect vision... each tends to ascribe to the other side a consistency, foresight and coherence that its own experience belies. Of course, over time even two blind men can do enormous damage to each other, not to speak of the room.[45]

C. Application of Our Explanatory Theory to Post-World War II History

During this period nations acted and reacted in an environment which discouraged decision-makers from adherence to such rational-moral principles as responsible use of power, devotion to peace, sensitivity to the opinions of others, or anything approaching the perfect use of the instruments of power.

Politically, anarchy envelops the planet in the same way as, meteorologically, atmosphere envelops the planet. Just as there are tiny centers of instability in the atmosphere which develop into low pressure areas and produce storms, so there are centers of instability in the planetary anarchy. Examples are divided Germany and Korea and Vietnam, as well as any nation involved in civil violence; the Suez and Panama Canals and any heavily-trafficked ocean strait; any border whatever between independent nations, but especially those in Central Europe, the Middle East, South Asia, Southeast Asia, Northeast Asia, and Africa where the great nations or their client states confront each other.

It was within this environment of anarchy that the Cold War developed. In the earlier years USSR occupied the most anxious seat. War-torn, isolated, and weaponless in the nuclear sense, its connections with most other nations in the system were negatively charged. Against Moscow's fears the Baruch and Marshall Plans could make little impression, for fear drives out reason.

Just as two great weather systems in the planet's atmosphere must interact, so did US and USSR necessarily interact. The deteriorating cycle of anarchy is essentially a phenomenon of reciprocal fear. As between the two great nations, the fear centered principally on Berlin and Germany. From 1945, as a low negative charge evoked a more highly charged negative response, the lines connecting Washington and Moscow mounted toward maximum negative charge. Impetus was added as the ante was raised from A-bomb to H-bomb to missile in the game of nuclear one-upmanship.

Negative charges increasingly polarized the two superpowers. Decision-makers at each polar node despatched along their cables to lesser nodes impulses positive or negative which resulted in a a two-power-dominant configuration of the international system. A constellation of lesser nodes grouped about each of the polar powers in what some call a bi-polar system. It was in this way that such examples of cooperation as NATO, the Baghdad Pact (CENTO), the Warsaw Pact, and SEATO came successively into being. The Marshall Plan, Western Europe's Common Market, and Eastern Europe's Comecon were in large part also responses to conflict.

The existence of two competing politico-economic ideologies played a role, especially in deciding the make-up of the constellations grouped around each superpower. Communist nations grouped around USSR while non-communist nations, especially the developed liberal capitalist ones, moved around US.

The significance of the ideological dimension can easily be overemphasized. True, communist Yugoslavia sided with USSR and joined the Cominform when Stalin re-constituted it. But the other East European countries were occupied by Soviet troops, hence had little choice. Also, the Cold War did not bring USSR to support its ideological comrades in China; instead, Stalin let the Chinese communists go it virtually alone until they won in 1949, then made common cause with them. But virtually a decade later Mao led China out of the Soviet coalition and in the early 1960s was challenging Khruschev and Moscow for leadership of the communist world.

Similarly, the liberal regimes in France and Italy embraced the anti-communist cause because in part they depended on US aid for reconstruction, while Britain pegged its whole foreign policy to Anglo-American cooperation with US as a senior partner. In Germany, anti-communism had historically had the status of a religion, but West Germany had no real choice, for it was occupied by Western armies. But ideology did not suffice to keep the US coalition intact, for De Gaulle virtually took France out of NATO and challenged US leadership in Europe. However, under subsequent French leaders the coalition has been somewhat repaired.

The polarization of the planetary system into two opposing constellations, with increasingly high negative charges, culminated in the crises of 1961 and 1962. Then, with Kennedy and Khruschev sending out positive charges toward each other, and going on to sign the Partial Nuclear Test-Ban Treaty, the Cold War waned as systemic pressures went down. Indeed, it was this that made Mao so angry at Khruschev. And it was this "thaw," with consequent loosening of both alliances, that gave De Gaulle the opportunity to play a lone hand, and the more so because he had just closed out France's final colonial war.

Systemic pressures revived during the Vietnam war, but mainly along the cables connecting Washington with Moscow and Washington with Peking, because most US allies stayed on the sidelines. The pressures never mounted so high as in 1961 and 1962, but they might have done so if it had ever appeared that US might defeat Hanoi.

The clearest of indications that anarchy between sovereign nations is ever so much greater a cause of war than is ideology is found in Nixon's new approaches to Moscow and Peking at the same time he was continuing to fight in Vietnam. Nixon, the great anti-communist ideologue, was announcing that he had finally learned that ideology distracts statesmen from their main job of enhancing the security and prosperity of the nation and leads them into disastrous ventures such as

Vietnam. In a way it is too bad that Watergate ended his career, just when he had learned this, for a reason that we'll discuss in our final chapter.

At any rate, the *detente* that Nixon initiated continued until 1979 when USSR intervened in Afghanistan. There was an immediate increase in negative charges along the cables connecting Moscow with Washington and the other NATO capitals but also with Peking and with many lesser nodes including Islamabad, Teheran, and even New Delhi. As between Moscow and Washington, pressures continued to increase with the advent of Reagan whose Cold War utterances have invited negative pressures from most nodes around the planet, including some in NATO.

As of 1985, then, the planet's developed nations are still divided into two opposing coalitions dominated by US and USSR, with China as a separate power off to itself, friendly toward US and, though moving away from socialist economics, improving its relations with USSR. Most of the other nations of Asia have connections, close or not so close, with US, USSR, or China, while most of Latin America and Africa cluster rather closely around the NATO coalition.

Given an anarchy intensified by nuclear weaponry, and the presence of competing ideologies, why has not World War III occurred? The other element in our explanatory theory is the dominance of at least one principal nation by an aggressive elite; this has been lacking.

From the viewpoint of the Western bloc, Stalin might be considered aggressive. He was comparable to Hitler in number of people liquidated, and he executed most of his early associates. But he was as defensive in managing foreign policy as he was aggressive in domestic policy. Even his war on Finland in 1939 can be seen as an effort to occupy frontier positions more easily defended. The Nazi-Soviet Pact of 1939 has been seen by most observers as essentially defensive—a buying of time after failure of USSR's military talks with France and Britain. At the end of the war, his reluctance to withdraw Soviet troops from Iran and his refusal to withdraw them from Eastern Europe are explainable as efforts to keep the defensive perimeter of USSR as broad as possible by flanking the Soviet Union with like-minded states.

The other candidate, from the Western viewpoint, would be Mao Tse-tung. But his preoccupation with internal affairs was almost total. His reincorporation of Tibet into the Chinese empire was implementation of long-term Chinese policy under Chiang Kai-shek and the Manchu emperors. In the border violence with India, Mao settled for far less territory than China's military superiority would have permitted, and this along a frontier never defined except unilaterally by Britain when master of India. Korea and Vietnam are too near China to impute aggressiveness to Mao by reason of China's intervention in the Korean War and its modest aid to Hanoi in the Vietnam War. The Maoist leadership tended to speak loudly in foreign affairs, especially during the early 1960s, while carrying a rather small stick.

From the viewpoint of the Soviet bloc and other communist states, only US can be seen as aggressive. Here the allegation is aimed at that alliance between the US military elite which seeks glory and rank in large budgets and foreign interventions and those industrialists and others who profit financially from defense expenditures and installations. But most US corporations do not benefit much from the Pentagon's budgets, while most military officers probably realize that they are living off the fat of the land, with generous pay, promotions and pensions, and do not welcome risky ventures such as Vietnam, even though they admittedly have a vast stake in a continuing Cold War posture toward USSR and communism.

If US qualified on the whole as an aggressive nation, then Barry Goldwater, who was a general as well as a senator and a hawkish hard-liner, would have done much better in the 1964 presidential election than he did. Reagan's election can be explained as the US public's reaction to defeat in Vietnam and to the incident of the hostages in Iran.

During this post-World War II period, statesmen have not been basically aggressive. They have been basically frightened—of other nations, of making mistakes, and of their own constituencies. Publics in turn have been equally frightened, believing their whole way of life threatened by other nations and ideologies.

However, nuclear weaponry, while aggravating the fears induced by anarchy and contrary ideologies, has imposed a ceiling of greater fear through which the lesser fears have not yet been able to penetrate. There is apparent paradox in that the level of violence is controlled by a greater level of potential violence, but the paradox disappears when the situation is viewed as a tension between fears.

We close this section by responding to the question, Why do wars occur in the nuclear age?[46] They occur because there is nothing in the Nuclear Balance of Terror to prevent the dynamic of anarchy from functioning as it always has done. The Balance inhibits only those wars in which nuclear weapons are apt to be used. But anarchy and ideology have proved strong enough, without the presence of an aggressor nation, to produce terribly destructive conventional wars as well as crises that have reached right up to the nuclear threshold.

Whether the Balance of Terror can forever inhibit the thrust of the world international system to extinguish itself will discussed in the next Chapter 7 on Prediction. First, we must take care of some unfinished business.

D. Untried Cures for War: Their Adequacy.

1. *Unilateral Disarmament.* This is a rather recent application of an old idea variously characterized as non-violence, civil disobedience, and pacifism, which draws on several religious-philosophical traditions.

The principled pacifism of the Gospels was by no means a theoretical one only, without any influence on the practical life of early Christians; evangelical recommendations were interpreted in conformity with the contents and followed. It is known, for example, that the Christian community in Jerusalem in 66 A.D. moved behind the Jordan to avoid participation in war. Christian writers of the first three centuries condemned wars as well as the military service. Origen was of the opinion that Christians were "sons of peace" and, in contradistinction to Moses' law, should not kill enemies, but use prayer as their weapon... Opinions were expressed that for this reason the Old Testament was anti-evangelical and should be rejected.[47]

Pacifism did not survive Christianity's becoming the Roman empire's state religion after Constantine's reign. The Church's position became one of an uncertain distinction between just and unjust wars, while fundamentalist sects today derive endorsement from the Old Testament for war. Nevertheless, in the Protestant-Catholic wars of the 16th and 17th centuries, a group called "eirenists" (literally, pacifists or "peaceniks") believed that for Christians all usage of weapons was prohibited. In England and Germany, pacificist sects such as the Quakers date from about that time.

The modern history of civil disobedience (non-violent or passive resistance), as distinguished from pacifism, begins with the essay "On the Duty of Civil Disobedience" by Henry David Thoreau, an American who opposed the Mexican War. His essay came to the attention of Leo Tolstoy, the Russian novelist and pacifist, from whose writings Mohandas Gandhi, the Indian, got the idea. In turn, a biography of Gandhi written by the American missionary, E. Stanley Jones, came to the attention of Martin Luther King, Jr., the American black leader. In this way the concept went around the world and back to its homeland.[48]

Passive resistance is very old, being found in ancient epics of India, among the ancient Greeks, and in early Scandinavian law as well as in medieval German thought.[49]

Gandhi held that every citizen is responsible for every act of his government. This is the most extreme doctrine of collective responsibility ever propounded. A truly just and democratic State deserves loyalty, but the citizen always retains the right to disobey particular laws that he regards as unjust and repressive. The citizen cannot relinquish even a portion of his ever-present moral responsibility in the name of the social contract, or legal sovereignty, or tacit consent, or the rule of law.[50]

The way in which non-violent resistance might be brought to bear on an international situation is indicated in these remarks concerning Rabindranath Tagore, an Indian poet and contemporary of Gandhi:

Hence though he at first doubted the full justification of the Gandhian non-cooperation movement, he later saw it as an intermediary step to be taken by our nation and by other unjustly treated nations till the wrong-doer had rectified his actions and opened the door for real cooperation. For him as for Gandhi justice could not be obtained by retaliatory injustice, wrong actions could not neutralize other wrong actions. Aggression by another nation-state or states had to be met by the united will and moral action of the trans-national community.[51]

Pacifism and civil disobedience are somewhat akin to international understanding and world public opinion, discussed among old cures for war, but they proceed more upon an awareness of a trans-national common humanity underlain by strong spiritual resources. Also, civil disobedience seeks actively to change public policy.

Civil disobedience is inherently limited in relation to international conflict. For it depends on an appeal to conscience and reason in a face-to-face confrontation. Draft-card burning in New York, being hustled off to jail for demonstrating in New Haven or West Berlin, being shot at Kent State University—these affect policy to the degree that protestors and policy-makers have some sort of proximity.

The trans-national impact is usually slight, and slightest when needed most—before the decision to resort to international violence has been made. Televised pictures of a Buddhist monk setting himself on fire can arouse people and affect national decision-making (in this case, the self-immolation probably affected the US decision to withdraw support from Diem's regime in Saigon). But there were no televised pictures of the decision-making process which began the US involvement in Vietnam.

Non-violent protest has therefore had its successes in primarily civil situations, in India and the US, and these successes depended on great leadership by Gandhi and King to keep the action mainly non-violent. Indeed, a scholar tells us that followers of Gandhi and Tagore practiced non-violence because the leaders told them to do it more than because they had any conviction that non-violence would convert the British.[52]

And it is significant that, so soon as British India was divided into two independent nations, India and Pakistan, the blood-letting was enormous, even though Gandhi and other leaders were still active.

Non-violent methods can have a certain applicability to international or quasi-international situations where Tagore's aggressor nation is actually on the scene, as the British were in India. The North Vietnamese and Vietcong might have gotten rid of the Americans more quickly if they had used passive resistance. But, even assuming that Tagore's trans-national community were united and vibrant with conviction, would this have a decisive effect on today's decision-makers? They are not intrinsically aggressive, as we have seen, but are genuinely frightened.

Unless the spiritual underpinnings of pacifism and non-violent resistance can so far change humans as to make them no longer afraid, this cure is not relevant to the causes of international conflict. Anarchy, ideological conflict and aggressive elites are—both in their becoming and in their being—alive with fear.

Unilateral disarmament has had little following except in Britain and US. From 1958 on for a few years it was hotly debated within the Labour Party. It was mainly concerned with nuclear disarmament, as the start toward total disarmament. The American Committee for Non-Violent Action produced a few examples of civil disobedience such as sailing into nuclear-testing zones, but it was Britain's Campaign for Nuclear Disarmament which for a time excited public attention and resulted in fairly widespread civil disobedience protests.

Unilateralism offers a basic criticism of power theory's strategy of negotiating from strength. It asserts that no real negotiations for disarmament have resulted and no real strength either. Unilateralists have cited the neutralization of Austria in 1955 which was possible only because USSR unilaterally reversed its position of strength.

Unilateralism seeks though political action within the nation, including civil disobedience, to convince decision-makers to abandon the nuclear-deterrence posture and do enough disarming to produce reciprocal disarmament by other nuclear powers. If there is no reciprocation, the true unilateralist believes his nation ought nevertheless to move on to disarmament.

Unilateralism also stresses the idea that a "garrison state" is one in which freedom and other human values cannot survive.[53]

Unilateral disarmament is not a very live issue in 1985. Its emotional content passed over into and was replenished by the anti-war movement of the 1960s and early 1970s, and in part undergirds the Nuclear Freeze movement of the 1980s.

Its intellectual content has provoked some interesting scholarly studies. Charles Osgood, a specialist in psychology and communications, suggests unilateral initiatives to break the armaments deadlock and says that these initiatives should be publicized, explicitly invite reciprocation, and be faithfully carried out in a series of progressive reductions, even though there is no reciprocation; provided however that the whole of these unilateral actions should not reduce a state's capacity to inflict unacceptable nuclear retaliation if an opponent should attack.[54] The Nuclear Freeze proposal is similar, except that most proponents stress early "mutual verification" that the Soviets are indeed reciprocating.[55]

This type of proposal would be valuable to decision-makers who, for the moment at least, are "transcendant" in their willingness to try to reverse the cycle of anarchy. But at best it amounts to no more than a partial disarmament with all its theoretical and practical inadequacies discussed in Chapter 5.

Unilateralism thus offers nothing already considered unless it goes all the way in case reciprocation is not forthcoming. Its chances of going all the way are remote so long as there is no genuine world security system to quiet fears of national insecurity; and if there were such a system, unilateralism would be beside the point.

The following remarks on non-violence in general apply not only to Americans but to all human beings because all are involved in the international predicament and its fears:

It would be difficult to persuade a nation like America, which has grown great through wars, to put its faith in nonviolent methods of combat. So far, nonviolence has appealed only to underprivileged groups without hope of achieving superior arms, for whom it offers enhanced self-respect and a new means of achieving their aims. Acceptance of nonviolence by Western nations would require changes in attitudes and values of the magnitude of the religious conversion of an individual or of a major revolution inside a country such as that which took place in Russia with the overthrow of czarism.

We do not know much about the conditions fostering either individual or group conversions... Sudden religious conversions occur typically in persons who have undergone a period of desperation, hopelessness, or panic... Even less is known about forces making for conversion of groups.[56]

This psychiatrist's words are not very comforting, but we might keep it in mind that "a period of desperation, hopelessness, or panic" could conceivably open the way to gain acceptance for some fairly drastic changes in the way the international system works.

2, *General and Complete Disarmament (GCD)*. This proposal, made by President Kennedy in 1962, would have required some drastic changes.

Disarmament, as usually proposed, fails to deal adequately with anarchy, as we noted in discussing old cures in Chapter 5. No proposal up to and including the Soviet proposal in 1959 for general and complete disarmament made provision for ensuring that a nation, once disarmed, would remain that way. The only safeguard was that if one rearmed other nations would do so too. Thus the USSR's proposal, mentioned again by a Soviet premier in 1974, suffers from the same light-minded optimism that curses all cures based on an exchange of paper promises. The 1960 British proposal for GCD went a bit beyond the Soviet one by providing for inspection.

But only Kennedy's proposal in 1962 grappled with the fear of rearmament and other fears. It included provisions that would have gone far toward providing what Kennedy called "a genuine world security system." His proposal alone—of all those made since the world became one international system—was based on the recognition that nations will fear each other and resort to armaments and violence unless and until they find some better source of security.

A fascinating account of the origins of Kennedy's plan for GCD and what happened to it has been provided by Charles Price, the former president of the American Chemical Society and peace activist mentioned in Chapter 5, as follows:

In 1961, after Kennedy's inauguration, John McCloy for US and

Valerian Zorin for USSR reached a remarkable accord on a Joint Statement of Agreed Principles for Disarmament Negotiations. It was endorsed unanimously by the UN General Assembly and was the basis for Kennedy's "Outline of Basic Provisions of a Treaty on General and Complete Disarmament in a Peaceful World" which was submitted at the Geneva disarmament conference on April 18, 1962. We shall summarize its provisions shortly.

According to Price, in subsequent negotiations USSR even agreed to accept "zonal inspection" as a basis for negotiations, meaning that each country would be divided into geographical zones and the other nation could pick a zone to inspect each year. But, by then, Kennedy was dead, and under Johnson the US withdrew from the negotiations. Arnold Wolfers and others, from "one of the university branches of the military-industrial complex," published a book rationalizing the US position.[57] Later, President Nixon refused a Soviet proposal that negotiations be renewed.

Price protested to Dr. Fred Ikle, head of the Arms Control and Disarmament Agency (where Kennedy's GCD proposal had been written) and Ikle responded that Price was naive, that the US never intended the McCloy-Zorin Joint Statement to be taken seriously, that it was just propaganda to counteract Soviet propaganda. Price makes the point that Ikle himself was a product of the military-industrial complex. But William Foster, who had been head of the Arms Control and Disarmament Agency during the negotiations with USSR, asserted that he and Kennedy had been completely sincere, and that his most difficult negotiations had been with the Pentagon, not the Soviets.

In 1977, Price goes on, in hearings in Senator Pell's Subcommittee on Arms Control, the US coordinator for the UN's Special Session on Disarmament said that US was still committed to the McCloy-Zorin agreement, but "Now, that implies a very considerable amount of reorganization of the world security system which frankly no one has a clear idea how to bring about." This was during the Carter administration and Price goes on to say that Carter's National Security Advisor, Brzezinski, was quoted by the *Philadelphia Inquirer* for May 18, 1980, as saying that one of his major accomplishments in office was "the decision to move ahead with the MX missile as a first-strike weapon."[58]

That USSR's invasion of Afghanistan probably had a lot to do with reviving the MX missile is simply another example of how, in our anarchic world, all things work together for the worst.

At any rate, when the GCD Outline was submitted at Geneva, Kennedy told a press conference that it was "the most comprehensive and specific series of proposals the United States or any other country has ever made on disarmament." It was.

Providing for disarmament in three stages, down to the level required merely for internal policing, the Outline went on to say:

> The verification of disarmament would be the responsibility of an International Disarmament Organization, which would be established within the framework of the United Nations. Reduction of armaments and armed forces would be verified at agreed locations; and limitations on production, testing, and other specified activities, at declared locations...

> By the end of Stage III, when disarmament had been completed, all parts of the territory of states would have been inspected...

> A United Nations Peace Observation Corps would be established in Stage I, and a United Nations Peace Force in Stage II. The United Nations Peace Force, which would be equipped with agreed types of armaments and would be supplied agreed manpower by states, would be progressively strengthened until, in Stage III, it would be fully capable of insuring international security in a disarmed world.[59]

The International Disarmament Organization (IDO) would be a separate organization from the UN, established by a new treaty, with a General Conference in which all countries would be represented and a Control Council on which the major nations would have permanent seats while others would be members from time to time as voted by the General Conference. An Administrator, nominated by the Council and approved by the Conference, would be Chief Executive Officer of the IDO and would be in charge of the actual verification and inspection process. The International Court of Justice (World Court) could be asked by the Conference or Council for interpretations of the IDO treaty.

The IDO would maintain close working arrangements with the UN. Moreover, if at the close of each stage the Control Council had decided by majority vote (no veto) that the disarmament agreed to for that stage had been carried out, any permanent member which disagreed could appeal to the UN Security Council where presumably the veto would still apply, so that any of the five permanent UN Council members could bring the disarmament process to a halt.

The Treaty would require the parties to act within the UN to establish the UN Peace Force during Stage II, but presumably this process too would be subject to the veto. If Stage I, which would take three years and involve a 30 percent reduction in non-nuclear armament, were carried out without a successful appeal to the UN Security Council, Stage II would then begin. It would require a 50 percent reduction in the non-nuclear armaments still left at the end of Stage I, as well as the building up of the UN Peace Force to whatever level might be agreed on in the UN Security Council.

Since the production of nuclear weapons would merely be stopped in Stage I and none gotten rid of until Stage II at the earliest, and since nothing is said about transferring such weapons to the UN Peace Force, apparently national power would still outweigh world power at the end of Stage II. Indeed, the Outline suggests that the degree of nuclear disarmament is left to be negotiated at the outsets of Stages II and III, so it appears national power would outweigh world power until some time in Stage III. This last stage is not fixed at three years, as are Stages I and II; its duration is to be negotiated at the end of Stage II.

It would seem then that all nations would still have the means of dropping out of the disarmament process until very late in the game, while permanent members of the UN Security Council could veto the process at any point by carrying their dispute from the veto-free IDO Control Council to the UN Security Council.

The Outline also makes some provisions for peaceful international change. It would require the parties to accept in Stage II the compulsory jurisdiction of the World Court to decide legal disputes. It also speaks of the development and codification of rules of international conduct relating to disarmament. Such rules would go into effect when approved by the IDO Control Council by the end of Stage II unless a *majority* of the parties signified their disapproval. Any nation could, however, give notice within a year that it did not consider itself bound by these rules.

The Kennedy proposal was bold enough to have fired the imagination of people around the globe. But Kennedy shortly became involved in the Cuba crisis, then in the test-ban treaty negotiations and its ratification. Then he was assassinated. And we have seen what happened to it under Johnson and Nixon.

The proposal was never intended to be complete in its details; those were left to be negotiated in the IDO Treaty itself. It was unclear even in some of its major suggestions, especially the awkward interface between IDO and UN. And the proposal that conventional arms be sharply reduced in Stages I and II while the parties would not even try to negotiate on nuclear weapons until Stage II probably did not appeal to USSR. On the other hand, USSR would have been permitted to retain its veto in the UN Council, and therefore a veto on the disarmament process.

Nonetheless, one of the very few scholars who commented on the GCD Outline was close to correct in remarking that "If, as some have suggested, general and complete disarmament would bring into existence a world state without a government, by Stage III there would presumably *be* a government."[60]

Even without the veto loophole, there is little hope that Stage III would ever have been reached. During the years before the UN Peace Force obtained the decisive margin in coercive force, there would have been too many opportunities for disagreement and too much room for a return to suspicion and fear.

We can thus identify the fatal flaw in the Kennedy proposal: it assumed that national states would be able to agree to give up—and then actually give up—approximately two-thirds of their non-nuclear armament before the new source of world security (the UN Peace Force and the machinery for peaceful change) was established and in being.

National fears engendered by anarchy cannot be allayed in this fashion. A military historian, writing two years after the GCD Outline was submitted, asserted that

> Today, general and complete disarmament is irremediably bogged in the old dilemma of disarmament conferences: By lending maximum political importance to the weapons systems they are tying to abolish, they automatically estop any progress toward their abolition. I think it quite impossible today to draft a general disarmament treaty so exactly balancing all the military factors— force levels, controls, inspections, and so on—that it will be generally acceptable either to the few military great powers or to the many smaller ones.[61]

This surely holds true for any arrangement which omits or postpones the creation of a genuine, full-fledged world security system. One scholar sees this clearly:

> No national statesman, Western, Soviet or neutral, has yet proposed a disarmament plan that has any chance of lasting success, and it is unlikely that any will until the basic crucial issue is faced squarely. In order to protect the people of a nation which has willingly surrendered its weapons, the UN will require a range of powers and a delegation of authority considerably greater than that now entrusted to it. To deal effectively with the armament-tension dilemma, the organization will need certain of the powers which have come to be associated with those of a federal government.[62]

GCD does not deal directly with ideological conflict or the rise of aggressive nations, although, if it were able to cope with anarchy, it would abate those variables because it would reduce those external pressures that radicalize nations.

If Kennedy had lived, and had continued to work with Khruschev, we might have gotten a GCD that would indeed have amounted to a genuine world security system, capable of coping with anarchy. But he didn't, and we didn't. Lacking that, what do the next twenty or twenty-five years hold in store for us?

Chapter 6 Notes

1. To avoid nuclear war, five steps are recommended: calm statesmanship, the building of a sense of predictability and mutual interest, weapons that do not give great first-strike capability, arms control and disarmament including sharing of information, and a good deal of luck (Bruce Russett and Harvey Starr, *World Politics: The Menu of Choice*, reviewed in *Journal of Peace Research* 19:2 (1982), 197-202).

2. S. B. Jones, "The Power Inventory and National Strategy," in James N. Rosenau, ed., *International Politics and Foreign Policy* (New york, Free Press, 1961), pp. 254-267.

3. Charles O. Lerche, Jr., and Abdul A. Said, *Concepts of International Politics*, Prentice-Hall, 1963.

4. *Ibid.*, pp. 184-187. Another writer suggests that rationality in foreign policy-making requires also that non-rationalistic capabilities such as intuition be recognized and developed (Miriam Steiner's "The Search for Order in a Disorderly World, *International Organization* 37:3, 373-413).

5. McGeorge Bundy, "The Uses of Responsibility," *Saturday Review*, July 3, 1965, pp. 13 ff.

6. J. W. Fulbright's "Christian A. Herter Lecture," at Johns Hopkins University, April 21, 1966.

7. Gar Alperovitz, *Atomic Diplomacy: Hiroshima and Potsdam* (New York, Vintage Books, 1965), especially pp. 226 ff.

8. Senator Clinton P. Anderson in his *Outsider in the Senate* (New York, World Publishing Co., 1970), pp. 67 ff.

9. See Allen S. Whiting's *China Crosses the Yalu* (New York, Macmillan, 1960) and I. F. Stone's *Hidden History of the Korean War* (New York, Monthly Review Press, 2d Ed., 1969).

10. Hans J. Morgenthau, "Roots of U.S. Failure in Vietnam," a paper presented at the 1968 meeting of the American Political Science Association. Tocqueville was a French political philosopher who visited the US during the 1840s. But it is clear that even in the pre-democratic era in Old Europe "perfect use" was rare and disaster frequent.

11. See Lincoln Bloomfield, "Planning Foreign Policy: Can It Be Done?" *Political Science Quarterly* 93:3 (1978), 369-392. He stresses that the long-term interest is usually sacrificed to short-term needs.

12. Stanley Hoffman, in *Gulliver's Troubles, or the Setting of American Foreign Policy*, New York, McGraw-Hill, 1968.

13. Harold Macmillan, in his *Tides of Fortune*, 1945-1955, New York, Harper & Row, 1969.

14. It has been argued that the British-French intervention was an example of decision-makers going against internal public opinion, but it is more accurate to say that public opinion was "permissive" until Eisenhower and Khruschev made public their attitudes toward the Suez intervention.

15. See Townsend Hoopes, *The Devil and John Foster Dulles* (Boston, Little Brown, 1973). Hoopes served in the Truman and Johnson administrations. Werner Levi argues in "Ideology, Interests, and Foreign Policy" (*International Studies Quarterly*, vol. 14, 1970, pp. 1-31) that statesmen protect national interests rather than ideology. But most decision-makers are True Believers like their fellow countrymen, and Dulles was surely a notable example.

16. *New York Times*, June 11, 1963.

17. Carl Marcy, "The Burdens of Power," *Saturday Review*, September 4, 1964, pp. 11 ff.

18. Harlan Cleveland, *The Obligations of Power: American Diplomacy in the Search for Peace* (New York, Harper & Row, 1966). Cleveland had formerly been Assistant Secretary of State for International Organization Affairs.

19. These tough-minded characters include, in addition to Bundy and Rostow, Henry Kissinger and Zbigniew Brzezinski, but many other scholars have done consulting or contract work for Washington bureaus. Rostow, from M.I.T., wrote in his *Law, Power, and the Pursuit of Peace* (New York, Harper & Row, 1968), published after he left the Johnson White House, that US was the only permanent member of the UN Security Council able to withstand aggression in Southeast Asia "condoned by the Soviet Union or Communist China" (p. 14). Rostow, who belongs to the sociological school of law mentioned in our discussion of international law in Chapter 5, says that "For twenty years we have sought to build coalitions which could make the precedents of restraint implicit in the Truman Doctrine into a common law of international behavior" (p. 119). For more "sociology of international law," see the remarkable works of Myres McDougal (his *Studies in World Public Order*, Yale University Press, 1960, and, in collaboration with Feliciano, *Law and Minimum World Public Order*, Yale University Press, 1961, which was mentioned in our Chapter 5.

20. Hans Morgenthau, in "Roots of U.S. Failure in Vietnam," a paper presented at the 1968 meeting of the American Political Science Association, said that the fact that most academic experts in international relations and Asian politics had either actively supported the government policies in Vietnam or had cast no public judgment on them had greatly contributed to giving these policies at least a temporary respectability. A meeting of the Peace Research Society (International) at Ann Arbor in November 1969 was marked by the number of scholarly papers bearing only the most peripheral connection with peace whose research had been funded by the US government, many by the Air Force. The meeting of the American Association for the Advancement of Science in Washington in January 1970 witnessed a sharp debate on military funding of academic research across the country.

21. Edmund Stillman and William Pfaff, *Power and Impotence: The Failure of America's Foreign Policy* (New York, Random House, 1966). They compare US messianism with Philip of Spain's fatal conviction in the 16th century that he was doing God's work. Walter Lippmann commented that the Pentagon Papers, whose unauthorized publication was a 1971 sensation, revealed a lot of intoxicated people playing for the first time in their lives with real power (Durham, D.C., *Morning Herald*, October 16, 1971).

22. An exception was the Canadian scholar, James Eayrs, in his *Right and Wrong in Foreign Policy*, Toronto, 1966.

23. The interchange was between Anatol Rapaport of the University of Michigan and D. G. Brennan, an employee of the Hudson Institute, published in *Bulletin of the Atomic Scientists*, December 1965. Another member of the Institute at that time, famous for its nuclear war scenarios written by Herman Kahn, was Henry Kissinger of Harvard.

24. George W. Ball has described how he resigned as Under Secretary of State in 1966 because the Johnson administration did not realize that Europe was paramount to US national interest while Vietnam was only peripheral (in his *The Discipline of Power*, Boston, Atlantic-Little Brown, 1968).

25. At a meeting of Peace Research Society (International) at Cambridge, Mass. in 1968, President Johnson was represented as having spoken, with respect to the Vietnam war, to the effect that "I'd like to stop bombing too, but if we stop and they don't then that's a little dangerous. When you duck and dodge and doubt and shimmy, every man and his dog gives you a kick."

26. Lucian Pye, in *The Spirit of Chinese Politics* (Cambridge, M.I.T. Press, 1968), says that with the breakdown of the traditional Chinese state, with its control of aggressive impulses, a flood of emotion was released which he describes as the discovery of hate.

27. A transcript of the hour-long interview was available from Bill Moyers' Journal, Box 345, New York, N.Y. 10011.

28. Jack Anderson's column, United Features Syndicate release, December 24, 1973.

29. Manuel Leguineche, "Kissinger y sus Libros," Guadalajara (Mexico) *El Informador*, June 16, 1974.

30. See Henry A. Kissinger, "The Policymaker and the Intellectual," in James N. Rosenau, ed., *International Politics and Foreign Policy* (New York, Free Press, 1961), pp. 273-278.

31. Kissinger's interview with James Reston of the *New York Times*, "Secretary of State Interview," Bureau of Public Affairs, Department of State, Washington, October 13, 1974.

32. Kenneth Boulding states that "From an economic point of view the scientific revolution has made power, in the sense of threat capability, relatively inefficient as a means of getting rich. History can be summed up in the aphorism, 'Wealth creates power and power destroys wealth'" (Paper presented at the Foreign Policy Association, May 29, 1968).

33. See Robert L. Osgood, *Alliances and American Foreign Policy* (Baltimore, Johns Hopkins Press, 1968) and Peter Mayer, *Cohesion and Conflict in International Communism* (The Hague, Martinus Nijhoff, 1968).

34. J. H. Plumb, in *Saturday Review*, January 27, 1968, pp. 26 and 28.

35. See Hedley Bull's "A View from Abroad: Consistency under Pressure," *Foreign Affairs* 57:3 (1979), 441-462, for a generally favorable view of Carter's foreign policy. However, another scholar concluded that Carter too was caught in the trap of equating national security with military hardware (Richard J. Barnet's "United States-Soviet Relations," *Foreign Affairs* 57:4, 1979, pp. 779-795).

36. George Kennan says that Soviet involvement with leftist factions in Third World countries is normal great-power behavior, proceeding less from aggressive than defensive motives, and is not apt to result in a major extension of Soviet power (his *The Cloud of Danger*, Boston, Little Brown, 1977, pp. 178-179). It can get ridiculous: Ethiopia was once a client state of US, while Somalia was a client of USSR; then a communist regime seized power in Ethiopia, which became a client of USSR, whereupon Somalia switched to US. Somalia is a good example of a corrupt socialist state, Ethiopia a fine example of an incompetent socialist state.

37. See *Israel's Lebanon War* (by Zeev Shiff and Yehud Yaari, New York, Simon & Schuster, 1984) for the role played by General Ariel Sharon in bringing about that war.

38. This quotation, as well as the paragraph on US troop commitment to NATO, is taken from Jonathan Rowe's article on foreign policy in *The Washington Monthly*, October 1984, pp. 40 ff.

39. Bruce D. Hamlett and Fred W. Neal, in "The Never-Never Land of International Relations," *International Studies Quarterly*, vol. 13 (1969), 281-305.

40. Joseph H. de Rivera, *The Psychological Dimension of Foreign Policy* (Columbus, Charles E. Merrill, 1968), Chapter 8.

41. Articles by Robert Jervis and by Ole R. Holsti in R. A. Falk and S. S. Kim, eds, *The War System: An Interdisciplinary Approach* (Boulder, Colo., Westview Press, 1980).

42. Yeheskel Dror, *Crazy State: A Counterconventional Strategic Problem* (Lexington, Heath Lexington Books, 1971).

43. Lloyd S. Etheridge, "Personality Effects on American Foreign Policy, 1898-1968." *American Political Science Review* 72:2 (1978), 434-451.

44. Saul Bellow, *Him With His Foot in His Mouth* (New York, Harper & Row, 1984), p. 101.

45. Henry A. Kissinger, *White House Years* (Boston, Little Brown, 1979), p. 522. His indebtedness to Butterfield's description of "the Hobbesian dilemma" is obvious.

46. The question is put by David V. Edwards in his review of *Contending Approaches to International Politics* (K. Knorr and J. N. Rosenau, eds., Princeton University Press, 1969) in *American Political Science Review*, vol. 68, 1969, p. 1345.

47. Remiguisz Bierzanek, "Some Remarks on the History of International Conflict Resolution," *Our Generation Against Nuclear War*, 3:2 (1964), p. 33.

48. As told to this writer by E. Stanley Jones. Thoreau's essay said in part: "A minority is powerless while it conforms to the majority; it is not even a minority then; but it is irresistible when it clogs by its whole weight."

49. Raghavan N. Iyer, in *Civil Disobedience*, an "occasional paper" of the Center for the Study of Democratic Institutions," Santa Barbara, Calif., 1966, p. 21.

50. *Ibid.*, p. 20.

51. Amiya Chakravarty, "Tagore's Concept of Internationalism and Gandhi's Support," *The Asian Student* (Asia Foundation, San Francisco), April 11, 1970.

52. Amrut Nakhre, "Meanings of Non-Violence: A Study of Satyagraha Attitudes," *Journal of Peace Research* 13:3 (1976), 185-196. "Satyagraha" can be translated as "soul-force."

53. Much of this summary of the unilateralist position has been taken from April Carter's contributions to a special issue on Unilateralism in *Our Generation Against Nuclear War*, 3:3 (1965), pp. 3, 64-68.

54. See Charles E. Osgood's *An Alternative to War or Surrender* (University of Illinois Press, 1962) or its Chapter 5 republished in *Peace Research Reviews* 8:1 (1979), 1-50.

55. Osgood's G.R.I.T. (graduated reduction of international tensions) receives some support from an application of the Prisoner's Dilemma game to a tit-for-tat process of conditional cooperation in disarming, provided it is assumed that each side can check up pretty well on the other (Steven J. Abrams, *et al*, "The Geometry of the Arms Race," *International Studies Quarterly* 23:4 (1979), 567-588). But this study is rebutted in the same issue (pp. 589-598) by Raymond Dacey who says Abrams did not handle the matter of detection properly.

56. Jerome D. Frank, "Human Nature and Nonviolent Resistance," in Quincy Wright, ed., *The World Community* (University of Chicago Press, 1948), pp. 192-205, 204. There is quite a large literature on non-violent resistance, perhaps larger than it deserves as a cure for war, but it is a topic with a lot of idealistic romance to it. Two recent articles are Lewis Lipsitz and Herbert M. Kritzer, "Unconventional Approaches to Conflict Resolution," *Journal of Conflict Resolution* 19:4 (1975), 713-733, and Gene Sharp, "Making the Abolition of War a Realistic Goal," *Peace Research Reviews* 8:5 (1980) 3-22.

57. Arnold Wolfers, *et al*, *The United States in a Disarmed World: A Study of the U.S. Outline for General and Complete Disarmament*, Baltimore, Johns Hopkins Press, 1966.

58. Charles C. Price, "The Case for Disarmament: Some Personal Reflections on the United States and Disarmament," *Annals of the American Academy of Political and Social Science*, vol. 469 (1983), 144-154, especially pp. 147, 149 and 150.

59. "Blueprint for the Peace Race: Outline for Basic Provisions of a Treaty on General Disarmament in a Peaceful World," United States Arms Control and Disarmament Agency Publication 4, General Series 3, Superintendent of Documents, Washington, D.C., pp. 3-4.

60. Lincoln P. Bloomfield, "International Force in a Disarming—but Revolutionary—World," *International Organization*, vol. 17 (1963), pp. 444-464, 464. Scholars were so leery of anything that smacked of prescriptive idealism at that time that Kennedy's revolutionary proposal went almost unnoticed in the academic periodicals.

61. Walter Millis, *The Demilitarized World (And How To Get There)*, Center for the Study of Democratic Institutions, Santa Barbara, Calif., 1964, p. 24.

62. J. David Singer, "Threat Perception and the Armament-Tension Dilemma," *Journal of Conflict Resolution*, vol. 2 (1958), pp. 90-105, 104.

PART III

SO WHAT
OF THE FUTURE?

Having applied our theory to the recent past in Chapter 6, we now attempt to apply it to the future. In Chapter 7 we assume that nothing will be done to keep the three causes of conflict from continuing to operate during the next generation—the next 20 to 25 years—as they have in the past, and we try to answer the question whether there will be a nuclear, third world war. But in the final Chapter 8 we discuss what could be done about the causes of war, if there were the willingness to do it, and we try to identify those elements of the human race who are willing as well as some who are apparently not.

Chapter 7

WHAT WILL HAPPEN IF THINGS GO ALONG AS THEY ARE?

A. Introduction

A prominent mathematician remarks that the "predictions of biological theory are not as neat and exact as those of physical theories" because in physics one can base theories on "situations where initial conditions can be precisely specified." Biology therefore has to depend on theories of larger speculative scope, in which "reasoning by imaginative analogy plays a more important role." In the social sciences, he says, this role must be even greater, because the more controlled and rigorous experiments in the social sciences tend to be the least relevant to the important issues.[1]

Economics is the most quantifiable and "scientific" of the social sciences. But a noted economist, speaking in 1972 of the difficulty of predicting the gap between the rich and the poor countries, said that "despite its vastly greater elegance, economics suffers from nearly as many complexities and handicaps as the other social sciences." He probably proved his own point by going on to say that "the notion of a world famine, arising from food scarcity and overwhelming us by 2000 A.D., seems to be altogether fanciful."[2]

The past chairman of Reagan's Council of Economic Advisers said that "One of the great mistakes of the last 30 years of economic policy has been an excessive belief in the ability to forecast." In 1984 *Time* magazine said that "this kind of professional performance is raising serious questions about the degree to which companies and governments should pay attention to economists at all."[3]

International relations is far less susceptible than economics of being reduced to meaningful numbers and equations, let alone biology or physics or mathematics. But for that very reason there is more room for common sense and ordinary reasoning processes. We would argue too, in keeping with Frederick Schuman's assertion in our Chapter 4 about international relations not being terribly difficult to understand, that the behavior of groups and of nations is far less complex than is the behavior of individual persons, and that the behavior of an international system is much simpler yet, therefore more predictable. Nevertheless, an expert in the field warns of "the impossibility of political prophecy" and gives many examples.[4]

Still, in Chapter 5 we developed an explanation of war that has only three variables. Or, alternatively as we said then, one constant and two variables. We ought to be able to manipulate just three variables. We ought to be able, if not to measure, at least to judge the intensities that each of these three will reach over the next 20 to 25 years.

Actually, we've already done a little bit of measuring. In elementary statistical language, we started our study with the lowest level of measurement there is: Waltz' three categories, as amended by us, which divided the task of seeking the causes of war and thereby made it manageable. This is called "nominal" measurement. After developing our three-variable theory out of those categories, we ranked them in order of their causal significance with anarchy first, the aggressive nation second, and the ideological package third. This ranking is called "ordinal" measurement. We then said that if anarchy were given a causal weight of, say, ten, then the aggressive nation should have a weight of no more than four, and ideological competition no more than three. This was an effort to achieve a higher precision called "interval" measurement.

We could now treat these as maximums, saying that 10+4+3=17, with 17 representing a nuclear World War III, while 14 or thereabouts might represent a conventional war of some kind. It is not difficult to give examples of intensities in anarchy from 1 to 10 (there is no such thing as zero between independent nations). In 1985, for example, Washington-Moscow relations stand at about 7, as do Peking-Moscow relations, while Washington-Peking is perhaps a 5. As for the aggressive nation, the Germany of Hitler and his Nazi Party would represent the maximum of 4; Napoleon's France, 3; Louis XIV's France, 2; and the Germany of Bismarck and his Junkers, 1. Maximum ideological competition was represented by fascism versus communism in the 1930's; an intensity of 2 by liberalism versus communism during Reagan's first term; and an intensity of 1 by liberalism versus Mussolini's fascism in the 1920s.

Such an exercise would enable us to carry "interval" measurement a bit further. The intensities assigned to a situation are a matter of judgment, obviously; it is not like counting pebbles or weighing stones. But students of international relations—whether Ph.D.'s or publicists or State Department hands—could probably agree on the intensities of each variable at any given time between any two nations, and possibly for the world system as a whole. This consensus technique is not unheard of in the "scientific" study of socio-political phenomena, when an "operational definition" is difficult to arrive at from objective data.[5]

At any rate, that is one way to go about the task of prediction. A simpler approach would be to take note of the fact that since World War II we have had anarchy, as always, plus two competing politico-economic ideologies, but we have not had a principal nation run by aggressive leaders and their supporting elites. Therefore, if our explanatory theory is correct and complete, and if anarchy continues, as it must, and if ideological competition continues, as it looks sure to do, then World War III will come if and when aggressive leadership takes control of at least one principal nation.

This approach is tempting, for it simplifies the task. The principal nations are few: US, USSR, China, Japan, West Germany, France, Britain, India. We could concentrate on the possibilities of future radicalization in these countries. And USSR and China have already been rather thoroughly radicalized, though USSR could return to Stalinism, which some call fascist communism, and China could relapse into Maoism and its peculiarities.

Unfortunately, that approach would require us to overlook the possibility that we could get a nuclear world war without any aggressive great nation. Anarchy does vary in intensity and we need to look at the situations and other elements that determine this. In that connection we must look at the potential for radicalization of lesser nations, for these radicalizations are apt to become points of conflict between the two coalitions. And we must look not only at weaponry and its technology but also at the world economy, for both these affect relations among nations but also are strong external pressures that enter into and radicalize nations internally.

We shall compromise. We shall not attempt to come up with numbers. We've tried it, and it borders on the farcical. But we shall discuss the elements that enter into the intensity of anarchy, in the next Section B. Then in Section C we'll look at how the external pressures are apt to combine with internal cleavages so as to bring to power aggressive elites and their ideologies, with particular reference to the principal nations. Finally, we'll give our best judgment as to the probability of a nuclear world war over the next generation.

Prediction is no picnic, true. But we approach it with some assurance. We've been at it for a good many years, and enough has come true to provide a modicum of confidence.

B. The Things That Will Determine Anarchy's Future Intensities

1. *Histories of Hostility*. NATO and the Common Market contain and restrain, at least for now, the very old hostility between Britain and France, France and Germany, and France and Italy. Similarly, the long hostility between Russia and Poland, as well as that among most Balkan

nations, is buried for now in Comecon and the Warsaw Pact.

Fortunately, among the nuclear nations, US-USSR hostility dates back only to the Bolshevik scare after World War I; the Chinese-Russian only to around the 1890s; the Chinese-Indian merely to the 1950s. British-Russian rivalry goes back to the early 1800s, but it declined with the dissolution of Britain's colonial empire, only to revive in the Cold War. France and Russia have had a distant amity since unification of Germany. India-USSR and India-US relations have been brief and ambivalent. Japan, which can become a nuclear nation when it chooses, has been a rival of Russia since the 1890s but its enmity with China is old. West Germany, too, can have nuclear weapons when it wishes, and its bitterest enemy is the Soviet Union. Pakistan is trying hard to match India's nuclear capability. Israel is nuclear capable and it destroyed Iraq's nuclear reactor, but Iraq may try again.

We can mention only some of the other old hostilities: Burman vs. Thai vs. Khmer vs. Vietnamese, making the Southeast Asian subsystem a kind of cockpit such as the Balkans used to be; also Vietnamese vs. Chinese. In the Middle East there is the old enmity between Arabs and Persians, its latest round being the Iraq-Iran war; also between the Turks and the Arab states which were formerly Ottoman domains, And there is the very old but still virulent hatred between Turkey and Greece, both members of NATO, and also a younger but strong enmity between Turkey and Russia/USSR. In southern Africa there are nearly four centuries of hate between white-dominated South Africa, which can have nuclear weapons when it wishes, and the black Africans who now have states of their own along South Africa's borders.

On the whole, the anarchic intensity is not high among the great nuclear nations on the basis of old hostilities. But much can happen. In predicting, we must focus on the probable, for it is paranoiac to focus on the merely possible, as a psychiatrist told us in Chapter 2. But it is not paranoiac to speculate that conditions might change enough—US for example, may become unable or unwilling to pay most of Japan's defense and much of Western Europe's—so that Japan or West Germany would decide to build nuclear weapons. What, then, of old hostilities, especially the German-Russian?

2. *Weaponry.* We focus on the Nuclear Balance of Terror that began in 1953 when USSR matched US by testing its first fusion device (hydrogen bomb), with some mention of the chemical-biological weapons.

Soviet physicist Andrei Sakharov wrote in 1983 that as of 1980 US and USSR had 50,000 nuclear warheads totaling 13,000 megatons. A megaton equals in destructive power one million tons of T.N.T., so the total was equal to 13 billion tons of T.N.T., or about three tons for each person on the planet. By comparison, only six million tons were used in World War II.

Both nations go on building these weapons, in what some describe as a mindless fashion like animals on treadmills. One scholar says that such quantities would be significant only in a long war of attrition, which seems so unlikely that it is not worthwhile spending large sums and running dangers to prepare for it.[6]

Both nations have intercontinental ballistic missiles (ICBMs) that can deliver warheads anywhere on the other nation's territory. These ICBMs are called "strategic" weapons. There are also intermediate-range missiles that might be used mainly in Europe, as well as short-range missiles for battlefield use that are called "tactical" weapons. The argument that both sides have too many nuclear weapons is negated somewhat by the fact that many missiles would be shot down so that only a certain percentage would reach their targets, hence the more you have the more will do their damage.

Back in 1967 a panel of experts named by the UN concluded that a 20,000-megaton exchange would kill 95 percent of Americans if unprotected by adequate shelters, and 90 percent of USSR's population; that a bi-nation exchange would probably become a worldwide nuclear war; and that non-belligerents and other survivors would suffer from windcarried debris, especially the long-lived Strontium 90. A 1977 estimate for the President placed US deaths at 140 million.[7]

China, with far fewer weapons, can deliver H-bombs on all Soviet cities and probably on West Coast American cities.

Britain and France have small but sophisticated nuclear arsenals. But in Europe the principal stand-off is between US intermediate-range missiles emplaced in certain NATO countries, now being supplemented by mobile Pershing-2 missiles and low-flying cruise missiles, and Soviet SS-20 intermediate-range missiles, some of which are emplaced in Warsaw Pact nations. NATO, weaker in conventional war capability than the Warsaw Pact, has refused to match the Soviet pledge of no nuclear first-strike in Europe, and some NATO generals believe there could be a "limited" nuclear war there.

India, which has tested a nuclear device, claims to have built no warheads, but it would quickly become capable of delivering small bombs by airplanes over cities in China, Pakistan, or Sri Lanka (Ceylon).

Population and industrial concentration make the nations vulnerable in this order: Britain, US, France, USSR, India, China.

Not much is known about the chemical-biological (CB) weapons. Chemical weapons are synthetics or inanimate agents which dissipate with time, but biological weapons are organisms which cause disease and may become more lethal with time. Bad publicity caused US in 1969 to announce that germ weapons were being phased out, and biological weapons were "prohibited" by an ambiguous, virtually useless treaty in 1972. Congress probably will up the Pentagon's budget for CB weapons to over $1 billion in 1985, including money for a "binary" nerve gas said to be safer to handle.

The CB weapons are said to be as destructive of life as nuclear weapons but far less destructive of property, which might make them desirable in certain situations. They are also far cheaper to make and easier to deliver secretly on targets than the "clean" neutron bombs which also destroy life rather than property.

Use of CB weapons would probably carry less onus than the use of nuclear weapons. But in 1984 an expert on "biochemical warfare" indicated that such weapons do not bulk large in nuclear-oriented US planning.[8] Still, as noted, US is seeking to expand its CB facilities. Also there is reason to believe, owing to reports of a 1979 anthrax accident at Sverdlovsk, that these weapons remain a lively option in USSR. US accuses USSR of using such weapons in Afghanistan. And their cheapness may appeal to lesser nations. Mustard and nerve gases have been used by Iraq on Iran, and phosgene gas by Vietnam in Cambodia. A UN conference to write a CB treaty is deadlocked.

It was Sakharov's opinion that a nuclear war could terminate all life. Then in 1983-84 we had the prediction of astronomer Carl Sagan and other scientists that a nuclear war would throw so much smoke, dust, and debris into the atmosphere for so long that the war would be followed by a "nuclear winter" that might make the human race extinct.[9] Edward Teller, a physicist who is often in the scientific minority on war-peace matters, says such predictions are based on faulty information and require more research. Yet there are scientists who say such a war might end all kinds of life, leaving Earth a dead planet. So Jonathan Schell's position, closely argued in books published in 1982 and 1984,[10] is probably the correct one for non-scientists to take: if there is respectable scientific opinion that a nuclear war might terminate the human species, then it is infinitely immoral for us who are alive today to risk the denial of life to all future generations.

What is wistfully called "Stable Nuclear Deterrence" means that "We won't fire first because we think that if we did you would still have enough to launch a devastating retaliatory attack on us, and you won't fire first because you'd better believe that if you did we'd still have enough left to wipe you out." Thus it is fitting that this strategy is also known as MAD, meaning Mutually Assured Destruction.

It is not probable that the balance will forever provide an umbrella of terror beneath which life can go on as usual, for the following reasons.

a. *The Logic of Probability.* One scholar says: "Deterrence will not deter unless it is credible; it will not be credible unless there is a positive probability of its failing; over the long run, therefore, it must fail. This logic seems to me irrefutable, and as Mr. Kahn himself has suggested, all that deterrence does is give us time to change the system, and we are not doing very much with the time that it gives us."[11]

But another scholar rejoins that "the prediction is mathematically impeccable but trivial... An equally impeccable bit of algebra would show that the outbreak of the rule of law and eternal peace is statistically certain—'sooner or later.' "[12]

But the histories of international systems suggest that the probability of another general war is much greater than that of "the rule of law"— unless that rule is imposed by world conquest.

b. *The Difficulty of Knowing When Balance Exists.* We mentioned this problem in Chapter 5 while discussing arms control and disarmament among the "old cures" for war.

The difficulty is threefold: (1) How does either side know whether a weapon is defensive or offensive, for so much depends on intent? (2) How can either side compare and balance out USSR's lead in quantity, that is, in total megatonnage of nuclear missile warheads, against US lead in quality, that is, in the sophistication, maneuverability, and accuracy of its missiles? (3) How does either side know for sure whether the other is cheating on the arms control agreements that are in effect? In 1984-85 both sides have been accusing each other of cheating. Difficulty (3) depends heavily on whether "unilateral verification" is adequate or whether there must be "mutual on-site inspection." We'll be discussing this again.

c. *The "First-Strike Problem.* Stability depends on neither side's getting enough missiles or other weapons with the power and sophistication to destroy all or nearly all of the other's nuclear capability. For this would mean that one could risk a pre-emptive first strike with little likelihood of sustaining unacceptable losses in return. Neither side can be sure the other may not have or be on the way to having a first-strike capability, so each must seek it. Ways of getting this capability include the following:

(1) *Infinitely impenetrable or infinitely mobile launching places.* Launching sites for missiles on land are "hardened" with many layers of protection, while mobility has been sought first with airplanes and then with submarines. "Cruise" missiles are themselves mobile in that they can evade attack and "home in" on their targets. MIRV missiles carry several independently targeted warheads, which is another kind of mobility. In the game of leap-frog which an arms race is, USSR is reported to be approaching US sophistication in cruise and MIRV missiles. But in the same game Reagan wishes to build 100 MX missiles in super-hardened land sites, though some say the MX is a "lemon," inferior to the submarine-launched Trident D-5. In the same game, USSR is putting its SS-24 ICBM on railroad cars and its lesser-range SS-25 on trucks; both are MIRV'd as well as mobile. But US has a new, mobile Midgetman ICBM; also powerful non-nuclear warheads.

(2) *Anti-ballistic missiles.* These ABMs are "defensive" missiles launched from the ground to intercept offensive ICBMs. After impact, the defending territory would suffer fall-out and radioactivity from *both* warheads. When USSR was detected in 1966 building ABM sites around

Moscow, the anarchy intensity bounced high in US and an ABM program was pushed through Congress. In MAD's warped rationality, one has to guess whether the enemy would use ABMs merely to defend his ICBM launching sites or to defend his cities. The latter could mean he is no longer willing to leave his population undefended as hostage to prove his defensive intentions. If he can defend a substantial part of his industry and people, he need not have a complete first-strike capability. One also cannot be quite sure that the enemy's ABMs are truly short-range defensive weapons instead of having intercontinental range.

In 1972 US and USSR reached agreement to put a very low limit on ABMs, but US has recently accused USSR of violating the treaty.

(3) *Nuclear shelters.* The "tedium of a long death watch" probably assures there will be no demand for adequate shelters until there is another nuclear crisis at the earliest. A shelter program for US would cost several hundreds of billions. There is no point, objectively, in building shelters to protect more people than the post-war economy could support. Shelters could possibly protect 80 percent of the population, but suppose only 50 percent could live off of what probably would be left? A less-than-universal program would pose the political question, Which individuals would be let into the shelters? It would be a comparatively lucky area that was attacked with CB weapons or neutron bombs which spare property.

So far as is known, no nuclear nation plans an adequate shelter program, but nothing could be more de-stabilizing than the suspicion that one is planned. For the nation which built it could launch a first-strike attack, knowing that enough of its people could survive retaliation and its aftermath to rebuild and carry on.

(4) *Technological break-through.* The principal candidate for this highly de-stabilizing event is Reagan's Strategic Defense Initiative, usually called "Star Wars," proposed in 1983. It has to do with lasers and particle beams based in outer space which destroy oncoming ICBMs. Expert opinion is sharply divided. Some say such weapons would become available only in the next century and even then would be vulnerable to less expensive Soviet countermeasures.[13] Another says that these weapons would violate the letter or the spirit of several arms control agreements and thus would surely be destabilizing of MAD. But he adds that they potentially could provide a defense against ICBMs while permitting a counterforce offensive capability that would not entail mass destruction of societies.[14] Still another says such a defense would not violate the ABM treaty and might make it possible to shift from MAD, with its built-in offensive arms race, to a defensive policy of Mutual Assured Survival.[15]

But yet another says that if too much of this and other military hardware were placed in orbit, we might have nuclear war by accident, owing to damage to any of the spy satellites on which both sides increasingly rely as their eyes and ears.[16] In this connection, given USSR's long opposition to verification by mutual on-site inspection, a C. I. A. expert wrote in 1980 that USSR evidently has not interfered with US "national technical means of verification," including surveillance by satellite, and he expected this tacit approval to expand.[17] Hence Star Wars might endanger even this minimal cooperation. And anyway both sides are testing "ASAT" devices to shoot down satellites.

The weightiest opposition to Reagan's proposal has come from four former high-level US officials who have been involved in arms control[18] and from six prominent scientists including Hans A. Bethe and Carl Sagan.[19] The scientists make these points: Star Wars would be no defense against low-flying delivery systems; USSR could keep ahead of any Star Wars system because it is cheaper to build new warheads than to shoot down old ones and easier to shoot down orbiting defense systems than incoming ICBMs; a Star Wars system could be "outfoxed" by thousands of decoys; such a system would cost from several hundreds of billions to one trillion dollars; and Soviet leaders see Star Wars as part of a US first-strike strategy, allowing US to launch a pre-emptive attack of offensive ICBMs, then destroy whatever counterforce ICBMs the Soviets might have left, hence USSR might decide on a pre-emptive strike of its own before the Star Wars system can be developed.

The possibility of a Soviet pre-emptive strike seems to have been recognized by Reagan who said in the autumn of 1984 that he would share the Star Wars technology with USSR. But this statement has not been repeated; the decision would be made by the then President, for the technology will be years in developing; and it is hard to imagine the US Pentagon giving up such a technological advantage. In all likelihood, anarchic mutual fears will prevent any such sharing. What is certain is that never in the entire Cold War period have Soviet officials been campaigning so energetically as they are presently doing, all over the world, against the Star Wars plan. Star Wars and other strategic weapons are presently up for US-USSR negotiations, with Chernenko's death bringing on scene the much younger and more vigorous Gorbachev. It will be interesting to see what happens.

This terminates our consideration of ways of obtaining a first-strike capability, and we return to other reasons why MAD may not long suffice.

d. *The Nth Country Problem.* Suppose a nuclear war were started by a small nation, perhaps one not known to have nuclear weapons. Would the great nations know where the attack came from? Would they wait until they found out? By 1985 the development in many nations of nuclear power projects, mainly for electricity, has made available weapons-grade plutonium sufficient for thousands of bombs a year. Presumably the technical know-how for assembling at least small A-bombs has already proliferated widely. The text of the Nuclear Non-Proliferation Treaty permits nations to drop out if they feel threatened; they would anyhow. And several key smaller nations have not agreed to the treaty.

The UN study mentioned early in this Section 2 concluded that the larger the number of nuclear nations the greater the danger of nuclear war through calculation, miscalculation, or accident; and that the introduction of even small "tactical" nuclear weapons (such as Dulles, Nixon, Goldwater and others thought of using in Vietnam) would lead to full-scale nuclear warfare. Kahn said the longer nuclear weapons are not used the greater will be the psychological pressure never to use them.[20] But an equally well informed British expert wrote years ago that the advent of ten or twenty nuclear *or* CB nations could render the Nuclear Balance obsolete.[21] In 1985, in addition to the six older nuclear nations, there were eleven "emerging" nuclear countries: Pakistan, Israel, Iraq, Syria, Egypt, Libya, South Africa, Brazil, Greece, Turkey, and Argentina. Seven have not signed the treaty. Israel has medium-range missiles.

So there is the possibility of the Nth country being poor, but able to build small bombs and deliver them modest distances, and quite able to produce and deliver CB substances in a manner relatively immune to aerial surveillance.

e. *The Accident.* In a best-selling novel of the early 1960s it was urged that malfunction in a tiny electronic component could prevent the recall of a nuclear bomber plane before it reached the "fail-safe" point, so it would go on to drop H-bombs on USSR and trigger a terminal nuclear war.[22] A political philosopher responded that the story rested on a "conjunction of unrelated improbabilities" and that "one can devise a great number of systems capable of reporting instantly the malfunction of any machine."[23]

The evidence is that although there have been accidents involving nuclear weapons none has approached the point of nuclear war. But in 1971 Polaris submarines are reported to have mistakenly signaled twice that submarines had been sunk by enemy action,[24] and a book published in 1984 asserts that from January 1979 to June 1980 there were 152 false alarms caused by computer failure, leading US forces to prepare for full-scale nuclear conflict.[25]

One must be guided by probabilities, not possibilities, but we are not quite sure what that means in this connection. And even if an accident is merely a possibility, its consequences terrify.

f. *The Crazy Man.* A popular motion picture around 1960 was *Dr. Strangelove* which featured an insanely anti-communist US general who set off in an airplane to nuclear-bomb the enemy into submission. This too is possible. As we have noted, individuals who reach high position often have interesting psychological histories. After Foster Dulles, Lyndon Johnson and Richard Nixon, not to overlook Stalin, Mussolini and Hitler, one must admit that anything *can* happen.

We do not quite put it within the bounds of the probable. But the reader may wish to speculate, for example, about the crazy chief of a smallish country who has accumulated a modest supply of those cobalt-jacketed nuclear bombs which could render the Earth uninhabitable. Or consider this comment by Kissinger at a conference he attended after he had left office: "Any military man at this conference will tell you that launching strategic forces on warning (of an attack) can be accomplished only by delegating the authority to the proverbially 'insane colonel' about whom so many movies have been made."[26]

g. *The Terrorist* In 1974 there was criticism in Congress that US nuclear weapons were stored abroad under such conditions that terrorists might be able to get them and use them for massive blackmail. Since 1974 the world's terrorist problem has worsened.[27] And how difficult would it be, really, for a terrorist group to steal plutonium from a Third World reactor and fashion a suitcase-size A-bomb? One wonders why it has not happened already.

Summary Comment on Weaponry. How would one measure this weaponry dimension of anarchy? We have described several ways in which the Nuclear Balance can go awry and produce war. Is it a matter of this way *or* that way? Or this way *plus* that way? Or perhaps even this way *times* that way, and so forth? Possibly this is a question for the experts in the algebra of probability, such as those mentioned in subsection (a), to argue about. But is would seem that "or" is the more appropriate connector. If war begins in a deliberately calculated pre-emptive strike, then it can't begin by accident or by the act of a crazy man.

It may be of some help to know that a scholar whose statistical studies of history have been noteworthy has concluded that in the very long run preparation for war does not make peace more likely.[28] Another statistical study of history concludes that if two powers are already in an arms race (as US and USSR are today), then a subsequent crisis is apt to escalate into war.[29] Still another statistical study suggests that the burden of proof is on those who argue that winning an arms race is a safe substitute for ending it.[30] Yet another empirical study provides modest support for the idea that extended nuclear deterrence has reduced the risk of war, but does not forever rule it out.[31] Schell believes that war, as a calculated act, is an option no longer available to the nuclear powers with respect to each other.

3. *Tension Points.* Divided Berlin and the two Germanies are not apt to cause the trouble they have in the past, thanks to Chancellor Brandt and his successors. But a divided Berlin is awkward and by its nature temporary, and it could come to crisis again along with a general heating up of the international system. Here the principal antagonists would be West Germany and USSR, backed by NATO and the Warsaw Pact, respectively, if those alliances endure.

In Southeast Asia, a divided Vietnam is no longer the problem. The problem now is whether Hanoi will be content with extending its rule over all of former French Indochina. This was rather to be expected, once Sihanouk's stable regime in Cambodia had been terminated.[32]

Vietnamese troops appear to have defeated Pol Pot's remaining Khmer Rouge troops, backed by China, as well as the two non-communist resistance groups (one of them headed by Sihanouk) which are backed by China and by the non-communist Southeast Asian nations. But defeat now does not rule out future guerrilla activity against Hanoi's puppet regime in Cambodia (Kampuchea). As USSR backs Hanoi, this is a tension point between two great nations, with US and the ASEAN states providing modest support to the non-communist groups.

Divided Korea will almost surely continue to be a tension point in relations among US, USSR, Japan and China, despite talk of peace between the two Koreas.

Communist guerrilla activity is increasing in the Philippines, while liberal opposition to Marcos is strong, but divided. This is a mess, in which US is apt to intervene at some point, possibly (but not probably) bringing on a confrontation with China or USSR. Communist insurgency may revive in Indonesia, Malaysia, and Thailand, three nations friendlier to US than to China or USSR.

Pakistan, with some support from China and US, lost East Pakistan (now Bangladesh) because India was backed strongly by USSR. US is building up Pakistan militarily, somewhat as it did the Shah of Iran, as well as using Pakistan as a conduit for aid to the Afghan guerrillas fighting USSR. Pakistan has not yet won in its military encounters with India, hence may at some point try again to take Moslem Kashmir from India.

Any US intervention on the Asian mainland might involve it with China or USSR, conceivably *with* China against USSR and India.

In the Middle East there are two focal points of tension, one centering upon Israel and the other upon the Persian Gulf. What with Arab intransigence, Israeli paranoia, Islamic fundamentalism, and oil, one could scarcely wish for a more fertile breeding ground for World War III. Syria is a USSR client-state while Israel holds itself out as the bastion of US influence, now that the Shah is no more. US builds up Saudi Arabia militarily, but the Saudi regime is shaky, partly because so many of the oilfield workers are Shiite Moslems, which is the predominant sect in militant Iran. There was once a strong communist movement in Iran. If it were to revive and try again for power, and if US suspected it was supported by USSR, a very ugly situation would result. Also, a further decline in the price of oil could further destabilize the whole area. On the whole, a US-USSR confrontation is likelier in the Persian Gulf area than in any other tension point.

Great power confrontation is unlikely in Northeast Africa even though Ethiopia is a USSR client and Somalia a US client, nor in Southern Africa despite the turmoil between South Africa and the Black African states. In North Africa, Libya is noisy but will not be taken too seriously unless it gets an A-bomb or two.

Central America is the most recent tension point, but its principal danger is that US may intervene in Nicaragua, and possibly El Salvador as well, with its own troops in a Vietnam-like process, with perhaps a Vietnam-type conclusion. USSR will continue to send aid but its leaders, no doubt mindful of Khruschev's mistake in Cuba, are unlikely to challenge US power in a direct confrontation. Still, we know from Chapter 6 how irrational statesmen can be.

We'll be talking later in this chapter about tension points that will arise from the radicalization of nations around the globe.

But the most critical tension points of course lie along the frontiers between the great nations, specifically the USSR-China border and the China-India border, and between the two great coalitions, especially West Germany's borders with the Warsaw Pact countries. Nor should we overlook the narrow seas that separate China from Japan. We shall recur to these in our summing up at the close of this chapter.

4. *Trade and Currency Imbalances, and Worldwide Depression.* A former Managing Director of the International Monetary Fund, no less, is reputed to have said that *"nobody* really understands the international monetary system."[33] Or perhaps every international economist understands it, but each one differently.

Trade balances are easy enough to understand. If a nation in a year sells abroad goods and services worth $1 billion more than it buys abroad, it has a "favorable" balance of $1 billion overall, though it likely had "unfavorable" balances with some nations.

Payments balances are different from trade balances. Our nation with a favorable trade balance will have an unfavorable payments balance (a deficit) if its $1 billion trade surplus is exceeded by the total of: money spent abroad by its tourists or invested abroad by its businessmen; money spent abroad by its government to support its troops there or for other purposes; and grants or loans made by its government or its banks to foreign nations or to private concerns within those nations. Our nation may have credit payments balances with some nations but it will have an overall payments deficit.

There is no world currency, so if you order something from a foreign seller you have to pay him in his nation's currency or in another currency he will accept. You go to a bank and write a check in your currency to buy a draft in that currency and send it to him. Thousands of these transactions work their way up through the banking system in each nation to the top where governments and their central banks can figure out where they stand overall and with respect to each other nation.

There are parts of the world that can produce better or cheaper products than others—for example, the German VW at one time, now the Japanese Datsun or Toyota. Some nations like Germany and Japan have more efficient industrial plants because the old ones were destroyed in World War II. Some, like Japan and Germany and Italy, have benefited financially from the US effort to make its military weight felt around the world. Mexico, Italy, and Greece get a lot of tourist business. Multinational corporations based in US, Japan, and Western Europe make large investments abroad which eventually start sending some profits back home. Over time, favorable or unfavorable payments balances build up. What is done about them?

After World War II, the principal non-socialist countries set up the International Monetary Fund (IMF), agreeing that rates of exchange between national currencies would be fixed ("pegged") more or less permanently. The bankers/governments would confer if, despite their buying and selling to keep things in equilibrium, problems arose. If a nation built up big payments surpluses, often there was no problem: the government or the corporations could use their credit balances to buy bonds or stocks in the deficit countries or to invest in new plants there or to give aid to them. But occasionally a nation was left, even after its debit and credit balances with other nations had been used to offset each other, with a deficit which it had to pay in something acceptable to the creditor nation or nations.

These payments traditionally had been in gold until the 1930s Depression, although there was no longer anything like enough gold in the world at the going price per ounce to settle the balances arising from vastly increased world trade and finance. And only US still promised, in certain circumstances, to pay gold for its currency on demand. So payment was usually in an acceptable currency, sometimes the British pound but more commonly in later years the US dollar. Indeed, the dollar became the world currency, for lack of anything better.

Then the dollar got into trouble in the later 1960s, owing largely to the Vietnam war, whose expense was on top of already large US spending and investing abroad. And it came when the US economy was already going full blast. Under Johnson and Nixon, the money supply increased more than twice as fast as the supply of goods and services. So a heightening inflation, added to high labor costs and inefficient management or obsolete industrial plant, began to price US goods and services out of world markets. US went into a trade deficit in 1971 and stayed there after 1973.

Lord Keynes' economics, calling for higher taxes, higher interest rates, and less government spending to slow down the economy and control inflation,* were abandoned by Johnson, then equivocated on by Nixon, for these would have meant unemployment and loss of votes.

---

*To speed up a stagnating or lagging economy, Keynesian economics prescribes lower taxes, lower interest rates, and more government spending.

During the Vietnam years, foreign bankers and governments, weary of the disruptions caused by the flood of dollars, wrung their hands because US would not put its house in order. France under De Gaulle gleefully tapped the US gold reserve, especially after Johnson refused to double the price of gold to $32 an ounce. But most nations forebore to do so, for US gold reserves were dangerously low, down to about a third of its short-term obligations alone (those due for payment within a year). They knew collapse of the dollar could evoke world financial crisis, strangle world trade, and might produce Great Depression.

But the foreign bankers and governments refused to upvalue their currencies in relation to the dollar, for this would make their exports more expensive. So individuals, banks, and multinational corporations continued transferring tens of billions from US to other nations, mainly in Western Europe and Japan. This increased *their* money supply and touched off serious inflation there; thus US, through the medium of its payments deficit, exported its inflation to much of the world. This also produced a phenomenon known as the Eurodollar, whereby private banks and government central banks, mainly in Europe but also elsewhere, accumulated the dollars sent to countries with payments surpluses by US to settle its payments deficit. These Eurobanks (which eventually included branches of US banks) began to treat these claims on the US Treasury as their "stock in trade," lending them out at interest to new debtors including other nations that were suffering payments deficits.

In 1969, after a small monetary crisis in 1968, the governments and bankers in the IMF created Special Drawing Rights (SDRs or "paper gold"). This in effect was a pool of strong currencies which nations in trouble like the US could borrow from for a few years until they got their houses in order.

But US did not get inflation down. In 1971 exchange speculation was rampant, US payments deficits were worse, and the price of gold on the world market went through the roof. Then Nixon, in violation of commitments and agreements, banned exchange of gold for foreign-held dollars, and later devalued the dollar officially in relation to gold. Finally, in 1973, US went off the gold standard entirely. Since then there has been no currency in the world backed by tangible value; there is no real money; there is no adequate adjustment mechanism, such as the transfer of gold from one nation to another, to put payments back into balance.

The IMF's fixed exchange rates were dead. Most currencies were "floating," meaning that the rate is determined within a range by its supply and the demand for it, and in 1977 the IMF officially accepted this floating. This is realistic but makes it difficult to sign contracts for future delivery, for nobody knows what the specified currency will be worth then. It also makes speculation in currency more dangerous; large banks in several countries have gone bankrupt that way.

The Vietnam war was the first major shock to the post-World War II international monetary system. The second was occasioned by the 1973 Arab-Israeli war which prompted the Arab oil embargo and resulted in an increase of the oil price from under $3 a barrel to nearly $12. This immediately produced enormous trade and payments surpluses for the OPEC countries. They required payment in dollars for their oil and deposited the proceeds in US banks, Eurobanks, and Japanese banks. Just as immediately, most oil importing countries began experiencing great trade and payments deficits, so they went to those banks where the OPEC dollars had been deposited and borrowed them, thus eluding the stricter lending standards of IMF and the World Bank. This second major shock was followed by an after-shock, the 1979 civil war in Iran, which sent the price of oil to over $30 a barrel before it settled down to somewhere around $26 as of 1985.

All this ought to have meant that international trade, except in oil and food, would dwindle to nothing. But that did not happen. The bankers had dollars to lend for almost anything any country might want. They even began "onlending" the petrodollars to Third World *governments* like Brazil's and Poland's on an unsecured basis. Meanwhile US still did not get its house in order. In the later 1970s inflation hit 13 percent and interest rates went over 20 percent briefly. But toward the end of his term Carter brought in Volcker as head of the Federal Reserve in an effort to get things under control. For a time the dollar was so weak that creditors took the West German mark when they could get it, but there wasn't enough of this or other strong currencies lying around.

With Volcker at the Federal Reserve, the Reagan administration put the US house in order, but a strange thing happened.

With tight money-supply controls, and a closer rein on non-defense government spending, inflation was brought down below five percent, and interest rates moderated somewhat. The cost was a big jump in unemployment and the third recession in ten years—the worst recession, in fact, since the 1930s Depression, and one which spread to the rest of the world.

But, because Reagan cut income taxes drastically, the US budget deficit jumped to about $200 billion a year. This caused heavy government borrowing which prevented interest rates from going down as much as inflation did. The resulting combination of high interest rates and low inflation, coupled with US political stability, proved irresistible to foreigners, and not just to oil-wealthy Arabs but also to Western Europeans and Japanese. They sent their money to US to be invested in US Treasury and corporate securities, including about half of Japan's annual $100 billion payments surplus.

So the strange thing that happened was that a very weak dollar changed into a very strong dollar and made US exports costly in the foreign currencies abroad while foreign exports are cheap in US when translated from those currencies into dollars. The result is that in 1984 the US trade deficit was $130 billion, twice that in 1983 and four times that in 1982, and 1985 is expected to be $160 billion. Many US exports had long been non-competitive owing to obsolete industrial plant and high labor costs; the overvalued dollar added a further burden.

US has had payments deficits before, and not just in wartime, but these were caused mainly by the very large investments being made abroad by US corporations. These investments eventually returned profits which, when brought home ("repatriated") and changed back into dollars, were enough to keep US in an overall payments surplus most of the time, even after it began running a trade deficit in 1971. But since 1981 US has been sustaining a payments deficit (also called a "current account" deficit) which in 1984 was about $100 billion. US foreign debt may reach $1,000 billion by 1990; indeed, all western DCs are now net borrowers of capital from Japan and the OPEC nations.

The worldwide recession of the early 1980s was so severe that many LDCs could no longer even pay the interest on their foreign debt. Oil prices dropped, owing to recession and to conservation, so that an oil exporter like Mexico fell into that predicament while other oil-exporting countries had to tighten their belts too. The banks, which made so many foolish loans while recycling petrodollars, are encouraged by the IMF and their own governments to lend still more to the LDCs so they can pay the interest and therefore, technically, not default, for this might bring down the whole world house of cards. Many banks are in bad shape; US banks, for example, have lent out $350 billion abroad, which is far more than their total capital.

The critical year thus far was 1983, when default was staved off. The same year, the US economy began a rather strong comeback, which may or may not prove to be merely cyclical. This recovery has spread, somewhat thinly thus far, to much of the rest of the world. But what of the next monetary crisis? We'll return to this shortly.

Meanwhile, a trade crisis is now a-building. Since World War II, under the 90-nation General Agreement on Tariffs and Trade (GATT), the world has achieved a relatively free-trade condition compared to the 1930s when high tariffs and other trade restrictions helped bring on the Great Depression. US tariffs will shortly average only about four percent of the value of the goods. GATT officials even hope to go beyond goods and negotiate on reducing trade barriers in services, meaning such things as engineering and insurance and transport services.

In theory, and probably in practice as well, free trade realizes the goal of the old Utilitarian slogan, "the greatest good of the greatest number." Free competition, without tariff or other barriers, will result in the production of any good or service by those who can produce it most economically. But, apart from the Arab oil exporters, most LDCs are weary of receiving so little for their exports that they can't buy oil and food and service their foreign debts, and they are weary of seeing their manufactured goods excluded from the DCs. More ominously for the world situation as a whole, some of the DCs including US and several Western European nations are getting tired of losing markets to the Japanese and the quasi-developed Pacific Rim countries, for this means their industries will fold up and their jobs will be "exported" to cheap-labor countries. In US, for example, the smokestack industries no longer attract new investment so they become even less competitive with foreign industries.

Tariffs are only one way to keep out foreign goods and services. There can be quotas regulating the quantity that can be imported or the amount of foreign currency that the importer will be permitted to buy to pay for his imports. There can be formal or informal agreements with other governments that limit imports, as US has done with respect to foreign steel and Japanese automobiles. There are more complicated arrangements involving specifications that foreign goods cannot meet. Exports are secretly subsidized and may be "dumped" abroad at less than cost. Ways are found to exclude foreign investors.

At any rate, protectionism is on the rise everywhere, but especially between US and Japan, which is probably the worst place it could happen in terms of future prosperity and peace. "Autarky," which means national self-sufficiency and is rather similar to "mercantilism" in 17th and 18th century Europe, has been dead since the 1930s Depression, but is reviving.

Moreover, the Arab oil-exporters and the Japanese and those few other nations that consistently earn a payments surplus are beginning to tire of supporting US and the many LDCs that consistently consume more than they earn and therefore keep piling up payments deficits. True, the surplus countries do get paid, usually in dollars. At least these debts are mainly denominated in dollars, though most of them are not US obligations. These are the Eurodollars we mentioned earlier, and nowadays Eurodollars is a rather loose term that refers to all those pieces of paper in several currencies that bounce around among banks outside US.

They may be promises, usually in dollars, backed by the "full faith and credit" of a national government which has no credit because nobody has faith in its pesos or zlotys. They may be promises in dollars backed only by the banks themselves, though they haven't enough dollars on deposit in US to redeem their promises. Perhaps we have come down to the point where the world monetary system consists of promises backed by other promises which go on receding back until they disappear in a murky realm out of which comes a recorded voice saying, over and again, "Nobody really understands the international monetary system."*

*One expert calls this a world of Einsteinian general relativity.

Well, why do these surplus countries keep on accepting these pieces of phony paper? One reason is that they pay interest, in fact a higher rate than if they represented a claim on something of intrinsic value. The other reason is, What else can they do? Get out of the game, quit exporting, and maybe cause a worldwide collapse that will wash them up on the beach too? Japanese prosperity is terribly dependent on world trade. And what have the Arabs got to sell besides oil?

What is likelier to happen is that as confidence in the US dollar goes down again, as it must, foreign investors will switch to other countries and currencies while creditor nations and corporations will begin requiring payment in marks, pounds or francs or yen instead of in dollars. The weaker dollar would enable US to sell more goods and services abroad, thus reducing the payments deficit. But another result would be higher interest rates in US, causing recession, higher unemployment, and higher budget deficits, with consequent inflation, making the dollar even less acceptable.

Whether in that crisis or the next, at some point nations will begin to raise tariffs or otherwise interfere with foreign trade, thus bringing about another 1930s type of deflationary World Depression. Or the phony money game will go on until some bank or some debtor government balks and there will be a default which will reverberate through the world financial structure and cause the same deflationary-type collapse. Or the game will go on, with governments "guaranteeing" new bad loans to LDCs and issuing new bad paper to cover payments and budget deficits, paying higher and higher interest rates, until we get a new phenomenon: a worldwide inflationary collapse, instead of those runaway inflations in the past that were limited to one nation or a few.

What can be done? International debt probably totaled between 1,500 and 2,000 billion dollars, as of 1984. Two international economists, Hogan and Pearce, estimate that, after correcting for the loss in the dollar's purchasing power, this debt is about ten times what it was in 1931 when the system collapsed in the Great Depression, or perhaps four times more onerous if one takes into account the increase in the capacity to pay (ratio of debt to production). But they add that the short-term method of finance (the bankers are lending long-term, then covering by borrowing short-term, the opposite of prudence) leaves the whole structure infinitely more fragile.

The SDRs or "Paper Gold" were a temporary expedient, proved ineffective in 1971. Robert Triffin, a highly respected international economist, has suggested that nations which have more of other currencies than they need could swap them for IMF long-term bonds. He saw this as one of the interim steps toward a single world currency which, he said, would require no more discipline than does the maintenance of free and stable exchange rates. But he did not expect to see a world currency by the year 2000.[33]

The two international economists just mentioned suggest a new international unit that would be defined as a fixed basket of goods such as those in a cost of living index. This "Commodity Pound" could always be turned in for precisely that basket of goods. Thus, with a true Standard of Value, payments imbalances would again be self-correcting, as they were when gold was the Standard, and nations could no longer consume beyond their earnings. Meanwhile, the present debt would be turned into long-term bonds.[34]

Comment. We believe international anarchy will continue to preclude any durable solution; that anarchy's intensity will be lifted high by trade and payments problems over the next generation, and probably soon rather than late; that we shall experience Great Depression, whether deflationary or inflationary. We expect Western DCs to be most affected, especially US and Japan. But the members of the European Common Market will be hurt too; their new ECU (European Currency Unit) is far from replacing their nine national currencies and may well be aborted; Britain has already opted out. The socialist nations will be least affected because their politico-economic system protects them to a degree from external collapse; on the other hand, their margins of prosperity tend to be slight. As for the LDCs, we shall be describing in the next Section C their manifold problems, which world depression will aggravate sorely.

5. *Trans-national Environmental Deterioration.* Environmental pollution owing to acts or omissions by other nations was recognized along the Rhine and Danube more than a century ago. And around 1960 the dangers of radioactive pollution from nuclear testing caused strong world opinion to form.

But the stepped-up pollution of the planet's atmosphere and oceans, and the depletion of its natural resources, have only recently been recognized. At the UN's Stockholm Conference on the environment in 1972 the LDCs were more interested in development than in pollution.

The DCs are indeed mainly accountable for worldwide pollution and resource depletion, for these are caused by their industries. If in fact pollution's "greenhouse effect" is heating up the planet's atmosphere—and in 1985 the experts are not yet agreed that it is—with accompanying drastic climatic changes, there will be the devil to pay.

But in India and in Africa's Sahel belt, as well as in other LDCs, overpopulation and overgrazing and the cutting down of forests have combined with drouth to change climate and create vast new deserts.

Since 1973 the UN Environment Program (UNEP), headquartered in Nairobi in Kenya, has been trying to do something. But, like other international organizations, it must make do on little money. In this case, contributions to the Program are entirely voluntary. The responsibility is therefore still in national hands, entirely.

So, the question is, as things get worse, which nations are going to bear how much of the vast economic cost of really cleaning up the environment and conserving natural resources? For example, Canadians are angry because US industry is producing acid rain that appears to be killing Canadian forests and lakes. Disputes of this sort, especially in Europe where pollution from NATO countries is deposited in Warsaw Pact countries, will add to the intensity of our anarchy component.[35]

And the effect of sovereign anarchy upon this problem is indicated by the refusal of three big polluters (US, Britain, Poland) to join 18 other nations in a 1985 treaty agreeing to a 30 percent reduction in sulphur dioxide emissions, believed the cause of acid rain; also by the failure, as of 1985, to reach an international convention on controlling damage by chlorofluorocarbons (CFCs, such as aerosols) to the planet's ozone layer. In this dispute, US and Canada, which have banned CFCs in aerosols, are opposing their NATO allies in the Common Market, which have not banned them because it would cost over $200 million to change to other propellants.[36]

Summary Comment on Section B, Anarchy's Future Intensities

We have the same problem here that we had in summing up on weaponry. Do we say that future intensities will be determined by Histories of Hostility *or* by Weaponry *or* by Tension Points *or* by World Depression *or* by Trans-National Environmental Deterioration? Or do we add up all five? Or perhaps even multiply them?

We don't know. But we believe something is to be gained by raising the questions of simultaneity and sequence of events. For example, a trade war may end the one-sided US-Japan alliance, and Japan would re-arm. What, then, of old Japanese-Chinese and Japanese-Russian hostilities, if the Korea tension point comes to crisis? A Great Depression would probably break up the Common Market and disrupt NATO too, so West Germany might rearm. What, then, of old German-Russian hostility focused on Berlin? A third example: a US technological break-through occurs, perhaps on Star Wars, or such an event is greatly feared by USSR, while crisis is occurring in the Persian Gulf tension point, with USSR backing the Iranian Shiites while Saudi Arabia and the other Sunni Arab states are backed by US.

C. Future Intensities
of Ideological Competition and Aggression.

As we noted earlier, throughout most of history aggressive leaderships have taken charge of nations for reasons unrelated to ideology or even to socio-economic problems. But in modern times aggressive elites and their messianic ideologies usually take control of a nation after civil conflict over internal problems caused by external as well as internal pressures. The civil conflict is a process of radicalization and polarization toward the extremes of Left and Right, with the moderate Center giving way.

History suggests that in a nation with a large middle class the process involves a short-term swing to the Left but is completed with victory by the Right. Thus there were strong communist movements in Italy and Germany in the 1920s before Mussolini and Hitler took over. But in a nation with a small middle class the short-term move is to the Right; the ultimate victory is to the Left. Thus Colonel Beck, Chiang Kai-shek, and Sergeant Batista had their day in Poland, China, and Cuba.

Spain thus far is an exception. It had a small middle class and moved sharply to the Left as the 1930s civil war went on, but the Right prevailed thanks to the Church and to the greater aid given General Franco by Mussolini and Hitler than that given the Republican regime by USSR and France.

At any rate, in our day aggressive elites and strong ideologies do move together to seize control of a nation. The new government becomes authoritarian if not totalitarian and acts more aggressively at the international level than a Centrist government does, but a Rightist or fascistic regime is more aggressive than a Leftist or communist regime.

1. *External Stresses.* These pressures from the international system which impinge upon a nation, and which its political system may not be able to cope with, are, as listed in Section D of Chapter 5: international violence and the expectation thereof, including the diversion of economic resources to defense and the possibility of outside intervention in the nation's affairs; international trade and currency imbalances, and worldwide depression; and trans-national environmental deterioration. All these were discussed fully in the preceding Section B.

International violence will bear most heavily upon the nations in the following international subsystems: the Middle Eastern including the Persian Gulf; the Southeast Asian; the South Asian (India, Pakistan, Bangladesh, Sri Lanka); the Central American.[37]

The expectation of international violence, even if the nation is not at war at the moment, bears heavily upon all nations that spend a substantial part of their economic product on war. Israel may spend half its product, Iraq and Syria perhaps a third. These three are kept going only by massive subsidies from other nations. USSR spends at least a sixth, US a tenth. The "protected" nations of West Germany and Japan spend only about a twentieth. But all the rest average six to eight percent of their economic product, including the LDCs that can ill afford to divert any resources from real needs. Defense spending provides incomes for people, but no products that anyone would want to buy, hence it causes inflation. The world's arms bill is nearly $700 billion, far more than the income of a billion LDC inhabitants, and half again as much as the world spends on education. In addition to the defense burden, there is also the strain of living in fear of war, for this too can radicalize a nation; for example, US in the 1950s, in the heyday of McCarthyism.

Intervention by other nations in a civil conflict means usually that the conflict will be longer and bitterer with consequent greater radicalization, witness France in the 1790s, the Allied intervention in Russia in 1918, the radicalization of the two Vietnams to opposite extremes, and present US intervention in Nicaragua which pushes the Sandinista regime leftwards.[38]

As for trade and payments imbalances, these external pressures bear most obviously upon those LDCs which—by reason of oil or food imports, or overquick development or other bad management—have run up foreign debts that they cannot pay. Some of these countries, like Mexico, probably can live with the austerity imposed by the IMF to get their deficits in hand. Others, like Brazil, probably cannot. But they bear heavily also upon some DCs, especially US whose payments deficit has been allowed to run so wild (partly owing to the peculiar position of the dollar as the world currency) that in 1985 its foreign debt will exceed its foreign investments for the first time in 70 years, with Japan as principal creditor. But beyond that, if we come to currency collapse and trade war, those DCs like Japan and the semi-developed Pacific Rim countries (South Korea, Taiwan, Hong Kong, Singapore) that depend most on foreign trade will be hurt worst. And on beyond that, if payments and trade collapse brings on world depression, as we think it would, every nation will suffer severe strain but especially those DCs which are least self-sufficient in terms of a balance between agriculture and industry, between production and consumption; these include Japan, Britain, and West Germany. The Common Market, if it could hold together, would be more self-sufficient than some of its members. The same is true of Comecon, which is far more self-contained as a whole than some of its members, especially USSR.

As for environmental deterioration, if a nation's government accepts the responsibility to stop trans-national polluting and to conserve natural resources, it must make do with fewer resources to meet other needs, hence new aggravants will be added to civil conflict. If it rejects this responsibility, this too is a source of civil discord. This problem, which enters also into the whole question of under- or over-development of the nation's economy, is sure to grow luxuriantly in future.

2. *Internal Stresses.* These, as listed in Section D of Chapter 5, are cleavages of class, of religion or ideology, of race or caste, and of language and culture, plus underdevelopment or overdevelopment. We shall deal with them in several subsections.

a. *Differences of Economic or Hereditary Class.* Hereditary social class structures are still well defined in most LDCs, although they are breaking down at varying speeds under the impact of other changes, primarily economic-technological ones. Social class is still apparent in all non-socialist DCs but it is mingled with and undergirded by economic class. Only in socialist nations, which have had the most thorough-going social convulsions, has class been abolished officially. Even there it is not obliterated; many sons of peasants are still peasants, looked down on by urban laborers who in turn look up to the new intelligentsia and officialdom.

Everywhere there is substantial social mobility between classes. But class remains a significant internal stress in Britain, West Germany, France, Italy and Japan, as well as in the LDCs. And there is no country where every group does not wish for higher relative status and greater prosperity, especially in LDCs where there is least of these values to go around.

As we expect the world in the future to offer fewer of these goods in relation to population, and since in class nations some obviously have more than others and will continue so unless it is taken away from them, we see class as a strongly radicalizing pressure.

b. *Differences of Religion or Politico-Economic Ideology.* Religious conflict is overt in several important nations including Britain (Ulster), India with its Moslem, Sikh, and other minorities, and Nigeria where the civil war was a Christian-Moslem split to a degree. It lies not far beneath the surface in Canada, the Netherlands, and West Germany. Anti-clericalism is still an issue in many predominantly Catholic lands such as France and Spain and Italy, Every Arab nation with a Sunni majority must worry if it has a sizeable Shiite minority. Islamic fundamentalism is focused now in Iran, Pakistan, and Malaysia, in several sects, and it could become a terribly divisive factor in any Moslem nation. Indeed, even in nations that appear homogeneous in religion, there are sects which can become conflictive when other stresses heat up the situation of if a sect feels oppressed. In Latin America, where the other stresses are substantial, Protestant gains alarm dominant Catholics. In predominantly Protestant US, the influx of Catholic refugees from Hungary and Poland, Cuba, and Vietnam, plus the flood of illegal immigrants from Latin America, has aggravated old anti-Catholic feelings, while the cleavage between Christians and Jews has widened owing to cost of US support for Israel in terms of taxes and oil prices.

Conflicting ideologies are a lively source of internal stress, because as civil problems arise groups embrace differing solutions offered by competing ideologies. A group may ask help from an outside nation that shares its ideology, then intervention can come in any of several forms open or secret. Nearly every non-communist nation has its liberals, its socialists, and its communists whether of the Moscow or Maoist variety. Some nations have fascists. Some have Buddhist Socialism, others Arab or Islamic Socialism, where belief systems are compounded of religio-socio-political elements. In some Protestant sects in US, Christianity and capitalism are mingled.

In each great nation there is a ruling ideology, though in several it is a blend of liberalism and democratic socialism, and in none is the ruling ideology absolutely secure. In other nations, including virtually all

LDCs, the ideological situation is more competitive or could become so.

Communist socialism, with its massive bureaucratic central planning, has not proved so productive as Marx prophesied, though it has done better in industrial development than in agriculture. Hungary has moved far toward market incentives; Yugoslavia is trying to. China has abandoned its collective-farm "communes," doubling its wheat production, and is trying to decentralize its industrial planning and find some way of introducing incentive, while still maintaining state ownership of the means of production. Its leaders say the ultimate goal is still communism, but one wonders. One wonders too how much appeal socialism will continue to have, even to the LDCs.

Perhaps the ideology has already been written that will seize groups and then whole nations. Existentialists and Teilhard de Chardin offer worldviews that might be altered into politico-economic ideologies, but they fit well enough as they are into democratic socialism. At any rate, we are skeptical that the next 20 to 25 years will see no more than the three present choices: communism on the left, liberalism in the center, and fascism on the right.

   c. *Differences of Race or Caste, Language and Culture.* Among the great nations, Japan is most homogeneous in these respects, followed by France, then Italy, West Germany and Britain, with China, US, and USSR bringing up the rear in about that order. India is a conglomeration of drastic linguistic and cultural diversities, with a complex hierarchy of hundreds of castes. Nearly every Southeast Asian nation has a sizeable Chinese minority; some have a Hindu minority. Burma is a federation of minorities that resent the dominant Burmans. Bangladesh, Pakistan, Iran, and the Arab nations are each fairly homogeneous in these respects. The Black African states are divided within by tribes, while South Africa is a white-dominated black country.

Most Latin American nations have a sort of caste system whereby those who claim "pure" Spanish or other European ancestry rank first, followed by mixtures between whites and indians or blacks, with the indians or blacks last. Argentina, Brazil, Uruguay, and Chile have many non-Iberian Europeans but these have been assimilated fairly well. Canada has its large French-speaking minority, the US its large black and Hispanic minorities.

Nations having overt difficulty with these cleavages include India, Sri Lanka (Ceylon), Burma, Philippines, South Africa, Israel, US, and Canada. But nearly all nations have cleavages along these lines that, like religious differences, could become important under pressure from other stresses.

   Comment on Subsections a, b, and c. A statistical study of four DCs (Belgium, Canada, South Africa, Switzerland), based on opinion surveys, found that religion was the strongest determinant of political party choice, followed closely by language, with class a distant third.[39] Another study concluded that the notion that civil violence derives from economic inequality may be in need of re-thinking, mainly because there are other cleavages—cultural, religious, racial, ethnic, linguistic—that may cut across the economic cleavage.[40] Maximum radicalization might therefore be expected in nations where these cleavages coincide instead of cross-cutting each other; and on that basis, among the great nations, India is in greatest present difficulty, and in USSR a relaxation of totalitarian controls might produce rebellion by the Moslem republics, but USSR is already thoroughly radicalized. The usual way of dealing with these cleavages is to set up a federal arrangement, with the boundaries of the constituent units drawn to coincide with the differences as nearly as possible. Thus India, USSR, Switzerland, Canada, and Yugoslavia are federations, as well as US.

d. *Underdevelopment, Including Economic Scarcity in Relation to Population.* The UN designated 1974 as World Population Year. To reach one billion population took from the beginnings of mankind to around 1830. In 1930 there were two billion; in 1960 three billion; in 1975 four billion. In the year 2000, at present growth rates, there will be 6.5 billion of us.

This explosive growth since World War II was caused by public health programs in the LDCs that cut the death rate while the birth rate remained the same, by the availability of further land for tilling, by cheap oil, and—in the words of columnist Paul Harvey—by "undisciplined, uncontrolled, malignant multiplication of population."

If a net reproduction rate of 1 for 1 were reached by the year 2000 we would achieve zero population growth around 2060 with 8.4 billion people. But if world fertility continues to decline only at the rate foreseen in current projections, population will reach 10 billion in 2030, according to President Carter's "Global 2000" study, then 30 billion by 2100. In 1956 the astronomer Fred Hoyle calculated, using rates that may be conservative, that by 3055 Earth's population would reach standing-room-only.

The DCs, with population growth of only one percent a year, are polluting the planet with wastes and are gobbling up its resources. The LDCs, with a growth rate of two to more than three percent, are polluting the planet with people for whom there are no resources.

The UN-related Food and Agricultural Administration estimated in 1966 that there were 12 acres of living space for each human: one was cultivated; two and a half more were cultivable though less productive. But, the FAO said, bringing new areas under cultivation requires great expense by poor LDC governments, and anyway most of the additional 2½ acres was located in DCs or in LDCs with no population problem yet.

The Ford Foundation, the World Bank, the US and other governments provide funding for family-planning programs in the LDCs where the people, based on generations of experience, have large families so there will be some surviving sons to support them in old age. In China the government is getting the birth rate under control. In Colombia, Mexico, and a few other LDCs half or more of the women of reproductive age now at least have access to birth control methods, but in most LDCs little or nothing is being done. Still, whereas at the 1974 UN conference the LDCs wanted to talk about development instead of population, the problem is being recognized in international conferences at Cairo in 1983 and at Mexico City in 1984.

But the Worldwatch Institute says that so many young people in LDCs will reach reproductive age even after the one for one replacement level is achieved that the population would eventually level off, if food were available, as follows: Bangladesh, 454 million, 4½ times present population; India, 1.7 billion, about 2½ times the present; Mexico, up more than 2½ times to 199 million; and Nigeria would grow to 618 million, more people than now live in all of Africa. Ethiopia, the focus of famine concern in 1985, has nearly 40 million people now, but this will increase six-fold to 231 million if the rest of the world sends enough food.[41]

The 1966 FAO report said that unless there were a revolution in agriculture, famines and civil disorders would take a heavy toll of human life. Well, there has indeed been a revolution. Mainly under Rockefeller Foundation auspices, far more productive strains of grains were developed: wheat in Mexico, rice in the Philippines, and then sorghum in Ethiopia; now cassava, yams, cowpeas, and corn.

Unfortunately, the new rice does best on hot, dry land, such as that in Northwest India and Pakistan, where irrigation is plentiful, but gives only moderate yields in the monsoon areas which account for most of India and for Southeast Asia. More unfortunately, the "Green Revolution" requires a technological revolution. Fertilizers or pesticides must be imported or produced in one's own factories. These require building materials, know-how, and above all petroleum now priced at just ten times what it cost back before the Arab-Israeli war of 1973. There must be trains and railroads, trucks and highways, credit, drying facilities, storage. In India, benefiting in recent years from favorable weather as well as the Green Revolution, much of the larger crop is eaten by birds and pests, and some of the rest rots for lack of storage and shipping. The farmer must be taught how to use the new strains and persuaded to change his ways of doing many things.

Still more unfortunately, the technological revolution that is behind this also implies a socio-political revolution. Large plots of land are needed, with mechanization, so small landowners and farm laborers leave the land and add to the restless, dispossessed millions around the urban fringes. DCs may give aid, but not often for industry; they want the LDCs to remain agricultural and buy their machinery and other needs from them; and they may be right because many a new nation has wasted its resources on ill-conceived industrial development programs while neglecting its farms. At any rate, there are few jobs in the cities.

A further advance in the Green Revolution is based on new knowledge involving genetic changes in plants which, for example, can then produce their own fertilizer, and on the introduction of natural pest-killers.

The World Food Assembly reported in 1984 that, except for Africa, world food production had increased more than population in the years since the 1974 UN meeting, yet the number of malnourished persons doubled to 800 million. Africa's food production per person fell eleven percent during the period 1970-1983, owing to the highest birth rates on the planet as well as to drouth. Lester Brown of Worldwatch Institute says we are still in the Oil Age, not the Nuclear or the Electronic Age, because of oil's importance to food production as well as to so many other things.[42]

The Green Revolution can, at best, do no more than buy a few years during which nations can try to get their population problems under control. Meanwhile the socio-political change it requires, combined with the task of finding food for a million new mouths every five days, radicalizes the LDCs from two different directions, so to speak.

The places where the population presses most heavily on the land are located in a belt reaching around the Earth from the Philippines to Central America, specifically the main island of Luzon in the Philippines, China, the main island of Java in Indonesia, Bangladesh, Pakistan, India, Iran, Turkey, Egypt, Black Africa, northeastern Brazil, Haiti, El Salvador, and Mexico.[43] This belt is the zone of maximum radicalization.

Conceivably, this suffering and radicalization could be prevented or at least substantially ameliorated by the DCs, though some LDCs may be already beyond hope. The UN General Assembly several years ago resolved that the DCs ought to give one percent of their gross national product to the LDCs. Preferably this would be given through world agencies rather than as the usual bilateral aid—so often misgiven and misspent. Actually aid by DCs averages only about one-half of one percent, a figure which is declining, and most of it is in loans rather than grants.[44]

A realistic figure in relation to need would be Sakharov's suggestion of 20 percent a year for 15 years.[45] But if the DCs were not generous when they were prosperous, they are not apt to be so now. They will no doubt continue to sell or give military aid, and they must continue to lend money to keep the LDCs from defaulting on old debts, but they will do little to foster economic development. True, the DCs will continue to send food when famine gets publicized enough, as in the case of Ethiopia in 1985, yet it is sad but true that the sending of food to an overpopulated land will result in a larger population that will starve in its turn.[46]

The present situation is that aid received by LDCs is more than offset by: their repayments of old loans, the widening gap between what they get for their exports (unless they export oil) and what they pay for imports, the cost of maintaining their military, and the flight of capital from LDCs to DCs. Most LDCs also suffer from a poor brand of capitalism at home: a focus on high profit margins and low volume in enterprises that survive only because the governments keep out more economically produced goods by high tariff and other measures. There is a general lack of entrepreneurship such as created the thriving capitalist economies. There is also the "brain drain," whereby many of their ablest and best trained go abroad where they can make more money. And, finally, there is the problem of political instability which deters investment by foreign capitalists.

Still, some LDCs are apt to make it, by reason of their attention to population control or special economic conditions or entrepreneurship or disciplined hard work. Candidates include China, Indonesia, South Korea, Taiwan, Hong Kong, Singapore, Vietnam and Cambodia, Thailand, and possibly Malaysia. Of these, China and Vietnam and Cambodia have already had their radicalizations to the extreme Left. In the Middle East, the oil exporting Arab states and possibly Iran as well; and similarly, the North African states of Libya, Algeria, and probably Tunisia and Morocco. In Latin America, Argentina, Chile, Brazil, Uruguay, Colombia and Venezuela have a chance, and possibly Mexico and Costa Rica too. Cuba has had its radicalization and will survive.

So the problem countries, in terms of scarcity in relation to population, are the Philippines, all of South Asia, maybe Iran, Syria, Turkey, Egypt, nearly all of Black Africa, Bolivia, Peru, Ecuador, Haiti and the Dominican Republic, Panama, Honduras, El Salvador, Guatemala, and perhaps Mexico. As for North Korea, Burma, and Paraguay, we don't know enough about them, and this is true too of several of the newer and tinier states. Israel and South Africa are DCs whose future hinges on stresses other than economic scarcity.

We expect that many of the nations covered in the preceding paragraph will eventually radicalize to the extreme Left, partly because of China's apparent ability to feed its people and get population growth down through the use of totalitarian controls. Whether they might then go on to follow China's present example by reducing central planning, introducing market incentives, and opening up to foreign investment is beyond our ability to foresee. But China's pattern since 1949, shorn of some of Mao's absurdities, ought to have great appeal for overpopulated LDCs; indeed it may be their only hope. China may equal USSR's living standards by the year 2000.

    e. *Overdevelopment, Including Overconsumption and Environmental Deterioration.* Here we can be brief. For reasons described earlier, environmental problems will increasingly exacerbate civil conflict in DCs over the questions, What and how much shall be done to clean things up, Who shall pay for it, and How much and what kinds of further development will be permitted? Intergroup and intergenerational conflicts will intensify, as fundamentally new notions question the "consumer society" and ask what constitutes "progress." US, with a twentieth of the world's population, consumes a third of the natural resources used each year. Japan and the Common Market nations are similarly greedy; the Soviet economic bloc only a little less so. The gloomy forecasts in 1972 and 1974 by the Club of Rome and in 1979 by Carter's Global 2000 Study are not everywhere welcomed. How can business firms, investors, and the capitalist psyche generally adjust to "no growth"? Or the leaders of USSR and other socialist states.?

These computerized forecasts are as gloomy for the DCs, almost, as for the LDCs. The Club of Rome report, for example, predicted that, barring radical reorderings of priorities, the world would breed, consume, and foul itself back into the Dark Ages within a century; that even if nuclear power were to give us unlimited energy the pollution curve would shoot lethally high—that sort of Hobson's choice. The Global 2000 said food output depends on petroleum fertilizers but that petroleum production will curve down in the 1990s while fuelwood needs will exceed supply in the LDCs; that water shortages will be severe; that 40 percent of LDC forests will disappear; that carbon dioxide and chemicals may change the world's climate significantly by 2050; that thousands of species will disappear. On the other hand, there are experts who disagree with all this gloom.[47]

Fortunately we have a 1985 article by a member of the Systems Dynamics Group at Massachusetts Institute of Technology which did the Club of Rome reports. She summarizes and reconciles twenty of these computerized global models of the future and concludes that: (1) existing resources and known technologies can support all the needs of the world's people today and for some time to come; (2) population and physical capital cannot grow forever on a finite planet; (3) no reliable, complete information is available about the degree to which the earth's environment can absorb the wastes created to meet human needs; (4) if continued, present policies will lead to an increasing gap between rich and poor; (5) technology can help but is not the answer; (6) the interdependence among peoples and nations is much greater than commonly imagined; (7) policy changes made soon are likely to have more impact with less effort than the same changes made later; and (8) the range of real possibilities includes the end of everything or a world at peace in which everyone's physical needs are met, and the difference will be determined by the way we understand our options and the way we act.[48]

What might be involved is suggested by two scholars in a book commenting on the Club of Rome reports. They say that the world is a system made up of interdependent parts that will collapse in the middle of the next century unless solutions are developed in a global context; that narrow nationalism is futile, that the development of a practical international framework is essential.[49]

We shall return to these future potentialities in the next and final Chapter 8. In this Chapter 7 our assumption is that not much will be done, that things will go on as they are, and our conclusion on this Section 3 is that internal stresses will be sufficient over the next 20 to 25 years to radicalize many if not most LDCs but not the DCS; their radicalization will turn more upon external stresses, as described in Section 1.

3. *Availability of Alternative Leaderships and Belief Systems.* Leadership for discontent is usually available. As we have seen, some individuals acquire early in life, through fear and frustration and a conviction of inferiority, an aggressive need to achieve, to excel, to lead and to use other people, to prove themselves and be recognized. There are those too who, through whatever psychological mechanisms, sympathize or empathize with the oppressed and disadvantaged. There are some few who are reared by their mothers or fathers to be "great." Some hear a call from on high.

A fruitful source of new leaders and ideologies in LDCs is the large number of highly trained individuals who are unemployed or underemployed. There is little place for them in the private sector of the economy, which is small in most LDCs, and they cannot all be absorbed in the already swollen government bureaucracies. They cannot or will not go abroad to work. So they stay home and become reformers and agitators. A DC stricken by depression will similarly turn up a large number of such individuals.

Aggressive individuals see their opportunity or their responsibility in discontent. If they do not have ready access to the Establishment—the prevailing elite—they are prone to embrace an ideology other than the prevailing one. Out of a ready-made ideology or some synthesis-scheme of their own, often some melange of nationalism or socialism with religion, they propose answers to the external and internal stresses we have described.

Some leaders are more capable—that is, intelligent, quick, articulate, ruthless—than others, so that a leader with a small following may overcome another with a large one. As civil conflict worsens, moderates will be ousted by extremists. Long-term wisdom—a vision of eventual outcomes—is probably a handicap. Old elites are dispersed or subordinated to the new elite.

Alternative leaders and ideologies are not always salient, by which we mean that they may exist but are not very prominent. Mexico, for example, looks to be in for deep trouble again, but no alternative leadership-ideology is visible. But if they become salient, they will interact with the masses, playing upon overt cleavages of class, race or language, or invoking latent schisms of religion, caste or culture. They will offer to defend the nation, throw out any interventors, and increase the defense budget while solving the nation's trade and currency problems and providing socio-economic justice to all or most.

If the stresses are bad enough, or become so through protracted civil conflict, the new leaders will cry not Reform but Revolution and the nation may be anarchized into two or more warring factions as we noted in Chapter 5. The faction that best persuades the people to the worldview personalized by its leadership will prevail, though it may have to win over a significant part of the military unless it can arm and train its own.

4. *Future Radicalization.* We expect the external and internal stresses discussed in Sections 1 through 3 to have the following effects some time within the next 20 to 25 years.

a. *In the LDCs.* These countries are of two categories: those which got their independence long ago, as in Latin America, plus those which like Thailand or Turkey were never colonies; and those which have gained independence since World War II. These latter have displaced their anti-colonial leaders with their liberal regimes and most of them are now under rightist military regimes or civilian regimes tolerated by the military. The post-colonial liberal governments fell owing to doctrinaire ideologies, corruption, unfamiliarity with the art of political compromise, and simple lack of know-how to develop their countries. Unfortunately, the military suffer from these same deficiencies.[50] Even more unfortunately, countries in the earlier category simply have longer histories of inadequate liberal regimes followed by inadequate military regimes. Our point is that the political systems in nearly all the LDCs are quite incapable of dealing with severe future stresses.[51]

Taking into account war and the cost of defense, and trade and payments problems, plus socio-economic cleavages, overpopulation, and the availability of new leaders and ideologies, we expect the following countries to radicalize eventually, within 25 years, to some version of the extreme Left: the Philippines, Bangladesh, Pakistan, India, Sri Lanka, Iran, Turkey, Egypt, Nigeria and several other black African states, Brazil, Chile, Bolivia, Peru, and Ecuador. We expect that most of these will adopt the Chinese or Cuban patterns (though each may call its version by a different name) because of their egalitarianism and relative moderation which are apt to be more attractive than the Soviet version of communist socialism.[52]

US and other NATO nations will intervene in some of these cases but will probably fail. US will intervene effectively, however, to stop thrusts toward the extreme Left in Central America, Mexico, or the Caribbean; those countries will be dictatorships, behind some facade of liberal democracy, receiving military and economic aid from US.

As each country radicalizes it will become a tension point between the Soviet and US blocs, plus China in some instances. This is especially true

of Philippines, Pakistan, India, Iran, Turkey, Egypt, Nigeria, and the
South American countries.

b. *In the DCs.* Radicalization here, with consequent intensification
of aggression and ideological competition, is likeliest to cause World War
III.

If the Common Market moves on from ECUs to a true common
currency, and from direct election of the European parliament to a full
federal political union, it can survive.[53] True, a federal Western Europe
might simply become a great nation contending with other great powers.
Anarchy's pull would be in that direction. But such a federation could
insulate its members to a saving degree from world depression.

But the Market, as it stands now, has been described by one scholar as
an economic giant but a political dwarf, and he doubts NATO could
survive a collapse of the Market.[54] The Market nations are not doing very
well these days; they suffer high unemployment and low growth in
productivity. They have trade and currency problems among themselves;
also with US and Japan. We believe that unless the Market's structure is
changed in time it will collapse—and NATO with it. West Germany will
rearm and move to some new version of fascism, followed by France and
possibly even Britain. But Italy, along with Greece, Spain and Portugal,
is apt to radicalize to the extreme Left next time. Remember: France and
Britain had fascist movements in the 1930s.

Among the communist-socialist countries we do not see further vast
upheavals. They are no longer peasant economies; they have
industrialized; most people are better off than their parents were; they can
probably improve their agricultural production; they ought not to have
to import much petroleum from outside Comecon; and their type of
economy insulates them to a degree against a general capitalist financial-
economic collapse. The means available to these governments to control
dissent are formidable, especially as USSR stands ready to supplement
them. Yet, many people do resent the lack of liberal freedoms, and several
of the governments wish to move further back toward market incentives,
thus we expect new moves to break away, perhaps by East Germany and
Czechoslovakia, both long-industrialized and more prosperous than
USSR, or by Poland where the Church is strongest and the farms have
never been collectivized. Or take the case of Yugoslavia, which is outside
Comecon and the Warsaw Pact. It is torn by religious, language and
cultural cleavages. Suppose, on top of those problems, its mounting
economic troubles cause a chaos out of which some reverse radicalization
back toward the liberal Center emerges? This could become a tension
point indeed between USSR and the West. At any rate, the worst we see is
a return to Stalinist repression, brought on in part by world depression,
and the best we see is a widespread reverse radicalization, permitted by or
even led by USSR under Gorbachev. In neither case do we see a severe
increase in aggression or ideological competition coming from this
quarter.

Whereas Gorbachev is young, Deng Xiao-ping is old and we can only guess what kind of leadership will succeed his. Our guess is that China will continue along its present liberalizing trend—reverse radicalization. China is tired of turmoil. Its people have no more desire to return to Maoism than the Russians wish to return to Stalinism. A world depression would hurt China, now that it is trading abroad and inviting foreign capital investment, but we believe the population problem will be solved and that a billion people will be clothed and fed. Domestically, any effort by Maoist elements in the party or the military to seize power will fail. Internationally, a strange thing could result from China's reverse radicalization: growing prosperity could encourage its leadership to become more aggressive along its borders with USSR.

In Japan, because we anticipate world monetary collapse and Great Depression, we expect radicalization all the way to the extreme Right this time. This will be a fascism pictured as a return to old traditions of Shogun, Daimyo, and Samurai—the familiar hierarchical and authoritarian pattern of Japanese life which has been disrupted by post-World War II prosperity.

Dozens of rightist groups have been formed. The dominant Liberal Democratic Party is a league of factions. Several of these may join with the nationalistic Komeito Party (based on a large Buddhist sect called Sokka Gokkai that appeals to uprooted countryfolk) in the usual fascistic alliance of upper class and lower middle class. With the military, they could seize the government. Japan would then rearm rapidly, partly to reduce unemployment, and develop its own nuclear and CB capabilities.

In US, blacks alternate between outrage and quiescence, as do Hispanics, while poor whites respond to populist appeals. The lower middle class, including European ethnic groups, feels threatened—by blacks and browns and simply in general. Members of the great middle class are frustrated and anxious. Prosperity, when they got it, did not satisfy, but it was all they had worked for, and now it may be disappearing. They largely support military spending and US interventions abroad; at home they want law and order more than they want justice. They seek places of withdrawal and retreat, but also scapegoats and ways to fight back. Frustration breeds fear and anger.

There is a reaching back to a time when things were simpler. In the search for emotional security, fundamentalist sects are growing. Glossolalia, the speaking in unknown tongues, has spread in thirty years into all the old main-line churches, recruiting the middle class away from the social gospel into an other-worldly conservatism. Many Catholics follow Pope John Paul II into ever deeper conservatism and anti-communism.

Conservative religion undergirds conservative politics. Biblical quotations are grounds for opposing integration, communism, sex education, abortion, feminism, welfare legislation and pacifism.[55] Evil is associated with change, or with that which is strange, for these threaten the sureties of religion and nation. Private censorship is on the increase, as is government secrecy. Loyalty is prized above reason, but loyalty can attach only to the static, not the dynamic. Reasoning may question that which is, hence is mistrusted.

As blacks and Hispanics move left, the Great Silent Majority moves right along with the Moral Majority, from the Democratic into the Republican Party. These conservatives gravitated also into the John Birch Society, the Minutemen, the Klan, and so forth, and they are joining the *Bruder Schweigen* (Silent Brotherhood), the Aryan Nations, the Posse Comitatus and other new rightist organizations as they are formed.

Many individuals and groups have private arsenals including mortars and bazookas; the number of guns in private hands is estimated at 90 million upwards.[56] Some plan to go hunting, but many are hoarding weapons against the day when They (meaning communists, liberals, humanists, Jews, Catholics, Hispanics, blacks) come to get Us.

It is the triumph of the New Right, funded by direct-mail contributions and by some very rich people, that it has captured the Catholic-based abortion crusade while capitalizing upon frustration among fundamentalist Protestants, enlisting both in its radical right-wing political movement.

Henry Kissinger, a Jewish refugee from Nazi Germany, was represented in 1972 by a reputable journalist as privately fearing a rightist revolution in US triggered by the tactics of the extreme Left.[57] Probably no such tactics will even be required; the Christian New Right has its own fearsome momentum.

The problems of race, poverty, urban decay and pollution can largely be solved by assigning resources to them. But US spending for defense (about half the world total) goes on unabated by a Congress still shackled by poor leadership, by bribery in the form of campaign contributions, and by fear of the military-industrial complex.

Radicalization of the political system has been occurring at a steady rather than a runaway pace. We anticipate the collapse of the world monetary system and Great Depression will inject a populist appeal into the rightist ideology. Fascism typically adds the economic to the nationalist-racist appeal. New extremist leadership will appear and extol the old virtues of god, race, and nation. It will be a fascistic ideology called Christian Americanism*—an Americanism shorn of its traditions of tolerance and fairness and the Bill of Rights but justified by national emergency. The thrust toward the extreme right is historically endemic in American society.[58] It will at last have its day.

And it's a crying shame. Because US could easily handle its internal

---

*Hitler sold Nazism as a bulwark against atheism.

stresses if the external stresses were lacking. But, as we have noted, the dynamic of anarchy sees to it that a great nation is at the vortex of a competing coalition. It suffers most from war and the fear of war, and the attendant diversion of resources. Moreover, US is at the heart of the anarchic trade and monetary system, and will suffer greatly in its collapse. Even the sturdiest political systems, namely the American and the British, cannot forever withstand the ravages of international anarchy.

D. World War III?

Of course, unless the international system is extinguished by agreement. We shall consider that possibility in the final Chapter 8. Here in Chapter 7 the question is, What will happen if things go along as they are? And the answer is, World War III. When? By the year 2010.

Why 2010? Because there are so many ways already visible that can cause war, and 25 years gives them ample time to happen. (In contrast, there is only one way to prevent it, and international history offers only slight hope of integration by agreement.)

Any person can see ahead for one generation. If his awareness is limited to his village, he can predict some things about the village and its groups with considerable confidence. If his awareness extends to the planet and its groups, he can do the same.

A man who is noted for his studies of trends says that political prediction is best concerned with the future state of the *milieu* within which decisions have to be made. The *milieu*, or ambience, that we have projected is one of anarchic fear, ruinous defense budgets, unstable weaponry, historical hostilities, tension points old and new, a crumbling ecology, trade wars, currency crises, Great Depression, raging internal upheavals, and the reintroduction of fascism into what was already an international witches' brew.

Earlier we raised the presumption that, since anarchy and competing ideologies are already present, World War III would occur when we got a great nation with aggressive leadership, and in this Chapter 7 we supplied that ingredient, saying that Great Depression would install fascistic regimes in Japan and US and, if the Common Market breaks up, in West Germany, France, and even in Britain. And fascism will intensify ideological conflict.

But we note that a nuclear world war can happen even if there is no great aggressive nation.

Consider now whether or not you agree with the following statements. World War III can happen:

a. By nuclear accident, insanity, or terrorism, without any technological breakthrough in weaponry;

b. By governmental decision, in fear of technological breakthrough;

c. By governmental decision, because it has made a technological breakthrough;

d. By great-power intervention in present tension points (Israel v. Arabs, Iraq v. Iran, Vietnam v. its neighbors, South Korea v. North Korea, and so forth);

e. By great-power intervention in future tension points caused by radicalization toward the extreme left in Philippines, Pakistan and/or India, Iran, Turkey (a NATO member), Egypt, Nigeria, or a South American nation.

With regard to (b) and (c) above, bear in mind that the leading research nations among capitalist DCs, and probably in the world, are US, Japan, West Germany and Britain, in that order (none in the Soviet bloc).

Consider now that:

f. Trade wars now under way between US and Japan, between US and the Common Market, and between Japan and the Common Market, aggravated as they are by payments deficits, may break up the US-Japan alliance and the NATO alliance, even without complete collapse and World Depression;[60]

g. And, in that event, Japan would surely rearm and contend with US, China, and USSR, awakening bitter old hostilities with perhaps a realignment of contending coalitions in which Japan and USSR are allies;

h. While West Germany would probably rearm, even if the Common Market remained intact, reviving the bitterest of old hostilities with USSR, especially because divided Berlin and Germany would become acute problems.

Clearly, items (f) through (h) add to the overall likelihood of a nuclear world war. Now, consider a different situation whereby:

i. World Depression comes, placing terrible stress on the liberal capitalist nations so that Japan goes its own fascist way while NATO and the Common Market are still more or less intact and the Western nations are trying to remain liberal, open societies;

j. But the quasi-developed NATO members begin to slide away, radicalizing toward the extreme left, first Turkey perhaps, if it isn't already gone, then Portugal, then Greece and Spain, with Italy leaning that way;

k. US and its NATO allies suspect USSR is sending aid to Turkish leftists across their common land frontier or by water or by air, or to Greek leftists through Bulgaria;

l. NATO intervenes, secretly or openly, and the Warsaw Pact responds; one side begins to lose, then uses tactical nuclear weapons, and so forth; or, instead of intervention, NATO sends an ultimatum, USSR and its allies respond in kind, and the dance may begin with strategic nuclear missiles.

The scenarios in (g) through (l) may never have their opportunity to come to pass; the world may be long gone before trade wars or World Depression have much influence. At any rate, the foregoing items can be separated into snippets and put back together, or they can be run backwards. For example, instead of NATO members radicalizing leftwards, the scenario can have Warsaw Pact members moving back toward the center ("counter-revolutionary" or moving to the right, from the Kremlin's standpoint), with aid from NATO, whereupon USSR intervenes or sends an ultimatum.

We think it will make little difference; there are too many ways and too many places for World War III to get started. We do believe another Great Depression bad enough to radicalize US and other Western liberal nations into fascism would be the "worst case," a final nail in the coffin. Yet we see no way to provide against that eventuality within a framework of sovereign, independent nations.

There is a school of thought, with which we tend to agree, that US and its NATO allies are too caught up in an analogy between anti-communism now and anti-fascism in the 1930s; that World War III may not come as World War II did, when appeasement of Hitler was seen to be futile, but as World War I did, that is, unexpected crisis, followed by mutual miscalculation or irrational reaction.[61]

And, finally, we note that public opinion polls indicate a general trend in North America and Western Europe toward greater expectation of nuclear World War III.[62] This suggests that many people are forgetting or are too young to remember what the last great war was like, that they are tiring of living under tension, and that they are resigning themselves to what they see as inevitable. So, if not by the year 2010, then a little later on.

E. Two Proven But Untried Cures

The old cures for war that we considered at the close of Chapter 5 and the untried cures we discussed at the end of Chapter 6 were found defective in the light of our explanatory theory. As for anarchy, either they do not deal with it at all or they rely upon mere agreements which nations can disregard, or which, in the case of disarmament, leave nations free to rearm. Even Kennedy's GCD proposal failed to create, early enough in the process, a genuine world security system.

All those cures take a gradualist approach to the control of international conflict.

Gradualism depends for its acceptance on a great folk myth which peoples everywhere share. Its logic is that many changes occur gradually, therefore all change must be gradual. What American could not agree with any Russian—what Moslem with any Buddhist, what capitalist with any socialist—that "one must crawl before one can walk," that "one must walk before one can run"? There is perhaps no language that does not contain the equivalent of "little by little does it."

Gradualists say, "Let us get to know each other better and adopt common ways, so we will one day live peacefully together" or "Let us exchange promises to do a little something, and if that turns out all right, then let us see if we can agree to exchange promises to do a little something more." How sweet; how reasonable. Gradualism, if it thinks of a world security system at all, invariably puts it at the end of a process, not at the beginning.

The central paradox which all gradualist approaches fail to face up to is the circumstance that national governments, which do in fact possess the coercive force in today's global system, will not surrender their ability to pursue an independent quest for security in favor of any "emerging world order" which cannot guarantee security in return. Instead, driven by a frantic search for security in a highly insecure world, they will violate any norms of international conduct and rupture any incipient strands of world community if the exigencies of the moment seem to require it.

The only condition necessary is that the perception of threat be great enough, and this condition is not lacking, given the advanced weapons technology and the psychology of anarchy. Gradualism is thus doomed by what Lasswell calls the self-confirming expectation of violence. This is the dilemma of gradualism; it cannot deliver the international system from fear.

It is this dilemma that world government offers to resolve.

The difference between world disorder and order is the same as between insecurity and security. This difference is in the nature of a gap or a chasm rather than a road or a pathway. If the chasm is indeed to be bridged at all, then as freedom of national action is left behind on this side, so must security be ready and waiting on the other side. The chasm is not to be bridged by a series of gradual steps placed along a pathway of time. Instead, the surrender of national responsibility for security and the acceptance of that responsibility by world instruments of security must transpire together in a vertical moment of time. One must leap. So nearly as is possible, the transfer of the security responsibility must correspond to the reassurance implicit in the old cry, "The King is dead, long live the King."

The opposite of anarchy is not disarmament, even "general and complete disarmament." It is not even law, because the only source of meaningful law is government. The opposite of anarchy, since anarchy means the absence of government, is of course the presence of government. If anarchy is the main cause of international conflict, it follows that international government is the indispensable remedy. Since the international system—the arena of conflict—is worldwide, a world government is required.

Government deals squarely with anarchy, by simply taking its place. It does not try to creep up on it, or to by-pass it, or to ignore it.

And, as we saw in Chapter 3, a new framework of government, however long it may have been in the preparation, is something that can be—and usually is—installed upon a given day at a certain hour.

Given government, the self-confirming fear of violence can no longer find confirmation because weaponry need not be feared, tension points cannot erupt, old hostilities can die out, and order becomes possible in trade and currency. Ideological conflict between nations cannot continue to feed on fear and thus is abated if not removed, while the radicalizing stresses which install aggressive elites and messianic belief systems are reduced sharply.

But we have two basic types of government to choose from.

In Chapter 4 we studied many writers who, because they know more about anarchy than they know about federalism, think in terms of a unitary world government if the world is ever to get any government at all. Hence they require a high degree of cultural community before there can be what they call a "world state."

A unitary state or a unitary government is one which possesses all authority except any that may be reserved to the people. This supreme authority is not shared with regional governments such as the West German *Laender* or the American states. The national government may give some authority to provinces or prefectures and to local governments. But it can constitutionally withdraw their authority or change their boundaries at any time. Most nation-states in the world system are unitary states.

Thus a unitary world government would preside over a globe whose national governments had been abolished, although nations or other geographical subdivisions might still be used as administrative units.

Any world government—unitary or federal, good or bad, just or unjust, democratic or autocratic, communist or capitalist—is theoretically feasible; that is, it answers to our explanation of war. But feasibility has that other meaning: is it practically feasible? What are the actual chances of its coming into existence in time to prevent a nuclear world war?

There is only one way that a unitary world government can be established and that is by conquest. Thus unitary world government as a prescription against violence is a prescription of violence. If the world gets that kind of government, it will be a post-World War III development.

As we have seen, the thrust of international conflict toward the integration and extinction of international systems is plain enough, usually through conquest. And Raoul Naroll finds from his study of past imperial cycles that the odds that there will be a world empire by conquest by the year 2125 are 2 to 3; by 2250, 5 to 3; and by 2375, 4 to 1. But he adds that a conquest state could well be forestalled by a world federation.[63]

A unitary world empire, barring a fanciful conquest by blackmail, could come only at terrible cost in terms of reversing the human venture. Indeed, the post-nuclear situation might not be a world empire but hundreds of tiny "nations" in dozens of little international systems playing the same silly diplomatic games—but on a ruined planet.

The only tolerable way of moving from conflict to integration is by agreement, and that implies a federal world government. It offers possibilities of reconciling many of the threads woven into our inquiry. It ought to have greater practical feasibility than unitary world government while sharing its theoretical adequacy.

Chapter 7 Notes

1. Anatol Rapaport, "The Search for Simplicity," *Main Currents in Modern Thought* 28:3 (1972), pp. 79-84, 81.

2. J. N. Bhagwati, ed., *Economics and World Order* (New York, Macmillan, 1972), pp. 2, 17.

3. Both quotations are from Greg Franzwa, "Bullish on America," *The Texas Observer*, February 22, 1985, p. 31.

4. Kenneth W. Thompson's review of General John Hackett's *The Third World War*, in *Political Science Quarterly* 94:4 (1979), 676-677. He says elsewhere that no task in political science is more baffling than that of political prediction (his *Understanding World Politics*, University of Notre Dame Press, 1975, p. 18).

5. See for example Hubert M. Blalock Jr., *Social Statistics* (New York, McGraw-Hill, 2d. Ed., 1972), p. 20. One actual effort at measuring hostility divides the number of hostile events between two nations in a year by the number of all events between them to predict the probability of war or peace between them. This "content analysis" study was by Gernot Koehler, "Events Data and the Prediction of War," *Peace Research Reviews* 5:4 (1974), 53-83. Another study takes military expenditures as a percentage of a nation's gross national product to predict the probability of its being at war within five years (Alan G. Newcombe, *et al*, "An Improved Inter-Nation Tensiometer for the Prediction of War," *Peace Research Reviews* 5:4 (1974), 1-52.

6. See Andrei Sakharov, "The Dangers of Thermonuclear War," *Foreign Affairs* 61:5 (1983), 1001-1016, and Robert Jervis, "Why Nuclear Superiority Doesn't Matter," *Political Science Quarterly* 94:4 (1979), 617-633. But Brian Martin, in "Critique of Nuclear Extinction," *Journal of Peace Research* 19:4 (1982), pp. 287-300, says a nuclear war might be a limited one and long drawn out.

7. See "The Nuclear Time Bomb," *Saturday Review*, December 9, 1967, pp. 16 ff., and U.S. National Security Council Presidential Memo #10, June 1977.

8. Interview with Matthew S. Meselson, *Omni* 7:3 (1984), pp. 104 ff.

9. See Carl Sagan, "Nuclear War and Climatic Catastrophe," *Foreign Affairs* 62:2 (1983-84), 257-292, and Lewis Thomas, "Scientific Frontiers and National Frontiers," *Foreign Affairs* 62:4 (1984), 966-994. Both articles draw upon a report by the Conference on the Long-Term Biological Consequences of Nuclear War. On March 14, 1985, the Pentagon said it accepts the Nuclear Winter theory but Sagan said the Pentagon was assuming a big nuclear war whereas he believes a small nuclear exchange would do.

10. See Jonathan Schell's *The Fate of the Earth* (New York, Knopf, 1982) and his *The Abolition* (New York, Knopf, 1984).

11. Kenneth E. Boulding, "Arms Limitation and Integrative Activity," *Peace Research Society (International) Papers*, vol. 6 (1966), p. 4. Kahn is Herman Kahn, famous for "thinking the unthinkable" in a Think Tank called The Hudson Institute.

12. Albert Wohlstetter, "Technology, Prediction, and Disorder," in R. A. Falk and S. A. Mendlovitz, eds., *Toward a Theory of War Prediction* (New York, World Law Fund, 1966), p. 103.

13. A. M. Weinberg and J. N. Barkenbus, "Stabilizing Star Wars," *Foreign Folicy*, No. 54 (1984), 164-170.

14. Donald M. Snow, "Lasers, Charged Particle Beams, and the Strategic Future," *Political Science Quarterly* 95:2 (1980), 277-294.

15. Ben Bova, "Feedback," *Common Cause*, September-October 1984, p. 6.

16. Bhupendra Jasani and Christopher Lee, *Countdown to Space War*, a book published by Stockholm International Peace Research Institute, according to an Associated Press dispatch published October 26, 1984.

17. Stuart A. Cohen, "SALT Verification," *Orbis* 24:3 (1980), 657-683.

18. Article in *Foreign Affairs* 63:2 (1984-85), pp. 264-278, by Robert McNamara, George Kennan, Gerald Smith, and our old friend from Chapter 6, McGeorge Bundy.

19. In a letter to *The Wall Street Journal* on January 2, 1985, republished in *The New York Review* for February 14, 1985.

20. Herman Kahn, *On Escalation: Metaphors and Scenarios* (New York, Praeger, 1964), Chapter 6.

21. Neville Brown, *Nuclear War: The Impending Strategic Deadlock* (New York, Praeger, 1965). Brown had been a research associate at the Institute for Strategic Studies in London. On nuclear proliferation see the entire vol. 430 of *Annals of American Academy of Political and Social Science*, March 1977.

22. Eugene Burdick and Harvey Wheeler, *Fail-Safe* (New York, McGraw-Hill, 1962). Burdick was a noted political scientist.

23. Sidney Hook, *The Fail-Safe Fallacy* (New York, Stein & Day, 1963), pp. 11-12, 31.

24. United Press International dispatch of January 16, 1974.

25. Helen Caldicott, *Missile Envy* (New York, Wm. Morrow, 1980).

26. Henry A. Kissinger, "NATO-The Next Thirty Years," *Atlantic Quarterly* 17:4 (1979-80), 464-475, 469.

27. On terrorism, see M. I. Midlarsky, *et al*, "Why Violence Spreads: The Contagion of International Terrorism," *International Studies Quarterly* 24:2 (1980), 262-298, an empirical study, and all of volume 463 of *Annals of the American Academy of Political and Social Science* (1980).

28. Raoul Naroll's, "Deterrence in History," in D. G. Pruitt and R. C. Snyder, eds., *Theory and Research on the Causes of War* (Englewood Cliffs, Prentice-Hall, 1969), p. 163.

29. Michael D. Wallace, "Armaments and Escalation," *International Studies Quarterly* 26:1 (1982), 37-56. See also Wallace and J. M. Wilson, "Non-Linear Arms Race Models," *Journal of Peace Research* 15:2 (1978), 175-192.

30. Michael D. Wallace, "Arms Races and Escalation," *Journal of Conflict Resolution* 24:2 (1979). In JCR 24:2 (1980), Erich Weede disagrees and Wallace responds (pages 285-292). Both are empirical scholars.

31. Erich Weede, "Extended Deterrence by Superpower Alliance," *Journal of Conflict Resolution* 27:2 (1983), 231-253.

32. See *My War with the C.I.A.*, by Prince Norodom Sihanouk as told to Wilfred Burchett (Penguin Books, 1974). Burchett, an Australian, is considered a leftist writer. Sihanouk spoke cautiously, however, in an interview published in 1985 (see "The Lesser Evil," in *The New York Review*, March 14, 1985, pp. 21 ff.)

33. W. P. Hogan and I. F. Pearce, *The Incredible Eurodollar* (London, Unwin Paperbacks, 1984), p. 145. Hogan is Australian; Pearce, English. For Triffin, see his "The International Monetary System of the Year 2000," in Bhagwati, *Economics and World Order* (New York, Macmillan, 1972), pp. 183-197.

34. Hogan and Pearce, *op. cit.*, pp. 180-192. The Atlantic Council's Working Group on International Monetary Affairs reported in 1983 that the problem was serious, yet the Group had no new proposal worth mentioning (*Atlantic Quarterly* 21:1, 1983, pp. 33-43.)

35. See Gunther Handl, "Territorial Sovereignty and the Problem of Trans-National Pollution," *American Journal of International Law* 69:1 (1975), 50-76.

36. See Iain Guest, "US and Common Market Take Opposite Sides in Ozone Dispute," *Christian Science Monitor*, January 31, 1985, p. 14.

37. A review of empirical and other studies concludes that external conflict increases internal cohesion if the group is an ongoing one with effective leadership and if the group is able to deal with the external conflict (Arthur A. Stein's "Conflict and Cohesion," *Journal of Conflict Resolution* 20:1, 1976, 143-172). A statistical study of five US wars (Spanish-American to Vietnam) concludes that those wars affected the level of domestic violence in US but in contradictory ways (Michael Stohl's "War and Domestic Political Violence," *Journal of Conflict Resolution* 19:3, 1975, pp. 379-415.)

38. A weak nation is apt to become a client state of some patron nation because it is first a vacuum (Michael Handel, *Weak States in the International System*, London, Frank Cass & Co., 1981).

39. Arend Lijphart, "Religious v. Linguistic v. Class Voting," in *American Political Science Review* 73:2 (1979), 442-458. But he adds that past conflict dimensions may be frozen in the party structure.

40. Lee Sigelson and Miles Simpson, "A Cross-National Test of the Linkage Between Economic Inequality and Political Violence," *Journal of Conflict Resolution* 21:1 (1977), 105-128.

41. "One-Child Family Looms as Possible Trend for Future," *Popline* 7:2 (Washington, The Population Institute, February 1985), pp. 1-2).

42. Lester R. Brown, *Population Policies for a New Economic Era* (Washington, Worldwatch Institute, 1983).

43. Ansley J. Coale, in "Population Growth and Economic Development: the Case of Mexico" (*Foreign Affairs* 56:2, 1978, 415-429), says Mexico in 1978 had a much larger industrial and agricultural output than in 1958, per capita as well as total, and literacy was more common, but the population doubled, unemployment became more acute, and the labor force grew so rapidly that in 1974 a constitutional provision was inserted giving every person the right to birth control information.

44. Bhagwati, *op. cit.*, p. 11. Switzerland, a prosperous state, gives 3/100ths of one percent. Bhagwati says that "Until we have worldwide government" aid will continue to be predominantly bilateral. Only 12 percent is presently multilateral.

45. See *The Widening Gap: Development in the 1970s* (Columbia University Press, 1971) by Barbara Ward, who originated the one percent idea; also *From Aid to Recolonization* (Pantheon Books, 1973) by Tibor Mende who stresses the "brain drain."

46. For a slightly optimistic view, see "The Impact of Good Aid on World Malnutrition," *International Organization* 35:2 (1981), 329-354. But the conclusions from this statistical study are suspect; the 1963-73 period was used, which ended just before the first great jump in oil prices. But any 10-year period is too short.

47. For contrary opinion, see N. G. Onuf's "Reports to the Club of Rome," *World Politics* 36:1 (1983), 121-146, and W. Beckerman's *In Defence of Economic Growth* (London, Cape, 1974). Still, the Global 2000 Report asserted that its conclusions were actually biased toward optimism (New York, Pergamon Press, 1980). The full original Club of Rome report is *The Limits of Growth* (New York, Universe Books, 1972) by Dennis L. Meadows, *et al.*

48. Donella H. Meadows, "Charting the Way the World Works," *Technology Review* 88:2 (1985), pp. 52 ff.

49. Mihajlo Mesarovic and Eduard Pestel, *Mankind at the Turning Point* (New York, Dutton-Readers Digest Press, 1974).

50. See Eric A. Nordlinger's "Soldiers in Mufti," *American Political Science Review* 64:4 (1970) 31-48, for a criticism of the military as modernizers and reformers.

51. LDCs are unstable because of the disruptive effect of change and the inability of the political system to satisfy wants, according to I. K. and R. L. Feirabend, in "Aggressive Behavior Within Polities," *Journal of Conflict Resolution*, vol. 10 (1966), 249-271. See also Daniel Katz, *et al*, "The National Role," *Peace Research Society (International) Papers* vol. 1 (1964), 113-127.

52. See Bhagwati, *op. cit.*, pp. 18-22; also the contributions to this volume by Thomas E. Weisskopf, pp. 43-77, and Stephen Hymer, pp. 113-140.

53. See Simon Veil, "The European Parliament," *Atlantic Quarterly* 18:1 (1980), pp. 98-101, and Ronald Iglehart, *et al*, "Broader Powers for the European Parliament?" *Atlantic Quarterly* 18:1 (1980), 102-117, for cautious hopes that the Common Market might become, in effect, a federal government.

54. Roy Jenkins, in "The United States and a Uniting Europe," *Atlantic Quarterly* 15:2 (1977-78), 209-220.

55. See Elbert W. Russell's "Christianity and Militarism," in *Peace Research Reviews* 4:3 (1971), 1-77.

56. Report by Associated Press Special Assignment Team, March 8, 1970.

57. Marquis Childs' column, Winston-Salem (N.C.) *Twin City-Sentinel*, February 1, 1972.

58. See Seymour M. Lipset and Earl Rabb, *The Politics of Unreason: Right-wing Extremism in America, 1790-1970* (New York, Harper & Row, 1970) and William W. Turner's *Power on the Right* (Berkeley, Ramparts Press, 1971), especially Chapters 10 and 11; also Studs Terkel's *Hard Times* (New York, Pantheon Books, 1970) for a look at US during the Great Depression.

59. Bruce M. Russett, "The Ecology of Future International Politics," *International Studies Quarterly*, vol. 11 (1967). pp. 12-31, 13. He adds that "Even rigor and information, the twin pillars of modern social wisdom, suffice only for limited tasks" (p. 17).

60. Eisenhower said that "the history of alliances is the history of failure" (quoted in *Nato's Future*, July 1985). The unreliability of allies is underlined by Edwin H. Fedder in "The Concept of Alliances," *International Studies Quarterly*, vol. 12 (1968), pp. 65-86. In a statistical study of "National Alliance Commitments and War Involvement, 1815-1945" J. David Singer and Melvin Small conclude that alliance predicts to war involvement, especially in the 20th century (*Peace Research Society International Papers*, vol. 2, 1966, pp. 109-140). A game theory exercise suggests that in opposing coalitions such as the US and USSR blocs, a war condition is more apt to result if the great nation in one coalition increases its power relative to the great nation in the other coalition (D. A. Zinnes, *et al*, "A Formal Analysis of Some Issues in Balance of Power Theories," *International Studies Quarterly* 22:3, 1978, 323-356). There is a large literature on alliances.

61. This is the thesis of Miles Kahler in "Rumors of War: the 1914 Analogy," *Foreign Affairs* 58:2 (1979-80), 374-396, and of Richard J. Barnet in "U.S.-Soviet Relations," *Foreign Affairs* 57:4 (1979), 779-796.

62. See *Public Opinion Quarterly* 45:1 (1981), 126-134.

63. Raoul Naroll, "Imperial Cycles and World Order," *Peace Research Society (International) Papers*, vol. 7 (1967), 83-101. Naroll says another alternative to a conquest state is a "world order" imposed by US and USSR. Cauley Sander, in "Economic Theory of Alliances," *Journal of Conflict Resolution* 19:2 (1975), 330-348, concludes that the optimal size for an alliance in this age of overkill is a worldwide alliance. But even an alliance of all against none would not serve unless there were overall government to abate mutual fears.

Chapter 8

IF WE DON'T WANT THAT
TO HAPPEN, WHAT CAN BE DONE?

A. INTRODUCTION

The closing section of Chapter 7 was headed, "Two Proven But Untried Cures." Government, whether unitary or federal, is "proven" because it is the way—and the only way—that people have found to live together without large-scale violence.

Government is a structure which may perform more than one function. But, as we noted at the close of the *Summary of International History*, it has had historically one basic function that is peculiarly its own. That is the maintenance of public order—keeping the peace in the sense of preventing violence. Those other functions that government must also perform if it is to perform this basic function vary with time and circumstance.

Government has been "tried" countless times as the cure for international conflict. It has been installed after conquest, and thereafter has succeeded in maintaining order among previously warring independent units. As we have seen, this is the way most international systems in history have been integrated. Governments installed after conquest are unitary. Ethnic diversities are repressed and over the long run tend to disappear, though some empires have used indirect rule through local princes.

But if a new central government is set up by agreement among the formerly autonomous units, it may be unitary, as for example in the case of Italy when unified in 1871, or it may be federal, as in the case of Germany in the same year. If the people and governments involved wish to retain as much political autonomy as is commensurate with the well-being of the whole, they will choose a federal arrangement.

Federal government has been "proven" by its overall success in Switzerland, US, Canada, Australia, West Germany, Malaysia, and India. And even where the overall success of the political system is more dubious, as in USSR, Yugoslavia, Burma, Nigeria, and several Latin American nations, the federal arrangement has mitigated internal ethnic conflict while acting as a check upon the central government.

268

But federal government is "untried" in the sense that it has never been applied to any well-developed system of warring nations—only to subsystems of quarreling nations or states. A federal arrangement of some sort or other was repeatedly suggested as the cure of war within the old European system, and similar arrangements for wars within the global system have been proclaimed, but to deaf ears, for only treaty-leagues have resulted.

However, the UN Charter is just as pre-nuclear as the League Covenant. And in our dread times there is an increasing openness, as we noted in Chapter 4, to the possibility of international institutions of greater strength and scope, reaching so far as world government. For example, Bruce Russett, a quantifier of trends in international relations, says that the need for new political forms is more pressing than ever; that no one has come up with a scheme for the year 2000 that really looks workable; and mentions world government rather wistfully.[1] Walter Isard, a prominent peace researcher, says we must consider the possibility of new levels of regional or world government.[2] Kenneth Boulding calls upon his fellow experts in conflict resolution to come up with a policy for peace and to make clear what world institutions are needed to make peace more probable.[3]

As the peoples and governments on this planet wish to keep their cultural peculiarities and political institutions that are so dear to them, but they also wish to live out their days and see the human venture go on, a federal arrangement is indicated. That is the only way they can have their cake and eat it too.

As we approach the task of prescribing a form of government, our grounds are simply stated: a world government must be based at its outset on community in the MacIver sense described in Chapter 4, that is, a common interest in the biological survival of the human race. It must be endowed with whatever grant of authority and coercive force may be necessary to enable it to guarantee that survival. All other authority not clearly related to that guarantee must be left in national and individual hands.

Community in the sense of cultural particularism must be left untouched and allowed to homogenize or not within a world environment of security. National politico-economic ideologies, and the elites that embrace them, must be left alone and permitted to lose their virulence within this governed world environment.

B: The Clark-Sohn Proposals

We are unable to say much about the informal institutions which might come into being and, together with the formal governmental institutions, make up a working world polity. We already have two sizeable world interest groups: the military, whose national components reinforce each other in their drive for big budgets and high status; and the peace movement, which is fragmented but nevertheless trans-national. But presumably both these groups would not survive the establishment of a world government. In a way, the Western and Soviet blocs, maneuvering for support from the neutral nations, are sort of embryonic political parties, as are the DCs versus the LDCs, and oil exporters versus importers. These distinctions probably would continue on into the post-anarchic period, along with cleavages along ideological lines.

However, the history of federal government in the Americas, India and elsewhere suggests one almost certain line of cleavage. This will be between those individuals, interest groups and national governments which generally support a broader role for the world government and those which support national authority. There is little doubt too, that, from the outset, particular issues will evoke particular interest groupings. Some of these groupings will almost surely be trans-national. But it is likely that clear-cut trans-national political parties will be a long while in emerging.

Turning from vague speculation to something more specific, the best known proposal for the authority and institutions of a world federal government is that in *World Peace Through World Law*,[4] first published in 1958. The authors were the late Grenville Clark, a practicing international lawyer, an American, and Louis B. Sohn, Polish-born professor of international law at Harvard and an authority on the UN.

Fortunately, the authors published revised editions in 1960 and 1966; by that time some of the recent world concerns other than nuclear war were coming to the fore. Whereas the earlier editions had offered a detailed revision of the UN Charter as the most likely route to world government, the 1966 edition included as an alternative "A Proposed Treaty Establishing a World Disarmament and World Development Organization"—presumably prompted by Kennedy's 1962 outline of a treaty on general and complete disarmament which we discussed at the end of Chapter 6. Sohn updated the work again in 1973 by revising the Introduction to *World Peace Through World Law*.[5] With his revisions, the main features of the plan are as follows, expressed for convenience's sake in terms of a revised UN.

(1) *Membership.* The new UN would come into being after the revised Charter has been ratified by five-sixths of the nations of the world, these nations to represent at least five-sixths of world population and to include the four most populous nations. All nations, whether members or not, would be required to disarm and abide by world law. The practical result would thus be little different from universal compulsory membership.

(2) *The General Assembly.* All the basic provisions of the disarmament process and the other main features such as the world police force, the

revenue system and the judicial systems are spelled out in the Clark-Sohn revised Charter. This is called "constitutional legislation" and its advantage is that all would know in advance of ratification just what the new world government in broad terms could do and could not do. The Assembly becomes the legislative branch, with power to name the executive, and is given final authority on the enforcement of disarmament and the maintenance of peace.

The formula for representation in the Assembly divides the 170-plus independent nations into seven categories according to population. The four largest (US, USSR, China, India) would have 30 seats each; the ten next largest (Indonesia, Japan, Brazil, Bangladesh, West Germany, Britain, Nigeria, Italy, France, Mexico) 12 seats each; and on down to the smallest with one seat each. A body of about 750 representatives would result.

In relation to population, the smallest nations would still have a disproportionately large voice, but far less so than under the present one-nation-one-vote rule. That rule has assured that the large nations will not give any real authority to the Assembly. For example, one reason US quit UNESCO was that the same rule gives a majority to nations which together pay only a tiny percentage of its budget.   Clark and Sohn studied many plans for representation by wealth, literacy, or other factors, as well as proposals for a two-house legislature. But they believe their arrangement is simpler and probably as fair as any other.

Representatives would be chosen for 4-year terms by their national legislatures at the outset, but by stages half and then all would be elected by popular vote, within no more than 40 years after the new Charter goes into effect. This is a compromise between present practice whereby all representatives are mere ambassadors of national governments and the principle that legislators ought to be responsive to people and their interests.

In addition to its legislative authority, the Assembly could make non-binding recommendations on other matters such as trade and immigration.

The Assembly would have full-time standing committees to (1) supervise disarmament and the UN Peace Force, and to (2) handle budget and finance.

Comment: Any serious effort to set up a world government would evoke bitter bargaining over representation in whatever body possesses real decisional authority. For example, when the Common Market nations decided to give the European Parliament some real budget authority in 1979 and to name its representatives by direct popular election instead of appointment, it was this kind of bargaining that led to agreement to give 81 seats to each of the four largest nations, scaling on down to six for Luxembourg.[6] The end result inevitably would be that each nation would accept representation that corresponds roughly to its true capacity to act independently in an anarchic system. By this gauge the Clark-Sohn formula looks good.

(3) *The Executive Council.* Elected by the Assembly for a 4-year term and removable by it, this body would replace the present Security Council and become the executive branch of the revised UN. Its 17 members would be selected from members of the Assembly. The four largest nations would be represented on the Council all the time; the next ten largest, half the time, in rotation. The other eight persons would be chosen from the rest of the world, with regard for regional diversity. Ordinary votes would carry by a vote of any 12, but on "important matters," specifically defined, the majority would have to include persons representing nine of the largest nations. But no one nation would have a veto. These provisions are a compromise between Big Power fears and Small Nation fears.

(4) *The Economic and Social Council, the Trusteeship Council.* These would be continued, but their members would be elected by the Assembly and responsible to it.

(5) *The Disarmament Process.* Beginning one year after ratification of the new Charter, a tenth of each nation's arms-production facilities would be destroyed, and a tenth of its armed forces disbanded, every six months, under supervision of a UN Inspection Service; except that some non-nuclear weapons and all nuclear materials from which weapons could be made would be turned over to the UN Nuclear Energy Authority. At the end of five years (six, from ratification) nations would have no armed forces except lightly armed internal police forces, unless the process were postponed by the Assembly for one or more periods of no more than six months while non-complying nations were being brought into line. The only military force in the world then would be the UN Peace Force.

The Inspection Service would be under an Inspection Commission of five persons from smaller nations nominated by the Executive Council and confirmed by the Assembly.

The Nuclear Authority would be under a Nuclear Energy Commission similarly chosen and charged with acquiring and controlling all nuclear energy for peaceful purposes. Similarly, a UN Outer Space Commission would control and operate in its field.

Comment: Whereas Kennedy's GCD proposal had a three-stage process which required a new international agreement at each stage, Clark and Sohn provide that, once the new UN is ratified, the disarmament process is entirely in its keeping and subject to no veto. Moreover, the Peace Force is in being from the outset, as is the Nuclear Authority, and both are receiving weapons from the first six months onward. The crucial period of disarming nations while arming the UN is cut to six years, essentially.

(6) *The UN Peace Force.* When completed at the end of the disarmament process this Force would consist, as determined by the Assembly, of a full-time professional force of 200,000 to 400,000, supplemented by a reserve of 300,000 to 600,000 persons. They would be

volunteers recruited individually, no more than three percent from any nation, with pay and allowances free from all taxes, and stationed at UN land, sea and air bases dispersed about the globe, but none in any of the 14 largest nations. It would be equipped with the most modern weapons except nuclear and CB weapons. It would be commanded by a UN Military Staff Committee recruited from the smaller nations and operating under the Executive Council, subject to review by the Assembly. The Force could be equipped with nuclear weapons by the Nuclear Energy Authority only if the Assembly declared that such weapons have actually been used or their use is imminently threatened.

Comment: Given the method of recruiting and paying the members of the Force, their loyalties would probably soon run to the UN and the human race instead of to the nation.

(7) *Judicial Organs.* In addition to a World Conciliation Board, to which nations might voluntarily submit their disputes, Clark and Sohn suggest two tribunals. For those disputes which can be decided on legal principles, an International Court of Justice (World Court) would have mandatory jurisdiction. It would interpret the revised UN Charter and legislation enacted pursuant to it; and other international agreements, including those which might conflict with the Charter. For those disputes which cannot be decided on principles of law, there would be a World Equity Tribunal whose decisions would be binding only with the consent of the parties unless the Assembly voted by a three-fourths majority (including two-thirds of all members from the 14 largest nations) that the Tribunal's ruling was essential to the peace. In that event, its ruling would become enforceable by the same means as a judgment of the Court.

Persons would be nominated to Court and Tribunal, and to regional UN courts, by the Executive Council and confirmed by the Assembly. They would serve for life unless declared unfit by their colleagues.

(8) *Enforcement.* Under a UN Attorney-General, named by the Council and confirmed by the Assembly, there would be a UN civil police force of not more than 10,000 persons. It would work with the Inspection Service and with national authorities in apprehending individuals accused of offenses against the Charter and the laws and regulations enacted thereunder.

If a nation were found to be directly or indirectly responsible for a serious violation, the Assembly could order economic sanctions against it. In extreme cases the Assembly (or the Council in an emergency and subject to immediate Assembly review) could order the UN Peace Force into action.

(9) *World Development Authority.* This authority would work under a World Development Commission nominated by the Economic and Social Council and confirmed by the Assembly. That Council would draw half its members from the DCs and half from the LDCs. The

Authority's function would be to remove the danger to world stability caused by the economic disparity between DCs and LDCs. Sohn suggested that the Assembly budget the Authority at about $75 billion annually (in 1973 dollars).

Comment: The rationale is that world disarmament would permit reallocation of funds to this end. $75 billion in 1973 equals about $200 billion in 1985, when the world's military expense is nearly $700 billion.

(10) *UN Ocean Authority.* Under an Ocean Council with full jurisdiction over the central part of the oceans, but sharing jurisdiction with national governments in the area between 12 and 200 miles from the coast, this Authority would regulate navigation and conserve but develop the resources of this "common heritage of mankind."

(11) *UN Environment Protection Authority.* Under an Environment Commission, this Authority would perform only a data-collecting and coordinating function for national environmental efforts, as envisaged by Sohn.

(12) *The Revenue System.*Sohn estimated the annual UN budget at around $90 billion in 1973 dollars (which, after correcting for inflation, is less than half of annual military expenditures now). Presently the UN depends precariously on annual contributions by member nations. The Clark-Sohn answer to the problem of a reliable and adequate source of revenue is a "collaborative" system whereby each nation would assign in advance to the UN all or part of certain taxes, collect them and pay them into a UN fiscal office in each nation, thus avoiding a UN Bureaucracy for this purpose. The revised Charter would limit the UN revenues to no more than three percent of the Gross World Product (total value of all goods produced and services rendered) in that year, and no nation would be assessed more than four percent of its Gross National Product.

(13) *Limitation and Guarantees.* The UN would be prohibited from usurping authority not granted in the revised Charter, and individuals would be guaranteed against violations by the UN (not by their national governments) of the rights and freedoms usually listed in liberal constitutions.

(14) *Amendments.* Amendments to the revised Charter could be proposed by two-thirds of the Assembly membership (or of a special General Conference called to amend) and ratified by four-fifths of the member nations including ten of the fourteen largest. There could be no one-nation veto of amendments as there is in the present Charter.

The Clark-Sohn proposal is superior to Kennedy's GCD proposal on several critical points. As already noted, Clark and Sohn transfer decision-making authority to the revised UN from the outset; there is no allowance for nations to reconsider at future stages in the disarmament process. There is no veto. There is a true legislative body with distinct executive and judicial branches such as are found somewhere in virtually all present-day national governments.

Clark and Sohn have designed a fairly typical federal republic, with a multiple executive like Switzerland's, but the executive is responsible to the parliament (the Assembly) as in Britain and many other nations. Yet their scheme is innovative, the balance provided for between great and small nations, between developed and developing counties, and among regions, is impressive. A world government endowed with the paramount military power in the world must be strapped round about with every safeguard that the mind of man can devise, and the Clark-Sohn plan is impressive on this score too.

We do find one possible fault: the "collaborative" system of collecting world revenues may depend too much on the willingness of nations—or even their ability in times of domestic turmoil—to collect and turn over the money to the federal government; this could be a source of future trouble.

With the revisions made by Sohn in 1973 the proposal is less susceptible to criticism as too "minimal" than were earlier versions. The truth is that all of us have been astonished by the number and weight of mounting world concerns and have had trouble keeping up with them. For example, the environmental movement is much stronger now than in 1973, and it has been joined by screaming concern over a population growth that can only be described as cancerous.

Other suggestions for change in the Clark-Sohn scheme will arise as we discuss shortly in Section D the authority that a world government for biological survival must possess. Here we take up the question of *simultaneity*, for which Clark and Sohn may have under-prescribed, and the question of *inspection*, for which some would say they have over-prescribed.

Their scheme, even as revised in 1973, may still fail to resolve the dilemma of gradualism whereby nations retain a practical veto of the disarmament process so long as they retain enough coercive force to make their non-compliance credible. Actually, *any* realistic process must come up to that critical point at which the coercive force under world control is about to become greater than the force still controlled by any one great nation and its sure allies. Only once past this "moment of truth" could disarmament move freely on down to the level required to maintain internal order and the world force be augmented freely to the point at which it could not be challenged.

It is difficult to say just when the critical point of no return would be reached, but it surely depends in part on how fast the UN Peace Force is built up. It might prove possible to approach the requirement of simultaneity as follows.

Let us project a situation in which the chiefs of several principal nations have, for whatever reasons, signed an agreement "in principle" to draft a revised Charter or an entirely new constitutional document. This in itself would put the UN Secretary-General and Security Council on notice that some advance planning was then in order.

Next, the signers of that agreement would send out invitations to a Charter review conference or a new constitutional convention. It is conceivable that those who respond and meet could, within six months to a year, agree on the new document and sign it, although ratification would be yet to come. This document could authorize the Secretary-General of the old UN to recruit men for the UN Peace Force, set forth tables of organization and equipment, and acquire bases, on a contingency basis until the required number of nations have ratified.

The new constitution could provide that, immediately upon adequate ratification, the Secretary-General is to take jurisdiction over (legal possession of) all nuclear missiles, aircraft and warships having a range of more than X kilometers. These weapons and their bases would then be transferred to the control of the new Assembly so soon as it has met. The Assembly would then create the Executive Council and the other organs, transferring the nuclear and CB weapons to the Nuclear Energy Authority and the missiles and other delivery vehicles to the UN Peace Force.

The rest of the disarmament process—the transfer or destruction of conventional weapons, the destruction or de-fusing of the nuclear and CB weapons, the dismantling of most bases, the mustering out of national armed forces could take place thereafter, perhaps over the five-year period Sohn suggests.

Given a delay of six months to a year, after the "in principle" agreement is reached, before the new constitution has been signed by most nations, there would be a further delay while enough nations ratified. In some, such as US, where ratification could properly come only through constitutional amendment, the process could be long. Much would depend on popular expectations and on the national decision-makers then in office, but a further lag of six months to a year would be likely. However, from the moment of requisite ratification to the meeting of the new Assembly, only a week or so need elapse, because all Assembly delegates will initially be named by their national governments. And the Peace Force and Nuclear Authority can be brought into being by the Assembly almost immediately, for the Force will have been recruited already and its bases decided upon.

Thus we are looking at an interim period of one to two years after the "in principle" agreement has been reached. But anarchical fears ought to be substantially less than they were just prior to that agreement. Admittedly, however, there will be critical moments just before the required number of ratifications has been reached, and immediately thereafter, when the great weapons are to be turned over to the old UN to hold for the new.*

A special way of handling the interim period is conceivable. US and USSR might, at the time they and others enter into the "in principle" agreement, exchange inspectors and act in effect as world policemen, using orbital surveillance and the like, until such time as the world police function can be discharged in the only way it properly can be—as the enforcement arm of a representative and responsible world government. A variation on this would be George Kennan's suggestion in 1982 that the fusion triggers on thermonuclear weapons be turned over to "bi-national or multi-national authority."[7]

With regard to Clark and Sohn's requirement of on-site inspection done by a new UN Inspection Service, it is true that orbital surveillance and other high-technology modes of verification have increasingly made it possible for US and USSR to check on each other without the on-site inspection which USSR has usually—but not always—refused to permit. A 1985 article by a writer who apparently is in position to know is reassuring but not quite convincing, perhaps because the full story is classified and he couldn't divulge all.[8] Similarly, a pamphlet circulated in 1984 by the Union of Concerned Scientists, while pushing for arms control agreements, admits that undetected cheating is possible.[9] And a political scientist made the point in 1983 that weapons such as the cruise missile that are small, numerous, and easy to hide cannot be made the subject of arms control agreements—what cannot be seen cannot be verified, hence cannot be agreed to.[10] Moreover, the research that might underlie Star Wars or some other technological break-through is not verifiable at all, at least up to the point where some sort of test would become detectable.

We believe that if governments and populations ever get around to putting an end to anarchy by instituting government they will leave nothing of this sort to chance. There will be on-site inspection of the most intrusive kind.

Before considering the optimum of authority which might be transferred from national governments to a world government, it is necessary to consider the degree to which public opinion is ready to

---

*It is often argued in connection with disarmament that the rapid shutting down of national defense industries would put national economies into collapse. For the view that dislocation can be handled and that an unprecedented growth and development would ensue, see Juliet Saltman's "The Economic Consequences of Disarmament," *PEACE RESEARCH REVIEWS* 4:5 (1972), which was based on her examination of the many studies on this problem.

confer upon a world government the irreducible minimum of authority—the authority to prevent international violence.

If Jonathan Schell knew how much public support there is, he might have stayed on the course suggested in his *The Fate of the Earth* in 1982. Instead, he decided that people hold national sovereignty dearer than life or posterity and in his *The Abolition* in 1984 he proposes an infinitely complicated nuclear disarmament, without any world security system, that he hopes would rule out nuclear war by miscalculation because of the lead-time required for nuclear rearmament—possibly some six weeks.[11]

C. Public Support for a World Government Able to Prevent War

Statements such as the following no longer astonish sophisticated persons:

> It seems highly probable that the development of nuclear weapons and missiles with a range of half the earth's diameter will do for the national state what gunpowder did for the feudal baron. It makes it only conditionally viable from the military point of view, and this in the long run will destroy its sacred character. When it becomes clear that your country can do nothing for you in the way of defense, the question of why you should do anything for it becomes perfectly sensible.[12]

But what continues to arouse astonishment and disbelief among the sophisticated is the evidence that the general public realizes as fully as they that national governments can no longer protect their populations and that therefore the function of providing order must be transferred to world hands.

A poll made much of by Hans Morgenthau as proof of the public's unreadiness for "the world state"[13] is one taken in 1947.[14] To the question, "Would you like to see the United States join in a movement to establish an international police force to maintain world peace?" 75 percent said yes, but only 15 percent would consent to US armed forces being smaller than the international force. Morgenthau said this meant Americans are unwilling to pay the price for world government. But the public opinion experts say that polls are more reliable as to ends (the 85 percent response) than to means (the 15 percent response). Actually, both reponses reflect the same fear of insecurity.

In 1946 the American Institute of Public Opinion asked a US sampling "Do you think the UN Organization should be strengthened to make it a world government with power to control the armed forces of all nations including the United States?" To this question 54 percent answered yes, 24 percent no, and 22 percent had no opinion. To a substantially similar question, Canadians responded in the proportions of 59, 29, and 12 percent, while in the United Kingdom the proportions were 50, 27, and 23 percent.[15]

In 1949, asked how rapidly steps ought to be taken to form a world government with US as a member, Americans responded to a Fortune Magazine poll as follows: "Right away," 34 percent; "more slowly," 34 percent; "not at all," 17 percent; "no opinion," 15 percent.[16]

Two samplings for differently-worded propositions were taken in the summer of 1949 by the National Opinion Research Center: "Some people say that the UN Organization should be made into a government of the entire world with power to control the armed forces of all nations, including the United States." 36 percent said this was a good idea, 53 percent that it was not such a good idea, and 11 percent had no opinion. However, to the question, "Would you approve or disapprove of the idea of a world government, assuming it could be worked out?" another US sampling returned a 56 percent approval as against a 27 percent disapproval, and 17 percent "did not know."[17]

In November 1949, the same Center found 58 percent of a US sampling in favor of a UN police force, 32 percent opposed, and 10 percent no opinion. Of the favorable 58 percent, 22 percent would let the UN call out American troops to put down an "aggressor," 32 percent would permit this only with Congressional approval, and four percent did not know.[18]

But in 1950 a referendum on world government was on the Oklahoma ballot. This was the heydey of McCarthyism, which was peculiarly vitriolic in that state. With every daily paper and every weekly save one opposed to the referendum question, often on the grounds that world government was a communist plot to sell out America to the Soviet Union, the question was defeated by a margin of more than three to one.

In September 1953, the Roper Poll gauged US "Attitudes about World Organization," learning that nine percent held isolationist views; 21 percent would leave the UN much as it was but gradually try to improve it; 35 percent opted for a stronger UN with enough power "to actually keep even a strong nation from starting a war;" 11 percent wanted a world government "in which every nation would in effect become a state, somewhat like the different states in this country;" six percent preferred a federal union of friendly democratic countries; and seven percent thought no reliance should be placed on the possibility of any stronger organization.[19]

These results, showing a stronger UN to be more popular than a world government, should be read in the light of the fact that a multiple-choice response does not shape and confine the responses as does a simple yes-or-no arrangement.[20] Moreover, Roper spelled out the stronger UN in terms which amount to a limited world government.

In a sampling of Minnesota residents after Pope John issued his *Pacem in Terris* encyclical in April 1963, this proposition was put:

Pope John has suggested a single world authority be set up to keep the peace. It would represent all nations and have more power than the present United Nations. Do you think such a world authority can be set up in the next several years, or not?

23 percent thought so, 69 percent thought not, with more Catholics than Protestants saying yes. Then the second question was asked:

Suppose that to set up an effective world authority to keep the peace, each nation must give up some of its right to decide how large its armed forces should be, or about developing nuclear weapons. If all other nations were willing to do so, would you be in favor of, or against, having the United States also give up that right?

To this, 70 percent replied affirmatively and only 21 percent negatively.[21]

This poll was graced by the aura of a pope who was liked by most Protestants. It was taken after the Cuba and Berlin crises of 1962 and 1961 but before the partial-test-ban treaty of 1963. There may have been an especially acute awareness that something needed to be done. At any rate, the second question seems to have been fairly phrased, emphasizing the "world authority" as a whole rather than its police force alone, with the military implications reasonably put forward. The negative response to the first question indicates that members of the public as well as scholars and other experts consider themselves readier than others to perceive the need for change. It is a case of "I see the need but I am sure the general run of people are not ready for it yet."

Somewhat similar irony is found in the results of a survey in 1960-62 of 100 students and 100 legislators in each of the following: Brazil, Finland, Germany, France, India, Japan, Spain, Puerto Rico, St. Croix (Virgin Islands), rural Arkansas, and rural Canada. It showed that 48 percent of the total (with little variance as between students and legislators) desired worldwide disarmament with UN police enforcement but that 55 percent expected the arms race to continue indefinitely.[22]

A Louis Harris poll in 1969 showed 90 percent of Americans supporting "an agreement reached between the U.S. and Russia to let the United Nations really do peacekeeping," with only five percent opposed, while 88 percent favored "an agreement with Russia to conrol nuclear weapons," with eight percent opposed.[23] In 1970 Gallup found Americans favoring a UN peacekeeping army by better than two to one.[24]

Turning now for the moment to non-scientific samplings, in 1965 a questionnaire was sent to some 600 residents of Missouri. Half were Missouri Methodists who had been included in a two-year "peace education" project sponsored by the Church; the other half were ordinary residents; both samples were chosen by random selection. 25 percent of Methodists favored a gradually strengthened UN; 17 percent of the non-Methodists. 24 percent of Methodists approved giving the UN authority "to prevent war by peaceful means or by force if necessary;" only 17 percent of the other group. 44 percent of the Methodists said US should work to change the UN into an "international governmental organization" with authority to keep the peace through a system of enforceable world law against aggression, binding on all nations and all people, and 30 percent of the other group.

The same questionnaire, sent in 1962 by Senator Joseph Clark to several thousand of his Pennsylvania constituents, had evoked responses more favorable to a stronger UN and to "international government" than those of the non-Methodist group in Missouri (where the John Birch Society, the Minutemen and similar organizations had been very active) but less so than those of the Methodists in Missouri. What is significant is that 68 percent of the Methodists selected the two strong options and that 47 percent of the Missouri rank-and-file selected them, with the Pennsylvanians in between.[25]

In 1960 Congressman William B. Widnell (Republican-New Jersey) learned from a questionnaire returned by 12,000 of his constituents that 77 percent favored the creation of rules of law backed by a world court and enforced by an international armed force, and that 76 percent favored using the American federal pattern to delegate to the UN the enforcement of worldwide disarmament and peaceful settlement of international disputes.

In 1962 Congressman James Roosevelt (Democrat-California) found that 85 percent of a sampling of his constituents approved total disarmament under rules administered by a world court and backed by an international armed force. Also in 1962, Senator Benjamin A. Smith (Democrat-Massachusetts) discovered that 72 percent of a sampling of his constituents supported a UN with constitutionally limited executive, legislative, judicial and police authority in the area of disarmament and peaceful settlement of disputes, patterned after the American federal system.[26]

Returning now to the professional polls, in 1974 Louis Harris Associates sampled public and elite opinion in US, finding that among the public 71 percent believed US ought to conduct its foreign policy through international organization, while 29 percent did not, and 49 percent agreed that the only way to keep the peace is through international organization, with 41 percent disagreeing. In 1978 the Gallup organization found 52 percent of Americans favored strengthening the UN, with 26 percent opposed. Both the Harris and the Gallup polls found elites more knowledgeable about international affairs and more aware of the interdependence of nations, but distinctly less supportive of stronger international organization, even though the public responses were definitely more chauvinistic than the elite responses.[27] These are extremely interesting findings, and the more so when one considers that the UN has dropped drastically in prestige over the past 20 years, at least among the sophisticated (the elites).

And, during the era of the nuclear-freeze movement which began in 1980, we have an NBC-Associated Press poll in May 1982 which found 50 percent of Americans in favor of mutually-verifiable nuclear disarmament with USSR, 28 percent opposed, 14 percent in favor of unilateral disarmament, and eight percent not sure.[28] And Yankelovich's Public Agenda Foundation reported in 1984 some rather surprising findings: Americans by 83 percent to 13 percent say "we cannot be certain that life on earth will continue after a nuclear war" and reject by 68 percent to 20 percent the notion that "if we had no alternative we could fight and win a nuclear war with the Soviet Union;" that for several years upwards of 75 percent have supported a bilateral and verifiable freeze while 56 percent favor an arms control agreement even if foolproof verification cannot be guaranteed.[29]

Taken as a whole, the foregoing polls show that probably somewhere between a very large minority and an outright majority of the American public favors a world government capable of preventing war. Opinion has been substantially consistent since World War II, with variations depending on existence of major crisis before the polls were taken. The polls in several other Western nations summarized above suggest a substantially similar degree of approval of world government. What is lacking is some better indication of public attitudes in the LDCs and, above all, in USSR and other socialist countries.

Japan is a special case, being a developed but non-Western nation. A sample of 3,144 Japanese highschool students was compared with 260 US highschool students. The Japanese were found to be more internationally tolerant, more politically sophisticated, more for peace and against war, less anticommunist, less nationalist, less racially prejudiced, and more in favor of the UN.[30]

As for the reliance we can place upon the scientifically-designed polls that we do have, two scholars say that

> the accuracy of poll predictions has been well established both empirically and statistically. An unbiased sample of over 900 people will represent the division of opinion of any size of population with less than a 5% error.[31]

And another group of scholars says that

> To define a social attitude, for example, solely by the character of responses to a list of questionnaire items is eminently legitimate— so much so that almost everything we know about attitudes comes from such research.[32]

An interesting inference from the polls we have summarized is that public opinion simply by-passes the stumbling block of "world community" so touted by sociologists and behavioralists generally. To use MacIver's terminology, the public unconsciously defines community as "any common interest" and goes on immediately to accept world government as a way of realizing the common interest in world order.

In a non-scientific survey of foreign students at the University of Colorado in 1965 it was found that the external aspect of sovereignty, as distinguished from the right to run one's internal affairs free of outside control, was held less dear by students from LDCs than by those from DCs. Various schemes for supranational integration were more acceptable to the former than to the latter. This suggests that people in the LDCs have few illusions about the ability of their states to go it alone at the international level, however much they prize deliverance from colonial status.[33]

Opinion polling is a recent development in the socialist countries. It appears not to have reached thus far to matters of political moment, except briefly in Czechoslovakia, and we know of no poll relevant to our study. As we have seen, communist theory has its own official theory of war: wars occur because of capitalism's competition for markets and raw materials, hence wars will cease when all the world has abandoned capitalism for socialism-communism. But the doctrine of "peaceful coexistence," based as it is on a text of Lenin, could be built into acceptance of a limited form of world government called a revised UN Charter or a scheme for general and complete disarmament along the lines of the McCloy-Zorin agreement.

In 1963 the then deputy editor of *Pravda* and a columnist for *Izvestia* were in New York and were asked whether they would agree that general and complete disarmament requires "some degree of supranational authority over all states." The *Pravda* editor replied:

> It is our belief that under general and complete disarmament there can and must be complete control in order to guarantee that the world remains disarmed. Will that make it necessary to give some functions of the nation-state to some supranational organs or authorities? Of course. We would like it to be understood that we are not opposed to such measures. Those functions ought to be transferred to some supranational authority.[34]

We should note that these newspapers are organs of the Soviet government and that this interview occurred the year of the test-ban treaty, 1963, a year after Kennedy's plan for GCD was proposed.

In 1968 the so-called Sakharov Manifesto was published in the *New York Times*. Written by Andrei D. Sakharov, member of the Soviet Academy of Sciences who made important contributions to the Soviet H-bomb and whom we quoted in Chapter 7 on weaponry, his essay asserts that the division of mankind threatens it with destruction; that intellectual freedom is essential to human society; that capitalism and socialism will converge, each borrowing elements from the other, in four stages; and that in the fourth stage, 1980 to the year 2000, convergence will "lead to creation of a world government and the smoothing of national contradictions."[35]

In 1973 Sakharov joined 120 world leaders in "Humanist Manifesto II" which called for "a system of world law and a world order based upon transnational federal government."[36]

Judging by contributions of Soviet citizens to the "Pugwash" and other non-official international meetings, and the wide if secret circulation of Sakharov's manifesto within USSR, his views are probably shared by most socialist intellectuals.

We conclude this survey of opinion by saying that it shows support only for a world government able to prevent war, although some of the questions to which the public was asked to respond to hint at a possibly broader grant of authority.

D. A World Government for Biological Survival

We are here concerned with the optimum of authority, not with the maximum which would make it a unitary world government, nor with the minimum which would enable it merely to prevent war. The Clark-Sohn proposal is by far the best known plan for a federal type of world government but it has not evoked widespread, close examination. Several scholars have referred to it but merely to dismiss it. Schell finds it too maximal, saying:

> We want relief from the nuclear peril, but if we sign up for world government as the means of getting it we find that global institution after global institution is inexorably delivered on our doorstep thereafter, each one equipped to meddle in some new area of our lives.[37]

If Schell still wants any world government at all, it is one whose authority is limited to banning nuclear weapons. On the other hand, Boulding has said that "The case for world government to police total disarmament as put forward for instance by Clark and Sohn seems to me absolutely unshakeable,"[38] but he has not gotten into the details of the proposal.

1. *Millard's Criticism of the Clark-Sohn Plan.* The most detailed criticism has come from Everett L. Millard. He for many years solicited and published the views on world government held by some of 800 political scientists, sociologists, lawyers, churchmen, and others in 22 countries. He said, of Clark and Sohn's early version, that they had proposed a police state. But he meant by this that the grant of authority was too narrow, being limited to the prevention of war. He asserted that "A world government with power to prevent war must necessarily govern in many other fields than armaments."[39]

Specifically, Millard argued that a world government should have jurisdiction over the high seas, Antarctica, and outer space, and some not too clearly defined authority over economics and commerce. In 1963 he reported that most of some 100 political scientists who had responded to his questionnaire agreed with him.[40] Presumably, Sohn's 1973 revision meets Millard's criticism so far as the high seas and outer space are concerned, but we shall discuss them further.

Millard did not require that a world government have authority to issue a common currency or provide for free immigration or free trade, or to eliminate discrimination or guarantee human rights.

He and his correspondents prefer a bicameral legislature, as in most federal states, but agree with Clark and Sohn that the executive should be the creature of the legislative branch. The Millard group attached great importance to a popularly-elected house, suggesting that if this one change were made in the existing UN it might lead to the vesting of decisive authority in the world body and thus to eventual world government. (As we have noted, the Common Market's Parliament was made subject to direct popular election in 1979 and was given some substantial budgetary authority.) In 1966 individuals calling themselves the "Peace-Keeping Ways and Means Committee" took full-page advertisements in the *New York Times* to promote this view. Sohn himself suggested a beginning might be made by adding to the UN a body of national parliamentarians, 25 from each of the great nations and ranging down to one from each of the least, which could advise on such problems as the General Assembly might refer to it.[41]

Is world jurisdiction over the high seas, Antarctica, and outer space essential to biological survival? Probably not. Yet a viable world government must have revenues. Licensing of Antarctica and the seas and seabeds for exploitation, collection of fees from craft traversing oceans and outer space, together with manufacture and sale of nuclear materials—these might go far toward meeting its needs. And it probably is not wise to leave a world government dependent, as Clark and Sohn do, on national governments to collect world taxes and pay them in. In certain situations the world body might have to threaten violence to get its dues.

Moreover, as a political scientist put it, "the international common agency must control something of value and importance to all—most anyway—of the member states if it is to succeed."[42] He mentions that the early US Congress controlled the public lands. The psychology expressed seems sound. International waterways probably ought also to be included, for revenue purposes and because they are fruitful sources of conflict, especially the Suez and Panama canals, the Dardanelles-Bosporus, and the Strait of Malacca, perhaps Rhine and Danube.

Anyhow, it is difficult to see how national governments can regulate the oceans, Antarctica, or outer space; the treaty process works too poorly.

Clark and Sohn do not envisage the world government guaranteeing any human rights except against the world government itself. But discrimination, whether based on race, religion, language, sex or something else, can in some circumstances become a threat to international peace by evoking civil war or by provoking neighboring nations to intervene. It can thus force the organs of a world government to become involved, whether merely to conciliate or to enforce a ruling by, say, Clark and Sohn's World Equity Tribunal. Perhaps discrimination is one of those items of authority best left a bit cloudy.

We turn now to three problems that have worsened dramatically in the years since Millard was debating with Clark and Sohn. They were described in Chapter 7 among the pressures that radicalize nations and make for war. They must at least be discussed in considering the grant of authority of any world federal government. They are: the planetary ecology; planetary overpopulation; and world trade and currency problems.

2. *The Ecology*. Environmental deterioration, if we are to believe the experts, is indeed a threat to biological survival. In 1977 an international relations journal devoted an entire issue to the problem. One article asserted that most solutions offered by technological optimists would only buy time, often at high social costs, but that there is real hope in proposals for large scale industrial expansion into space using "non-terran" energy and materials, a development possible within 20 to 30 years. In theory, polluting industries could be exported to outer space.[43]

Environmental deterioration is a threat to international peace, as we have noted, because other nations suffer from the failure of any nation to conserve its environment. Few nations are so large or so removed that their populations do not suffer from pollution of air and rivers in neighboring nations, and of course damage to the earth's ozone layer affects the whole planet, as does the "Greenhouse effect" which we have described.

Such an ecological problem as overfishing the seas is recognized, and conferences are held, but little results. The 1974 Conference on the Law of the Seas met year after year until it finally hammered out a new treaty to replace the 17th century sea code still in use, but US and other nations have refused to sign it. The rather futile Stockholm Conference on the environment is another example.

In effect, nations meet but reach disagreement rather than agreement. Lacking a centralized decision-making apparatus, there is no way to move the problems on to resolution. It is true that national legislatures are reluctant to face up to problems, and their consideration of them is overlong. But the mechanism is there if the majority wishes to press on to decision, whereas in the treaty process each nation has an absolute veto as to its participation so there is little pressure to accept compromise. And of course, so long as anarchy persists, a nation can ignore or denounce or interpret for itself any treaty it has signed and ratified.

One difficulty, which we noted in the 1985 summary of computerized models of the planet's future, is that much information about the degree and rate of ecological decline is simply lacking; for example, no reliable data exist on soil erosion, groundwater pollution, or disposal or radioactive waste.[44] Clark and Sohn's UN Environment Protection Agency would be merely a coordinator of national plans, but it might very well see to it that the information gap is closed. And national governments, freed of military burdens, would have far greater resources to spend on the ecology.

Is this enough? Probably not. But if the World Court had the authority to interpret and enforce treaties in general, and not just those that might conflict with the revised Charter, this might suffice. And this appears to be what Sohn's 1973 version provides for. Presumably a national government would rather negotiate a treaty it can live with than risk being hauled before the World Equity Tribunal where the whole matter could be decided by others, then the decision enforced against it. Certainly, if treaties were at last going to become truly binding and enforceable, national governments would be more careful what they sign.

3. *Overpopulation and Immigration.* However much injustice there may seem to be today in the unequal distribution of human beings in relation to resources, there is no possibility that a world government would be given authority to regulate immigration. Too many key nations—US and USSR, for example—would not consider it. Why, the DCs ask, should they take the surplus people the LDCs are producing? Here there is no world community even in the MacIver sense of a common interest.

Fortunately, there is increasingly a perceived common interest in preventing starvation anywhere, though the task admittedly is increasingly difficult. And we can assume that few of the deprived would wish to emigrate if things were going to get better at home. For that matter, there is not enough transport in the world to transfer South Asia's surplus people to happier lands, even if there were places where they would be welcomed. Given an adequately financed World Development Authority, plus vast national efforts to reduce population growth, the ravages of famine and pestilence can be limited. And a world government could play a considerable educative role while making family planning measures available at no cost on request. In 1984 French scientists announced a "countergestation" pill that interrupts pregnancies of fewer than eight weeks with 100 percent effectiveness, and it will be tested in India and China in 1985.

At best, there may be tens of millions of premature deaths. Yet, overpopulation is a threat to the biological survival of only a part of the human race, not to the human venture as a whole, so far as we can see now.

4. *World Trade and Currency.* Obstacles to trade frustrate the optimal distribution of the world's goods and services. Two factors will hamper any World Development Authority in improving the living standards in the LDCs. These factors are (1) non-competitive cost and quality, and (2) inequitable terms of trade. Bargaining power of LDCs (except oil-exporting countries) over the terms of trade has proved weaker than that of DCs. Moreover, the same two factors will aggravate international

conflicts among DCs. And, brooding on top of these two factors is the
crisis-ridden international monetary system described in Chapter 7.

Nations are not apt to give a world government full authority to
increase, reduce, or abolish obstacles to trade. Yet, fortunately, within a
true world security system, nations would tend toward freer trade, for
self-sufficiency in the interest of national defense would no longer be an
excuse for propping up non-competitive industries by excluding
imports.

World trade seems a logical source of revenue for a world government.
The constitutional document could provide (a) that some of the worst
trade abuses such as quotas and dumping are no longer legal, and (b) that
the world government may collect for itself or otherwise dispose of
one-half the tariffs then levied by nations and three-fourths of any
increase in tariffs. This would discourage the raising of tariffs while
enabling the world government to ease the terms of trade in particular
instances by forgiving or refunding all or part of its share. LDCs thus
might be able to buy, on better terms, some of the additional food that US
and other countries can produce by cultivating idle acreage. Also, these
tariff revenues could be applied through the World Development
Authority to subsidize purchases of food and petroleum by LDCs.

Perhaps a world government ought to regulate multinational
corporations. This could be done through a treaty enforceable in the
World Court or perhaps under the world government's jurisdiction over
the oceans, the atmosphere above the oceans, other international
waterways, and outer space. But this likely would raise the question of
world regulation of the monopoly trading corporations used by USSR
and other socialist countries. And what of cartels like OPEC?

Regulating world trade would be a tricky matter, for human ingenuity
can devise many obstacles to trade, including substitutes for tariffs which
could deprive the world government of any tariff revenues while giving a
nation an advantage over other nations. The World Court, the Equity
Tribunal, and the Assembly itself would be the arenas of many an
economic struggle.

There is no way that world trade can run smoothly unless there is a
drastic reform in the international monetary system. Overpopulation,
together with other pressures, can produce radicalization in LDCs to the
extreme left, thus intensifying anarchy, ideological conflict, and
aggression. But, as we have seen, the maximum danger lies in the
radicalization of DCs to the extreme right, for they are the nations that
have the nuclear capacity to bring on a nuclear, third world war.
Probably only Great Depression can cause this radicalization in the DCs,
and probably only trade and currency problems can produce Great
Depression. Moreover, even within a governed and peaceful world,
mismanagement of national economies, usually in response to domestic
political pressures, would evoke trade-currency crises with serious

implications for the world political system that would underlie and undergird the world government.

Two experts tell us that an international monetary system that works must have:

(a) international money, based on something of real value;

(b) an adjustment mechanism, whereby a nation cannot forever buy more than it sells; and

(c) coordination from the center.[45]

While it is not possible to assert that a world currency would be essential to biological survival in a world no longer anarchic, it seems obvious from looking at (a), (b), and (c) that an international currency is a prime example of something a world authority could handle infinitely better than national governments do or ever can do.

Moreover, lacking a world currency, in what national currencies would a world government pay its civil servants and armed forces? In which national currencies would it collect its revenues? Which currencies would it accept in payment of licenses and royalties for the exploitation of the seas or for atomic energy or for manufacturing rights in outer space? Would it accept all currencies at the going rates as determined by supply and demand, or at "pegged" rates which may be unrealistic? How could it obtain the proper amounts of the particular currencies needed to discharge its responsibility for developing the LDCs? Would its currency reserves be used to bail out some distressed national regime to prevent, say, anti-federalist politicians from coming to power in that nation? What would be the politics of this sort of thing in a world federal legislature?

Above all, why permit the likelihood that even in a governed and peaceful world currency crises will still occur for lack of a world currency? It seems prudent to foresee the strains that might be placed on a world government in its infancy and to make provision against them. Accordingly it may be wise to transfer the currency-issuing authority from national to world hands. Triffin and other experts have recommended this.

It might be enough that a world currency would be backed by the "full faith and credit" of the world government. It would hold its value to the degree that people had faith in it. A world currency would probably have high credibility at the outset and, if responsibly administered, would be a continuing symbol and asset of the world government. But it would be better to base it on something of real value such as the "Commodity pound" recommended by Australian and English experts which would be based on a commodity index.[46] Triffin says there would be complex calculations and endless controversy over the honesty of the index,[47] but there would be less of this if it were the only world currency, for there would be no quarreling over its ratio to national currencies. That is a problem that afflicts the IMF's "Paper Gold" and the Common Market's

ECU, both of which are expressed in terms of a basket of national currencies. And no national currency is tied to anything of real value, whereas the "commodity pound" would be. Conceivably, it could even be tied to gold.

A compromise might be the issuance of a federal currency to circulate along with national currencies and perhaps gradually displace them as the medium for settling international balances. Another alternative arises from a suggestion by two students of federalism who recommend, with respect to a future European federation, that a single currency for the federation be postponed until free trade throughout the area is achieved but that, meanwhile, the federal government have authority to fix and alter exchange rates among national currencies.[48]

5. *Functional Agencies Related to the UN.* Several of these would be absorbed into the institutions provided for by Clark and Sohn: the Food and Agricultural Organization, the World Bank, and the International Development Association would presumably become part of the new World Development Authority. The International Monetary Fund and the General Agreement on Trade and Tariffs should become part of the new world body with their officials nominated by the Executive Council and approved by the General Assembly. But others, such as the International Labour Organization, the World Health Organization, and the bodies dealing with telecommunications and meteorology could remain as independent treaty organizations which merely send reports to the UN. However, if anything adequate is going to be done about overpopulation some organization such as *WHO* must have far greater resources to work with.

Conclusions. One might properly infer from the foregoing discussion that a world government for biological survival would require a little more authority than that set forth in the 1973 revision of the Clark-Sohn plan. We say this even though further authority would accrue anyway to a Clark-Sohn world government through its control of nuclear energy, the oceans, and outer space and through the decisions made by the Court and the Tribunal. Bearing in mind that the authority actually set forth in a new constitutional document will be the product of the bitterest bickering, we suggest that the Assembly might well be given *some* legislative authority over

    (a) international waterways in addition to the oceans, and Antarctica;

    (b) international aspects of environmental deterioration;

    (c) international trade, and real money to settle payments imbalances;

as well as authority to provide for

    (d) adequate and absolutely dependable sources of revenue.

Such a world government would seem able to assure that the human venture will survive the nuclear-CB threat. It would be only moderately well equipped to cope with the twin problems of overpopulation and "limits to growth" that are foreseen in the computerized studies of world futures. But, once installed, such a government would be likely to take the early initiatives that those studies tell us are so vitally important if the problems are to be solved at all.

Such a world government could do something about economic inequities between DCs and LDCs but little about such inequities within nations. It could assuage social injustice—the treatment within nations of racial minorities and castes, the status of women, child labor, and the like—only through education and recommendation. It could not guarantee free speech to the individual or save him from torture, or even assure him of an education, much less of adequate medical care.

But on the whole nations would be happier places to live in—freed largely from the external stresses discussed in Chapter 7, and with the internal stresses at least mitigated.   If such a world federal government could get through its first difficult years, nations and peoples might become willing to vest additional authority in it. As a scholar of federalism says,

> ...federalism is more fully understood as it is seen as a process, an evolving pattern of changing relationships... This finding ought not to be misunderstood as meaning that the rules are insignificant; far from it. What it does mean is that any federal relationship requires effective and built-in arrangements through which these rules can be recurrently changed.[49]

In this connection, the amendment process suggested by Clark and Sohn seems to strike a proper balance: amendment is made difficult, but by no means impossible. World law would also accrue in small increments through decisions by their Court, Tribunal, and other organs.

E. The Likelihood of Civil War

Most objection to world government on the grounds of civil war rests on the assumption that what have been international wars would simply become civil wars between the member-nations of a world government. We suggest that such wars would not be tried because the world government would have a monopoly on large-scale coercive force and the possibility of subverting any considerable part of a Peace Force recruited, trained, and dispersed around the globe as provided by Clark and Sohn is remote. But the main assurance is of course that the principal cause of international conflict—anarchy—would have have been removed and the other two causes so abated that the deteriorating cycle of fear would no longer operate.[50]

Another possibility is that broad trans-national elements of the world population might raise an insurrection against the world government or go to violence against other broad elements; in these situations, nations as nations might play little role. Here again, success would depend upon subverting part of the world Peace Force. As for the argument that guerrilla insurrections have succeeded without disaffection of the armed forces, students of guerrilla warfare say success depends on support from outside in terms of a supply base and and a sanctuary. In a governed world, where would "outside" be?

There remains the case of civil wars within nations. These will continue despite the elimination or mitigation of the external and internal stresses. Civil war in misgoverned nations might be more frequent because rebels would have a better chance against lightly armed national police forces in a disarmed world. Civil war is the ultimate way of deciding great issues or rivalries in nations, however much citizens of long-stable nations may deplore the fact. Thus it would seem wise to let these affairs run their courses unless they become threats to international peace in the judgment of the General Assembly along the lines recommended by Clark and Sohn. Order could then be restored pending adjudication or mediation of both the international and civil aspects.

Yet there is no doubt that the world organs must exercise their authority with that degree of wisdom and justice which will preclude reliance on coercive force of the world government save in rare instances. It is probable that national governments will accept some perceived injustice at the hands of the world government rather than provoke its coercive force.

But, if all else fails and force must be applied, it is important that in a truly federal system the general government can arrest and bring to trial the individual persons who threaten the peace, whether they be terrorists with suitcase A-bombs or national officials. Then the situation will not come to war unless a national government intervenes to prevent the arrest.

This brings us to a discussion of the principles which distinguish the federal form of government from other forms.

F. The Theory of Federal Government

The world federal arrangement we have discussed would be different from any present federation but its form would correspond to what most scholars consider the standard federal principle.

K. C. Wheare, whose work on federalism is probably the best known, says that "The modern idea of what federal government is has been determined by the United States of America."[51]

Farrand's records of the convention in Philadelphia in 1787 show that the debate ranged over almost the entire field of political philosophy and was replete with examples from earlier "federations" or "confederations;" the delegates made no distinction between those two terms.[52]

The outcome was a new principle in political theory. It was an arrangement whereby the general government would be federal (or confederal) in so far as it operated on state governments, but national (or unitary) in so far as it operated directly on the people within its own grant of authority. The idea was to get away as far as possible from what Madison described as

> a sovereign over sovereigns, a government over governments, a legislation for communities, as contradistinguished from individuals; as it is a solecism in theory, so in practice it is subversive of the order and ends of civil polity, by substituting violence in place of law, or the destructive coercion of the sword, in place of the mild and salutary coercion of the magistrate.[53]

Madison means here that one ought not to expect order if the general government must ask the state governments to do thus and so, and, should they refuse, have then to make war to compel them. That sort of arrangement is now called a confederation. The alternative was to give the general government authority to act directly on individual persons within a specified authority, bypassing the state governments. Madison coined the term "national-federal" to describe this arrangement, but nowadays it is simply called federal.

Since 1787 the arrangement has been considered a "true federation" and the following nations have organized substantially on this principle: Mexico, Venezuela, Argentina, Brazil, Switzerland, Bismarck's Second German Empire, Canada, Australia, USSR, the present West German Federal Republic, Yugoslavia, Burma, India, and Nigeria. Such an arrangement is often called a federal union, emphasizing that there is diversity as to some items of authority but unity as to others.[54]

NATO and the Warsaw Pact are properly called alliances, which is the loosest form of integration. The Holy Roman Empire, the League of Nations, and the present UN are properly called leagues, for lack of the centralized decision-making apparatus characteristic even of confederations. Confederations have seldom lasted much longer than leagues or alliances; they tend to move on to federal union or break up; there is no current example of a confederation—the European Community (Common Market) is the nearest approximation.

Wheare asserts that the amount of authority given the general government is not decisive in determining a true federation. Nor does it matter whether the "residual powers" (those not specified as belonging to either) lie with the general or the state governments. What is required is that neither "general nor regional government is subordinate to the other."[55] Similarly, William Riker says that each level of government must have "at least one area of action in which it is autonomous."[56] Whereas an arrangement in which the state or regional governments can dominate the general government is called a confederation, an arrangement in which the general government can dominate the state governments is usually called a quasi-federation.

Thus a world government such as we have described is a true federation. Unlike a confederation, it not only has a centralized decision-making apparatus but also has enforcement powers backed by superior coercive force and can exercise its authority on individuals without having to threaten war on national governments—unless they intervene to shield individuals. Unlike India, which is sometimes classified as a quasi-federation, it lacks authority to suspend state governments in the discharge of their authority.

A world federation along the lines suggested would be unlikely to break up as alliances, leagues, and confederations do, because the items of authority vested in it, though few, are critical for preserving order and dealing with other crucial world problems which are not manageable under anarchy. That its authority is indeed limited to a few items is indicated in a study by Bowie and Friedrich of the US, Swiss, Canadian, Australian, and West German federations: they conclude that each of these federal governments has broad authority to regulate interstate commerce and ensure free interstate trade, to tax and to spend, to issue a single currency and regulate banking and credit, to enact labor and social security legislation, and to provide for free immigration within the federation. All these powers are in addition to exclusive control over military and foreign policy matters.[57] In most federations not included in their study, the general government has even more authority; several, under stresses external, have become quasi-federations. In USSR, virtually all authority is exercised by the Party through the federal and regional Soviets, though a high degree of regional cultural autonomy is permitted.

That such a world federal government would not become tyrannical is suggested not only by its relatively narrow grant of authority but by the fact that the external stresses that so often have evoked tyrannical national governments could not operate on a planetary government, while the internal stresses would continue to affect primarily the national governments, though at reduced intensities.

Moreover, Riker has found that constitutional guarantees which federal arrangements have given to states have usually enabled them to frustrate policies favored by majorities at the federal level, despite the superior coercive force which the federal governments always possess.[58] This has been true of Canada, even though its constitution gave broad powers to the federal level; and it is hoped now that the constitutional reforms of the 1980s will check the rising regionalism and provincialization.[59] That federal governments do not necessarily increase their authority at the expense of state authority is seen also in the Yugoslav federation where, since 1966, substantial authority has been transferred back to the constituent republics and provinces.[60]

Samuel Beer suggests that US, through constitutional amendment and judicial interpretation, may have become a quasi-federation over the course of its 200 years, for there are few powers left that belong exclusively to the state governments, yet he says that federalism "still divides and organizes power so as to avert the evils and realize the benefits of free government."[61] In US, West Germany, and most federations, federalism is considered a guarantee against tyrannical government.

Thus world government may not mean more government overall, but less. Alexandre Marc, France's foremost student of federalism, holds that federalism is the natural enemy of that statism (*etatisme*) by which national governments have arrogated to themselves greater and greater power over their citizens. Only within the framework of a government for world affairs can national governments be reversed in their apparently inexorable trend—under anarchy—toward total control over the human spirit. Freedom in community is not possible except anarchy be ended.

Wheare says the desire of states to enter into a federation may be rooted in the need for a common defense, for independence from a foreign power, for bringing about a common economic advantage, or in recognition of a commonalty of previous association or of political institutions.[62] If, by the term "common defense," one includes the need of all nations to be defended from other nations, then this need is present to maximum degree in the present international system; also present is the "common economic advantage." The only "commonalty" of association is that all are embarked on the common human venture.

Wheare believes federation can succeed in spite of dissimilarity of social institutions although he does not believe autocratic or dictatorial units can be federated successfully with "democratic" units.[63] Riker assumes some sense of common interest, expressed in a bargaining process between (a) politicians who wish peacefully to form a federation to accomplish expansion of territory and (b) those representing units that accept federation out of pressing need for the military and diplomatic strength it would bring.[64]

The impulses toward federation mentioned by Riker are substantially the same as Wheare's need for a common defense. This *is* the principal common interest in the international system today, though not the only one. As we noted, the authority and institutions of a world government will be decided by the most bitter bargaining. The dissimilarity in terms of ideology, economy and government is best seen as an argument not to give a world government authority to determine these for its member-nations. At the same time it is fortunate that, as mentioned earlier, virtually all nations today have the form of republican government if not its substance, hence have some experience in representative government.

Karl Deutsch and others have laid down nine conditions for the "amalgamation" of nations:

(1) mutual compatibility of main values; (2) a distinctive way of life; (3) expectations of stronger economic ties or gains; (4) a marked increase in political and administrative capabilities of at least some

participating units; (5) superior economic growth on the part of at least some participating units; (6) unbroken links of social communication, both geographically between territories and sociologically between different social strata; (7) a broadening of the political elite; (8) mobility of persons, at least among the politically relevant strata; and (9) multiplicity of ranges of communication and transportation.[65]

These conclusions were based on a study confined to the historical "amalgamations" in Europe and North America, and it was probably only historical coincidence that conditions (4) through (7) were present at the same time as the other conditions more directly related to integration. Moreover, the study included the merger of states into unitary states as well as into federations, hence all these conditions can scarcely be made prerequisites for federation. Conditions (3), (8), and (9) are probably sufficiently present in the world today.

Deutsch's conditions are not expressed clearly and few seem pertinent to transforming the international system into a true federation. Moreover, Deutsch was primarily interested in the political integration of the North Atlantic area, somewhat along the lines of Streit's Federal Union movement that will be described in our next section. Nevertheless, his conditions remind us again that the height of any reasonable scheme of world federal government must be proportionate to the depth of the common interest which provides its foundations. Even Dante, perhaps the first prophet of world government since the Stoics, stipulated that only matters of world concern be brought before his World Monarch for decision.*

India is the most interesting federation from our viewpoint. Its federal authority is quite broad, and it came into being in a way that does not tell us whether a world government is feasible in the sense of getting agreement to set one up, but it does tell us something about whether a world government would prove to be workable.

India contains about one-sixth of the planet's population and is a world in miniature in terms of differences of language, race, religion, customs—in virtually all factors of cultural particularism. Yet India has managed to maintain a centralized and enforceable decision-making apparatus for nearly two generations, despite enormous external and internal stresses. As indicated in Chapter 7, we do not expect this success to continue. But if India did not perceive itself threatened by Pakistan and China, and if it could get its population growth under control, the federation might well endure.

---

*Interestingly enough, Dante's *De Monarchia*, on world government and the proper relationship between Universal Church and Universal State, was proscribed as heretical by Pope John XXII and the next pope of that name, John XXIII, issued a call for world federal government in his *Pacem in Terris* in 1963, six centuries later.

India suggests a point that some students of federalism have raised: does a federal government need more authority in proportion to the degree of diversity it must preside over and reconcile? If the answer were yes, then a world federal government would require far more authority than the Clark-Sohn plan, as amended by us, provides. But this argument might better be restated to assert that any government, federal or unitary, needs heavy authority to cope with the external and internal stresses India faces, hence our prediction that India will radicalize to the totalitarian left. But a world federal government would face comparatively simple problems, once it were set up.

A world government would not suffer from a defect found in the old United Provinces of the Netherlands and in Bismarck's German federation. This is the presence of one state so powerful that the rest cannot counter-balance it. There would be no state comparable to the House of Orange or the Kingdom of Prussia. Nor would it have the somewhat similar defect that some have noted in the federation of Nigeria: too few states to elicit a lively process of countervailing power, compromise, and balance.

The great difficulty with a world federation lies in getting it agreed to and established, not in making it work. And that is the subject of our next and final section.

G. But Can We Get a World Government?

Recalling now the polls summarized earlier which showed an astonishing degree of public support for a world government able to prevent war, Dr. George Gallup says:

> I see over and over again how sound the collective judgment is and how much ahead of elective representatives of the country the people are. On almost all issues the public is ahead by months and sometimes decades.

> The public has its own peculiar way of making up its own mind on how to vote. We may disagree with this choice on occasion—but the interesting thing about this process is that it is far more rational than emotional. It is usually a pretty intelligent choice.[66]

What is lacking is presidents and prime ministers who will catch up with the public and then go on and behave like leaders. Yet the world has twice come close to building supranational institutions: the Baruch Proposal for the international control of atomic energy, put forward by the Truman administration after World War II but turned down by Stalin; and Kennedy's proposal in 1962 for general and complete disarmament, followed by his speeches in June and September of 1963.

Clement Attlee and Charles De Gaulle asserted outright that world government is the only answer. But neither mentioned it while heading the British and French governments. Dwight Eisenhower wrote in 1948 that the value learned in the war of pooling national independence in a single headquarters was not applied in creating the UN:

> Its application would have meant some form of limited, federated world government which...was politically unacceptable to any of the great nations concerned...the world is now too small for the rigid concepts of national sovereignty... No radical surrender of national sovereignty is required—only a firm agreement that in disputes between nations a central and joint agency, after examination of the facts, shall decide the justice of the case by majority vote and thereafter shall have the power and the means to enforce its decisions.[67]

He too was silent while president except for vague statements about world law. His second Secretary of State, Christian Herter, called while in office for world law backed by a world court and an armed force superior to any national threat, but his speech strangely got little attention.[68] Britain's Labour Party adopted a world government plank but it was never reflected in Harold Wilson's subsequent prime ministership.

We noted earlier that the problems of the moment always bulk too large; there is no time or energy to attempt fundamental change; assuming the role of national decision-maker seems to blind the individual to any alternative to the anarchic power struggles of the moment. Occasionally a decision-maker comes along who can rise above all this—Kennedy, Khruschev, Brandt, Sadat, possibly Carter—but as of 1985 there is no such Transcendant Leader on the scene.

Fortunately, in liberal republics private individuals can join together to arouse the public and put pressure on so-called leaders. As John Stuart Mill said, one individual with a cause is worth a hundred with merely an interest to protect.[69]

The Association to Unite the Democracies is the present name of Clarence Streit's "federal union" movement which dates from the publication of his book *Union Now* in 1939.[70] Scholars say Streit draws too neat a parallel between the union of the 13 American states in 1789 and his proposed union of the seasoned liberal democracies now. Ernst Haas, a noted functionalist, says for example that "The community of the American people antedated the American state, as a world community must antedate a world state."[71] But these scholars ought to go on and explain why, with all that community, the 13 states still could not get along as a confederation but had to go on to federal union.

Streit's movement was important on both sides of the Atlantic during and after World War II, until the McCarthy era. In 1940, when France was about to fall, a French follower of Streit made a suggestion to Jean Monnet (later known as the father of European integration) which resulted in Churchill's proposal of a federal union with France. But the French government declined and surrendered.[72]

Streit's movement has persisted because he has been able to attract at least the nominal support of many notables. There is a story that in 1949

Justice Owen J. Roberts of the US Supreme Court went to President Truman and suggested he move for a federal union of the Atlantic democracies; Truman asked Secretary of State Acheson, who said the most they could hope for was an alliance; and NATO was the result.[73]

In 1973 Streit's resolution for a NATO conference to explore federal union was endorsed by President Nixon and it passed the Senate and the House Foreign Affairs Committee. But Nixon's affairs went awry and it was defeated in the house. President Ford, when House Republican Leader, had voted for the resolution, but it seems not to have remained a live issue after Nixon.[74]

Streit's Association publishes a newsletter, *The Federator*, from Washington, encourages schools and colleges to emphasize federalism in the American experience, still hopes to call a NATO convention to discuss federation, and cooperates with the Union of European Federalists whose special concern is changing the Common Market into a federal union.

A federation of liberal capitalist nations might inspire a counter-federation of the Warsaw Pact nations, possibly making the two blocs even more dangerous to each other. But any federation, say of the Common Market nations, would be desirable in that it might set a trend toward transcending anarchy by abridging sovereignty.

We've seen there is worry that the Common Market might break up, partly because each nation has a broad veto. One scholar says that the decline in nationalism seems not to have produced wider loyalties to Western Europe as an entity.[75] But a 1985 poll shows that a majority of Common Market residents support "a kind of political union like there is between the 50 states of the U.S.A. or the 10 provinces that form Canada."[76] A Draft Treaty of European Union, supported by the Union of European Federalists and others, was overwhelmingly approved in 1984 by the European Parliament which wants union when half the member states representing two-thirds of the Community's population ratifies. But the 1985 Community summit meeting in Milan failed, with Britain, Denmark and Greece objecting to closer union. It is possible the others may proceed without them. As *The Federator* remarked (June 1985), "Common assemblies are the birthplace of initiatives to unite polities.... Summits of heads of governments are the graveyard of such initiatives."

NATO, which includes the Common Market members (except Ireland) and several other West European nations plus US and Canada, is also in trouble, as we saw earlier. There is the feeling that it must become more than an alliance, else it will break up. One scholar wrote in 1970 that there must be an integrated army subject to the direction of a supranational, multifunction Western European Union.[77] But that did not happen and in the 1980s there are articles with such titles as "The Crumbling Alliance," "The Alliance in Disarray," and "NATO: Can the Alliance Be

Saved?" A former US foreign service officer wrote in 1983 that the alliance is drifting toward nationalism and a loss of common purpose; he wishes to shore it up with a Council of Democracies to include Japan, Australia and New Zealand.[78]

Lincoln Bloomfield, one of the few scholars who paid any attention to Kennedy's GCD plan, reports that there is little interest in Western Europe in the UN, that "Western Europeans are, as before, waiting for the United States to give the lead in any new phase of global institution-building."[79] And it is true that there is rising opinion in the First-World liberal capitalist nations that the UN is dominated by Third-World countries (LDCs) that, owing to population and other problems, are probably beyond hope.

Hence there might be strong support, in the next crisis or the one after that, for a federal union of the NATO nations plus Japan and a few more. These nations have enough in common to meet nearly all the requirements for federation listed by Wheare, Riker, and Deutsch. Moreover, unlike a union of the Common Market members only, such a federation would be world-dominant in every respect except weaponry.

There might even be some support for inviting the Second-World socialist nations to join the federation. These too are developed, industrial countries. But the differences in ideology, economy, and political system would argue for a federal government of narrower authority than if it were a union of liberal capitalist nations only.

Still, the argument for a worldwide federation is based solidly in the principle that a government cannot guarantee peace unless it has jurisdiction over the entire arena of conflict. Thus, as a minimum, any federal union of liberal capitalist nations should be left open for others to join, once they meet certain criteria. Even Streit's plan provided for this. And it might be prudent as well as gallant for such a federal union to take on the burden of India as a founding member, if at that time India still practices representative government.

World Federalists U.S.A. dates back to two organizations formed in World War II, one of them largely made up of Streit supporters who had come to believe that world wars proved the need for world instead of partial federation. These two merged in 1946 to form United World Federalists, which under the leadership of Vernon Nash and others had a sizeable and influential membership and made a considerable impact on some sectors of the US public. It was helped by the efforts of Robert Lee Humber who persuaded several legislatures to pass resolutions calling for world federation. At one time Ronald Reagan was a member of United World Federalists, and its president around 1950 was Alan Cranston who, as a senator from California, ran in 1984 for the Democratic presidential nomination on a nuclear arms-control platform.

But the United World Federalists too never recovered their following and influence after McCarthyism and the Korean War hit them in the early 1950s. They are still in nominal existence as World Federalists U.S.A, with an office in Washington, and are related to groups in Japan and Western Europe, with a straggling of members in LDCs, in the World Association of World Federalists.

Senator Joseph Ball, a Minnesota Republican, in 1944 had led a bipartisan but unsuccessful effort to incorporate an international peace force into the UN.[80] In 1945 Grenville Clark called the First Dublin (N.H.) Conference which asserted the UN was not enough, and he was a founder of United World Federalists. Thus the Clark-Sohn plan is substantially in keeping with the proposals of world federalists over the years. In 1965 Clark convened the Second Dublin Conference which repeated the call for world government and emphasized the need for a World Development Fund. The Grenville Clark Institute for World Law was set up; it sought adherents to the Dublin Declaration from notables around the world and came up with an impressive list, including five members of a recent British Cabinet.

In 1969 the UN Assembly voted to place on the agenda of the 1970 25th anniversary session an item calling for a review of the Charter. In the crucial committee vote on the item, the socialist states except Yugoslavia voted no; the LDCs plus Japan voted almost solidly for it; but most nations where the federalist movement is strongest (US and Western Europe) abstained; only Ireland and Italy voted yes.

Carlos Romulo, Philippine delegate, pleaded for "a fundamental review of the structure," saying "none of us who signed the Charter in San Francisco knew anything about the atom bomb."[81] Charles Yost, the US delegate whose personal views are rather similar to Romulo's,[82] dutifully spoke for the State Department, saying "We have in fact only just begun after 25 years to implement our Charter. Perhaps it needs in some respects to be amended, but more important and urgent, it needs to be implemented."[83] Presumably, Nixon and Kissinger did not favor a stronger UN; their interest was limited to an Atlantic federation.

When the item on Charter review came before the 25th anniversary session, the Assembly sent the issue back to the member states for restudy.

In 1974 *Members of Congress for Peace Through Law*, a group formed in 1947 and composed in 1974 of 35 senators and 117 representatives, introduced a resolution saying that in a world without war

nations will rely for their external protection on world institutions strong enough to stop any nation from making war, capable of assuring peaceful and just settlements of international disputes, and reliable enough to be entrusted with such powers

and asked that US policy seek such institutions.[84] The resolution died. But, for what it may be worth, Congress in 1984 created an "Institute of Peace."

In 1977 a committee of the Atlantic Council, composed of executives, scholars and others interested in international relations, suggested changes in the UN system but they were minor because, as Chairman Yost said, the UN reflects "a world of nation-states jealous of their sovereignty and fearful of their neighbors."[85]

In October 1985 the UN will celebrate its 40th anniversary and many chiefs of state are expected to be present. There is talk of a "summit of summits" but very little talk about amending the Charter.[86]

The calling of a UN review conference under Article 109 cannot be vetoed. Once called it could meet and consider amendments. This process, once entered upon, might take on a momentum of its own. A delegate to the UN discharges a role which tends to shape him toward wanting a more effective world body, as one can tell from the utterances of Stevenson, Goldberg and Yost, though not from those of Kirkpatrick. Thus it is conceivable that delegates might outrun their briefings and produce a radically new document, which might then elicit public support. But much would depend on the key presidents and prime ministers then in office.

The holding of a review conference could follow some new crisis prompting US, USSR and other great nations to reach the "Agreement in Principle" mentioned in Section C of this chapter. It would not matter that the Charter permits the veto when amendments are referred back to nations for ratification. The new document could ignore the old one by simply providing it would go into effect when X number of nations representing X percent of the world population ratified it.

Whereas the world federalists have looked mainly to transformation of the UN, and Streit's supporters have tried to transform NATO, both by action through national governments, the Denver-based World Committee for a World Constitutional Convention sought to by-pass national governments by holding a People's Convention. Here again, an impressive list of notables endorsed the idea, agreeing to serve as delegates to a Convention. So far as is known, the Denver group is inactive, but there is general agreement among federalists that some sort of people's world convention might have value, serving as a "preview conference" and evoking interest in a more official conference.

In the universities radical questions are asked because professors have the time and inclination to concern themselves with the whys of current institutions and practices. The word "radical" has to do with the roots of things. It is for this reason that most new knowledge comes out of the universities, especially in the physical sciences whose discoveries are provable and point in themselves toward solutions.

Social scientists have better luck at analysis, which produces questions, than at synthesis, which produces solutions. Among social scientists solutions are suspect because, as we saw in Chapter 3, agreement is lacking as to the methods by which knowledge can be discovered; and this is true even among statisticians who criticize each others' data bases and correlations. Nevertheless, not only the "peace research scientists" but scholars generally who have concerned themselves with nuclear war and peace have been willing to bruise their own brains and to engage their students in the search for solutions.

Materials produced by the Institute for World Order (formerly World Law Fund) have been received into the curricula of dozens of colleges and universities and into some secondary schools. Earlier materials had a distinct world-federalist tinge, and the two American scholars who compiled them were criticized by other scholars who consider "normative" or "prescriptive" theorizing unscholarly and who anyway believe world government is a "simplistic" solution; that is, insufficiently complicated.[87] Later materials, known as the World Order Models Project (WOMP) reports, especially those written by scholars from LDCs, have veered off into questions of socio-economic justice and cultural differences, evoking the criticism that nearly every problem is being raised to the status of a global concern.[88]

Still, the WOMP reports are being published in several languages and are probably having an overall positive effect, for scholars and students need to run down all the blind alleys before they can come back to the simplistic principle that public peace is produced by government.

Robert M. Hutchins, University of Chicago president, wrote in the late 1940s that "Before the atomic bomb, we could take world government or leave it. We could rely on the long process of evolution to bring world community and world government hand in hand. Any such program today means another war, and another war means the end of civilization."[89] Hutchins went on to found the Center for the Study of Democratic Institutions which devised materials that pointed toward world government.

Many of those materials were taken from deliberations at the three *Pacem in Terris* convocations called by the Center. They have been read by many scholars and publicists, and in this way they reach into the intellectual bloodstream. It is unfortunate that Pope Paul had little to say about world government other than endorsing John 23d's encyclical, and John Paul II nothing at all. But the encyclical has found its way into many Catholic educational institutions, and perhaps it undergirds the recent declaration by US Catholic bishops in favor of nuclear disarmament.*

Most scholars wish to be seen as realists rather than as idealists, and perhaps that is why the Bundys and Rostows and Brzezinskis act so tough

---

*Pope John is said to have decided to issue this encyclical calling for world federal government after he read the Fatima prophecy on war and peace, which had been sealed in the Vatican since the "Miracle at Fatima" on October 13, 1917. The present writer, though Protestant, was born that day, and would like very much to know what it was that John read. John died in June 1963, five months before John kennedy. The "era of the two Johns" was brilliant, but brief.

when they occupy the seats of power. Still, there are indications that, having examined the "blind alley" cures and found them lacking, the scholarly community may be working around toward an eventual neo-realist consensus. As mentioned earlier, we are seeing in the last dozen years far more mention of anarchy and the need to limit sovereignty than we saw in the preceding twenty years ushered in by McCarthyism.

Lester Brown, demographer and agricultural expert, wrote in 1972 that the world's manifold problems require supranational institutions—agencies that exercise the sovereignty of governments.[90]

Two scholars mentioned earlier concluded in 1974 that narrow nationalism is futile and that development of a practical international framework is essential if problems are to be solved and a new mankind emerge.[91]

Another wrote in 1977 that what is required first is a minimal world government because in the early stages it is more important to establish conflict control than to try to solve all social problems, but that progress has been slow because the world's idealism has focused on equality instead of on preserving humanity.[92] One hopes the WOMP scholars will see this.

An expert in demography wrote in 1977 that the world needs population control but that the world cannot take this good advice because it is not yet a decision-making unit.[93]

In 1980 a scholar asked how George Kennan in his book *The Cloud of Danger* could envision mass weapons abolished, even though national arsenals and sovereign nations would persist.[94]

Also in 1980 two scholars published a book giving good coverage of some "old cures" and discussing the world federalist and Streit movements as well as the WOMP reports. They conclude that "The piecemeal attack on sovereignty remains the method of practical choice, despite the increasingly urgent need for major transformation of the international system."[95]

In 1981 a long-time power realist was still contemptuous of world federalists but found himself saying that "Increased authority must be bestowed on supranational agencies by states yielding portions of their cherished sovereignty."[96] No doubt the way to get a world federation is not to call it that.

The same year two textbook writers dealt at length with the WOMP reports and world government. They did not take a position but they quoted Kennedy as saying that "the untouchability of national sovereignty" is a "myth," and Kissinger as calling the national state "inadequate" and the emergence of a global community "imperative."[97]

A scholar concerned about nuclear proliferation wrote in 1981 that he was not predicting that the world's horror would produce world government but that it would lead to a truncation of a portion of nations' sovereignty—the right to nuclear weapons.[98] Here again, any arrangement that can disarm nations and keep them disarmed is properly called world government.

Also in 1981, the head of "The Dimensionality of Nations Project" at the University of Hawaii concluded in his final report on the project that there must be a minimal world federal government authorized to set up a police force to keep the peace, with disarmament to the level required for internal order.[99]

In books published in 1981 and 1983, and widely read, a scholar named Mandelbaum says anarchy is the root of our nuclear predicament, whereby each nation must be a "vigilante," and that world government is the cure, but he sees no clear precedent in 2,500 years of history for such a surrender of sovereignty.[100] He is wrong here; the unifications of Germany and Italy are ready examples.

In 1983 Roger Sperry, a Nobelist in biology, inferred from his science a global ethic whereby it is sacrilegious to make war, pollute, deplete, or otherwise damage the biosphere and said that this ethic requires world government.[101] Sperry's ethic could become the ideology of world government. Also in 1983, Raoul Naroll, noted for his statistical studies of history, wrote in his *The Moral Order* that the key values are peace, order, and a tolerance of diversity, and that these must be enforced by a central authority.

In 1984 a textbook with the catchy title *Games Nations Play* gave anarchy a thorough treatment and discussed several "old cures" for war, then concluded somewhat wistfully that world federation does not seem feasible.[102]

Such wistfulness among scholars is common enough. Karl Deutsch, who in 1953 looked forward eventually to a world government, wrote in 1979 that the world is now too international to permit a naive nationalism to flourish without limit but it is too national to permit a supranational government, a common currency, a common electorate, or a supranational tax system.[103]

If the scholars are having trouble reaching consensus on the simplistic idea of world government, perhaps there is hope in the *judges and lawyers*. Some 3,000 of them from 121 nations attended a World Conference on World Peace Through Law in Washington in 1965. It was the result of the efforts of Charles C. Rhyne, former head of the American Bar Association. At that time he prescribed treaty and judge-made law, without the legislative and enforcement functions which a world government would provide. The conference heard some strong emphases on enforceable world law and at least one plea for a world federation along Clark-Sohn lines.[104] Chief Justice Warren of the US Supreme Court seemed to have governmental institutions in mind when he said:

> Achieving and maintaining a rule of law strong enough to rule the actions of nations and individuals in the world community is no more dreamy, impossible or impracticable than was the idea of splitting the atom, or sending a missile to Mars a few years ago.[105]

Warren spoke again to this point during the conference at Belgrade in 1971.[106]

Rhyne himself in 1971 proposed establishing a set of international laws acceptable to all nations, with courts in every nation, backed by "an effective international police force."[107] The Sixth World Peace Through Law conference met at Abidjan, Ivory Coast, in 1973. It resolved that the UN Charter be amended to require all nations to submit all disputes to mandatory peaceful resolution.[108]

It appears that the World Peace Through Law concepts are finding their way into law schools in US and abroad. Young lawyers may in time realize that you get peace at the international level the same way you get it at the national, state or provincial, and local levels—by government.

International Physicians for the Prevention of Nuclear War, organized by an American and a Russian physician, now has a membership of more than 100,000 from many nations and has become an important factor in the peace movement. But thus far these physicians have limited their public pronouncements to estimates of casualties and other damage in a nuclear war, and the need for arms control.

As for the churches, we have already mentioned Pope John's encyclical[109] and the action by the American bishops. In the 1960s the Methodist Church had what amounted to a world federation statement in its *Discipline*. As part of the nationwide shift to the political right, this statement was watered down. But in general the main-line Protestant churches can still be counted upon to support institution-building at the world level. The same is true of most Jewish ecclesiastical organizations as well as the Quakers and the Fellowship of Reconciliation.

Columnists, commentators, and other publicists, who were important in the federalist movement during and after World War II, have not thus far played much role in its revival. Harry Reasoner came out in 1974 for world government on ABC's evening news telecast. But most publicists seem unable to get beyond reporting anti-nuclear demonstrations or commenting pompously on the charade of arms control negotiations. For example, James Reston wrote in 1985 that if the UN has failed the fault lies with its member nations "and not with the principles of its Charter;"[110] some people never learn.*

In 1982 Jonathan Schell published his *The Fate of the Earth*, in which he seemed to say that if the race is to survive national sovereignty must go, but in the sequel, *The Abolition*, published in 1984, he recommended the abolition, not of sovereignty, but of nuclear weapons, by a mere treaty which would also stipulate the limits on conventional arms, permit anti-nuclear defensive forces such as Star Wars, provide for inspection to

---

*But in late 1985, PBS began showing a TV series on war, done by Canadian Gwynne Dyer and already aired in six other nations, which appears to teach that some sovereignty must be transferred if any world organization is to work.

prevent cheating, and permit the formation of alliances to discourage aggressors from building nuclear weapons anew. Schell was driven to this awkward solution, which does something about nuclear fears but nothing about anarchic fears, because he thinks people will die rather than give up national sovereignty. As we said earlier, he seems not to know what the opinion polls reveal on this point.

But part of his problem is suggested by his statement that, in his solution, nations "would agree to have not world government, in which all nations are fused into one nation, but its exact opposite—a multiplicity of inviolate nations pledged to leave each other alone."[111] So it may be that Schell, a publicist, shares with many of the younger scholars a weakness in federal theory, which permits sovereignty to be divided.

Apart from Schell, the only thing we are indebted to the publicists for lately is a reminder in *The Washington Monthly* in 1984 that Section VI of the Nuclear Non-Proliferation Treaty of 1968 calls upon US, USSR, and the other signatories to pursue in good faith a "treaty on general and complete disarmament under strict and effective international control."[112]

The 1984 edition of the Encyclopedia of Associations lists 84 peace organizations in US, most of which have no idea that government has anything to do with public peace, but which might be able to learn. Many of these, plus hundreds of others, support an umbrella organization called *Nuclear Weapons Freeze Campaign* with headquarters in St. Louis. Dating back to 1980, the freeze campaign gained impetus from Schell's first book and from the "nuclear winter" warnings of Sagan and others. Its agitation for a mutually verifiable freeze on the testing and deployment of warheads and delivery vehicles enlisted the support of many notables including more than 200 members of Congress. Even the old Cold Warrior, evangelist Billy Graham, is a convert. The campaign may have pushed Reagan to change his rhetoric toward the Soviet Union. At the campaign's convention in late 1984 the delegates were told that Yankelovich, the pollster, says fully 90 percent of Americans now believe the arms race is very serious and that they will not survive a war—that the freeze campaign has "altered history as no other movement has."[113]

But Mandelbaum believes the US freeze campaign will die down. As for the nuclear protest movement in Europe, he says it seems much more extensive in the Protestant north than in the Catholic south, but adds that agitation for a nuclear-free Europe is part of the left-wing politics in southern Europe.[114]

Of all the peace-oriented organizations, those of the scientists have greatest prestige. These include *Council for a Livable World*, which tries to elect disarmament-minded candidates to the US Senate; the *Bulletin of the Atomic Scientists* which, like the Council, has worked for 40 years to avert nuclear war, and the newer *Union of Concerned Scientists*, which claims to represent some 6,000 scientists. In 1983 about 500 scientists from

20 countries met in Washington for a "World After Nuclear War" discussion, the essence of which was that nobody can escape its effects and nobody can win.

An international newspaper called *WorldPaper* is published in three languages and reaches 800,000 readers in 19 countries as an insert in local newspapers. It is the brainchild of Harry Hollins, an old world federalist who founded the Institute for World Order which publishes the WOMP studies. There is also the *World Press Review*, with a circulation of 100,000, published by the Stanley Foundation which was set up by a former president of United World Federalists.

There is some indication that the peace movement in the West has struck sparks in the Soviet bloc. During the past four years peace groups have been founded in Moscow, Budapest, Prague, the Soviet Baltic republics, and East Germany. It is possible that the peace issue in Eastern Europe has turned from official propaganda window-dressing into an authentic popular movement. Soviet bloc leaders may fear this, for it was Lenin's "bread and peace" campaign that destroyed the Russian army's fighting morale in World War I.[115] The tip-off may come in Gorbachev's treatment of Sakharov, the physicist and Nobel Peace Prize winner, who was banished from Moscow to the city of Gorky in 1980, presumably for his advocacy of human rights, peace and world government.

But US is the key to federation, whether worldwide or of the "democracies" only. We place a good deal of hope in *the Vietnam generation*. They, with others of their cohort in Western Europe and elsewhere, made the late 1960s and early 1970s a decade of protest against war. They will be taking over the levers of power by the year 2000, though by then it may be too late: this planet may have already ripped its fabric.

We are told that "the distributional pattern of personality types" evolves fast enough so that generational changes may be detected, hence we should examine the younger generation to detect coming changes.[116] Another study shows that the young agree with their parents on political values to only a small or moderate degree.[117] We know from US polls that the silent majority in the universities overwhelmingly supported most of the positions taken by student leaders in the late 1960s, and that their attitudes spread in the early 1970s to the young who did not go to college.[118] In a 1972 poll, 65 percent of male students and 73 percent of female students agreed that "the real enemy today is no longer communism but rather war itself" as compared with 26 percent of males and 37 percent of females in 1962.[119] A scholar studied the polls and reported in 1972 that it was only during the Vietnam period that people under 30 were more pacifist than those over 50.[120]

The Vietnam period was a hopeful one, in a way, with the coining of such phrases as Mankind II, Consciousness III, The Greening of America, Children of the Eighth Day, Humanity's Phase Four, and The New Morality. But will the commitment of the Vietnam generation last as it becomes middle-aged? One study suggests it will, judging from attitudes in US of varying cohorts (persons born at about the same time) toward national security policies.[121] But another asserts that the Vietnam generation will not be of one mind when it takes over US leadership.[122]

Our own observation is that the young people whose views were molded in the Vietnam era retain them unchanged into the 1980s. True, most have married and must make a living. But they are the people behind the nuclear-freeze movement. Many of them who were in graduate school instead of Vietnam are now the younger scholars who do peace research. A sociologist who has tracked 200 of these former protesters said in 1985 that they have held their political convictions while succeeding in society; that they haven't as much time for political activism, "but the notion that you change your attitude as you get older isn't true."[123] He also tracked many Vietnam war veterans who, he says, are coming to terms with the past. Their experiences in the most wretched of wars may make them as peace-minded as the protesters.

And those who despaired of the post-Vietnam "Me Generation" can take hope from a 1985 survey of 180,000 college freshmen. They are materialistic, as has been true of students since the Vietnam furore died away, but approximately two-thirds oppose greater military spending while believing that "the federal government is not doing enough to promote disarmament."[124]

We ask the men and women of the Vietnam generation to keep it in mind that:

> People and groups of people have never at any time or any place lived peacefully together except under government, hence they must rid themselves of that hatred of governments that they learned in the Vietnam years, realizing that only in a governed world will national governments cease to seize ever greater control over their minds and bodies; and that
>
> If they do nothing, the present global international system, like all its hundreds of lesser predecessors, must pass away—by nuclear conquest and integration, or by nuclear dissipation—for no world security system will have been put in place to stop the inexorable processes of conflict.

Who, then, will oppose such a federal world government? Those in Europe and the Third World who accept Lenin's explanation of war and who are preoccupied with the economic and social problems which Marxism offers to solve. Those, too, in US and other liberal capitalist nations whose short-term interests would be directly threatened, mainly corporations that live off of military contracts, the military, the intelligence services, their legislative allies, the veterans organizations, all whose ideology consists of a brass-bound anti-communism, and those other elements mentioned in Chapter 7 who might move their nations on into fascism.* And these will be joined in their opposition by Second World military men, officials in the defense ministries, and others whose rigid anti-capitalism or short-term interests are threatened by the outbreak of peace.

But in the First World these elements would be far less opposed to a Streit-type federal union of liberal capitalist nations. For one thing, the military would still be needed. For another, Streit's idea has always appealed to The Establishment. But, for that matter, many conservatives over the years have embraced the world government concept for its "law and order" appeal.

For world federation to have a chance, probably a terrible crisis will be necessary. Then the outcome will turn on whether we have any Transcendant Leaders of the Kennedy-Khruschev stripe. As General MacArthur said in 1955:

> When will some great figure in power have sufficient imagination and moral courage to translate this universal wish for peace—which is rapidly becoming a necessity—into actuality? It is the leaders who are the laggards. The disease of power seems to confuse and bewilder them. Never do they dare to state the bald truth that the next great advance in the evolution of civilization cannot take place until war is abolished.[125]

And, really now, which is the more incredible—a governed world or a gone one?

Beyond the fear that the human race will commit suicide, which we have dealt with head-on, and the fears associated with population, pollution, and depletion, which we have dealt with so far as we think any probable world polity can, there is a plenitude of other fears: of sickness, old age, death, ugliness, ignorance, loneliness—and of oneself. Science and especially genetics now offer intimations of hope for some of these. Para-psychology, now that it has become almost a respectable science, may some day remove, not death but the fear of death.

Beyond those developments are others that only Mankind II will be able to imagine. We know that humans live far below their potential but we can scarcely conceive what life might become if that potential began to be used. If, as one scientist has predicted, Earth's magnetic field will collapse by the year 3500, allowing radiation from the sun to cook the planet,[126] our descendants, if any, may already have devised means of transferring themselves to planets with better prospects. In December 1984 astronomers announced discovery of the first planet outside our solar system; it is 126 trillion miles from here.

All that is proposed here is a prescription whereby the world will not

---

*In the State of Washington in 1985 a "global education" bill was defeated in the legislature by New Christian Right groups as a step toward one-world government.

end with a bang, as in nuclear war, or with a whimper, as in starvation. It is a suggestion for taking care of ourselves in the only home we have now. At Christmas in 1973 astronaut Edward G. Gibson looked at Earth and said, "You don't see any dividing lines.... We really are in this together."[127]

And we may be quite alone in the universe. Our most powerful radio telescopes are exploring in all directions on all frequencies and radio bands, searching for intelligent life. Thus far, nothing. But, the astronomers say, it is too early to despair.[128]

Chapter 8 Notes

1. Bruce M. Russett, "The Ecology of Future International Politics, *International Studies Quarterly*, vol. 11 (1967), 21-31, pp. 21, 30.

2. Walter Isard, "Toward a More Adequate General Regional Theory and Approach to Conflict Resolution," *Peace Research Society (International) Papers*, vol. 10 (1968), 1-21, 1. A "region" could be Western Europe or the North Atlantic.

3. Kenneth Boulding, "Future Directions in Conflict and Peace Studies," *Journal of Conflict Resolution* 22:2 (1978), 342-354.

4. Grenville Clark and Louis B. Sohn, *World Peace Through World Law*, 3d. Ed., Harvard University Press, 1966.

5. Louis B. Sohn, *Introduction to World Peace Through World Law*, Chicago, World Without War Publications, 1973.

6. M. L. Balinski and H. P. Young, "Fair Representation in the European Parliament," *Journal of Common Market Studies* 20:4 (1982), 361-373.

7. George Kennan and Noel Gayler, "How to Break the Momentum of the Nuclear Arms Race," *New York Times Magazine*, April 25, 1982. Kennan was not quite recommending world government, however.

8. David Hofmeister, *et al*, "The Verification of Compliance with Arms Control Agreements," *Scientific American*, 252-3 (1985), 39-45.

9. "Can We Trust the Russians?" Union of Concerned Scientists, Cambridge, Mass.

10. Michael Mandelbaum, *The Nuclear Future*, Cornell University Press, 1983, p. 71.

11. Jonathan Schell, *The Fate of the Earth*, New York, Knopf, 1982, and *The Abolition*, New York, Knopf, 1984. Schell may be playing the devil's advocate with respect to world government, even though he says his solution is the middle way between war and government, the two methods of deciding quarrels. A scholar wonders if the revival of world order utopia writings, and their urgency, is based in a clear view of doomsday or in *fin de siecle* (and millenial) despair. (Ian Clark, "World Order Reform and Utopian Thought: A Contemporary Watershed? *Review of Politics 41:1 (1979), 96-120.*

12. *Kenneth E. Boulding, "Technology and the Love-Hate System," Columbia Journal of Business* 3:1 (1968), p. 48.

13. Hans J. Morgenthau, *Politics Among Nations* (New York, Knopf, 3d. Ed., 1960), p. 330.

14. Reported in *UNESCO and Public Opinion Today* (Chicago, National Opinion Research Center, 1947), Report No. 35, pp. 12 ff.

15. *Public Opinion Quarterly*, vol. 10, p. 618.

16. *Public Opinion Quarterly*, vol. 13, 176.

17. *Public Opinion Quarterly*, vol. 15, pp. 400 ff.

18. *Public Opinion Quarterly*, *ibid.*

19. *Public Opinion Quarterly*, vol. 17, p. 408. Elmo Roper was a prominent member of Streit's Federal Union organization.

20. See Clarence Schettler's *Public Opinion in American Society* (New York, Harper, 1960) for a discussion of these factors.

21. The Minnesota Poll, *Minneapolis Sunday Tribune*, June 9, 1963.

22. J. Nehnevajsa, "Prospects for Disarmament," a paper presented at the meeting of Scientists on Survival, New York, June 1963, and reported in Wm. Eckhardt and T. F. Lentz, "Factors of War-Peace Attitudes," *Peace Research Reviews* 1:5 (1967), pp. 18-19.

23. Louis Harris report published in Louisville (Ky.) *Courier-Journal*, May 9, 1969.

24. Reported in Honolulu *Star-Bulletin*, October 23, 1970.

25. The questionnaire was devised by Senator Clark's staff.

26. *The Federalist*, October 1967.

27. Discussed in R. W. Oldendick and B. A. Bardes, "Mass and Elite Foreign Policy Opinions" *Public Opinion Quarterly* 46:3 (1982), 368-382.

28. Reported in the December 1984 newsletter of the Council for a Livable World, Boston.

29. D. Yankelovich and John Doble, "The Public Mood: Nuclear Weapons and the U.S.S.R.," *Foreign Affairs* 63:1 (1984), 33-46.

30. Wm. Eckhardt and T. F. Lentz, "Factors of War-Peace Attitudes," *Peace Research Reviews* 1:5 (1967), pp. 18-19.

31. *Ibid.*, pp. 7-8.

32. Eugene J. Webb, *et al*, *Unobtrusive Measures: Nonreactive Research in the Social Sciences* (Chicago, Rand-McNally, 1966), p. 172.

33. This survey was done by the writer for a graduate seminar paper.

34. *War/Peace Report*, January 1964, p. 4.

35. *New York Times*, July 22, 1968. The essay was later published in a book, *Progress, Coexistence and Intellectual Freedom* (New York, Norton, 1968) with introduction and notes by Harrison E. Salisbury. See especially pages 81-89.

36. New York Times News Service dispatch, Eleanor Blau's byline, in Winston-Salem (N.C.) *Journal-Sentinel*, August 26, 1973.

37. Jonathan Schell, *The Abolition* (New York, Knopf, 1984), p. 87. But a game-theory exercise tends to show that inspection is not enough; that disarmament must take place within a framework of enforcement. At the critical point (their tenth move?) the UN must be stronger militarily than any probable combination of states that might challenge it (Marc Pilisuk and Anatol Rapaport, "A Non-Zero-Sum Game Model of Some Disarmament Problems," *Peace Research Society Papers*, vol. 1, 1964, pp. 57-78.

38. Kenneth E. Boulding, *Conflict and Defense* (New York, Harper, 1962); p. 334.

39. Everett Lee Millard, *Freedom in a Federal World* (Oceana Publications, 3d. Ed., Revised, 1964), p. 105. Millard's survey of opinion was called CURE, which used a newsletter, *One World* (published at 4030 Irving Park Road, Chicago) to distribute questionnaires and summarize opinion.

40. Gerald G. Grant and Everett L. Millard, "Some Proposed Jurisdictions of World Law: A Report," *Background* (now *International Studies Quarterly*), vol. 7, no. 3 (1963), pp. 137-149.

41. Louis B. Sohn, "The Need for the Democratization of the United Nations," *The Federalist*, January-February 1966.

42. Robert E. Rosack, in Millard and Grant (Note 40), p. 145. See also Herbert C. Kelman's "Compliance Identification and Internalization: Three Processes of Attitude Change," *Journal of Conflict Resolution*, vol. 2 (1958), 50-60.

43. Regarding the effects of environmental deterioration and economic scarcity, see all of *International Studies Quarterly* 21:4 (1977), especially the article by Jack D. Salmon, pp. 701-720. Also, volume 444 (1979) of *Annals of American Academy of Political and Social Science* is devoted to environmental problems,

44. Donella H. Meadows, "Charting the Way the World Works," *Technology Review* 88:2 (1985), p. 60.

45. W. P. Hogan and I. F. Pearce, *The Incredible Eurodollar* (London, Unwin Paperbacks, 1984).

46. *Ibid.*

47. In John Adams, ed., *The Contemporary International Economy* (New York, St. Martins Press, 1979), pp. 350-351. Triffin also says "the gold-convertible dollar standard" relieved US of adjustment pressures until 1971, then US in 1972-74 still avoided adjustment by borrowing from foreign central banks, then all deficit nations avoided it by borrowing from the Eurobanks.

48. Robert R. Bowie and Carl J. Friedrich, eds., *Studies in Federalism*, Boston, Little Brown, 1954.

49. Carl J. Friedrich, *Trends in Federalism in Theory and Practice* (New York, Praeger, 1968), p. 173.

50. Boulding says "the diminution of violence involves (a) an increase in the strength of the system and/or (b) diminution of the strain of the system," (In his "Twelve Friendly Quarrels with Johan Galtung," *Journal of Peace Research* 14:1 (1977), 75-86.

51. K. C. Wheare, *Federal Government* (New York, Oxford University Press, 4th Ed. Rev., in Galaxy paperback, 1964), p. 1.

52. Max Farrand, *The Records of the Federal Convention*, Yale University Press, in four volumes, 1911 and 1931.

53. James Madison, Federalist Paper No. 20, in J.E. Cooke, ed., *The Federalist* (Wesleyan University Press, 1961), pp. 128-9.

54. Wheare (Note 51), p. 10. Edward A. Freeman, writing in 1862, distinguished the U.S. system from a "system of Confederated States" where the central power deals only with the state governments, calling it the "Composite State" where the general government acts directly on citizens (his *History of Federal Government*, London, Macmillan, 1893, pp. 8-9).

55. Wheare (Note 51), p. 12.

56. William H. Riker, *Federalism: Origin, Operation, Significance* (Boston, Little Brown, 1964), p. 11.

57. Bowie and Friedrich (Note 48), *ibid.*

58. Riker (Note 56), p. 155.

59. Richard H. Leach, "Canadian Federalism Revisited," *Publius* 14:1 (1984), 9-19. Leach says Canadian federalism has been based, not in any shared political philosophy of federalism, but in a pragmatic desire to work out a way to live together.

60. Steven L. Burg, "Republican and Provincial Constitution-Making in Yugoslav Politics," *Publius* 12:1 (1982), 131-153. This devolution of authority has been backed by the Communist Party.

61. Samuel H. Beer, "Federalism, Nationalism, and Democracy in America," *American Political Science Review*, 72:1 (1978), 1-21.

62. Wheare (Note 51), p. 44.

63. Wheare (Note 51), p. 44

64. Riker (Note 56), pp. 12, 10.

65. Karl W. Deutsch, *et al, Political Community and the North Atlantic Area* (Princeton University Press, 1957), p. 58. Deutsch in 1953 looked forward eventually to world government (see final chapter, his *Nationalism and Social Communication*, M.I.T. Press, 1953).

66. Gallup's interview with Jeffrey St. John for the Copley Newspapers, published in Honolulu *Star-Bulletin*, August 5, 1970.

67. Dwight D. Eisenhower, *Crusade in Europe*, (Garden City, Doubleday, 1948), pp. 459, 477.

68. Reported in *Transition*, January 1975, published by Institute for World Order, New York.

69. In F. Scott Fitzgerald's *This Side of Paradise*, page 276, Amory is told there are things that always have been and always will be. He responds, "What this man here just said has been for thousands of years the last refuge of the associated muttonheads of the world."

70. Clarence K. Streit, *Union Now* (New York, Harper, 1939). For other early proposals for federal unions, see Howard O. Eaton, ed., *Federation: the Coming Structure of World Government*, University of Oklahoma Press, 1944. After the Canadian provinces federated in 1867 there was a movement for federating the British Empire, later expanded to include US in an English-speaking union. The idea scarcely survived World War I but its supporters were brought into Streit's movement after 1939.

71. Ernst B. Haas, *The Uniting of Europe*, (Stanford University Press, 1958), p. xiii.

72. James R. Huntley, *Uniting the Democracies* (New York University Press, 1980). p. 11.

73. According to Professor Neal Potter, who spoke at a meeting called by the Association for Uniting the Democracies, among others, held in the Senate Caucus Room, Washington. in September 1984.

74. *International Movement for Atlantic Union*, a newsletter then edited by Clarence Streit, 1736 Columbia Road, N.W., Washington DC 20009.

75. Michael Howard, "War and the Nation-State," *Daedalus* 108:4 (1979), 101-110.

76. Associated Press dispatch, Robert Burns byline, published in Odessa (Tx.) *American*, January 30, 1985. The poll was published by the Market's Executive Commission. Of the leaders of the Market countries, Britain's Thatcher is least in favor of moving on to federal union. Public opinion has been favorable for a long while (see Ronald Iglehart's "Public Opinion and Regional Integration," *International Organization* 24:4 (1970), 764-795.

77. Edwin H. Fedder, ed., *NATO in the Seventies* (Center for International Studies, University of Missouri at St. Louis, 1970), p. 274.

78. Robert K. Olson, "Community of the Democracies Faces New Challenge," *NATO Review* 31:2 (1983), 17-22. A good many former US foreign service officers favor something along the lines of Streit's federal union.

79. Lincoln P. Bloomfield, "Western European Reactions to 'The Future of the United Nations' " *Atlantic Quarterly* 15:4 (1977-78), 489-498, 492. Former UN Secretary-General Kurt Waldheim published in 1984 a sad report on the UN but no plea for amendment to make it work (his "The United Nations: The Tarnished Image," *Foreign Affairs* 63:1 (1984), 33-46).

80. *The Washington Monthly*, October 1984, p. 44).

81. Reported in *One World* 17:8 (March 1970), pp. 2-3.

82. See Charles Yost's *The Insecurity of Nations*, New York, Praeger, 1968. He later went on the Board of the Institute for World Order.

83. *One World* 17:8 (March 1970) and 13:3 (December 1970/January 1971).

84. *The Christian Science Monitor*, January 31, 1974, Dana Adams Schmidt byline.

85. "The Future of the United Nations: A Strategy for Like-Minded Nations," *Atlantic Quarterly* 15:1 (1977), 7-17. The main recommendation was for "regimes," each to be agreed to by interested nations, to take care of problems that neither individual nations nor the UN or other large international organizations can handle.

86. *The Christian Science Monitor*, March 7, 1985, Louis Wiznitzer byline.

87. In his "The Greening of the Globe," (*International Organization* 31:1, 1977, 130-147) Tom J. Farer criticizes *On the Creation of a Just World Order*, Saul H. Mendlovitz, ed. (New York, Free Press, 1975). Richard Falk, Mendlovitz' partner and contributor, responds (*International Organization* 32:2, 1977, 531-545), denying that he is a world federalist, and saying he would prefer muddling through with the nation-state system to "its displacement at this historical junction by any plausible form of world government." Later, in a reader edited by him and Samuel S. Kim (*The War System: An Interdisciplinary Approach*, Boulder, Westwood Press, 1980), Falk in his Introduction again denies forcefully that he favors world government.

88. So asserted by Stanley J. Michalak Jr. in "Richard Falk's Future World: A Critique of WOMP-USA," *Review of Politics* 42:1 (1980), 3-17. Falk replied in the same issue, pp. 18-30, that *A Study of Future Worlds* belongs to WOMP's earlier period and was a reaction against the world federalist "legal tradition" as in the Clark-Sohn plan. Apparently Falk, if not Mendlovitz, repents their publications in the 1960s that sounded sort of world governmental. At any rate, Falk (see Note 87) has denied world government thrice. Francis A. Beer, in "World Order and World Futures," *Journal of Conflict Resolution* 23:1 (1979), 174-192, reviews five books by WOMP scholars and suggests that future world order studies address more explicitly the differences between federalist and functionalist solutions.

89. In Hans Morgenthau and Kenneth Thompson, eds., *Principles and Problems of International Politics* (New York, Knopf, 1950), p. 143.

90. Lester R. Brown's *World Without Borders*, New York, Random House, 1972.

91. M. Mesarovic and E. Pestel, *Mankind at the Turning Point*, New York, Dutton-Readers Digest, 1974.

92. Emile Benoit, "Kenneth Boulding as Socio-Political Theorist," *Journal of Conflict Resolution* 21:3 (1977), 551-560. Avicenna, the Islamic philosopher, wrote a thousand years ago that politics "contributes to the human end indirectly through securing the low but necessary end of survival and political stability which, in turn, make possible the direct pursuit of other human goals." (In Miriam Galston, "Realism and Idealism in Avicenna's Political Philosophy," *Review of Politics* 41:4 (1979), 561-577.)

93. W.T.R. Fox, "Population and World Politics," *Journal of International Affairs* 31:1 (1977), 101-139. Fox says Eisenhower came to see population control as the world's most critical need.

94. Louis J. Halle, "A Hopeful Future for Mankind," *Foreign Affairs* 58:5 (1980), 1129-1136.

95. Steven J. Rosen and Walter S. Jones, *The Logic of International Relations* (Cambridge, Mass., Winthrop Publishers, 1980), p. 486.

96. John H. Herz, "Political Realism Revisited," *International Studies Quarterly* 25:2 (1981), 182-197, 195.

97. C. W. Kegley Jr. and E. R. Wittkopf, *World Politics: Trend and Transformation* (New York, St. Martin's Press, 1981), especially page 495.

98. George H. Quester, "Preventing Proliferation," *International Organization* 35:1 (1981), 213-240.

99. Rudolph J. Rummel, in the final volume 5, *The Just Peace*, of the Dimensionality of Nations Project (Beverley Hills, Sage Publications, 1981).

100. Michael Mandelbaum, *The Nuclear Future* (Cornell University Press, 1984), pp. 18-19. He, perhaps in contrast to Schell, realizes that although "Sovereignty is very old," it is not immutable. "It is not etched in the genes of the species *homo sapiens*." And he sees that sovereignty must be abolished. However, he seems to have little appreciation for the divisibility of sovereignty through a federal arrangement.

Similarly, an Australian scholar writes that "the only way to remove the anarchy is to destroy the units that produce it, namely the states" (in Ian Clark's *Reform and Resistance in the International Order*, Cambridge University Press, 1980, p. 26.)

101. Roger Sperry, *Science and Moral Priority: Merging Mind, Brain, and Human Values* (New York, Columbia University Press, 1983), especially pp. 46, 115.

102. John W. Spanier, *Games Nations Play*, 5th Ed., New York, Holt Rinehart and Winston, 1984. He also discusses "interdependence," which appears to be the same thing some scholars call "macropolitics," as something that carries with it the hope that since world problems of war, population, pollution, and resource depletion are so grave, people will demand and get global action to cope with them, though without global governmental institutions.

103. K. W. Deutsch and R. L. Merritt, "Trans-National Communications and the International System," *Annals of the American Academy of Political and Social Science*, vol. 442 (1979), 84-97.

104. *New York Times*, September 16, 1965, p. 24.

105. Associated Press dispatch, Boulder (Colo.) *Daily Camera*, September 15, 1965.

106. *Saturday Review*, October 23, 1971, pp. 16-18.

107. Associated Press dispatch, Honolulu *Star-Bulletin*, May 24, 1971.

108. Letter from Charles S. Rhyne to *Christian Science Monitor*, January 30, 1974.

109. For a summary of Pope John's argument for world federal government, see Hallock Hoffman's *On the World Community*, published by the Center for the Study of Democratic Institutions, Santa Barbara, Calif.

110. James Reston's column published in San Angelo (Tex.) *Standard*, January 4, 1985.

111. Jonathan Schell, *The Abolition* (New York, Knopf, 1984), pp. 114-148. But on page 160 there is a suggestion of federalism.

112. *The Washington Monthly*, October 1984, p. 40.

113. *The Texas Observer*, January 11, 1985, pp. 22-23.

114. Michael Mandelbaum (Note 100), pp. 116-117.

115. "The Peace Issue Goes East," *National Review*, January 11, 1985.

116. Kenneth W. Terhune, "From National Character to National Behavior: A Reformulation," *Journal of Conflict Resolution* 14:2 (1970), 203-263.

117. Article by Nieme, Ross, and Alexander in *Public Opinion Quarterly* 42:4 (1978), 503-520.

118. D. Yankelovitch and R. Clark, *The New Morality*, New York, McGraw-Hill, 1974. In 1970, in so embattled a country as Israel, there were anti-war demonstrations by Israeli youth (*Between-the-Lines*, August 1, 1970, p. 3) and one observer concluded in 1970 that young Arabs as well as young Israelis might be more peacefully inclined than their elders (Paul Jacobs, *Between the Rock and the Hard Place*, New York, Random House, 1970).

119. Roger B. Handberg Jr., "The Vietnam Analogy: Student Attitudes on War," *Public Opinion Quarterly* 36:4 (1972-73), 616-627.

120. Hazel Erskine, "The Polls: Pacifism and the Generation Gap," *Public Opinion Quarterly* 36:4 (1972-73), 616-627.

121. D. B. Bobrow and Neal E. Cutler, "Time-Oriented Explanations of National Security Beliefs," *Peace Research Society (International) Papers*, vol. 8 (1967), 31-57. Cohorts correlate with beliefs more than do "life-stage" (present age) or "situation" (events).

122. Ole R. Holsti and J. N. Rosenau, "Does Where You Stand Depend on When You Were Born?" *Public Opinion Quarterly* 44:1 (1980), 1-22.

123. Associated Press dispatch, "America Grapples with Vietnam Legacy," San Angelo (Tex.) *Standard*, April 15, 1985. p. 4A.

124. Associated Press dispatch, "Making Money Ranks High with Freshmen," San Angelo (Tex.) *Standard*, January 14, 1985, p. 7A.

125. Douglas MacArthur, speaking at Los Angeles on January 26, 1955, as quoted in Frederick A. Schuman's *International Politics* (New York, McGraw-Hill, 6th Ed., 1958), p. xi.

126. The scientist is Dr. B. B. Goodfellow, Director of IBM's Toronto Laboratory (Associated Press dispatch, *Denver Post*, June 22, 1969).

127. Associated Press dispatch, Winston-Salem (N.C.) *Twin-City Sentinel*, December 25, 1973.

128. Hubert Reeves, *Atoms of Silence* (Cambridge, Mass., M.I.T. Press, 1984.).

INDEX

As this book is concerned with solutions to war, the index stresses ideas toward that end and the people who have them, therefore few princes or potentates are listed.